FRENCH FASHION

WOMEN & THE FIRST WORLD WAR

FRENCH FASHION WOMEN & THE FIRST WORLD WAR

MAUDE BASS-KRUEGER & SOPHIE KURKDJIAN, EDITORS

Maude Bass-Krueger
Johanne Berlemont
Jérémie Brucker
Margaret Darrow
Susan Grayzel
Sophie Kurkdjian
Michele Majer
Anaïs Raynaud

Published by Bard Graduate Center, New York
Distributed by Yale University Press, New Haven and London

This book is published in conjunction with the exhibition *French Fashion, Women, and the First World War* held at the Bard Graduate Center Gallery from September 5, 2019 – January 5, 2020.

Exhibition curators and catalogue editors: Maude Bass-Krueger and Sophie Kurkdjian

Project director: Nina Stritzler-Levine
Assistant curator: Emma Cormack

Book designer: Irma Boom Office
Copy editor: Barbara Burn
Manager of photographic rights and reproductions: Alexis Mucha

On the cover: Jeanne Paquin. Photographs of designs "Cachemire," "Matin," and "Marmouset" deposited for copyright at the Parisian Copyright Office in 1917. © Archives de Paris / Roger-Viollet, RV-101320-25, RV-101322-7, RV-101320-1.

Chapter 9 is extracted from Maude Bass-Krueger, "From the 'union parfaite' to the 'union brisée': The French Couture Industry and the midinettes during the Great War," *Costume* (2013) 47:1, 28–44.

Library of Congress Cataloging-in-Publication Data

Names: Bass-Krueger, Maude, 1985– editor. | Kurkdjian, Sophie, 1985– editor. | Bard Graduate Center for Studies in the Decorative Arts, Design, and Culture, organizer, host institution. Title: French fashion, women, and the First World War / Maude Bass-Krueger and Sophie Kurkdjian, editors. Description: New York: Published by Bard Graduate Center, [2019] | "This book is published in conjunction with the exhibition French Fashion, Women, and the First World War, held at the Bard Graduate Center Gallery from September 5, 2019-January 5, 2020." | Includes bibliographical references and index.Identifiers: LCCN 2019023995 | ISBN 9780300247985 (cloth) Subjects: LCSH: Fashion-France-History-20th century. | Women's clothing-France-History-20th century. | World War, 1914–1918-Social aspects-France. | Women-France-Social conditions-20th century. Classification: LCC TT504.6.F7 F743 2016 | DDC 746.9/20944-dc23 LC record available at https://lccn.loc.gov/2019023995

Distributed by Yale University Press, New Haven and London

ISBN 9780300247985

Printed in the Netherlands

Support for *French Fashion, Women, and the First World War* is generously provided by The Coby Foundation, LTD. with additional support from Mission du centenaire de la Première Guerre mondiale and other donors to Bard Graduate Center.

THE COBY FOUNDATION, LTD.

CONTENTS

FRENCH FASHION: ADAPTING TO CRISES

Director's Foreword

SUSAN WEBER

25 Years! A particular focus of Bard Graduate Center Gallery publications over the past quarter century has been on the work of women designers. Many titles on our distinguished backlist elaborate on how women have enhanced design practice. In 2000, *Women Designers of the Twentieth Century* was an encyclopedic and groundbreaking study of the field. Other diverse titles featuring women followed, including *Marimekko: Fabrics, Fashion, Architecture*; *Sheila Hicks: Weaving as Metaphor*; *Dutch New York Between East and West: The World of Margrieta van Varick*; *Knoll Textiles, 1945–2010*; *Staging Fashion, 1880–1920: Jane Hading, Lily Elsie, Billie Burke*; and *Artek and the Aaltos.* To commemorate Bard Graduate Center's twenty-fifth anniversary, we are adding a new book to our list on this subject. Edited by Dr. Maude Bass-Krueger, a graduate of our PhD program, and Dr. Sophie Kurkdjian, *French Fashion, Women, and the First World War* contributes new research in multiple fields. The words *French fashion* and *First World War* in the same title may well provoke surprise, even skepticism by the reader. However, it is the weaving together of these narratives about the place of French women in the Great War that makes this such a fascinating book. This project is the outgrowth of the 2017 exhibition at the Bibliothèque Forney in Paris, where it was organized to celebrate the centenary of the First World War. The exhibition in New York not only enabled the publication of the first English-language book on the subject, but it also expanded the checklist with new loans from collections in the United States and France.

As Director of the Bard Graduate Center, I have the pleasure of thanking the many individuals and institutions who have shared their knowledge and experience with us and whose work on our behalf has contributed to the success of this project.

I want to begin by acknowledging the superb work that has been done by Drs. Bass-Krueger and Kurkdjian, who served as co-editors of this book and co-curators of the exhibition it accompanies. My thanks also go to the authors Johanne Berlemont, Jérémie Brucker, Margaret Darrow, Susan Grayzel, Michele Majer, and Anaïs Raynaud, whose essays in this volume have enlightened us about the wartime experiences of French women. Barbara Burn, our wonderful copy editor, was an indefatigable asset to this book.

Molly Stevens and Tristan Bass-Krueger undertook the complex task of translation. We are thrilled to have produced this book with Irma Boom Office. Irma Boom created the remarkable design, with the assistance of Eva van Bemmelen, who also undertook the challenging task of typesetting with great skill and affability. Our longstanding photographer Bruce White took many of the magnificent photographs of the garments and accessories featured here. I would also like to express our gratitude to the Roger-Viollet photography archive in Paris, whose incomparable collections were the source of many of the period photographs.

It would have been impossible to realize this project without our lenders, among them institutions that deserve to be better known outside France such as the Bibliothèque Marguerite Durand, whose collections are dedicated to the preservation of work by women. We are indebted to each of the institutions and individuals identified here for loans to the exhibition, many of which have never been shown before: Association Pour l'Histoire de la Mode (APHM); Hollis Barnhart; Bibliothèque Forney; Bibliothèque Marguerite Durand; Christine Edmonson; Chanel Heritage Department; Patrimoine Lanvin, Paris; Béatrice Cornet; Diktats bookstore; Fédération de la Haute Couture et de la Mode (FHCM); The Metropolitan Museum of Art, The Costume Institute and Watson Library; Musée des Arts Décoratifs, Paris; Musée de la Grande Guerre du Pays de Meaux; The Museum at the Fashion Institute of Technology; Palais Galliera – musée de la Mode de la Ville de Paris; Smith College Historic Clothing Collection; Special Collections & College Archives, Fashion Institute of Technology; Waleria Dorogova; and Western Reserve Historical Society, Cleveland, Ohio. Individuals in France and the United States facilitated our loan requests and others offered invaluable support to the curators and to our Gallery Director while they were organizing this project. We are grateful for the assistance of Miren Arzalluz (Palais Galliera); Antoine Bucher and Nicolas Montagne (Diktats bookstore); Hélène Fulgence, Odile Prémel, Julie Deydier, and Sarah Piettre (Chanel Heritage Department); Olivier Gabet, Marie-Sophie Carron de la Carrière, and Myriam Teissier (Musée des Arts Décoratifs, Paris); Christophe Guglielmo (Roger-Viollet); Laure Harivel (Patrimoine Lanvin, Paris); Max Hollein and Sarah Scaturro (The Costume Institute, The Metropolitan Museum of Art); Annie Metz (Bibliothèque Marguerite Durand); Pascal Morand and Guillaume Robic (Fédération de la Haute Couture et de la Mode); Elena Le Gall, Johanne Berlemont, and Anaïs Raynaud

(Musée de la Grande Guerre du Pays de Meaux); Eric Rivet (Western Reserve Historical Society, Cleveland, Ohio); Kiki Smith (Smith College Historic Clothing Collection); Ken Soehner (Watson Library, The Metropolitan Museum of Art); Valerie Steele (The Museum at the Fashion Institute of Technology); Karen Trivette (Special Collections & College Archives, Fashion Institute of Technology); and Lucile Trunel (Bibliothèque Forney).

A remarkably dedicated team at the Bard Graduate Center Gallery participated in the production of this book and the organization of the exhibition. Nina Stritzler-Levine provided the overarching leadership. As the assistant curator, Emma Cormack used her own knowledge of fashion history while attending to innumerable details with great skill and a truly remarkable demeanor. She was also a major contributor to the production of this book. Marianne Lamonaca assisted with the complex task of confirming loans and was a great help to the proofreading effort of this book. Alexis Mucha compiled the photographs and secured the rights. Caroline Hannah also helped with the catalogue production. Emily Reilly, Carla Repice, and Kristen Owens organized programs, tours, and other special events that enhance the Gallery's engagement with the public. Amy Estes and Hollis Barnhart created the dynamic marketing campaign. Jocelyn Lau created many of the marketing printed materials. Hellyn Teng enlivens the exhibition website. Benjamin Krevolin and Amy Brady collaborated on the fundraising effort with the assistance of Minna Lee. Tim Ettenheim and Mohammed Alam together with Rita Niyazova, Samantha Baron, and Miao Chen assisted with finance and administration. James Congregane and Chandler Small with the facilities and security teams provide extensive support with Gallery operations.

Ian Sullivan created the beautiful and thoughtful exhibition design. Laura Grey and Irma Boom designed the graphics in the exhibition. Tae Smith led the team that did the complex job of mounting the garments. Eric Edler coordinated the assembly of this complex project, and Alexander Gruen led our incomparable crew of installers. Jesse Merandy, assisted by Emma Cormack, created the digital media for the exhibition.

On behalf of our entire team I would like to conclude these acknowledgments by thanking our donors, to whom we owe an enormous debt of thanks. In France, Mission du centenaire de la Première Guerre mondiale realized the merits of this project when it was first proposed at the Bibliothèque Forney and then provided funding specifically for this catalogue.

We are also the grateful recipients of a generous grant from the Coby Foundation, LTD., whose unique mission advances research and scholarship on fashion and textiles. As we celebrate the twenty-fifth anniversary of Bard Graduate Center, I want to thank our Board of Trustees and express my appreciation to the entire staff and faculty.

Gallery Director's Foreword

NINA STRITZLER-LEVINE

Woman . . . cannot be seen as a fixed, pre-existing entity or frozen "image," transformed by this or that historical circumstance, but as a complex, mercurial and problematic signifier, mixed in its messages, resisting fixed interpretation or positioning despite the numerous attempts made in visual representation literally to put "woman" in her place. Like the woman warrior, the term "woman" fights back, and resists attempts to subdue its meaning or reduce it to some simple essence, universal, natural, and above all, unproblematic. LINDA NOCHLIN[1]

Both the content and design of this book substantiate the argument made by the late eminent art historian Linda Nochlin that *woman* defies simple, neutral, or narrow explanation. The French women who appear in this book—many of whom are anonymous, some of whom achieved great fame—embody Nochlin's notion of the "woman warrior." So too do the women editors, Maude Bass-Krueger and Sophie Kurkdjian, who investigated and wrote most of the content and assembled the contributors, and the woman graphic designer, Irma Boom, who interpreted the meaning of the content in the book design. During Nochlin's highly influential and prolific career, she challenged the conventions of what it means to be an art historian. As she explained in her book *Representing Women*, interpreting images of women in French painting demanded a different way of "doing history." This book, *French Fashion, Women, and the First World War*, is a different way of doing history in the Nochlin sense. On the one hand, it expands upon work that has been done on women and fashion in wartime, especially in Great Britain and the United States, and on the other it forges new ground by using fashion as a means of producing knowledge about the shifting attitudes toward women and their changing identities during the First World War in France, where this subject is seldom, if ever, discussed. The contributors to this volume raise many questions about French women and fashion in wartime, such as what French women wore; how what they wore changed in wartime; how what they wore came to signify their plight; and how French society perceived what they were wearing. The authors of these essays "do history" through the wartime lens of French fashion and women. They tell moving stories, some of them deeply troubling, as when we learn that France, the epicenter of the war, first extolled the woman warrior and then suppressed her ambitions.

Ultimately, the question of greatest significance here is: does it matter whose voice the historian allows to speak? This book responds unequivocally that it matters a great deal. Beginning with the cover, the graphic design of *French Fashion, Women, and the First World War* evokes the words of Linda Nochlin quoted above. We wonder who are the women wearing distinctive wartime tailored suits? They are posed looking away from us and gazing directly at us. What are these women thinking? Irma Boom's treatment of the cover and the texts directs us to "do history differently." Boom explains her approach with a brief commentary on the history of typography:

On Typography: After the Gutenberg Bible (1455), the structure and type of the printed book still looked very much like manuscripts. Movable type was structured as a block of text with a pilcrow (¶) as separator to indicate paragraphs, mainly in red and added by hand. Around 1500, books started to develop, and around 1520, the pilcrow was not always filled in any more. What was left were blank spots. These blank spots were an inspiration for the paragraphs for this book.

This explanation reflects Boom's ability to tell an author's story graphically through typography and by manipulating the relationship between word and image on the page.

Midway through the gestation of this book, Maude Bass-Krueger had a baby. I share this with the reader because it relates to the subject matter this book investigates and the persistence of the struggles it elucidates. Maude's becoming a mother while engaged in the demanding work of making this book and the exhibition it accompanies reveals how even today, in what we consider to be more enlightened times than the period examined here, the conflicting demands of womanhood persist. By that I mean contending with the multiple and at times opposing needs of motherhood and work. As many of the visual representations in this volume poignantly show, women in France during the First World War had to navigate many unprecedented situations—nursing wounded soldiers, driving trams, mourning their dead husbands, fathers, and brothers, and even nursing babies while working in munitions factories. There has never been an easy solution to the conflicting demands of being a woman, especially in bearing children. Among women's duties in wartime had been to work in previously male sectors of society, and at the same time to purchase and wear clothing made in France. As the visual representations in different media presented here reveal, those activities elicited both praise and disdain. Then, at the end of the war, French women were told that childbirth was critical to saving the nation. When they accepted being at home with their children, ostensibly out of desire and duty, women lost the power of agency to fight back against being relegated to secondary status in French society. Their voices went silent.

Finding a way to be the woman warrior in both wartime and peace poses an ontological dilemma for many women. The questions raised by this book about that pursuit and about being individuals, mothers, citizens, and workers among other roles continue to speak loudly to women today.

1 Linda Nochlin, *Representing Women* (New York: Thames and Hudson, 1999), 7. Nochlin died in late October 2017. For a tribute to her, see Mignon Nixon, "Women, Art, and Power After Linda Nochlin," *October* 163 (Winter 2018), 131–32.

Editors' Acknowledgments

French Fashion, Women, and the First World War originated exactly ten years ago, in 2009, as Maude's master's thesis for the Institut d'Études Politiques in Paris.[1] The First World War, with its relatively contained time span of four years, made an interesting case study in which to investigate the relationship between French politics, nationalism, and fashion. Taking Dominique Veillon's book *La mode sous l'Occupation* as an example of the kind of serious history that could come from researching the French fashion industry during the war—the Second World War in Veillon's case—Maude's thesis was the first comprehensive analysis of the development of the French fashion industry during the First World War and the relationships between fashion, gender, and wartime society.[2]

That work provided the backbone for the 2017 exhibition *Mode & Femmes 14/18*, which opened at the Bibliothèque Forney in Paris, and has served as the guide for both the exhibition and the catalogue at the Bard Graduate Center Gallery. While aspects of Maude's thesis are published here for the first time, this catalogue expands and broadens its scope. To that end we invited scholars working across academic disciplines, including the renowned World War I historians Margaret Darrow and Susan Grayzel, the World War I curators Johanne Berlemont and Anaïs Raynaud, fashion and textile historian Michele Majer, and cultural historian Jérémie Brucker. Sophie's knowledge of the press and the couture syndicates adds yet another dimension to this complex topic.

The next step in this project occurred as the centenary of the war dawned. In 2014, we organized the first international study day on fashion and World War I as part of the monthly seminar Sophie and Thierry Maillet were directing at the Institut d'Histoire du Temps Présent in Paris.[3] Along with our scientific committee—Professor Lou Taylor in Brighton; Dr. Adhelheid Rasche, then at the Lipperheidesche Kostümbibliothek in Berlin; and Dominique Veillon in Paris—we sent out an international call for papers for a conference on "Fashion, Dress, and Society in Europe during World War I" in February 2014, with the expectation of receiving a relatively small number of responses. We were astonished when more than one hundred submissions began pouring in. In all, sixty-four speakers from all corners of the world convened at the Institut Français de la Mode in Paris on December 12 and 13, 2014, to deliver papers on subjects ranging from handmade textiles to couture, from photographs to fashion magazines, from accessories to uniforms, and spanning the countries of France, England, Spain, the United States, Belgium, Sweden, the Netherlands, Greece, and French Sudan.[4] After the conference, we began reaching out to French museums, offering ideas for an exhibition on the topic of French fashion during World War I. Our hopes were fulfilled when the Bibliothèque Forney in Paris expressed interest. Working closely with Béatrice Cornet, the library's director of exhibitions, we chose fashion engravings, postcards, posters, and department store catalogues from their archives that houses one of the largest collections of printed documents related to fashion, women, and the Great War in France. Moreover, since the exhibition was organized under the auspices of the City of Paris, we were granted privileged access to the city's extensive network of archives in order to complement the material at Forney. The Archives de Paris (ADP), the Bibliothèque Historique de la Ville de Paris (BHVP), the Bibliothèque Marguerite Durand, Roger-Viollet, and the Palais Galliera – musée de la Mode de la Ville de Paris lent us photographs, printed materials, and garments. We were able to display many of the sources Maude had discussed in her thesis, as well as new ones to which she had not had access at the time, particularly clothing and accessories from the Palais Galliera – musée de la Mode de la Ville de Paris. Loans from the Chanel Heritage Department; Patrimoine Lanvin, Paris; Diktats bookstore; Waleria Dorogova; and Yves Aublet enriched the exhibition immeasurably. We also amassed our own collection of magazines, fashion illustrations, postcards, photographs, and newspapers that were shown. Following this period of intensive research, our exhibition, *Mode & Femmes 14/18*, inaugurated the new exhibition space at the Bibliothèque Forney in February 2017 (the exhibition was on view from February 28 to June 17, 2017). Then a fortuitous set of events further expanded our work on French fashion and the Great War. After seeing the exhibition at Forney, Nina Stritzler-Levine, Director of the Bard Graduate Center Gallery, approached us about bringing it to New York City where Maude had completed her doctoral work. This opportunity that we enthusiastically accepted reenergized our curatorial thinking. We were able to consider the exhibition from an American perspective. We were also given the opportunity to expand the selection of wartime garments with rarely seen loans from the Musée des Arts Décoratifs, Paris; The Costume Institute at the Metropolitan Museum of Art in New York; and The Museum at the Fashion Institute of Technology in New York. This reimagining of the material for Bard Graduate Center Gallery also incentivized us to recontextualize the exhibition for an American public by adding more information about the First World War itself, which has been largely overshadowed by the Second World War in the American cultural imagination, as well as providing more information about the relationship between France and America during the war.

It took a village to help make this book and the exhibition a reality. None of it would have been possible without the support of Susan Weber, founder and director of the Bard Graduate Center, or without Nina Stritzler-Levine, who ardently supported its transatlantic move and who helped to shape and edit this book. Special thanks go to Emma Cormack, whose masterful coordination made everything possible. Emma contributed substantially to the editing of this volume, assembled the checklist of the exhibition published here, and assisted with the exhibition design and interpretation. Much credit is due to Barbara Burn for her excellent copyediting, to Molly Stevens and Tristan Bass-Krueger for their translations. Alexis Mucha sourced illustrations and acquired reproduction rights for the many images in this book. Adèle Massias performed the complicated task of proofreading the French text.

Working with Irma Boom on the book design has been a wonderful experience—what a thrill it was to open up the first page proofs and discover her pioneering layout for this book. Eva van Bemmelen of Irma Boom Office was the lead designer of this book.

The knowledge and expertise of our contributors—Margaret Darrow, Susan Grayzel, Jérémie Brucker, Michele Majer, Johanne Berlemont, and Anaïs Raynaud—have expanded its scope immeasurably.

On the exhibition side, we are grateful to Ian Sullivan for his beautiful and thoughtful design. Tae Smith and her team made most of the clothing forms used in the exhibition and were essential contributors to the installation.

Many individuals on the staff of the Bard Graduate Center assisted us. Marianne Lamonaca helped facilitate loans and assisted with the production of this catalogue. Amy Estes and Hollis Barnhart have done a splendid job with the marketing and communications, while Benjamin Krevolin and Amy Brady led the fundraising campaign.

The Mission du centenaire de la Première Guerre mondiale has been an ongoing source of financial and moral support, from the 2014 conference in Paris through the exhibition at the Bibliothèque Forney to the Bard Graduate Center. We warmly thank Joseph Zimmet, Quentin Tissot, and Laurent Veyssière for their trust in us and our projects. We want to thank the Coby Foundation, LTD. for its generous support of the project.

At the Institut d'Histoire du Temps Présent, our institutional "home base" in Paris, Christian Delage, Henry Rousso, Pascal Maytraud, and Jean-René Borelly have supported us throughout. We are honored to have taken over the seminar from Dominique Veillon and are proud to continue her hard-fought legacy.

It was a thrill to present garments and ephemera at the Bibliothèque Forney in Paris in 2017 that had rarely, if ever, been on view before. We thank Lucile Trunel, Béatrice Cornet, Véronique Minot, Justine Perrichon, and Anne Gratadour for their help and hard work in bringing *Mode & Femmes 14/18* to life. Jeff Gaudinet was our masterful graphic designer in Paris. The support of Carole Medrinal, Hélène Dhoosche, and Annabelle Allain at Bibliocité was instrumental in bringing the Parisian exhibition to fruition as well. We sincerely thank those lenders who have allowed their objects to be presented on both sides of the Atlantic: Laure Harivel from Patrimoine Lanvin, Paris; Emmanuel Coquery, Odile Premel, and Sarah Piettre from Chanel Heritage Department, Paris; Aurélie Perreten, Johanne Berlemont, and Anaïs Raynaud from the Musée de la Grande Guerre du Pays de Meaux; Antoine Bucher and Nicolas Montagne from Diktats bookstore; Miren Arzalluz, Sophie Grossiord, and Sylvie Roy from the Palais Galliera – musée de la Mode de la Ville de Paris; Nathalie Doury and Christophe Guglielmo from the Parisienne de la Photographie / Roger-Viollet; Laurence Engel, Sylvie Aubenas, and Dominique Versavel from the Bibliothèque nationale de France; Emmanuelle Toulet, Pauline Girard, and Elisabeth Beilin from the Bibliothèque Historique de la Ville de Paris; Annie Metz from the Bibliothèque Marguerite Durand; Guillaume Nahon, Jean-Charles Vimaux, and Dominique Juigné from the Archives de Paris; and last, but certainly not least, Waleria Dorogova for photographs from her personal collection.

We are delighted to have added new objects to the exhibition at the Bard Graduate Center, and we sincerely thank our lenders for allowing us to enrich and broaden the exhibition with their loans. Thank you to Andrew Bolton, Sarah Scaturro, Lauren Birely, Elizabeth Arenaro from The Costume Institute and Ken Soehner from Watson Library at The Metropolitan Museum of Art; Valerie Steele, Colleen Hill, Sonia Dingilian, and Michelle McVicker from the Museum at the Fashion Institute of Technology; Karen Trivette, April Calahan, and Emily Arbuckle from the Special Collections & College Archives at the Fashion Institute of Technology; Olivier Gabet, Marie-Sophie Carron de la Carrière, Myriam Teissier, Marie-Pierre Ribère, and Emmanuelle Beuvin from the Musée des Arts Décoratifs, Paris;

Pascal Morand and Guillaume Robic from the Fédération de la Haute Couture et de la Mode; Kiki Smith and Rebecca Shea from the Smith College Historic Clothing Collection; Kelly Falcone-Hall, Eric Rivet, Patricia Edmonson, and Danielle Peck from Western Reserve Historical Society, Cleveland, Ohio; Hollis Barnhart; and Christine Edmonson.

Sophie would like to thank all the people who have been by her side helping to navigate the transatlantic ship through both the calm and turbulent waters of organizing a major international exhibition and of co-writing and co-editing an exhibition catalogue. Her gratitude extends to Catherine, Daniel, Alexandra, Thomas, Annie, Agnès, Romain, Louise, Théo, Waleria, Anna, Pierce, Johanna, Emanuele, Sandrine, Steve, Géraldine, Céline, Myriam, Sylvie, Aurélie, Etienne, Laurie, Élise, Antoine, Rezvan, Sarah . . . and all the others! Beyond the work of research and curating, these friends and family have provided unfailing support and were also available to share wisdom. They accompanied Sophie on the long and winding learning path of teamwork, especially in a country other than her own, a genuine initiatory journey that taught her a lot about herself and about others. And now, as Eugène de Rastignac in *Le Père Goriot* by Balzac said, relying on his newfound experience and strength as he prepared to conquer Paris, "À nous deux maintenant!"

The presentation of the exhibition at the Bard Graduate Center enables Maude to thank Peter Miller and Michele Majer for their incredible support and encouragement over the years—their mentorship has shaped her career since completing her dissertation in 2016. Judith Toledano, Elise Meyer, Nikki Petersen, Sophie Keller, and Rebecca Appel have provided the most pleasurable respite from the work. Roberta Krueger, Thomas Bass, and Tristan and Julian Bass-Krueger are the backbones that keep the whole enterprise supported with the utmost love. If a book is like a baby, then Maude has had the pleasure of birthing both at exactly the same time: her love goes to her partner, Benoit Alegre, and their son, Oren Joseph Alegre-Bass. What a joy to see you grow in this world.

Our deepest thanks to all who have made this project possible in Paris and New York City.

1 Maude Bass-Krueger, "La mode en France durant la Première guerre mondiale: approches d'histoire culturelle," vols. 1 and 2, master's thesis, Institut d'Études Politiques, 2009.

2 Dominique Veillon, *La mode sous l'Occupation* (Paris: Payot, 1990; repr. 2001, 2014).

3 The Institut d'Histoire du Temps Présent (IHTP) is the modern history laboratory of the French National Center for Scientific Research (Centre National des Recherches Scientifiques or CNRS).

4 The conference "Fashion, Dress, and Society in Europe" was held on December 12 and 13, 2014, at the Institut Français de la Mode in Paris with the support of the Mission Centenaire and l'Oréal Research & Innovation. The program can be found online at www.wwifashion.com. A selection of papers will be published in the volume *Fashion, Society, and the First World War*, ed. Maude Bass-Krueger, Hayley Dujardin, Amy de la Haye, and Sophie Kurkdjian (London: Bloomsbury, forthcoming).

Illustrated Chronology, 1914–20

MAUDE BASS-KRUEGER & SOPHIE KURKDJIAN

JUNE – NOVEMBER 1914

CAPTIONS ON P. 494

KEY DATES RELATING TO THE FIRST WORLD WAR IN FRANCE

JUNE 28, 1914
Archduke Franz Ferdinand of Austria and his wife, Sophie, are assassinated by a Bosnian Serb nationalist in Sarajevo.

FIG. T-3

AUGUST 1, 1914
Germany declares war on Russia and mobilizes. France mobilizes.

AUGUST 4, 1914
President Raymond Poincaré uses the term "sacred union" (*union sacrée*) in a speech read to the government. During the war, the term will come to represent a political truce in which the left-wing agrees not to oppose the government or call any strikes.

AUGUST 3, 1914
Germany declares war on France. German army invades Belgium.

JUNE 1914 — JULY 1914 — AUGUST 1914

KEY DATES RELATING TO FRENCH FASHION AND FRENCH WOMEN

JULY 5, 1914
Between 2,000 and 6,000 suffragettes march for voting rights in Paris.

FIG. T-1

FIG. T-4

AUGUST 1914
Last issue of the *Gazette du Bon Ton*, edited by Lucien Vogel. The luxury magazine ceases publication at the start of the war.

AUGUST 3, 1914
Theaters, cinemas, and music halls close their doors. 75,000 people are out of work in Paris alone. The Comédie-Française reopens on December 6, 1914, the Odéon theater on May 20, 1915, and the Opéra on September 9, 1915.

FIG. T-2, FIG. 5.2

AUGUST 1–23, 1914
Most couture houses remain open to present their new collections to buyers who have remained in Paris. Some houses show the new bell-shaped or "crinoline" line, while others fall back on the previous season's silhouettes in order to reassure nervous buyers.

FIG. T-6, FIG. 1.2

END OF AUGUST
Mass exodus of 1.5 million Belgian refugees toward France, the Netherlands, and England. 350,000 Belgian refugees will stay in France for the duration of the war.

SEPTEMBER 2, 1914
The French government, led by President Raymond Poincaré and Prime Minister René Viviani, relocates to Bordeaux for three and a half months.

SEPTEMBER 6–12, 1914
First battle of the Marne, which resulted in an Allied victory against Germany and halted the advance of German troops through France. Beginning of the trench warfare that typifies the next four years.

FIG. T-8, T-9

OCTOBER 11–13, 1914
German bombardment of the northern city of Lille begins. 5,000 shells are dropped and 800 buildings destroyed. Lille surrenders on October 13.

NOVEMBER 5, 1914
Britain and France declare war on the Ottoman Empire.

NOVEMBER 8, 1914
French government returns to Paris.

SEPTEMBER 1914 — **OCTOBER 1914** — **NOVEMBER 1914**

AUGUST 7, 1914
Prime Minister René Viviani delivers his call "Aux femmes françaises," summoning France's 3 million farming women to harvest the fields in the place of the men who had been called off to fight.

FIG. T-5, FIG. 4.2

AUGUST–SEPTEMBER 1914
Paul Poiret is mistakenly jailed for insubordination and then assigned to the 119th infantry regiment as a tailor.

SEPTEMBER 1914
German troops begin to occupy and destroy French cotton and wool factories in the northeastern regions of France. By the end of September, a handful of silk factories in Lyon adapted their looms in order to weave wool fabrics.

FIG. T-10, FIG. 5.15

FIG. T-7

FIG. T-12

DECEMBER 20, 1914
Beginning of the first battle of Champagne, the second Allied offensive against Germany since the battle of Ypres in Flanders (October 19–November 22, 1914). Mobile warfare has given way to trench warfare with the Allies on the offensive to push Germany out of northeastern France.

FEBRUARY 4, 1915
Germany declares a war zone around Britain and begins unrestricted submarine warfare.

DECEMBER 1914 — **JANUARY 1915** — **FEBRUARY 1915**

DECEMBER 1914
Several theaters reopen, including the Comédie-Française.

Poiret offers to help the government by designing a new uniform for the soldiers. This single-breasted "capote Poiret" uses less fabric than the previous model, designed in 1877. The uniform turns out to be too light, and as a result soldiers fall ill with pneumonia in the winter of 1914–15. The coat is discontinued shortly afterward.

FIG. T-11

DECEMBER 21, 1914
The Chambre Syndicale de la Couture Parisienne is disbanded in order to "purify" its membership of foreign couturiers.

JANUARY 1915
Women begin to replace men in jobs previously held exclusively by men. These female *remplaçantes*, or replacements, are hired for only the duration of the war.

FIG. T–13, FIG. 4.1d

FEBRUARY 1915
Germany tries to launch its own couture industry.

Leading Parisian couturiers Beer, Callot Sœurs, Chéruit, Dœuillet, Doucet, Jenny, Jeanne Lanvin, Martial & Armand, Paquin, Premet, and Worth show fashion models at the Panama–Pacific International Exposition, a world's fair held in San Francisco from February 20 to December 4, 1915.

FIG. T-15

APRIL 22, 1915
Second Battle of Ypres, Belgium, begins with a German offensive. The German army initiates the modern era of chemical warfare by launching a chlorine attack on two French colonial divisions at Ypres.

APRIL 24, 1915
Beginning of Armenian genocide perpetrated by the Turkish.

MAY 7, 1915
German torpedo attack sinks the RMS *Lusitania*, killing 1,198 passengers and leaving 761 survivors. This act helped turn public opinion against Germany.

MAY 23, 1915
Italy joins the war on the side of the Allies in return for Austrian territory around the Gulf of Venice.

FIG. T-16, FIG. 3.24

JULY 1, 1915
General Joseph Joffre allows all French soldiers to have a short leave of absence from the trenches of six to eight days, called a *permission*. Soldiers on temporary leave are called *permissionaires*.

MARCH 1915 **APRIL 1915** **MAY 1915** **JULY 1915**

MARCH 7, 1915
The "Drecoll Affair" begins, in which the Parisian couture house Drecoll is falsely accused of being led by German designers.

FIG. T-14, FIG. 7.2

MAY 5, 1915
The Chambre Syndicale de la Couture Parisienne is reorganized with only French-born members.

MAY 1915
Creation of the Photographic—and then Cinematographic—section of the Army.

Christoff von Drecoll sues Jean Aine-Montaillé and the *Le Figaro* newspaper for slander.

JULY 1915
Launch of *Le Style Parisien*, a new fashion magazine edited by Lucien Vogel.

JULY 15, 1915
Gabrielle Chanel opens her first couture shop in Biarritz. This is her third store, following a hat shop in Paris in 1910 and another in Deauville in 1913.

SEPTEMBER 25, 1915
Launch of French and British offensive attacks at Champagne, Loos, and Artois. The French and British gain a few miles, but at the cost of many casualties.

OCTOBER 29, 1915
René Viviani resigns as Prime Minister following a series of French defeats. Aristide Briand is elected in his place and holds the position until March 17, 1917.

NOVEMBER 25, 1915
Launch of the first war bond scheme, or *emprunt de la Défense nationale*.

AUGUST 1915 — **SEPTEMBER 1915** — **OCTOBER 1915** — **NOVEMBER 1915**

AUGUST 1915
Lucien Vogel and Condé Nast join forces to publish a special double issue—one French version and one English version—of the *Gazette du Bon Ton* in honor of the Panama–Pacific International Exposition in San Francisco.

FIG. T-17, FIG. 6.3

AUGUST 16, 1915
After the failure of Poiret's single-breasted uniform, the French Army returns to using the classic double-breasted uniform in "horizon blue" fabric.

NOVEMBER 1915
Armament manufacturers begin recruiting women, informally called *munitionnettes*, or female munitions workers.

The Syndicat de Défense de la Grande Couture Parisienne organizes a "Fête Parisienne," a French fashion party in New York. 100 couture ensembles are presented in various manners, including in a play written by Roger Boutet de Monvel about the financial plight of the *midinettes*, or couture seamstresses.

DECEMBER 2, 1915
General Joseph Joffre is elevated to Commander in Chief of the French Armies.

DECEMBER 1915

EXCELSIOR
Journal Illustré Quotidien
L'armée protège l'arrière : l'arrière travaille pour l'armée

FIG. T-18

FIG. T-19

FEBRUARY 21, 1916
The Battle of Verdun begins. The battle, which lasted for 303 days, was the longest of the First World War—it was also one of the most costly battles in human history. 275,000 French soldiers and 240,000 German soldiers are killed.

FEBRUARY 1916

FEBRUARY 1916
The textile manufacturer Rodier launches a new *djersette* fabric, with a warp fiber from silk and a weft from wool. In 1915, jersey was a novel fabric for use in casual daywear. By 1916 it was increasingly being used for dresses and suits.

Facing competition from the publishing house Hachette, *Le Style Parisien* issues its final number.

APRIL 1916

APRIL 1916
Lucien Vogel and Hachette launch a new fashion magazine, *Les Élégances Parisiennes*. Vogel stops publishing *Le Style Parisien* in order to devote himself to this new magazine.

FIG. T-20, FIG. 5c.37

MAY 16, 1916
Sykes-Picot agreement is signed and ratified in secret. In accord with Russia and Italy, the United Kingdom and France sign a treaty to define their mutually agreed spheres of influence and control in an eventual partition of the Ottoman Empire.

MAY 1916

MAY 1916
Jersey daytime suits by "Gabrielle Channel" (*sic*) are featured in *Les Élégances Parisiennes*.

FIG. T-21

JULY 1, 1916
Beginning of the Battle of the Somme, fought by British and French armies against the German Empire.

NOVEMBER 7, 1916
Woodrow Wilson is elected President of the United States.

JUNE 1916 · JULY 1916 · OCTOBER 1916 · NOVEMBER 1916

JUNE 1916
Les Élégances Parisiennes takes stock of the French fashion industry: lingerie exports had fallen since the start of the war, due to the loss of British and Belgian buyers; silk exports had increased since 1913; new markets were opening in Brazil and Argentina; 113 million francs of couture were exported in 1915, a decrease from 217 million francs in 1913.

JUNE 24, 1916
Women's Wear Daily reports on a new "Unis France" label created by an alliance of French fashion and textile syndicates to ensure the originality of French fashions against counterfeits and copies.

JULY 1916
Three jersey seaside suits by "Gabrielle Channel" (*sic*) are featured in *Les Élégances Parisiennes*.

FIG. T-22, FIG. 5c.43

OCTOBER 1916
British *Vogue* also features jersey fashions by "Channel" (*sic*).

FIG. T-23, FIG. 5a.3

FIG. T-24

DECEMBER 25, 1916
Robert Georges Nivelle replaces Joseph Joffre as Commander in Chief of the French army.

JANUARY 1917
Intense cold and worsening food and coal shortages.

MARCH 1, 1917
Sugar rationing cards are issued.

FIG. T-26, FIG. 8.2

MARCH 8, 1917
Start of the February revolution in Russia (named according to Russia's use of the Julian calendar). First phase of the more sweeping Russian Revolution of 1917.

MARCH 15, 1917
The Czar Nicolas II abdicates. Crowned ruler of Russia since 1894, the czar is replaced by a provincial government.

DECEMBER 1916 **JANUARY 1917** **FEBRUARY 1917** **MARCH 1917**

DECEMBER 1916
Paul Poiret makes plans to open "Poiret Incorporated" in New York. The store is designed to sell a limited number of styles that can be officially "copied" for American clients, a precursor to the ready-to-wear system. Poiret abandons the project when the Ministry of Defense refuses to grant him a leave of absence.

DECEMBER 1916 – JANUARY 1917
Parisian designers launch the new "barrel" silhouette, which uses less fabric than the bell or crinoline style but requires clients to update their wardrobe.

FEBRUARY 1917
Callots Sœurs, Chéruit, Edouard, Lanvin, Paquin, Poiret, Rodier, and Worth begin monthly deposits of photographs, illustrations, and textile swatches at the Parisian Copyright Office (*Conseil de Prud'hommes*) in an effort to protect their designs.

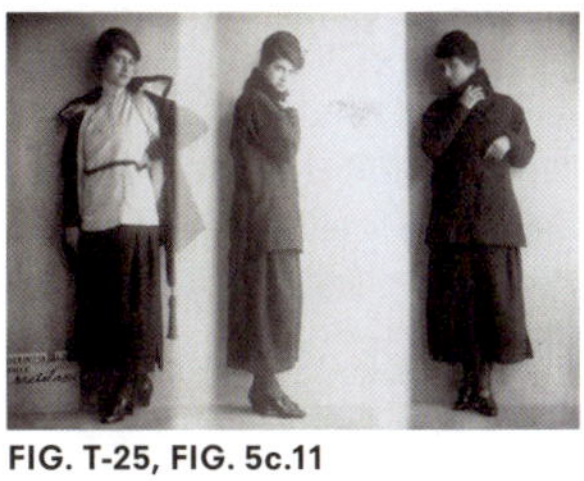

FIG. T-25, FIG. 5c.11

FIG. T-28

APRIL 6, 1917
The United States formally declares war against Germany and enters the conflict. The U.S. has a standing army of 127,000 officers and soldiers. By the end of the war, four million men will have served in the U.S. Army, with an additional 800,000 in other military service branches.

APRIL 16, 1917
Second Battle of the Aisne begins (*Bataille du Chemin des Dames* in French), a disastrous Franco-British offensive attack.

MAY 4, 1917
Soldiers begin to reject attack orders following the unsuccessful and costly Second Battle of the Aisne. The mutinies are kept secret from the Germans.

MAY 15, 1917
General Philippe Pétain replaces Robert George Nivelle as Commander in Chief of the French army.

MAY 1917
General John Joseph "Black Jack" Pershing is designated Commander of the American army in France and the American Expeditionary Forces (AEF) are created.

APRIL 1917

MAY 1917

APRIL 1917
New designs are shown at Paris couture shows. *Vogue* reports that the silhouette is longer and straighter than the previous season—a precursor to the postwar *garçonne* style.

FIG. T-27, FIG. 5c.24

MAY 1917
The Syndicat de Défense de la Grande Couture organizes a two-week exhibition of French fashion in Madrid.

MAY 11, 1917
180 seamstresses (*midinettes*) from the Jenny couture house strike for better wages and reduced work hours (called an "English work week").

10,000 midinettes from thirty-two couture houses join the Jenny strikers. By the end of May, more than 31,000 female workers from the dress, textile, and leather industries are striking for wage increases.

FIG. T-29, FIG. 9.1

MAY 22, 1917
The Chambre Syndicale de la Couture Parisienne cedes to the midinettes' demands and agree to pay the English week as well as a pay increase.

FIG. T-30

MAY 29, 1917
Pay increase for couture workers is voted into law and adopted without modification by the Senate on June 7, 1917.

OCTOBER 1917
First Division of the AEF enters the trenches in Nancy, France, the beginning of American involvement in trench warfare. From October 1917 until the summer of 1918, American divisions were usually employed to augment French and British units in defending their lines and staging attacks on German positions. Thereafter AEF commanders increasingly assumed sole control of American forces in combat.

FIG. T-31, FIG. 8.10

JUNE 26, 1917
The first 14,000 American soldiers begin arriving at the port of St. Nazaire in France.

JUNE 1917 — AUGUST 1917 — SEPTEMBER 1917 — OCTOBER 1917

JUNE 1917
Workers from seventy-one branches of French industries, including metalworkers, join the seamstresses on strike; a majority of the 133,000 strikers are women. This is the biggest labor strike Paris has known, as well as the most feminine.

AUGUST 1917
The U.S. imposes a ban on imported garments that use more than 4.5 meters of fabric.

The Chambre Syndicale de la Couture Parisienne elects Jeanne Paquin to replace Jean Aine-Montaillé as President.

SEPTEMBER 1917
Poiret is named head tailor of the Army.

The Chambre Syndicale de la Couture Parisienne sends a telegram to the American fashion press to assure them that the new couture models fall within the U.S. textile limit of 4.5 meters.

NOVEMBER 2, 1917
The British issue support for the establishment in Palestine of a national home for the Jewish people in the Balfour Declaration.

FIG. T-33

NOVEMBER 6–7, 1917
October Revolution. The Bolshevik Party seizes power in Russia in the second and final phase of the Russia Revolution.

NOVEMBER 16, 1917
Georges Clemenceau is appointed Prime Minister of France.

DECEMBER 15, 1917
Armistice between Soviet Russia and the Central Powers is concluded. Peace negotiations begin in Brest-Litovsk.

JANUARY 8, 1918
Fourteen Points address by President Wilson to a joint session of Congress outlines his proposal for a postwar peace settlement.

FEBRUARY 23, 1918
Food rationing cards are distributed.

NOVEMBER 1917 | **DECEMBER 1917** | **JANUARY 1918** | **FEBRUARY 1918**

NOVEMBER 1917
The government begins planning a "national fashion," or fixed price textiles, garments, and shoes, in order to help impoverished civilians and soldiers purchase new clothing.

FIG. T-32, FIG. 8.6

FIG. T-34

JANUARY 15, 1918
Vogue reports on the all-female drivers of the American Motor Corps created by the National League for Women's Service to transport patients, supplies, and personnel for the Red Cross, YMCA, and U.S. Army. 300 women served in France.

FIG. T-35

FEBRUARY 6, 1918
British women over the age of 30 obtain the right to vote in the Representation of People Act.

The Maison Chanel moves into new quarters at 21, rue Cambon.

MARCH 3, 1918

Treaty of Brest-Litovsk is signed by Soviet Russia on one side and the German Empire, Austria-Hungary, Bulgaria, and the Ottoman Empire on the other. The treaty marked Russia's withdrawal from World War I on harsh terms.

MARCH 21, 1918

Germans begin using long-range "Big Bertha" gun in an attempt at psychological warfare. The first shell lands in Paris on the Quai de Seine. 320 to 367 shells are fired, with a rate of around 20 a day. 250 people are killed and 620 wounded in all.

Beginning of the Spring Offensive, or Kaiserschlacht (Kaiser's Battle): A series of German attacks along the Western Front, in an attempt to break through Allied lines, outflank the British forces, and defeat the British Army before fresh American troops arrive.

FIG. T-36

MARCH 29, 1918

German shell hits a church in Saint-Gervais-et-Saint-Protais in Paris, killing 91 and wounding 68.

JULY 15, 1918

Beginning of the Second Battle of the Marne, the last major German offensive on the Western Front. The German defeat on August 6, 1918, marks the start of a relentless Allied advance, which culminates in the Armistice.

JULY 17, 1918

Execution of Nicholas II and the Russian Imperial Romanov family by Bolshevik troops.

MARCH 1918 — MAY 1918 — JUNE 1918 — JULY 1918

MARCH 1, 1918

Vogue inaugurates a new column, "Dressing on a War Income," for women who want to dress fashionably on a "war-reduced income."

MAY 1918

Les Modes publishes an article about "The Parisiennes Under the Bombs," illustrated with an image of a bomb shelter decorated by Poiret's Maison Martine. *Women's Wear Daily* reports that some Parisian couture houses were debating whether or not to leave Paris.

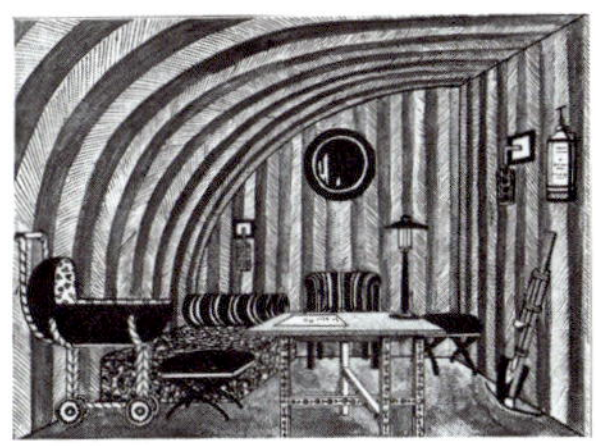

FIG. T-37

JUNE–AUGUST 1918

Some couture houses close their stores in Paris and open branches in Deauville and Biarritz.

AUGUST 8, 1918
The Battle of Amiens, also known as the Third Battle of Picardy begins. It is the opening phase of the Allied offensive, which begins in August and ultimately leads to the end of the war about 100 days later (Hundred Days Offensive).

SEPTEMBER 12, 1918
Battle of Saint-Mihiel, during which General Pershing commandeers the American First Army in the largest offensive operation ever undertaken by the U.S. armed forces.

EXCELSIOR
CE QU'ILS ONT SIGNE

FIG. T-39

SEPTEMBER 27–OCTOBER 6, 1918
General Pershing leads the successful Battle of Argonne offensive, commanding more than one million American and French soldiers. Allied forces recover more than 200 square miles of French territory from the German army.

NOVEMBER 9, 1918
Abdication of Wilhelm II and end of the German Empire.

NOVEMBER 11, 1918
Armistice is signed between the Allies and Germany, and fighting on the Western Front is suspended three times before peace was finally ratified with the Treaty of Versailles six months later.

AUGUST 1918 — **SEPTEMBER 1918** — **OCTOBER 1918** — **NOVEMBER 1918**

SEPTEMBER 1918
Couture houses hold openings despite bombing. *Vogue* reports that the "silhouette will be narrower than ever."

FIG. T-38, FIG. 5a.6

NOVEMBER 12, 1918
German women obtain the right to vote.

Women's Wear Daily reports that Spring couture openings are expected "to be the biggest in history of women's wear trade."

Poiret returns to Paris and encounters financial difficulties. He travels to Morocco in order to clear his mind of the war.

FIG. T-42

JUNE 28, 1919
Treaty of Versailles is signed after six months of Allied negotiations. The Treaty ends the state of war between Germany and the Allied powers, and imposes a number of harsh penalties on Germany.

DECEMBER 1918 — FEBRUARY 1919 — MAY 1919 — JUNE 1919 — AUGUST 1920

DECEMBER 19, 1918
Austrian women obtain the right to vote.

FEBRUARY 19, 1919
Callot Sœurs presents its first postwar collection: 400 models in a range of silhouettes, from wide bell-shaped to narrow.

FIG. T-40, FIG. 1.22

MAY 20, 1919
The *Assemblée Nationale* votes to allow female suffrage, but the *Sénat* rejects the law in November 1922. French women cast ballots for the first time on April 29, 1945.

FIG. T-41, FIG. 10.3

AUGUST 18, 1920
U.S. Congress ratifies the 19th Amendment granting women the right to vote.

Introduction

MAUDE BASS-KRUEGER

War changes everything, even what is furthest away from it.
(La guerre change tout, et jusqu'aux choses les plus éloignées d'elle.)

—JEAN RICHEPIN, *PROSES DE GUERRE*, 1915

In the winter of 1914, the French photographers and brothers Jules Séeberger, Louis Séeberger, and Henri Séeberger set out to photograph society women in the latest fashions. In one of the images from this series, two women pose for the camera wearing smart walking suits—their long jackets, closed with decorative buttons, are worn over crisp white blouses. FIG. I-1 They both wear fashionable hobble skirts, whose narrow circumference altered their gait and forced them to walk in small, mincing steps. Large fur coats, elaborate feathered hats, and a large fur muff for the woman on the left complete the look. If there were hints of an impending war on the horizon, they are not visible in this photograph, which reveals the absence of such concerns in high society. Four and a half years later, with the Great War over and Henri and Louis safely back from the trenches (Jules was not mobilized), the brothers took up fashion photography once again. In the first postwar photographic series, the Séebergers captured two women strolling in the woods. FIG. I-2 The season is the same, but the style has noticeably changed: the women's suits are plain, the skirts are cut to the calf, and the jackets are belted at the waist. The jackets no longer fit closely to the women's bodies but hang away from them like men's suits. The women carry nothing in their hands, save a walking stick for the woman on the right. Their clothing, shoes, and hats are simpler, with fewer embellishments and trimmings. When viewed next to each other, these two photographs make it clear that one era has ended and a new era has begun. The contrast in these images raises a central question that drives this book: What happened during the four years of the Great War to create such a vivid shift in the fashions, and what kind of impact did this shift have on the women themselves? Through print and visual culture, as well as garments, textiles, and accessories, this volume seeks to raise questions and to propose answers by exploring the relationship between fashion and war and the ways in which women, as well as the fashion and textile industries, negotiated both at the same time. *French Fashion, Women, and the First World War* goes beyond a mere examination of the economic system in which fashion and textiles were produced between 1914 and 1918. At its core, it looks at how women negotiated the tensions between fashion and war, and also how ideas, attitudes, and social mores were projected onto clothed women. Society held women to double standards when it came to getting dressed during the war: they were told to be elegant, yet were disparaged for appearing frivolous; they were encouraged to consume, yet were criticized for the financial independence their purchases suggested; they were told to look seductive in order to appeal to soldiers on leave, yet were castigated for unfaithfulness or, worse, prostitution. Few women escaped criticism about how they dressed—not the nurse, charity worker, factory worker or *remplaçantes* (women who replaced men who had been mobilized), and not even the widow. Wartime newspapers and satirical magazines abound with endless critical discourse about what women wore, how they wore it, and what their clothes meant. Representations of women wearing "questionable" clothing—too elegant, too extravagant, too feminine, too masculine, too ugly, too shoddy—permeated wartime visual culture in France.

Unfortunately, women's voices about what clothing meant to them in their wartime lives are hard to come by. We can assume that most working- and middle-class women purchased what was necessary for daily life, adding a few relatively inexpensive new things from time to time. Food, coal or firewood, and other household necessities undoubtedly came first. Women of means may have purchased new garments during the war, but they also might have mended and reused older garments more than in their prewar lives. Nurses, factory workers, and some remplaçantes were obliged to purchase specialized clothes or accessories for their new jobs. Uniforms and work wear could be bought ready-made at department stores or fashioned from widely available patterns. Widows were supposed to purchase several sets of appropriate black mourning garb from specialty stores, department stores, or their local seamstress, but some women simply wore black armbands to indicate their bereaved status—a more economical way of signaling their grief. In all cases, the criticism and anxious rhetoric that was projected onto clothed women was likely far removed from the actual experience these garments engendered in the women wearing them. The study of fashion during the war offers a new understanding of the ways in which French women, like the French textile and fashion system, were tasked with negotiating these new wartime realities.

There is nothing contradictory about uniting the terms *fashion* and *war*. This publication shows that this is particularly true in France. French fashion survived, and even thrived during the First World War. And this despite the massive destruction of the

FIG. I-1 Séeberger Frères. Two women at the races wearing tailored suits with hobble silhouettes, January 1914. Silver gelatin print. © Bibliothèque nationale de France, Département des Estampes et de la photographie, 0A 38 boîte 2 (janvier 1914, n°1, photo n°22).

FIG. I-2 Séeberger Frères. Two women wearing tailored suits with short skirts, January–February 1919. Silver gelatin print. © Bibliothèque nationale de France, Département des Estampes et de la photographie, 0A 38 boîte 2 (janvier - février 1919, n°1, photo n°39).

textile industries in the north of France; the general mobilization of French male textile and garment workers; a surfeit of problems relating to wartime exports, customs, and transport; economic inflation; and the devastation of caring for 4.2 million wounded French soldiers and mourning France's 1.3 million dead.

During the four years between 1914 and 1918, the French couture industry was the only luxury industry that the French government allowed to function without forcing it to close. The economics of the garment and textile trades were far too important for France's financial security for the government to impose undue constraints and regulations. Likewise, a robust and respected couture industry was essential for French morale. The French had dominated the global fashion scene before the war, and Parisian couturiers were concerned about the need to maintain this position despite the conflict. At the start of the war, workers, employees, and consumers formed alliances in order to stem the initial losses. However, as the war ground on, certain cracks began to appear: discontent among the workers, which ultimately led to the 1917 strike, and government plans for fixed-price clothing, textiles, and accessories as a way to address growing desperation caused by consumer price inflation. Women were central to this narrative: Jeanne Lanvin led the fight against counterfeiting; Jeanne Paquin helped negotiate the end of the strike by the *midinettes* (French couture seamstresses) in 1917 and was subsequently elected president of the Chambre Syndicale de la Couture Parisienne; Gabrielle "Coco" Chanel forged the foundations for her clothing business during the war. Female journalist Camille Duguet was an important voice in promoting fashion to French women during the war. Female workers were the beating heart of the fashion and textile industries during the war, stepping in to replace mobilized men in the male-dominated tailoring departments, leading the fight for better wages and hours during the 1917 strike, and working valiantly despite experiencing deep loss and grief. New fashion magazines, styles, and textiles were created and launched. Wartime designers did not, however, "liberate" women through their garments, as some historians have suggested. Wartime fashions followed the general tendency of the fashion cycle to renew itself every few years, war or no war; wartime styles were no more freeing than the prewar ones. The biggest change was the designation of the tailored suit as the "uniform of the home front," particularly for upper-class women. FIGS. 1-3–1-5 Working women had worn skirts, blouses, and jackets throughout the day for a long time, and this did not change in wartime. Upper-class women, accustomed to changing outfits as often as five time a day before the war, began to simplify their wardrobes, adopting the tailored suit in the morning and afternoon as the most practical garment for helping the war effort through charity work. FIG. I-6 The simplification of the silhouette that occurred between 1914 and 1918 helped usher in the new postwar look. The essays in this book examine representations of nurses, widows, elegant Parisiennes, humble midinettes, and hard-working women in order to understand how, during the First World War, they used fashion to shape their identities, but also how fashion was often used against them as a reflection of larger social anxieties. Women who went into nursing during the war often stemmed from the upper classes and were frequently featured in fashion magazines in their uniforms; this engendered disdain from the general public, who accused them of seducing soldiers for pleasure or of using their uniforms as a fashion statement. Widows, especially young ones, were also accused of appearing too fashionable in their black dresses; the most violent public rhetoric condemned young widows as prostitutes, their black dresses signaling to men that they were newly "available." Elegant Parisiennes were advised to purchase Parisian couture as a patriotic duty to the industry and were then attacked for their frivolity when they did so. Working women and remplaçantes were accused of "interfering" with gender norms when they donned work-issued outfits and coveralls. Fashion was a vital component of the French wartime economy and a lightning rod for male discourse; as the war progressed, men were increasingly anxious about the changes that were happening in front of their eyes. FIGS. I-7, I-8 This book is the first comprehensive study of French fashion during the First World War. Historians have written rich accounts of French war culture and French wartime gender relations, but very little on fashion. Although several articles on French wartime fashion exist, no volume has been devoted to the subject. This book is the first to weave an analysis of French fashion through the existing wartime historiography. Sources that had been overlooked for what they might say about fashion were reviewed, and new sources were found.

The agenda of French historiography of the Great War has been irrefutably set by the research on "war culture" conducted by Stéphane Audoin-Rouzeau and Annette Becker, former directors of the Historial de la Grande Guerre in Péronne. Defining war culture

FIG. I-3 A woman speaks to one of the marine riflemen who replaced the police in Paris, September 1914. Silver gelatin print. © Préfecture de Police, Service de l'Identité judiciaire / BHVP / Roger-Viollet, RV-76463-22.

FIG. I-4 Three women wearing blouses and tailored skirts, September 19, 1915. The woman seated in the middle wears a red, white, and blue ribbon fastened to her blouse. Silver gelatin print. Private collection.

FIG. I-5 A group of women wearing different versions of the ubiquitous tailored suit, date unknown. Silver gelatin print. Private collection.

FIG. I-6 Charles Lansiaux. An *ouvroir*, or charity sewing workshop, organized by Madame the Comtesse de Ricci within the rooms of the Musée de Sculpture Comparée, Palais du Trocadéro in Paris, October 7, 1914. © Charles Lansiaux / BHVP / Roger-Viollet, RV-73697-18.

FIG. I-7 Maurice Leroy. A female tramway conductress, from a series of postcards featuring women in different wartime roles (adoptive mother, letter writer, farmer, nurse, etc.), Paris: P.J. Gallais, ca. 1914–18. © BHVP / Roger-Viollet, CP 1328 a.

FIG. I-8 Albert Guillaume. Cartoon reflecting the underlying anxiety that men felt about women replacing them in their jobs and becoming more "masculine" in doing so. "I told you to wake me up at the Gare de l'Est, but that isn't a reason to shake me around like that!" exclaims the male passenger. "No, but really? . . . What did you expect? . . . That I was going to kiss you on the neck?" "Conductrice," *Le Rire Rouge*, November 27, 1915. Private collection.

as "many varieties of representation through which the French understood the war and their commitment to winning it," Audoin-Rouzeau and Becker's publications on the war methodically studied war violence and bodily damage, propaganda and popular culture, mourning, and private practices of memory and commemoration.[1] Excellent work by Antoine Prost and Jay Winter on civil society, identity and war, and sites of memory has greatly enriched the field as well.[2] These historians rely heavily on government war archives, war journals, police archives, trench journals, and printed ephemera and do not specifically address sources relating to the clothing or the fashion industry. Yet, when these same sources are examined for information about fashion, they yield rich results.

A variety of excellent publications on the male and female experiences of war have also come out of gender studies, some of them to coincide with the centenary. The collected essays in *Gender and the Great War*, edited by Susan Grayzel and Tammy Proctor, offer a transnational perspective to the gendered experiences faced by both men and women during the conflict.[3] Adding to the conversation, Tammy Proctor's *Civilians in a World at War, 1914–1918* explores the tension between how civilians "became central to the conflict as real targets and as justification for war" while also becoming marginalized.[4] Kimberly Jensen's *Mobilizing Minerva: American Women in the First World War* illuminates the American side of the story.[5]

Several collections of essays contain brief discussions about French fashion and clothing. These include Françoise Thébaud's groundbreaking *Les femmes au temps de la guerre de 14* (1986), followed by Susan Grayzel's *Women's Identities at War* (1999), Jean-Yves le Naour's *Misères et tourments de la chair: les moeurs sexuelles des Français, 1914–1918* (2002), and *Hommes et femmes dans la France en guerre* (2003) by Luc Capdevila, François Rouquet, Fabrice Virgili, and Danièle Voldman.[6] The first chapter of Mary Louise Roberts's *Civilization without Sexes* (1994) is instrumental in framing how fashion can be used to study the "reconstruction" of gender in interwar France.[7] Florence Brachet-Champsaur's essay "De l'odalisque de Poiret à la femme nouvelle de Chanel: une victoire de la femme," in the book *1914–1918: Combats de femmes* (2004), edited by Evelyne Morin-Rotureau, provides a contained study of fashion during the First World War.[8] New scholarship from fashion historians in Britain has enriched the historiography of World War I fashion studies. Nina Edwards and Lucy Adlington, a cultural critic and a dress historian, respectively, have published two helpful general-interest books on fashion during the war: *Dressed for War: Uniform, Civilian Clothing and Trappings, 1914 to 1918*, which examines military and civilian clothing in England, France, and Germany, and *Great War Fashion: Tales from the History Wardrobe*, which explores the lives and clothing of British women during the conflict. These works provide important leads on sources relating to women and World War I, including fashion magazines, postcards, published diaries, photographs, and archives relating to women's wartime work.[9]

The surprising lack of work on French wartime fashion cannot be attributed to the paucity of sources. The Archives Départementales de Paris has precious photographs and textile swatches for copyright deposit from the designers Worth (1917–30), Rodier (1917–34), Paquin (1917–34), and Callot Sœurs (1917–36).[10] FIGS. I-9, I-10 The Archives Nationales houses police reports on *habillement* (clothing) in the series F7 and records of commerce and industry in the series F12.[11] The Archives de Police reveal records of employment and activity within the couture houses, as well as a rich trove of documents related to women who stole garments from department stores during the war.[12] Documents held at the Bibliothèque Forney in Paris prove to be some of the most useful for research, from department store catalogues (Le Bon Marché, Le Printemps, Les Galeries Lafayette, Le Louvre, La Samaritaine) to the archive of postcards and fashion magazines. FIG. I-11 The Centre des Documentation des Musées—Musée des Arts Décoratifs (MAD) has documents on designers, and the Historial de la Grande Guerre in Péronne has archives on women and the war, fashion, postcards, iconography, and some working-class women's clothing.

French libraries and archives hold wartime issues of *Les Arts Français* (1918), *La Baïonnette* (1914–18), *Le Bon Ange du Foyer* (April–June 1917), *Chiffons* (October 1916–December 1917), *Les Élégances Parisiennes* (1916–19), *Femina* (July 1914; May 1917–December 1918), *La Femme de France* (1915–19), *Le Figaro* (1914–18), *La France Universelle* (July 1916–July 1918), *La Gazette du Bon Ton* (summer 1915), *La Gazette du Bon Ton: 1915 Mode as Shown by Paris* (1915), *L'Illustration* (1914–18), *J'ai Vu* (1915–18), *The New York Times* (1914–18), *La Midinette* (February 1914–April 1915), *La Mode Illustrée* (1914–18), *La Mode Pratique* (1914–18), *Les Modes* (1915–17), *L'Oeuvre Française* (December 1918), *L'Opinion: Journal de la Semaine* (1914–18), *Le Sourire de France*, 1914–18), and *Le Style Parisien* (July 1915–July 1916). FIG. I-12 Finally, the wartime registers of the Chambre Syndicale de la Couture Parisienne, held

FIG. I-9 House of Worth. "Grenadier" coat, named after a specialized soldier known for his red uniform, with textile sample for copyright deposit, February 21, 1918. Coat: wool, mousseline, silk embroidery; sample: paper, ink, wool swatch, mousseline swatch. © Carole Rabourdin / Archives de Paris / Roger-Viollet, RV-157094-4.

FIG. I-10 Paquin. "Marmouset" afternoon dress in blue poplin for copyright deposit, August 13, 1917. Silver gelatin print. © Archives de Paris / Roger-Viollet, RV-101320-1.

GRANDS MAGASINS DU LOUVRE - PARIS
COSTUMES TAILLEUR
65804.
65805
65804.
65805.
65804.
COSTUME
tailleur
en draperie fantaisie
et damier noir et blanc,
jaquette
doublée sergé mi-soie.
65805.
COSTUME
tailleur
en damier noir et blanc
et serge marine et noire,
jaquette
doublée soie.
65801. COSTUME tailleur en serge et draperie fantaisie, jaquette doublée sergé mi-soie . . . . Le costume 69. »
En serge ou gabardine, très belle qualité jaquette doublée soie. Le costume 89. »
Le costume . . 79. »
En gabardine, jaquette doublée soie.
Le costume . . . 95. »
65802. COSTUME tailleur en damier noir et blanc, serge et draperie fantaisie, jaquette doublée soie.
Le costume. . . . 89. »
Le costume . . 98. »
Le même, en toile blanche et couleurs.
Le costume . . 49. »
65708. COSTUME tailleu
marine et noire, et très be
noir et blanc, jaquette dou
Le costume . . . . . .

CC 268 "1916" févr

GRANDS MAGASINS DU LOUVRE - PARIS I

COSTUMES TAILLEUR

65704.

65703

65704.

65703.

65704.
COSTUME
tailleur
en serge et très beau
damier,
noir et blanc,
passepoils couleur,
gilet piqué blanc,
jaquette doublée soie.
Le costume 145. »

65703
COSTUME
tailleur
en belle serge marine
et noire et gabardine,
bordé tresse Réal,
col faille blanche,
jaquette doublée soie.
Le costume 175. »

. COSTUME tailleur en serge marine
oire, garni galon, col organdi,
ette doublée soie Le costume 125. »
abardine . . . . 135. »

65702. COSTUME tailleur en draperie fantaisie et serge marine et noire, jaquette doublée soie Le costume 135. »

65706. COSTUME tailleur en gabardine et serge marine et noire, gilet soie fantaisie, jupe haute nouveauté, jaquette doublée soie. Le costume 215. »

Tous nos Articles confectionnés se recommandent par leur bon goût et leur exécution.

FIG. I-11 Grands Magasins du Louvre department store catalogue showing tailored suits, February 1916. © Bibliothèque Forney / Roger-Viollet, RV-203791-8.

at the Fédération de la Haute Couture et de la Mode, are a particularly rich resource for the study of the structure of the French couture industry during the war. The findings from these registers are published for the very first time in this book. The two main sections of this book, although interconnected, constitute a specific area that provides larger contextualization for the contributing essays and case studies. Case studies of specific garments or designers complement and enrich several of the essays.

Margaret Darrow, in "French Women and the First World War," provides the book with a central narrative for the roles that French women took on during the war and the response that they engendered in doing so. CHAPTER 1 Asked to "embody the nation that French men defended," women were expected to fulfill conflicting desires: to be frivolous yet defiant, fashionable while upholding traditions, family oriented but sensual. Darrow's essay provides an important overview of how female factory workers, peasants, remplaçantes, midinettes, war charity volunteers, and nurses engaged in the war effort. For some women the war opened up new social, economic, or political opportunities, Darrow concludes, whereas for others, "war service seemed a parenthesis rather than a life-changing experience." FIG. I-13

Johanne Berlemont and Anaïs Raynaud, curators at the Musée de la Grande Guerre, in Meaux, France, examine two nurse's uniforms from their collection through the lens of the history of French female nursing in the first case study. CHAPTER 1a Berlemont and Raynaud, like Darrow, reveal the tension between the sacrifice and selflessness of these "white angels" and the criticism they received for appearing too "frivolous," "fashionable," or "seductive" in their pristine white uniforms. Susan Grayzel's essay, "'Needles En Avant!': The Militarization of Women's Sewing and Knitting during the First World War in France, Great Britain, and America," examines how the militarization of women's domestic labor—especially sewing and knitting—became one of the more ubiquitous and significant ways in which women contributed to the war and by which the war came home. CHAPTER 2 Postcards depicting women knitting reinforced gender roles, in which they were expected to provide material and emotional support. Grayzel, who enlarges the scope of this book with an important transnational perspective, also writes of the failure and futility of such work in preventing suffering and loss. In "Fashion, Gender, and Anxiety," I look at how caricatures, postcards, and writing about wartime fashion reveal deep unease about what women were doing while men were at war. CHAPTER 3 Commentary on fashionable women and fashionable dress masked anxiety about women who no longer "needed" men, had forgotten them, or else were enamored with officers and foreign soldiers rather than the common French infantryman, or poilu. Fashion, when refracted through the lens of war, bore the brunt of wartime anxiety around reconfigured gender roles. FIG. I-14 The problem with women's clothed bodies extended to mourning garments as well, which I examine in a case study that charts the simplification of wartime mourning fashion and the critical discourse it raised in light of male anxiety about being forgotten or replaced. CHAPTER 3a Mourning clothes, like nurse's uniforms and female work wear, were imbued with complex and often contradictory ideas about female emancipation, frivolity, and sexuality. FIG. I-15 This section concludes with two essays on clothing for the working woman. Kurkdjian's essay on the representation of working women in the photographic archive of the *Excelsior* newspaper argues that the mise-en-scène of these remplaçantes was intended to feminize their appearance, to appease male anxiety about working women, or to encourage more women to apply for these jobs. CHAPTER 4 Jérémie Brucker's case study on female work overalls, or *combinaisons de travail*, charts the history of how this garment was used by women during the war against its perceived "masculinization" of the female body. CHAPTER 4a Like Kurkdjian, Brucker notes the prevalent "feminization" of women wearing work overalls, both through photographic techniques and the manufacture of a new, more shapely pair of overalls designed specifically for the female body. In the alternating essays in the section entitled "French Fashion: Adapting to Crises," Kurkdjian and I examine the development of the fashion industry and the fashion press from the first "war crinoline" collection in August 1914 to the midinette strike in 1917 and its aftermath. The first chapter of this section traces the French wartime fashion industry from the chaotic first months of the war, during which nearly half of the French textile industry was destroyed by the German occupation of northeastern France, to the slow rebuilding of the textile and garment trades, thanks to Lyon-based silk manufacturing, new "war crinoline" and "barrel" silhouette collections, and the collective efforts by couturiers and manufacturers to market their styles abroad. CHAPTER 5 AND FIG. I-16 In "Jeanne

N° 172 LES MODES 1917

DIRECTION ET RÉDACTION
15, rue de la Ville-l'Évêque, Paris

ABONNEMENT ET VENTE
24, boulevard des Capucines, Paris

ADMINISTRATION
15, rue de la Ville-l'Évêque, Paris

Photo Henri Manuel.

LA BOUTIQUE DE « *ROSE BERTIN* »

L'EXPOSITION DU SYNDICAT DE LA PRESSE PARISIENNE EN FAVEUR DES ÉPROUVÉS DE LA GUERRE

AU PETIT PALAIS

FIG. I-12 Front cover of the fashion magazine *Les Modes* from 1917, featuring a photograph from a charity exhibition organized by the Syndicat de la Presse Parisienne (Union of Parisian Press) to donate money to those affected by war. *Les Modes: revue mensuelle illustrée des Arts décoratifs appliqués à la femme*, 1917, no. 172. © Bibliothèque nationale de France, FOL-V-4312 - 1917 (N172).

FIG. I-13 Satirical postcard entitled "Women's Place" mocking the new jobs for women: "Make Way for Women: We already have women doctors and lawyers, conductors, postal workers, drivers, etc. Tomorrow we'll have female Ministers. Minister of Supply: Will lead by example and guarantee milk. Minister of Finance: Unmatched in making the taxpayer settle up. Minister of War: Knows better than anyone else how to reduce bulges and protect lines. Minister of the Navy: Has a gift for getting ships quickly out to sea and the masts up." Paris: A.H. Katz, ca. 1914–18. © BHVP / Roger Viollet, CP 1720 a.

LA BAÏONNETTE

(Dessin d'Armengol.)

SOUHAIT IMPRÉVU

— *Je voudrais bien que mon mari revienne.*
— *Pour vous remplacer ?*
— *Non, pour garder les gosses !*

— 334 —

FIG. I-14 Henri Armengol. "Souhait Imprévu," a cartoon published in the satirical magazine *La Baïonnette*, which was founded during the war (1915–20) and published thematic issues. Women workers were often satirized for their supposedly masculine behavior, as in this example, entitled "Unexpected Wish: 'I would like my husband to return.' 'To replace you?' 'No, to babysit the kids!'" *La Baïonnette*, November 18, 1915. Private collection.

FIG. I-15 Mourning ensemble, 1916–17. Jacket: silk, wool beads; dress: cashmere, silk, wood beads. Paris, Musée des Arts Décoratifs, UF 70 45 4 a,b.

FIG. I-16a, b. Front and back view a suit of tailored wool twill, probably French, 1915. Wool twill. The Metropolitan Museum of Art, Gift of Mme. Louis Cerlian, 1940, C.I.40.90.7a,b.

Paquin, Jeanne Lanvin, Jenny, and Gabrielle Chanel, 1914–18" Kurkdjian provides an overview of the businesses and designs of the leading female designers in Paris—Jeanne Paquin, Jeanne Lanvin, Jenny Sacerdote, and Gabrielle Chanel. CHAPTER 5c Paquin, Lanvin, and Sacerdote were already smart businesswomen before the war, and the four years of hostilities did nothing to diminish their dominance on the international scene. Chanel rose to prominence as a couturier during the war, as her simple jersey suits were emblematic of the new era. Michele Majer's essay on the wartime suit distinguishes between the simple *tailleur classique* and the more complex *tailleur couturier*, both of which adapted themselves to the war through their use of textiles (silk and jersey), silhouettes (larger pockets), and trimmings (patriotically named colors and detailing). CHAPTER 5d AND FIGS. I-17, I-18 The garment's appropriateness to wartime realities made its influence ubiquitous throughout the war and into the interwar period. Kurkdjian's former position as archivist at the Fédération de la Haute Couture et de la Mode in Paris, where the wartime archives for the Chambre Syndicale de la Couture Parisienne are held, allowed her to expand upon the work I had done in the archives as a master's student, adding a new storyline with the Syndicat de Défense de la Grande Couture Française. She looks at how both the Chambre Syndicale and the Syndicat were restructured during the war and how they concentrated on promoting French fashion overseas. CHAPTER 6 Kurkdjian's expertise in the twentieth-century fashion press provides the basis for her chapter "Copying is Stealing!," in which she examines the phenomenon of German fashion magazines and fashions that marketed themselves as French. CHAPTER 7 She also charts the history of how two new magazines were launched during the war: *Le Style Parisien*, which had a print run of seven issues between July 1915 and February 1916, and *Les Élégances Parisiennes*, published between April 1916 and February 1924. The two following chapters outline the economic strain of the war, which forced the French government to plan a fixed-price "national fashion," and the hardships faced by female workers during the war, which led to the 1917 seamstress-led general strikes. CHAPTERS 8 AND 9 The demands of 180 midinettes from the Jenny couture house for better wages and working hours inspired more than 133,000 women from all industries to to go on strike during May and June of 1917. FIG. I-19 I argue that although this strike was instrumental in helping the midinettes achieve better working conditions, it also created resentment between women of different classes once the strike was over, particularly between the wealthy Jeanne Paquin and her working-class employees.

Finally, "Returning to the Gender Question" revisits the question of female emancipation in light of wartime fashion.

CHAPTER 10 The wartime fashions were not emancipatory per se, but they signaled female emancipation for contemporary commentators. Did the shifting silhouette reflect the social changes engendered by the war, or did women actively seek out certain fashions in order to claim new freedoms? In conclusion, Sophie and I argue that any perceived liberating effects of wartime fashion were not only offset by other sartorial or corporal constraints (heavy styles, high boots, makeup, dieting), but were also tempered by the larger socioeconomic reality of postwar France: the rights women gained during the war were revoked as soon as the Armistice was signed. Repopulating the country was more important than female suffrage in the interwar period—French women had to wait until 1945 to have the right to vote for the first time. The politics of fashion during the wartime period suggests that women's clothing had great power to incite public discussion, generate apprehension and unease, and perhaps even foster individual feelings of independence.

FIG. I-17 Grands Magasins du Louvre. Tailored suit with sailor-style collar, ca. 1915. Linen, cotton, metal buttons and buckles. Paris, Musée des Arts Décoratifs, 2012.115.18.1,2.

FIG. I-18 Tailored suit with sailor-style collar, 1915–16. Cotton, organdy. Paris, Musée des Arts Décoratifs, UF 90.52.28.AB.

6 Mardi 22 mai 1917

ANNONCEURS !... Vous êtes-vous aperçus de l'impulsion nouvelle donnée à ce journal? — **Profitez-en...**

EXCELSIOR

LA PUBLICITÉ ne crée pas le succès là où il n'y a pas d'éléments de succès. Elle ne fait qu'accélérer et augmenter le succès des produits qui en sont dignes.

APRÈS LES COUTURIÈRES, LES MODISTES SE SONT MISES EN GRÈVE

RUE RICHEPANSE, DES MODISTES BARRENT GAIEMENT LE CHEMIN A L'UNE DE LEURS CAMARADES QUI SE RENDAIT A SON TRAVAIL

Le mouvement s'étend : après les ouvrières de la couture — dont le conflit avec leurs patrons continue, bien qu'on s'attendît hier à une solution définitive — celles de la mode, présentant des revendications identiques, se sont mises en grève. Ayant quitté leurs ateliers, elles ont manifesté dans la rue hier, cherchant à débaucher celles de leurs camarades qui travaillaient encore. Pour pénétrer dans les maisons de mode fermées, l'une d'elles sonnait, s'introduisait prestement et montait aux ateliers faire de la propagande.

LE ROI D'ITALIE INTERROGEANT UN SOLDAT PENDANT L'OFFENSIVE

ENTOURÉ D'OFFICIERS ANGLAIS ET ITALIENS, LE SOUVERAIN CAUSE FAMILIÈREMENT AVEC UN COMBATTANT. — A DROITE, LE GÉNÉRAL PORRO

Le roi Victor-Emmanuel a suivi de très près les différentes phases de l'offensive déclenchée contre les Autrichiens, de Tolmino à l'Adriatique, et qui, à l'heure actuelle, coûte à l'ennemi plus de 30.000 hommes en morts, blessés et prisonniers. On le voit ici devant son quartier général, demandant des renseignements sur la bataille à un combattant qui revient des premières lignes. Derrière lui se tiennent des officiers de sa suite et des officiers d'une mission britannique. A droite, le général Porro, chef d'état-major général.

FIG. I-19 Front cover of the newspaper *Excelsior*, May 22, 1917, showing female hat makers on strike. "After The Seamstresses, The Hat-Makers Have Gone On Strike." Private collection.

1 The original French definition of *culture de guerre* proposed by Audoin-Rouzeau and Becker was "Le champ de toutes les représentations de la guerre forgées par les contemporains: de toutes les représentations qu'ils se sont données de l'immense épreuve, pendant celle-ci d'abord, après celle-ci ensuite." Stéphane Audoin-Rouzeau and Annette Becker, "Violence et consentement: la 'culture de guerre' du premier conflit mondial," in *Pour une histoire culturelle,* ed. Jean-Paul Rioux and Jean-François Sirinelli (Paris: Seuil, 1997), 252. The translated definition comes from the introduction of Leonard V. Smith, Stéphane Audoin-Rouzeau, Annette Becker, *France and the Great War* (Cambridge: Cambridge University Press, 2003), 3. Both Audoin-Rouzeau and Becker have extensive bibliographies of books on the First World War.

2 Notably, Antoine Prost and Jay Winter, *Penser la Grande Guerre: un essai d'historiographie* (Paris: Seuil, 2004).

3 Susan Grayzel and Tammy Proctor, ed., *Gender and the Great War* (Oxford: Oxford University Press, 2017).

4 Tammy Proctor, *Civilians in a World at War* (New York: New York University Press, 2010), 268.

5 Kimberly Jensen, *Mobilizing Minerva: American Women in the First World War* (Champaign: University of Illinois Press, 2008).

6 Françoise Thébaud, *Les femmes au temps de la guerre de 14* (Paris: Stock, 1986); and subsequent re-edition Françoise Thébaud, *Les femmes au temps de la guerre de 14* (Paris: Payot, 2013); Susan Grayzel, *Women's Identities at War: Gender, Motherhood, and Politics in Britain and France during the First World War* (Chapel Hill: University of North Carolina Press, 1999); Jean-Yves Le Naour, *Misères et tourments de la chair durant la Grande Guerre* (Paris: Aubier, 2002); *Hommes et Femmes dans la France en Guerre, 1914–1945,* ed. Luc Capdevila, François Rouquet, and Fabrice Virgili (Paris: Payot, 2003).

7 Mary Louise Roberts, *Civilization without Sexes: Reconstructing Gender in Postwar France, 1917–1927* (Chicago: University of Chicago Press, 1994).

8 Evelyne Morin-Rotureau, *1914–1918: Combats de Femmes: Les Femmes, Pilier de l'Effort de Guerre* (Paris: Autrement, 2004).

9 Nina Edwards, *Dressed for War: Uniform, Civilian Clothing and Trappings, 1914 to 1918* (London: I.B. Tauris, 2014), and Lucy Adlington, *Great War Fashion, Tales from the History Wardrobe* (London: The History Press, 2014).

10 Archives Départementales de Paris. The Worth archives contain 332 models from 1917 and 1918 and are located under DEM 397/4439-4580, DEM 398/4587-4694, DEM 399/4707-4850. The Rodier archives contain four drawings of scarves from 1917, DEM 326/4529. The Paquin archives contain 154 photographs from 1917 and 1918, DEM 249/4540-4551 and DEM 250/4693. The Callot Sœurs archives contain 656 models from 1917 and 1918, under DEM 48/4546, DEM 50-55/4684-4698, DEM 56/4710, DEM 57-61/4774-4775, DEM 62-62/4792.

11 Archives Nationales, F7/13.740/1–3 for notes on the Congrès National de la Fédération de l'Habillement; F7/13.741/4–6 for the Syndicat de la Chapellerie; F7/13.880/1–3, F7/13.881/4–7, F7/13.882/8-12 for the Grève des ouvriers: chemisiers, chapellerie, coupure, bonnetière, tailleurs, lingères, etc. F12/7684–7697 had helpful documents on all branches of the textile industry during the war.

12 Archives de la Préfecture de Police, Paris, BA 1376 (Habillement, 1917–1918), BA 1423 (Les Syndicats de l'Alimentation et de l'Habillement), BA 1564 (Vols dans les magasins, jusqu'à 1915).

I

French Women and the First World War

MARGARET H. DARROW

It seems paradoxical to unite these two words: woman and war.

FIG. 1.1 So mused François de Witt-Guizot in a 1912 speech intended to answer the question "How can a woman serve France in wartime?"[1] This question had puzzled commentators since the disaster of the Franco-Prussian War in 1870. A spate of books publicized the heroic actions of French women during that war, while magazine articles, plays, and textbooks celebrated France's historic war heroines, including several more or less mythical women soldiers of the revolutionary wars and, of course, Joan of Arc.[2] In 1910, feminist Marguerite Durand had campaigned for a national service requirement for young women that would be equivalent to the obligatory military service of young men. But none of this actually answered the question of what French women's duties were to their country in wartime. Witt-Guizot, a Red Cross promoter, at least had a concrete response: French women were to nurse the wounded. However, even he admitted that only a few highly trained women could fill this role. For most French women, the paradox remained: in wartime, especially when France was invaded and besieged, its national existence in danger, women should do something! But what? The two terms, woman and war, remained irreconcilable. As a result, any action that women took, any wartime role they assumed, garnered both applause and criticism.

Entry into War

When Germany attacked France in August 1914, the French government had no plans to involve most French women in the national defense. In 1907, in the Moroccan campaign, the French Red Cross for the first time had been authorized to provide nurses for military medical facilities, although not in the battle zones; in 1914 some 23,000 Red Cross nurses were "mobilized" along with the soldiers.[3] But otherwise, the only French women to whom the government made any appeal were peasants, who were implored by Prime Minister René Viviani on August 7 to bring in the harvest. Women who bombarded the Ministère de Guerre (Ministry of War) with offers to drive ambulances, fly planes, set up hospitals, and form military auxiliaries like those in Britain were either turned away or ignored. Women were to remain at home to embody what French masculinity was defending in battle. For women to intrude upon the war would presumably weaken rather than strengthen the French war effort.

An early, strange but significant manifestation of the antithesis between femininity and war in the French mindset was the sudden appearance of a mysterious lady in a hat. The outbreak of war in August

1914 had caught many people, both French and foreign, while vacationing at France's beaches, mountains, and resorts. But the public was sure that this woman was no innocent vacationer! For a few weeks in August, she appeared to be ubiquitous; people spotted her dozens of times across the country from the Marne in the northeast to the Lot-et-Garonne in the south.[4] She reportedly drove a powerful car, her face discreetly hidden by a large, fashionable hat. Some officials claimed she scrutinized railway lines and bridges; she asked for directions in a strange accent. Others accused her of contaminating wells or giving poisoned candy to children. She was mobile, fashionable, independent—out of place! Of course, she must be a German spy! This mythic threat found perfect embodiment three years later in Mata Hari, a Dutch exotic dancer executed for espionage on the flimsiest of evidence, more for what she appeared to be than for anything she had done.[5]

If women travelers stirred up such fears, women who found themselves in the war zone attracted even more suspicion. Not even nurses were exempt. One general stormed: "Now the whole country is full of secretive females with fancy Red Cross outfits, subject to no form of control. Many undesirables must be included among their activities, and it is an obvious means of access for hostile agents."[6]

As the German invasion swung through Belgium and into northern France, many women were caught directly in the war without having any choice in the matter. Forced to decide whether to flee or to stay put, women heard conflicting advice. Sometimes French officials identified women in the war zone as citizens whom it was the army's duty to defend, and sometimes they were regarded as nuisances, "useless mouths" who should be removed in the interest of greater military efficiency.[7] Women's feelings of duty to their families and to France could pull them in both directions. For example, Marguerite Lesage, the wife of a sugar manufacturer in the Oise, weighed her responsibility to keep her husband's business in operation against her duty to her young children to remove them to a safer place.[8] Families who fled became refugees, at first met with solicitude and charity, but later, in the words of historian Annette Becker, "they became useless mouths, nuisances, incompetents, poor. In short, foreigners," labeled "Boches du Nord" and targets of xenophobia.[9] FIG. 1.2

Women who remained in their homes in the war zone on the French side of the lines faced ambivalence from Allied armies. In the summer and fall of 1914, the people of northern France welcomed the arrival of soldiers, whether French or British,

FIG. 1.1 Two women with a soldier wearing the standard-issue military coat designed by Paul Poiret, ca. 1915. Postcard. Private collection.

FIG. 1.2 Agence Rol. "Fleeing from the barbarians (civilians fleeing on foot)," 1914. Negative print on glass. © Bibliothèque nationale de France, Département des Estampes et de la photographie, EST EI-13 (408).

and did their best to accommodate them. But as the war dragged on, feelings on both sides soured. Incidents of pilfering and property damage by soldiers tainted the armies' reputations. Marguerite Lesage's sugar refinery was alternately occupied by German and French troops, and she found the passage of the French troops as devastating as that of the Germans.[10] The soldiers' views of war-zone civilians also plummeted when they did not meet with the gratitude they thought they deserved. And women were often at the center of this fraught relationship. The popular song "Quand Madelon" idealized the war-zone waitress as every soldier's sweetheart:

But your girl is far away, too far for you to tell her — Everything you'd do when your group gets back. — You sigh as you count the days, and when time seems to drag — Everything you could not say to her, you can say to Madelon.[11] FIG. 1.3 But in their diaries, memoirs, and novels, soldiers depicted women in the war zone as war profiteers, making the soldiers pay dearly for such "luxuries" as straw for bedding, eggs, bread, and wine.[12] So out of place did women seem that innocuous behavior, such as listening to soldiers' conversations, running errands, hanging out laundry, or the simple fact that a woman's home had not been shelled by the German artillery, raised suspicions of collusion with the enemy.[13]

The assumption that women should not be in the war legitimated sexual assault for some soldiers, who assumed that they were as entitled to sex as they were to lodging and food and that women in the war zone were required to provide all three. One British soldier who witnessed a screaming girl in a hay loft trying to get away from two soldiers justified the fact that he did not intervene by concluding that she was putting on "a farcical act of fraudulent innocence."[14] Women in the war zone were out of place, suspect, and thus fair game.

Occupation

Women in French territory that was invaded and then occupied by the German army faced all of these difficulties and more. FIG. 1.4 The most dangerous periods were the summer and fall of 1914 and the spring of 1918, during German invasions, and the summer and fall of 1918, during the German withdrawal and Allied advance. Although many of the atrocity stories reported in the press in the summer and fall of 1914—bayonetted babies, crucified Canadians—were propaganda, German soldiers did take civilian hostages, shot suspected snipers, burned villages, and raped women. As in the Allied war zone, there are no reliable statistics of the incidence of rape in Occupied France;

sexual assault was seriously underreported both because of women's shame and because they assumed that officials would not take such accusations seriously. The position of German soldiers as conquerors heightened their sense of entitlement. Here, rapes were likely to be public affairs, witnessed by other soldiers and by civilians to underline the reality of conquest.[15] As historians John Horne and Alan Kramer remind us, "Rape demonstrated in the starkest possible way that the relationship between invader and invaded was also one of gender."[16]

The narrative of Occupation was gendered in such a way that it endangered women. Women were not only the majority in occupied populations, but they also figured symbolically as the quintessential innocent victims of the enemy's barbarism.[17] The most publicized example of the latter was the German requisition of labor during Easter week in 1916. Military patrols went from house to house in Lille, Roubaix, and Tourcoing conscripting residents for work in agriculture and construction. Although most were men and boys, it was the conscription of young women, called by the French press an "*enlèvement*" (i.e., an abduction), that engendered outrage. According to government propaganda, widely distributed especially in the United States, this was "the most brutal and most revolting" of German war crimes.[18]

But while women were the exemplars of innocent victimhood, they were also the heroic standard-bearers of French patriotism and civilization. The reverse of atrocity stories were the many stories of heroines of the invasion publicized in the first year of the war.[19] The story of Clotilde Boucry, a peasant girl, is a good example. According to the tale, Boucry duped a patrol of German cavalry, then led them into an ambush by French soldiers, and finally intervened with their captors to save their lives: "'I only ask,' she said, her voice becoming grave, 'that you don't harm the prisoners.' Unshaken and compassionate, as incapable of cruelty as of disloyalty, . . . such is the soul of our women."[20] In this way, the story uneasily reconciled wartime violence with femininity.

FIG. 1.5

Stories like this created a conundrum for women in the occupied territory. Resisting German demands extracted a heavy price. Celebrated British nurse Edith Cavell was not the only woman who paid with her life for helping Germany's enemies.[21] Even trivial offenses, such as failing to deliver requisitioned goods, impertinence, and wearing tri-colored ribbons, earned fines and prison terms.[22] On the other hand, in order to survive and especially to provide for their families, women often had to accommodate the occupying forces, such as lodging German troops, which then

FIG. 1.3 Gus Bofa. Soldiers marching through a French town singing "Quand Madelon." Captioned "And this evening on the front lines they will sing too..." *La Baïonnette,* October 3, 1918. © BHVP / Roger-Viollet, RV-203792-2.

FIG. 1.4 Map of French territory occupied by the German army (in green), 1914–18. Courtesy of Jonathan Chipman, Citrin GIS/Applied Spatial Analysis Lab, Dartmouth College.

FIG. 1.5 F. Fau. The wartime heroine Clotilde Boucry faces the German cavalry. Captioned "'Halt!' cries an Uhlan," this image refers to the story of Boucry duping a German patrol and leading them into an ambush by French soldiers. Charles Guyon, *Les Enfants héroïques de 1914* (Paris: Librairie Larousse, 1915), 15. © Bibliothèque nationale de France, NUMM-9680148.

could be construed as unpatriotic or even treasonous. Louis Revault, a legislator from the Meuse, worried in 1916 that people in the occupied region, including the Meuse, were becoming "too accustomed to the German occupation."[23] The most serious transgression was sexual intimacy with the enemy; in the weeks that followed the armistice in November 1918, women suspected of what in the Second World War would be called "horizontal collaboration" were denounced as traitors. Some Belgian women were publicly stripped and paraded through the streets with their heads shaved. Historian Annette Becker has found no such extreme retribution in France, but there were instances of boys shouting insults, breaking windows, and tearing down flags from suspected women's homes in Lille; sometimes they were denied food distributed by relief organizations. Historian Jovana Knežević asserts: "The anxieties of the nation were borne particularly by women."[24]

Homefront

Women who lived outside the war zone, on the home front, in what the French called the *arrière*, of course faced far fewer dangers, but they also wrestled with the question of how they should respond to the war. French women were to embody France: home, family, heritage, civilization—a passive role but one nonetheless difficult and fraught with pitfalls and controversy. Were women to embody a gay, fashionable, frivolous France, the epitome of style and sophistication, of beauty, romance and sexuality, as depicted in fashion magazines?[25] FIG. 1.6 Or were they to be the France of tradition, bravery, endurance, and defiance, the France of Joan of Arc? Commentators recommended and criticized every possibility. French women were to be exquisitely feminine, but practical, not frivolous. Fashion writers attempted to sell the crinoline styles, already designed before the war broke out, as liberating women for their more active wartime lives. As a cartoon in *La Baïonnette* suggests, not everyone was convinced![26] SEE FIG. 3.1b
And the French woman was to be deeply patriotic but never militaristic. "The little touch of the martial" promoted in fashion magazines in the fall of 1914 came in for scathing criticism; its mimicry of military glory was an insult to France's heroic soldiers, some claimed. Critics even looked askance at widows' weeds; if "excessive," they would damage morale.[27]

Women in the War Economy

But French women were not content simply to embody the nation that French men defended, however one defined that nation; they wanted to do something. In fact, many of them needed to support themselves and their families. Confidently expecting a short war, French authorities envisioned a country frozen in place until the glorious victory. Financial markets, banks, theaters, and other entertainment venues closed; the government requisitioned the railroad, but also horses, thus hamstringing agriculture, and of course it mobilized men without regard to their economic roles.[28] As men went off to war, shuttering workshops behind them, thousands of women not only lost the income normally brought home by husbands and sons but they also lost their own jobs. On August 5, 1914, the government authorized military allowances to soldiers' dependents, essentially women and children, but the payment—1.25 francs per day for an adult, plus an additional 50 centimes per child—was only about half the typical male wage. Parisian seamstress Louise Delétang wrote in her diary on August 8: "Everywhere it is a ceaseless chase for work. Worry about tomorrow deadens the anguish over separation. So many women say to me: 'If I had work, I wouldn't ask for anything more.'"[29] Charitable women tried to fill the gap by setting up work rooms where impoverished women could earn a pittance, or perhaps just get a meal and, as the war dragged on into winter, a warm place to spend the day.

FIG. 1.7

One group of French women had no doubts about how to respond to mobilization as well as an abundance of work: peasants. The war began in the midst of the harvest season; the crops had to be brought in. And when the war outlasted the year, new crops had to be planted. On small farms in particular, women took on what had traditionally been men's work, such as haying and plowing. Emilie Carles recalled: "I was not tall. I remember we had an ordinary plow, the swing type, with a handle designed for a man. It was far too high for me. When I cut furrows with that contrivance, I got the handle in the chest or face every time I hit a stone. For me plowing was the road to Calvary."[30] As the war stretched into three more seasons of planting and harvesting, peasant women's lot became increasingly difficult. Faced with shortages of manpower, draft animals, fertilizer, and an abundance of requisitioning and price controls, some abandoned the struggle. As one war widow explained in 1915, "At present, I can only sow wheat in two-thirds of the land that should be planted in grain. Thus certain deficit for next year. If I stay on, the little that my husband left to his children will be swallowed up."[31] Agricultural production fell and peasant women, celebrated as heroines of the harvest in 1914, were vilified as shirkers who were responsible for the high prices and shortages.

In the cities, the unemployment crisis did not ease until the

FIG. 1.6 Georges Lepape. "Longchamp (II), or She lost!" Fashion plate showing crinolines by Jenny, Beer, Worth, Dœuillet, Chéruit, Premet, and Martial and Armand at the fashionable Longchamp racetrack. *La Gazette du Bon Ton*, Summer 1915, pl. 5. © Bibliothèque Forney / Roger-Viollet, RV-157813-3.

FIG. 1.7 A workroom installed in the restaurant Le Doyen on the Champs Elysées, Paris (8th arrondissement), August 1914. Silver gelatin print. © Préfecture de Police, Service de l'Identité judiciare / BHVP / Roger-Viollet, RV-76464-10.

spring and summer of 1915, when the reality of a long war finally made itself felt in policies to revive industry. The Sous-secrétaire d'État de l'Artillerie et des Munitions (Undersecretary of Artillery and Munitions), Albert Thomas, a socialist, began to push munitions firms to expand production by hiring women. Contemporaries believed that French women were "torn from the hearth," in Thomas's words, to be thrust into the wartime labor force.[32] In fact, the majority of women who worked in industry during the war had worked *before* the war as well, mostly in female-dominated professions: domestic service, textiles, and garment-making. What was new in 1915 and 1916 was the visibility of working women in the press and in public, performing jobs previously held by men. In 1915 and 1916, the press enthusiastically described the newly minted female letter carriers, tram conductors, metro workers, gas inspectors, and so on. Their tailored uniforms were "coquette," their peaked caps jaunty, their faces charming and cheerful. In one article, the author imagined that he had fallen asleep in September 1914 and awakened in 1916 to the "curious spectacle" of myriad women doing men's jobs.[33]

Journalists and artists celebrated these *remplaçantes*, the women who replaced men in the labor force, for their pluck, patriotism, and especially their devotion to their men. FIGS. 1.8a–d "In working in [munitions plants] where she can risk her health or even her life, in the ultimate act of tenderness, she also puts her heart on the line by cooperating to safeguard the one who is as dear to her as her country's safety."[34] Such paeans underlined the expectation that women would leave the labor force when the war was over. However patriotically women responded to the war emergency and however well they did their new jobs, their true place, such comments implied, was in their homes. Although labor remained in short supply, especially during and after the summer of 1916's enormous death toll at Verdun, women earned at most only two-thirds of male wages. Employers not only believed that women's work was less valuable then men's, but they also feared that high wages would emancipate women now that their natural protectors, their husbands, brothers, and fathers, were absent. This anxiety broke into public discourse in 1916–17 in a torrent of accusations that working women, especially munitions workers, were, in fact, war profiteers. According to the critics, women workers squandered their "fantastic wages" on luxurious food—chickens, pastries—and inappropriate clothes—high-heeled boots, silk stockings. One journalist claimed that *munitionnettes* accessorized their boiler suits with diamond combs in their hair! Such attacks came from the Left as well as from conservatives; labor leaders expressed their anxiety over the disruption of traditional gender dynamics in attacks on working women. Confédération Générale du Travail (General Confederation of Labor) militant Raymond Péricat snorted: "Go in the industrial suburbs and see them coveting furs and wearing boots that go up to their knees! At the cinema, the theater, they all laugh, they all enjoy themselves . . . Their sons, their husbands, their fiancés fall, cut down by machine-guns, and they all accept the fact without flinching."[35] Peasant women were accused of price gouging, smugly accumulating nest eggs, and driving up the cost of living.[36] Hostility turned to near panic in response to a wave of strikes in 1917 and 1918. The strikes began in the garment industry; seamstresses, nicknamed *midinettes*, parading their demands in the street, initially attracted sympathy and support, and much press coverage celebrating their charm and chic.[37] However when munitions workers followed suit, demanding shorter hours (they were working eleven to twelve hours a day with, if they were lucky, one day off every two weeks), higher wages, and an end to the war, the government reacted swiftly. With the example of revolution in Russia before them, as well as the widespread mutiny in the French army, the government kept reports of the strikes out of the press and stepped in to arbitrate, imposing improvements in wages and hours. However, although most of the strikers achieved a six-day week and higher wages, they still did not earn as much as men, nor, of course, did the war end.[38] FIG. 1.9

Women in the Military?

Many middle-class and upper-class women who did not need to work to support themselves were convinced that they must serve France's war effort. But what could they do? In the decade prior to the war, a few had already contemplated this question. In 1913, novelist and archaeologist Jane Dieulafoy proposed that the French army should establish a women's auxiliary to take over non-combat jobs, an idea endorsed in a number of newspaper articles, but mocked in others.[39] In January 1916, Mme Arnaud, the widow of a French officer, attempted to carry out Dieulafoy's proposal. She recruited a women's militia, the Corps de Défense Nationale Volontaire des Femmes Françaises et Belges (Volunteer Corps for the National Defense of French and Belgian Women) and petitioned the Ministry of War for official status, proposing that her corps could take over many non-combat jobs such as kitchen work and laundry, but also guard depots and escort prisoners. Ministry officials refused to meet with her.[40]

FIGS. 1.8 a–d Fare collector of the Metropolitan subway. Étienne Adrian Drian. Uniformed *remplaçantes* from *La Femme et La Guerre*, 1920. Lithographs. © Bibliothèque Marguerite Durand / Roger-Viollet, RV-157633: 7-10.

Letter carrier of the PTT (Postal Service)

Tramway driver

Delivery woman carrying hatboxes

FIG. 1.9 Women on strike for the "English work week" and against the high cost of living. Employees of the Société Générale gather in front of the Paris Opéra before marching to the Bourse du Travail. *Excelsior*, May 26, 1917. © Excelsior–L'Équipe / Roger-Viollet, RV-72189-51.

At the same time, the Ministry of War was contemplating recruiting women, not as uniformed auxiliaries as was the case in the British and later the American armies and as Mme Arnaud urged, but as civilian employees. At first the army envisioned hiring women only for clerical positions; the war brought an upsurge in paperwork that required the introduction of typewriters, and, in Ministry minds, typewriters and women went well together. However, by the beginning of 1916, Minister of War General Joseph Gallieni ordered his staff to plan for "the replacement of military personnel by women in all possible posts and employment."[41] Although most commanders accepted, albeit reluctantly, this innovation in order to maximize combat strength, a few vehemently opposed the introduction of women into the masculine world of the military. One of the most hostile was General Pierre Ruffey; in his view, women's lack of discipline, their propensity for "vapors" and "periodic indisposition," their inherent laziness and indiscretion made them not only completely unsuitable for army employment but actually dangerous.[42] On the other hand, some, such as Captain Le Lorrain of the Automobile Service, appreciated and defended their female employees. In response to a questionnaire from the Ministry, Le Lorrain praised the work of his women drivers. He could not, he reported, state with any exactitude how many hours they worked a week because "[it] is impossible to limit [their work]; the maintenance of their vehicles, as well as the services they provide to the medical teams and following evacuations require their permanent availability and cause daily unforeseen demands . . . Moreover, they are exposed in all weather, often in danger at night in locations under bombardment."[43]

Nearly as contentious as hiring women was the question of what they should wear. Le Lorrain and other officers in the Automobile Service reported with frustration that their women drivers were frequently stopped and detained because of their unofficial appearance; the officers lobbied the Ministry of War to put women drivers in uniform. However, in the decades prior to the war, the main argument against women's suffrage had been that women did not deserve to vote because they did not perform military service and were therefore not full citizens. Thus, anything that implied women were "in" the military set off alarm bells. Finally, late in 1917, the Ministry authorized uniforms for women drivers. With navy blue coats and skirts, the new official costume prioritized femininity over practicality—even motorcyclists were supposed to wear skirts—and clearly distinguished the army's women employees from the gray-blue clad soldiers.[44] FIG. 1.10

The Volunteers

Most affluent French women, while desiring to help the war effort, did not seek to join the army. A much more popular—and more acceptable—feminine response to the outbreak of war was to volunteer at a war charity. While some, such as the three branches of the French Red Cross, predated the war, many others emerged in 1914 and 1915. Large and small, national and local, they responded to the crisis, some to help refugees or the unemployed but most to aid France's soldiers. The Duchesse de Clermont-Tonnerre recalled that canteens run by a new charity, the Croix Verte (Green Cross), were "springing up in all the train stations; girls spend the night there, their mothers knitting and tending to the stove while their daughters supply food to the convoys of wounded or pass through civilian trains, carriage by carriage, shaking their little metal bowls: 'For our wounded, please.'"[45] Other charities set up reading and recreation rooms for the soldiers or sent them writing paper, towels, books, food, cigarettes, religious medals, and clothing. Women founded organizations to support prisoners of war, to visit wounded soldiers in hospitals, and to help rehabilitate them when they were discharged. To fund these efforts, women appealed to wealthy patrons but also collected money in the street as well as on trains: "Accosting passers-by, acquaintances, strangers, loquacious, drunk . . . for the first time and the tenth, repeating the same plea that you vary among two or three phrases, requesting, being refused, offering again, thanking: it's like that from morning to night."[46] FIG. 1.11 A compendium published in 1915 by the Office Central des Oeuvres de Bienfaisance (Central Office of Charities), listed hundreds of such organizations in Paris alone.[47]

Women knitted scarves, balaclavas, and sweaters for their relatives and friends and sent them parcels. In January 1915, for example, peasant Marie Pireaud sent her soldier husband two rabbits cooked in fat, a bottle of wine, and a winter vest; the following month she sent more warm clothing, a chicken, more wine, brandy, and apples.[48] Newspapers advertised products—flea powder, knives, waterproof socks—that women should purchase to send to their men at the front. And, of course, women sent letters—approximately four million letters went to and from French soldiers every day of the war.[49] In the spring of 1915 the press promoted a new initiative, that women should "adopt" soldiers from the area of France occupied by the German army as

FIG. 1.10 Female automobile driver of the French army in uniform, Paris, December 27, 1917. © Bibliothèque de documentation international contemporaine, VAL 381/089.

FIG. 1.11 Henri Rachou. Poster to promote charity work for the "wounded, mutilated, orphaned, imprisoned, and those sick with tuberculosis in the Haute-Garonne." *Semaine de la Haute-Garonne,* March 5–12, 1916. Paris and Toulouse: Imprimerie Sirven, 1916. © BHVP / Roger-Viollet, RV-101384-5.

correspondents to support the morale of men who could not communicate with their families. The project, soon baptized *marraines de guerre* (war godmothers), quickly expanded to include prisoners of war and then any soldier who solicited such a pen pal.[50] FIG. 1.12

As women's wartime volunteer work proliferated, so did criticism of it. In response to a number of scams and also concerns that private fundraising was interfering with the government's bond drives, the legislature voted in May of 1916 to register and regulate all charities. The Left also worried that the Catholic Church was using women's charities to proselytize and accused some organizations of refusing aid to non-communicants.[51] Humor magazines trivialized charitable organizations; *La Vie Parisienne* jokingly imagined a new charity, the Pink Cross, to provide women deprived of their husbands and lovers by the war with escorts to help them through "their momentary widowhood."[52] But there were serious criticisms as well; medical authorities reprimanded the Green Cross for serving coffee and wine to injured soldiers for whom such stimulants could be dangerous.[53] But mostly the critics suspected women's motivations; they claimed that feminine volunteering sprang not from patriotism but from boredom, that women soon abandoned charity work when it impinged upon their social lives. The marraines de guerre scheme in which women wrote letters to soldiers came in for the most sustained attacks. It was, critics declared, simply a medium for flirtation, a way for women to consort with strange men via correspondence while their husbands and fiancés were away. They accused women of collecting war "godsons" as social capital to display to their friends, and of weakening rather than strengthening soldiers' morale. In their eyes, such dubious correspondence undermined the seriousness of the war effort by infusing it with illicit romance.[54]

Nursing

Of these varied programs, only that of the Red Cross initially found official favor. FIGS. 1.13–1.15 Thanks to a 1913 agreement, when the Ministry of War mobilized men for the war, it also called up Red Cross nurses. One of these was Léonie Godfroy, who later wrote in her memoirs: "A young girl in ordinary life is nothing or next to nothing. For the first time I was going to be someone, I would have a personal role to play, I would count in the world."[55] Meanwhile, the French Red Cross organizations were swamped with middle- and upper-class women who wanted to learn to nurse—as quickly as possible.[56] FIGS. 1.16 One such woman was journalist Maria Léra who rushed back to Paris from her summer vacation in order to volunteer as a nurse. After several days of besieging the Red Cross headquarters, she managed to sign up for classes with one of the society's branches, the Union des Femmes de France (Union of French Women), that would enable her to work as a nurse's aide. However the classes were so overcrowded, with three hundred or more women in each session, that although Léra could hear the lectures, she could not see the demonstrations that accompanied them.[57]

Confronted by petitions from wealthy women to set up hospitals in their châteaux and even in their Paris apartments, as well as by a deluge of more modest requests to drive ambulances, staff first-aid stations, and nurse the wounded, the French government at first hesitated. The prewar agreement with the Red Cross relegated volunteer nurses to auxiliary hospitals in the *arrière,* barring them from the war zone. However, the rapid advance of the German army into France and the enormous casualties of the first two months of the war eroded this ban. FIG. 1.17 Mme Colombel's memoirs of the auxiliary hospital her mother had set up in Arras, a town close to the Belgian border, describes this situation. After securing the use of a convent; collecting funds, linens, and medicine; and recruiting a group of well-to-do women as nurses, Colombel and her mother spent two weeks practicing bandaging as they nervously awaited their first patients. On August 28, a flood of horribly wounded men arrived, dirty, bloody, and screaming; there were many more patients than the 180 beds that had been prepared could accommodate. The supply cupboards stocked with sheets, bandages, and morphine were emptied by noon; then, at seven in the evening, another fifty wounded men arrived. Overwhelmed, Colombel collapsed in tears.[58] Nursing wounded soldiers turned out to be far more horrifying, exhausting, and difficult than anyone, including France's doctors, had imagined. Some women, unable to cope with its demands, guiltily withdrew to find other less taxing ways to satisfy their need to be useful. Confronted with her first sight of a naked, mutilated, and bloody male body, Louise Weiss was nearly paralyzed with fear and disgust. When her father asked her to accompany him to Bordeaux, where the French government had gone into brief exile, she hastily abandoned her nursing career. On their return to Paris, although her mother continued to volunteer in a hospital, Louise volunteered instead at a charity that collected clothing for prisoners of war.[59] More than 70,000 Red Cross volunteers did stay the course, however. Military doctors

FIG. 1.12 A *marraine de guerre* (war godmother) contemplates sending a balaclava to her soldier pen pal to keep him warm in the trenches.
Postcard, 1914–18. © Roger-Viollet, RV-1721-4.

FIG. 1.13 Maurice-Louis Branger. Henriette of Belgium, the Duchesse of Vendôme, working as a nurse, 1915. © Maurice-Louis Branger / Roger-Viollet, RV-88814-11.

FIG. 1.14 Nurse's bag, 1914–18. Cotton canvas, felt emblem on wool patch. Paris, Musée des Arts Décoratifs, 53 290.

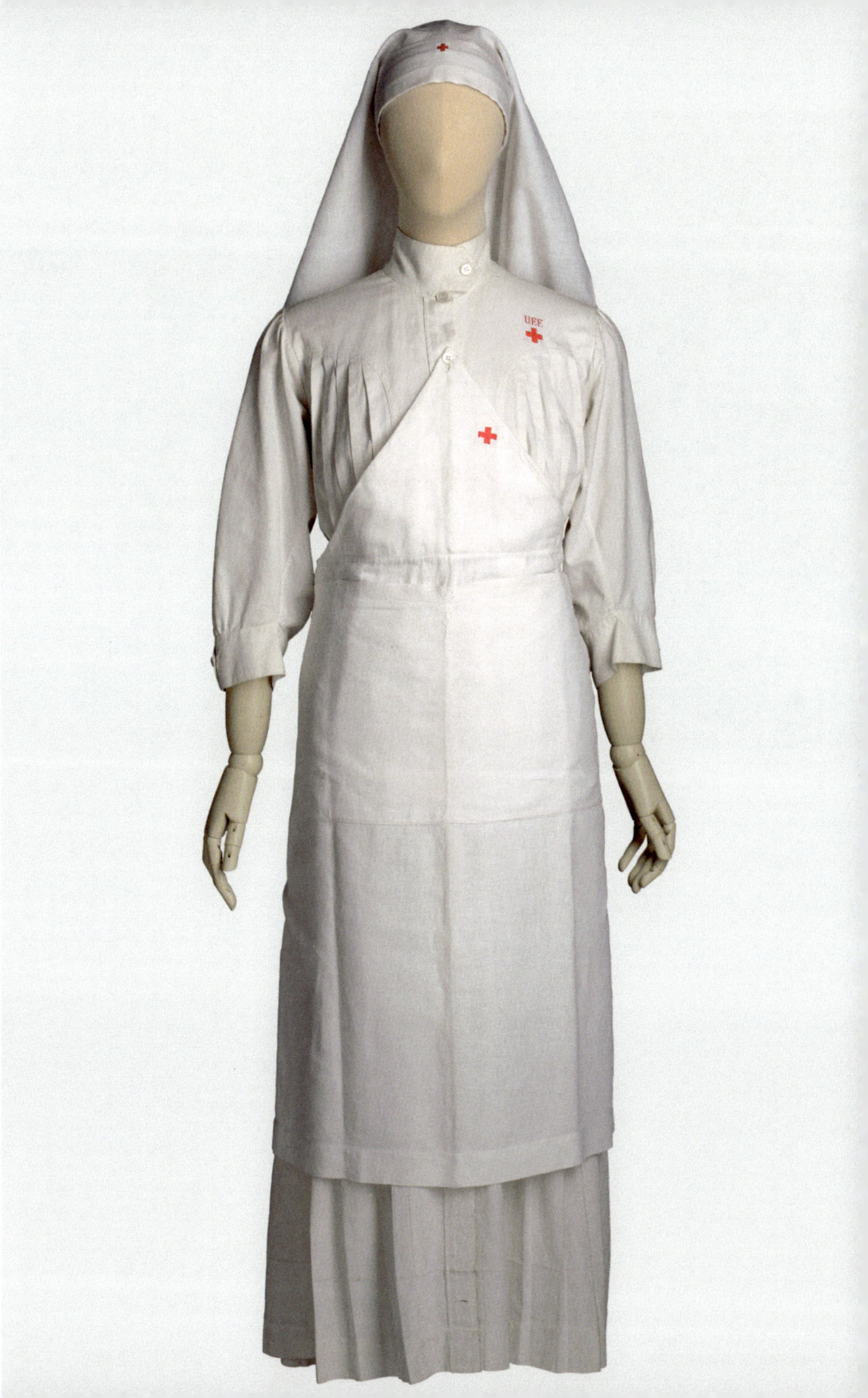

FIG. 1.15 Croix Rouge nurse's uniform, 1914–18. Cotton canvas. Paris, Musée des Arts Décoratifs - collection UFAC, UF 73 28 27 ABCDEF.

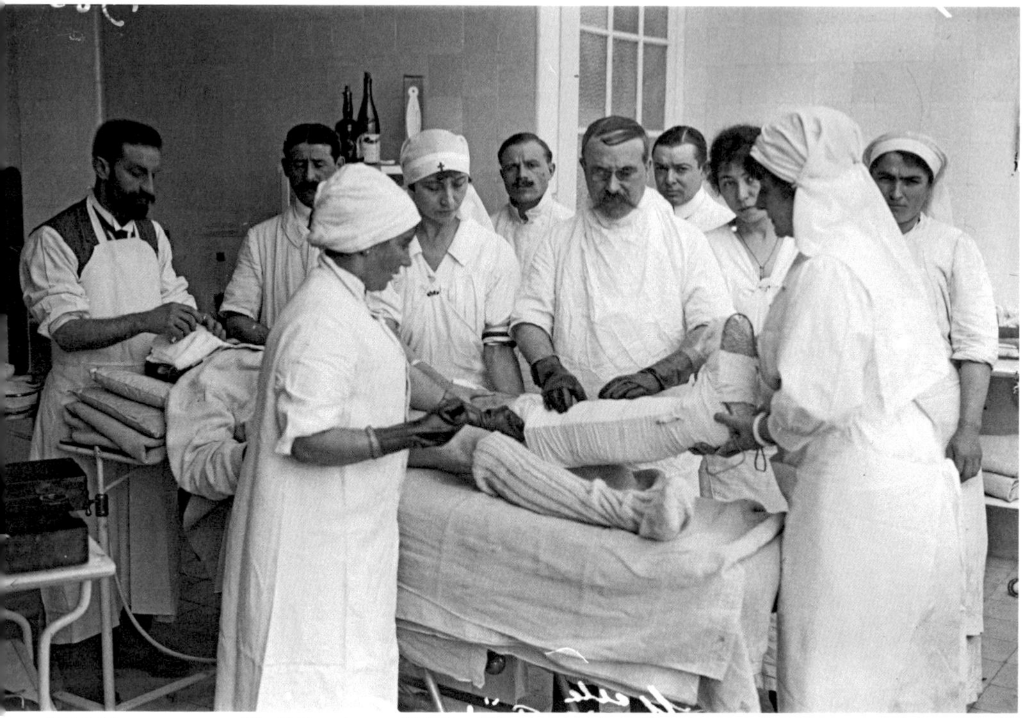

FIG. 1.16 The Italian dancer Aïda Boni (front, center) working as a nurse at the annex of the Val-de-Grâce military hospital, Villa Molière, Paris, captioned "Those who heal our wounded." *Excelsior*, October 4, 1915. © Wackernie / Excelsior–L'Équipe / Roger-Viollet, RV-70555-6.

FIG. 1.17 Lucien Jonas. Poster publicizing the work of the French Red Cross in villages devastated by the war, *Société Française de Secours aux Blessés Militaires: Les Permanences de la S.B.M. dans les Villages Dévastés*, 1917. Lithograph. © Bibliothèque Forney / Roger-Viollet, RV-86432-31.

like Alfred Mignon grew to trust experienced volunteers so implicitly that when they were transferred to war zone hospitals, they insisted on taking their nursing teams with them, despite Ministry of War rules to the contrary.[60] Most of the French women who published war diaries or memoirs were volunteer nurses. Those published during the war tend toward the propagandistic, full of noble suffering and feminine consolation. However, some, especially those published after the war, leave no doubt about the harrowing nature of their experiences: mud, blood, pain, disease, insufficient supplies, incompetent physicians, inefficient administration, long hours, inadequate food, emotional and physical exhaustion. Many nurses paid a heavy price. Léonie Godfroy, who went off to war exultant at being able to be useful, ended up in a German prison camp. Jeanne Antelme, a volunteer nurse who accompanied the French expeditionary force to Greece, where she battled heat, dust, polluted water, and typhoid, suffered a mental breakdown. Nearly all of the nursing memoirs report episodes of deep depression and illness. Nurses succumbed to the diseases that flourished in the war zone, especially typhus, an infection caused by lice, and then, in 1918, influenza. More than three thousand were injured or medically discharged; six hundred died.[61] But despite their hard work and sacrifice, not even nurses were exempt from criticism. It was claimed that their image of pure feminine patriotism actually masked feminine seduction or, worse, hypocrisy. FIG. 1.18 Critics accused women of "playing" at nursing as a new addition to their social calendars. "With sounding horn and sparkling brass, the limousine advances ceremoniously down the teeming street. Inside, bosom high, all in white, pearls at her ears, a Red Cross nurse . . . Grave gentlemen gallantly salute the *grande dame* who is playing at angel."[62] A more serious criticism was that "fashion-plate" volunteers saw nursing as a way to flirt with officers. FIG. 1.19 Dr. Edouard Toulouse commented dryly: "The husband hunt has become a big deal for the young woman and remarkably assists her duty to aid the wounded."[63] FIG. 1.20 Whereas the true nurse was selfless, dutiful, and devoted, the false nurse was self-centered, frivolous, and wanton. She disregarded doctor's orders, sought admiration and publicity, and fled in disgust at the sight of blood. In their memoirs, nurses also leveled criticism, but usually at hospital administration and the military rather than at their fellow nurses. However, most acknowledged that the rivalry among the different nursing corps was a problem. Each of the three branches of the Red

Cross enrolled its own volunteers, and there was little cooperation between them: "'That's the enemy society that competes with us and steals our patients, a worthless society, Johnny-come-latelies . . . civil servants' wives and shop girls.'"[64] Plus, there were paid army nurses and also nursing nuns. Social class caused some of the cleavages; religion created others, as did the type of training, length of service, and where nurses had worked. Battle-zone nursing experience, for example, gave a nurse prestige. One memoir, titled *Croix et Cocarde* (Cross and Cockade), details the havoc that these rivalries created, to the detriment of patient care.[65]

Volunteer nursing was the most celebrated of French women's war work; nearly one thousand Red Cross nurses were awarded the Croix de Guerre and 375 received the Légion d'Honneur.[66] In the view of Red Cross promoters, the volunteer nurse upheld French society, which before the war had been threatened by socialism and feminism. "Because of her, yesterday's wounded who is tomorrow's electorate will, after the war, mistrust revolutionary doctrines and be saner and clear-thinking."[67] One fictional nurse proclaimed that her war work had taught her "man is our champion, our hero, even our god. A poor god who dies for us, to save us from the Beast's fury! Woman realizes what she owes to him."[68] The extent of criticism, however, suggests that many in France were not convinced. Red Cross nurses, like women factory workers, tram conductors, pen pals, invasion resisters, and military drivers, raised deep anxieties about how, and even if, French women should be at war.

Demobilization

Just as the French government had had no plans to mobilize women in 1914, it made no plans to ease their demobilization after the armistice on November 11, 1918. Instead, the public services, the army, and the defense industry immediately began to fire women employees. The Ministère de la Défense (Ministry of War) fired the female clerical staff in the first months of 1919, and this was followed by a purge of all women workers.[69] Citroën, a major war contractor, laid off all of its more than three thousand women workers by February. Transportation and the postal service followed suit more gradually and selectively, firing women tram conductors and letter carriers but retaining clerical workers and telegraph operators.[70] Women were told to "return" home and have babies; postwar legislation encouraged childbearing by awarding medals for motherhood, criminalizing birth control, and mandating instruction in infant care for all school girls. FIG. 1.21

If women really did need to support themselves—many

Femina

5

(Phot. du peintre Harry-B. Lachman.)

LE JOUR DE CONGÉ

FIG. 1.18 Harry B. Lachman. "The Day Off Duty." *Femina,* June 1917. © Diktats bookstore.

FIG. 1.19 G. Léonnec. "The Coquetry of an Angel: Regulations did not foresee this!" *La Vie Parisienne*, May 13, 1916. © Bibliothèque Forney / Roger-Viollet, RV-157622-11.

LA BAÏONNETTE

(Dessin de Icart

LA DOUBLE BLESSURE

— *Oui, il a reçu deux balles dans la tête.*
— *Et combien de flèches dans le cœur ?*

— 245 —

FIG. 1.20 Louis Icart. "The Double Wound," showing a wounded soldier in bed attended by a nurse while a fashionably dressed woman looks on. "Yes, he received two bullets to the head." "And how many arrows in the heart?" *La Baïonnette*, October 21, 1915. Musée de la Grande Guerre du Pays de Meaux, CAPM.2006.8.3.0.

FIG. 1.21 Poster for the “National Day for Mothers of Large Families.” “France needs children. Let’s honor large families and help those who are in need. It is our duty. It is in our interest. Thus France will be stronger, more prosperous, and glorious. Let us all give to our children...” ca. 1920. Lithograph. © BHVP / Roger-Viollet, RV-101749-2.

recognized that the war had deprived some women of masculine support—they should seek feminine work, such as garment making and domestic service, or perhaps artistic trades like bookbinding or ceramics.[71]

The volunteer work of middle- and upper-class women also dwindled. Some charities shut down, but the wounded and disabled as well as soldiers awaiting demobilization still needed a variety of services, as did residents of the formerly occupied region. Increasingly, however, government workers and professionals replaced volunteers. The war had drawn thousands of women into volunteer nursing, but it had also increased the ranks of professional nurses; after the war, as the need for nurses decreased, the latter replaced the former.[72] Even more than working-class women, middle- and upper-class women were urged to devote themselves to home and family in order to rebuild France.

In some areas, the purge of women was effective and long-lasting. In transportation, women disappeared so completely from public view that fifty years later journalists would celebrate the "first" woman hired as a driver, ignoring her predecessors in 1916.[73] In others, the initial wave of firings in 1918–19 was followed by gradual rehiring, although in more limited job categories. During the war, women had been praised for taking on "men's work;" now they were pushed back into "women's work," but what qualified as women's work had subtly changed. The war had accelerated trends already present in the prewar economy, such as assembly-line production in manufacturing and clerical work; both drew upon women workers. The French army, overwhelmed by the paperwork of demobilizing millions of soldiers, began to rehire women file clerks and typists as early as the spring of 1919. Manufacturing, as it painfully shifted from producing armaments to producing consumer goods, also re-employed women; for example, by the end of 1919, Citroën was hiring women again to work on its new automobile assembly line. A variety of "light" industry jobs became defined as naturally feminine.[74] Employment opportunities for middle-class women also reopened in the civil service and in education in response to growing bureaucracies and the shortage of manpower. Education reform in 1925 instituted the same *baccalauréat* for girls and boys, facilitating women's entry into university and the lower echelons of the professions.[75] In general, France's postwar labor market remained quite rigidly divided by gender, and women's share decreased from wartime highs; however, it did not fall back to prewar levels.[76]

How did French women respond to the First World War? There are, of course, nearly as many answers as there were French women. For most, the war was traumatic; men for whom they cared—husbands, fiancés, brothers, cousins, friends—departed, were wounded, taken prisoner, and killed. Women's ordinary domestic responsibilities became much more difficult as prices rose and food and fuel ran short. And often women had to juggle new responsibilities as the family's primary breadwinner. Yet for some women, the war opened up opportunities, to "count in the world," as Léonie Godfroy wrote. Their war work was often criticized—munitions workers were unfeminine, peasant women were profiteers, Red Cross "ladies" were frivolous—but it was also praised; they were heroines, patriots, true daughters of Joan of Arc. The war had also engendered new opportunities for female community in the strikes of garment and munitions workers, for example, and in the female-run volunteer organizations, particularly the Red Cross. In the aftermath of the war, volunteer nurses formed nursing veteran organizations to lobby for benefits but also to maintain contact with other women who understood their experiences.[77] Their contributions to the war effort gave women a platform to push a claim for full citizenship; bills enfranchising women passed four times in the Chambre des Députés (Chamber of Deputies) by large majorities only to be rejected by the Senate.[78] FIG. 1.22 However, for some women, war service seemed a parenthesis rather than a life-changing experience, at least in the eyes of their families and community. One such was Red Cross nurse Mireille Andrieu, who had been awarded the Croix de Guerre for her service in war-torn Soissons. Although she contributed to a small volume of war reminiscences, she rarely talked about her experience to her family and friends; her grandchildren, interviewed in 2006 by a TV documentary crew, were astonished to learn of her war record.[79]

FIG. 1.22 Maurice Barbey. Poster for the Society for the Improvement of the Status of Women and the Demand for Women's Rights, ca. 1925–28. © Bibliothèque Marguerite Durand / Roger-Viollet, RV-54759-5.

New Era, New Suffrage

Women Must Vote

in order to avoid war
protect childhood
improve hygiene
eliminate slums
curb immorality
reform the Civil Code
increase the standard of living
combat alcoholism and infectious diseases

Everyone should join a feminist group in order to demand voting rights for women.

Society for the Betterment of Women and the Defense of Women's Rights

Minimum dues
5 francs per year

1 François de Witt-Guizot, *La femme et la guerre: Comment une femme peut-elle servir la France en temps de guerre? Deux conferences données à l'Action sociale de la Femme, Paris, 25 avril–6 mai, 1912* (Autun: Imprimerie Pernot, 1913), 12.

2 For example, on Franco-Prussian War heroines, Joseph Turquan, *1870–1871: Les Femmes de France pendant l'invasion* (Paris: Berger-Levrault, 1893); on Revolutionary War heroines, Emile Cère, *Madame Sans-Gêne et les femmes soldats: 1792–1815* (Paris: E. Plon, Nourrit, 1894).

3 L. Ruault, *Cents ans de Croix rouge française au service de l'humanité* (Paris: Hachette, 1963), 37.

4 Yves Pourcher, *Les jours de guerre: La vie des français au jour le jour entre 1914 et 1918* (Paris: Plon, 1994), 49–57; Reports from Prefets of the Lot, Lot-et-Garonne and Lozère, August 1914, Archives Nationales (hereafter abbreviated AN) F7 12938.

5 Julie Wheelwright, *The Fatal Love: Mata Hari and the Myth of Women in Espionage* (London: Collins & Brown, 1992).

6 Ibid., 125.

7 Rapports des préfets, AN F7 12937-8 guerre de 1914.

8 Marguerite Lesage, *Journal de guerre d'une française* (Paris: Editions de la diffusion du livre, 1938), 3–6.

9 Annette Becker, *Les Cicatrices rouges 14–18: France et Belgique occupées* (Paris: Fayard, 2010), 73.

10 Lesage, *Journal de guerre*, 94–99.

11 Charles Rearick, "Madelon and the Men—in War and Memory," *French Historical Studies* 17, no. 4 (Fall 1992), 1003.

12 The two best known are Henri Barbusse, *Under Fire*, trans. W. Fitzwater Wray (London: Dent, 1926), 73–81; and Roland Dorgelès, *Les Croix de bois*, (Paris: Albin Michel, 1919), 106–14.

13 Margaret H. Darrow, *French Women and the First World War: War Stories of the Home Front* (Oxford: Berg, 2000), 106: Craig Gibson, *Behind the Front: British Soldiers and French Civilians, 1914–1918* (Cambridge: Cambridge University Press, 2014), 57.

14 Gibson, *Behind the Front,* 281.

15 John Horne and Alan Kramer, *German Atrocities, 1914: A History of Denial* (New Haven: Yale University Press, 2001), 196–200; Becker, *Les Cicatrices rouges*, 23–24.

16 Horne and Kramer, *German Atrocities*, 199.

17 Jovana Knežević, "Gender and Occupation," in *Gender and the Great War*, ed. Susan R. Grayzel and Tammy M. Proctor (Oxford: Oxford University Press, 2017), 133–48.

18 Darrow, *French Women*, 117–22; [Ministère des affaires étrangères], *The Deportation of Women and Girls from Lille* (New York: George H. Doran, 1916).

19 Darrow, *French Women*, 106–13.

20 "Le Livre d'or," *Lectures pour tous* (January 15, 1916), 592; "Héroïque conduite de Mlle Clotilde Boucry," *La Mode* (January 10, 1915), 634. The first account apparently appeared in the *Chronique Angevine* of November 3, 1914.

21 Recent biographies have brought attention to Louise de Bettignies, who died in a German prison, and Gabrielle Petit, a Belgian woman who was executed; both had been convicted of spying. Réné Deruyk, *Louise de Bettignies (1880–1918)* (Hazebrouk: La Voix du Nord, 1998); Sophie de Schaepdrijver, *Gabrielle Petit: The Death and Life of a Female Spy in the First World War* (London: Bloomsbury Press, 2015); Kathryn J. Atwood, *Women Heroes of World War I: 16 Remarkable Resisters, Soldiers, Spies and Medics* (Chicago: Chicago Review Press, 2014).

22 Becker, *Les Cicatrices rouges*, 125, 254.

23 Ibid., 155.

24 Knežević , "Gender and Occupation," 141; Becker, *Les Cicatrices rouges,* 244–47.

25 Patricia Tilburg, "Mimi Pinson Goes to War: Taste, Class and Gender in France, 1900–18," *Gender & History* 23, no. 1 (April 2011), 92–110.

26 Maude Bass-Krueger, "From the 'union parfaite' to the 'union brisée': The French Couture Industry and the Midinettes during the Great War," *Costume* 47, no.1 (2013), 33.

27 Joanna Shearer, "Dressing Up For War: Women and Militarism in the Writings of French Women Journalists in the First World War," *Minerva: Journal of Women and War* 1, no. 2 (July 2008), 71–73; Darrow, *French Women*, 66–68.

28 Bruno Cabanes, *August 1914; France, the Great War, and a Month that Changed the World Forever*, trans. Stephanie O'Hara (New Haven: Yale University Press, 2016).

29 Louise Delétang, *Journal d'une ouvrière parisienne pendant la guerre* (Paris: Eugène Figuière, 1935), 16.

30 Emilie Carles, *A Life of Her Own: A Country Woman in Twentieth-Century France,* trans. *Avriel H. Goldberger* (New Brunswick, NJ: Rutgers University Press, 1991), 60.

31 Réné Bazin, "'Tenir' aux champs," *L'Écho de Paris*, October 26, 1915.

32 Marcel Frois, *La santé et le travail des femmes pendant la guerre.* Carnegie Endowment for International Peace, Histoire économique et sociale de la guerre mondiale, no. 23 (Paris: Presses universitaires de France, 1926), 138.

33 Margaret H. Darrow, "Mademoiselles in Uniform," in *Cutting a New Pattern: Uniformed Women in the Great War,* ed. Bart Hacker and Margaret Vining (Washington, DC: Smithsonian Institution Scholarly Press, forthcoming).

34 Paul Strauss, "Le travail féminin dans les usines de guerre," *Revue philanthropique* 19 (1917), 119.

35 Cited in Jean-Louis Robert, "La CGT et la famille ouvrière 1914–1918: première approche," *Le Mouvement social* 116 (July–September 1981), 62.

36 Darrow, *French Women*, 198–202.

37 Bass-Krueger, "From the 'union parfait.'"

38 Laura Lee Downs, *Manufacturing Inequality: Gender Division in the French and British Metalworking Industries, 1914–1939* (Ithaca, NY: Cornell University Press, 1995), 129–46.

39 Darrow, *French Women*, 40–42.
40 Darrow, "Mademoiselles in Uniform."
41 The correspondence from the Ministry of War about female employment is contained in the archives of the Service Historique de l'Armée de Terre, Château de Vincennes (hereafter SHAT) 7N 159 main d'oeuvre féminine. This circular is dated January 26, 1916.
42 Main d'oeuvre féminine, November 1916, SHAT 7N 495.
43 Direction Service Automobile [hereafter DSA] personnel féminin. June 20, 1918, SHAT 16 N 2767.
44 Darrow, "Mademoiselles in Uniform."
45 Elisabeth de Gramont, Duchesse de Clermont-Tonnerre, *Mémoires: Clair de lune et taxi-auto* (Paris: Brasset, 1932), 84–85.
46 Maïten d'Arguibert, *Journal d'une famille française pendant la guerre* (Paris: Perrin, 1916), 116.
47 Office central des oeuvres de bienfaisance, *Paris charitable pendant la guerre* (Paris: Plon, 1915).
48 Martha Hanna, *Your Death Would Be Mine: Paul and Marie Pireaud in the Great War* (Cambridge, MA: Harvard University Press, 2006), 59.
49 Ibid., 9.
50 Darrow, *French Women*, 79–86.
51 Ibid., 75.
52 Pompon, "La Croix Rose," *La Vie parisienne* 53, no. 2 (January 9, 1915).
53 Darrow, *French Women*, 86.
54 Ibid., 86–89; Susan R. Grayzel, *Women's Identities at War: Gender, Motherhood, and Politics in Britain and France During the First World War* (Chapel Hill, NC: University of North Carolina Press, 1999), 30–33.
55 Léonie Godfroy, *Souvenirs d'ambulance et de captivité* (Paris: Librairie de "L'Eclair," [1917?]), 6.
56 There were three rival branches of the Red Cross in France at this time. The oldest, most aristocratic, and least open to women was the Société de Secours aux blessés militaires, founded shortly after the creation of the Red Cross in 1864. The Association des Dames Françaises, founded in 1877, and the Union de Femmes de France, founded in 1881 both focused on nursing.
57 Marc Hélys, pseud. of Maria Léra, *Cantinière de la Croix-Rouge 1914–1916* (Paris: Perrin, 1917), 7.
58 Marguerite (Mme Emmanuel) Colombel, *Journal d'une infirmière d'Arras: août-septembre-octobre 1914* (Paris: Publications Bloud et Gay, 1916), 37–40.
59 Louise Weiss, *Mémoires d'une européenne. I: 1893–1919* (Paris: Payot, 1968), 182–220.
60 Alfred Mignon, *Le Service de Santé pendant la guerre 1914–1918*, vol. 4 (Paris: Masson, 1926–27), 195–96.
61 Margaret H. Darrow, "French Volunteer Nursing and the Myth of War Experience in World War I," *The American Historical Review* 101, no. 1 (February 1996), 160; Alison S. Fell, *Women as Veterans in Britain and France After the First World War* (Cambridge: Cambridge University Press, 2018), 123.
62 Marcelle Capy, *Une voix de femme dans la mêlée* (Paris: Librairie Paul Ollendorff, 1917), 84–85.
63 Dr. Edouard Toulouse, *La réforme sociale: Question sexuelle de la femme* (Paris: Bibliothèque Charpentier, 1918), 71–72; 150.
64 Juliette Martineau, *Journal d'une infirmière* (Angers: Imprimerie G. Grassin, 1916), 2–3.
65 M. de La Boulaye, *Croix et cocarde* (Paris: Plon-Nourrit, 1919).
66 Ruault, *Cent ans de Croix-rouge*, 51.
67 Comtesse Roger de Courson, *La femme française pendant la guerre* (Paris: P. Lethielleux, n.d.), 41–42.
68 Maxime Formont, *La dame blanche* (Paris: A. Lemerre, 1917), 25.
69 Andrew Orr, *Women and the French Army during the World Wars, 1914–1940* (Bloomington, IN: Indiana University Press, 2017), 44.
70 Darrow, *French Women*, 216.
71 Karen Offen, *Debating the Woman Question in the French Third Republic, 1870–1920* (Cambridge: Cambridge University Press, 2018), 587–89.
72 Yvonne Knibiehler et al., *Cornettes et blouses blanches: Les infirmières dans la société française (1880–1980)* (Paris: Hachette, 1984), 106–8.
73 Press clipping [1965?] Bibliothèque Marguerite Durand, dossier 331.
74 Downs, *Manufacturing Inequality*, 204–8.
75 Evelyne Héry, "Quand le baccalauréat devient mixte . . ." *Clio: Histoire, Femmes, Société* 18 (December 2003), 77–90.
76 Laura Levine Frader, *Breadwinners and Citizens: Gender in the Making of the French Social Model* (Durham, NC: Duke University Press, 2008), 46–49; Siân Reynolds, *France Between the Wars: Gender and Politics*, (London: Routledge, 1996), 92–108.
77 Fell, *Women as Veterans*, 95–106.
78 Christine Bard, *Les Filles de Marianne: Histoire des féminismes, 1914–1940* (Paris: Fayard, 1995), 145–49, 331–61.
79 Camille Clermont, *Souvenirs de parisiennes en temps de guerre* (Paris: Berger-Levrault, 1918), 6–70; *Edwardians in Colour: The Wonderful World of Albert Kahn*. Programme 5; "The Civilian Story." BBC Arts, 2007.

1a Nurses' Uniforms

JOHANNE BERLEMONT & ANAÏS RAYNAUD

Clothing Charged with History In France, care of the sick has traditionally been the privilege of female religious orders. The practice dates back to the sixth century with the establishment of the Hôtel-Dieu in Lyon in 540, which took in and treated the sick and destitute and was run by nuns.[1] Even though the medical profession gradually opened to laypeople, caregiving continued to be the responsibility of nuns, who wore specialized religious habits while they worked. These ensembles consisted of a long robe, a mantle, and a coif, or cap, and were often dark in color. FIG. 1a.1 During the French Revolution, however, nuns were expelled from all the hospitals, along with the rest of the clergy. They later returned and resumed their work in clinics, but the rise of liberals who championed the secularization of society challenged their monopoly on nursing. Radical republicans were opposed to the nuns, whom they perceived as bigots with narrow moral conceptions, and they campaigned from 1848 and particularly after 1871 to secularize public health. Nuns were gradually removed from military hospitals, an operation that ended in 1904 with the last expulsions from the naval hospitals. Training of secular nurses in military hospitals began in 1909; these nurses then passed *concours*, or state competitions, which enabled them to join the army's health services. Public authorities also championed training programs, first within public hospitals and then through specialized schools, such as the Salpêtrière, which opened in 1907.[2] The secularization promoted by public authorities was preceded by a number of private initiatives. As early as 1866, the Société de Secours aux Blessés Militaires (Society for the Relief of Wounded Soldiers, SSBM) drew inspiration from the experiences of the British nurse Florence Nightingale in the Crimean War (1853–56) and began to train nurses in new caregiving practices during wartime.[3] The recruits came from aristocratic circles, which, according to its founders, was a guarantee of the morality of the aspirants. The rejection of less privileged women led to the formation in 1879 of the Association des Dames de France (Association of French Women, ADF) and then to the Union des Femmes de France (Union of French Women, UFF) in 1881. The three associations, working under the aegis of the Red Cross, expanded their schools across the country and were the only organizations permitted to intervene in wartime.

With a focus on training nurses for the military, programs ranged from assistant nurse to head nurse, which involved two years of training and internships. The combination of private initiatives and proactive public policy led to an increase in the number of professional nurses. In 1884, France had forty-three certified nurses; in 1912, there were more than 6,600.[4] Drawing on the medical discoveries of Louis Pasteur, all the schools taught their nurses how to sanitize a patient's environment by sterilizing and regularly cleaning instruments and also by maintaining personal hygiene, which influenced what nurses wore. Nuns preferred dark habits, which hid dirt, but hygienic doctors rejected these because it was difficult to detect possible soiling, and so the white cotton apron replaced the dark wool dress. Cotton was chosen for its easy cleaning and maintenance. Even though the length of skirts and coats was not specified, photographs show that they were worn to just above the ankle. Veils were simplified so that nurses could work with ease, but eventually they were replaced by a cap that hid the hair for hygienic as well as moral reasons. Because nurses were expected to suppress any hint of sexual passion, hair, a traditional agent of feminine seduction, was hidden in order to conform with the moral restrictions placed on women working in such close proximity to men. Despite such changes, work parameters for nurses remained unclear. Practices were not often described in terms that specifically defined the missions and responsibilities of the role. However, uniforms were required (as of a decree issued on May 2, 1913) and always included a dress, an apron (sometimes bibbed), and a veil, complemented for outdoor wear by a cape and a coif made of a dark fabric, a vestige of the religious habit. The public nursing schools and the three associations connected to the Red Cross did not provide the uniform, and so it was the responsibility of each nurse to acquire one. FIG. 1a.2 For this purpose, every nurse received a fixed stipend of 100 francs in 1916.[5] The only rules of standardization concerned the veil. The one worn by secular nurses in military hospitals, a corps founded in 1909, was distinguished by a tricolor rosette on the left.[6] A decree on March 19, 1915, further specified that the red cross on veils would be reserved for nurses who belonged to the SSBM, the ADF, and the UFF. This enabled nurses to wear a red-on-white cross topped by the initials of their respective organization on their chest or coat, as can be seen on Sidonie Pocquet's uniform discussed below.

FIG. 1a.1 "Hymn to France: France counts on them / This duty is sweet to them." Postcard. Musée de la Grande Guerre du Pays de Meaux, CAPM.2006.1.14235.037.

FIG. 1a.2 At the Galeries Lafayette, the elegant outfits on sale for women have been replaced by nurses' coats, August 1914. Silver gelatin print. © Préfecture de Police, Service de l'Identité Judiciaire / BHVP / Roger-Viollet, RV-76464-5.

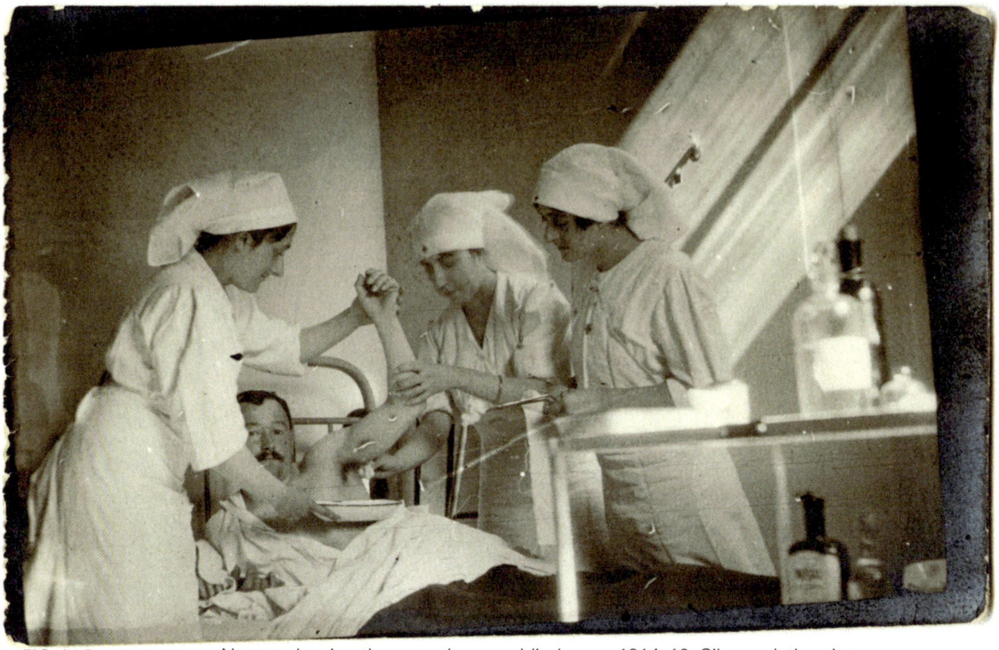

FIG. 1a.3 Nurses cleaning the wound on a soldier's arm, 1914–18. Silver gelatin print. Musée de la Grande Guerre du Pays de Meaux, CE20019.2.2.

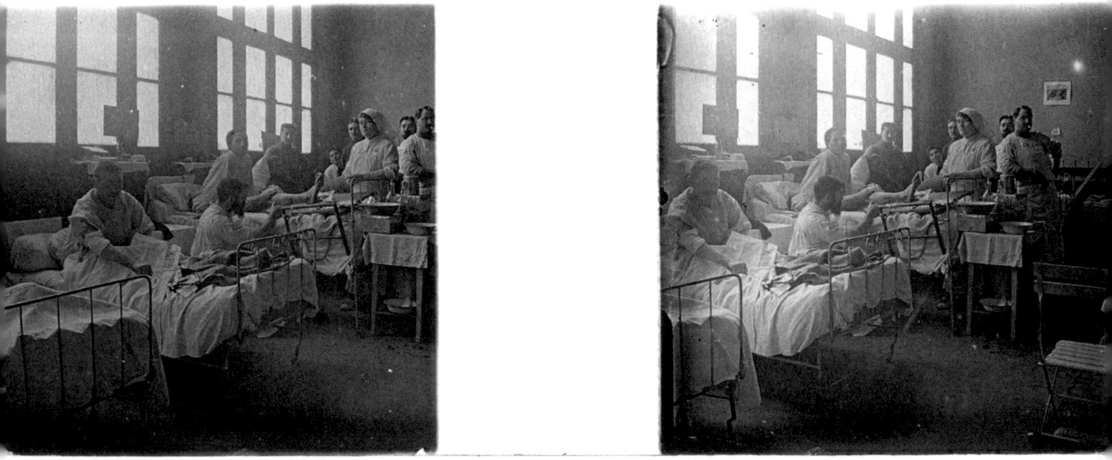

FIG. 1a.4 Treatment room at a French military hospital, 1914-18. Stereoscopic plate. Musée de la Grande Guerre du Pays de Meaux, 2006.1.4972.

FIG. 1a.5 Georges Lepape. Illustration of a French nurse entitled "The White Birds." *Femina,* June 1, 1917. © Bibliothèque Forney / Roger-Viollet RV-157622-9.

FIG. 1a.6 Léo Fontan. "The most beautiful fashion," showing several French Red Cross nurses in uniform. *La Baïonnette*, October 21, 1915, 244. Private collection.

Missions and the Organization of Nurses during the Great War

On August 2, 1914, secular nurses from military hospitals were drafted into service and integrated into the military's emergency and first aid departments. They were dispatched to hospitals and to the front. Nurses worked under the direct authority of doctors, either in the hospitals or at the front line, and did not report to the general health service. The war's duration, as well as its unprecedented scale and the gravity of injuries, made it necessary to establish a temporary corps of nurses from military hospitals to join the nurses already in service.[7] Civilian nurses were recruited, on the basis of competence, from the public nursing schools and the Red Cross branches. They wore the same uniform as the military nurses already in service, and their rank was made clear by the rosette on their veils. However, there were not enough reinforcements, and the French government made a call to non-professional volunteers to care for the wounded at home, behind the lines, and to help them recover. These were most often women from wealthy circles who could afford to offer their free time. Trained quickly, they were nevertheless unprepared to face the horrors of a war that for the first time included modern weapons and trench warfare that produced heavy artillery wounds and shell shock. For some upper-class women, serving as nurses meant that they could exhibit their charity in broad daylight as they cared for the wounded. However, as a group they were frequently mocked by their colleagues and by the press who were unable to see beyond social hierarchies to the sincere and important involvement of volunteers. Many worked with ambulances on the front line and in hospitals at home, and their work enabled the health-care system to function. Such volunteers also included nuns who, despite their forced expulsion from military hospital structures, were eager to continue serving their country by offering their skills. Nurses assisted doctors, even in operating rooms, where they wore an additional coat on top of their dress and apron to guarantee that the environment remained sterile. They monitored patients on a daily basis, tending to treatments and bathing the wounded. FIG. 1a.3 Photographs show that nurses' long shirt sleeves were rolled back, probably because it was convenient but also to ensure better hygiene between patients. FIG. 1a.4 Nurses stood in for pharmacists to prepare medications and ensure proper dosage, and they accompanied doctors on their rounds and recorded observations. They also joined related services, such as radiology. Marie Curie proposed to furnish ambulances with radiology equipment so that soldiers could be examined without being moved, and helped train the nurses in this practice.[8] In addition, as the war profoundly changed the nature of injuries and necessitated modified evacuation procedures, nurses helped organize relief efforts. The nurse emerged in France as both the kingpin and the backbone of military hospitals and ambulances, fully deserving the name paramedic and the recognition of hospital personnel and patients.

The White Angel

The nurse in World War I immediately brings to mind the image of the "white angel," the devoted and competent woman who washes and bandages patients, aids the suffering, and sometimes attends to soldiers as they succumb to their wounds. FIG. 1a.5 The maternal instincts, tenderness, and feminine gentleness of these nurses emerge in accounts by wounded soldiers or soldiers who hoped for a "good wound" that would take them away from the front lines and into the care of a nurse. Nevertheless, some soldiers reacted violently to nurses, who were occasionally insulted or defied by patients.

The nurse, an essential and influential figure in French wartime society, inspired illustrators, artists, writers, and the press to portray her as an elegant, gracious, and sometimes, even naughty, woman. SEE CHAPTER 1, FIG. 1.20 Illustrated postcards conveyed men's fantasies, sometimes explicitly, by taking advantage of the separation of the two sexes. Women's magazines frivolously appropriated the image of the nurse, whose uniform quickly became fashionable; the Minister of War even had to regulate when it could be worn in a decree dated March 19, 1915.[9] FIG. 1a.6

However, in stark contrast to popular imagery, the daily life of nurses among the wounded, especially in military zones, was exhausting and difficult. Aside from the indispensable medical role they played, nurses served as confidantes, witnessing the misery of men, sometimes during their final moments of agony. FIG. 1a.7 It was through their involvement with hospitals, as well as the recognition of their work and virtues, that nurses were able to make progress toward economic and educational reform for women. Nurses proudly wore the uniforms they purchased in department stores or that they themselves made from patterns. The comfortable and simple silhouette allowed for great freedom of movement, and the uniforms were suitable for a wide variety of wartime tasks and responsibilities. The professionalization of nursing that the Great War enforced was reflected in its clothing. In that respect, the evolution of the nurse's

FIG. 1a.7 A group of French soldiers in convalescence posing with nurses, July 7, 1915. Postcard. Musée de la Grande Guerre du Pays de Meaux, CAPM.2006.1.14129.033.

FIG. 1a.8 A French nurse smoking a cigarette. Photograph on cardboard. Musée de la Grande Guerre du Pays de Meaux, CAPM.2006.1.14129.019.

FIG. 1a.9 Nurse’s blouse and apron belonging to Louise Daniel. Musée de la Grande Guerre du Pays de Meaux, CE2019.1.1, 2.

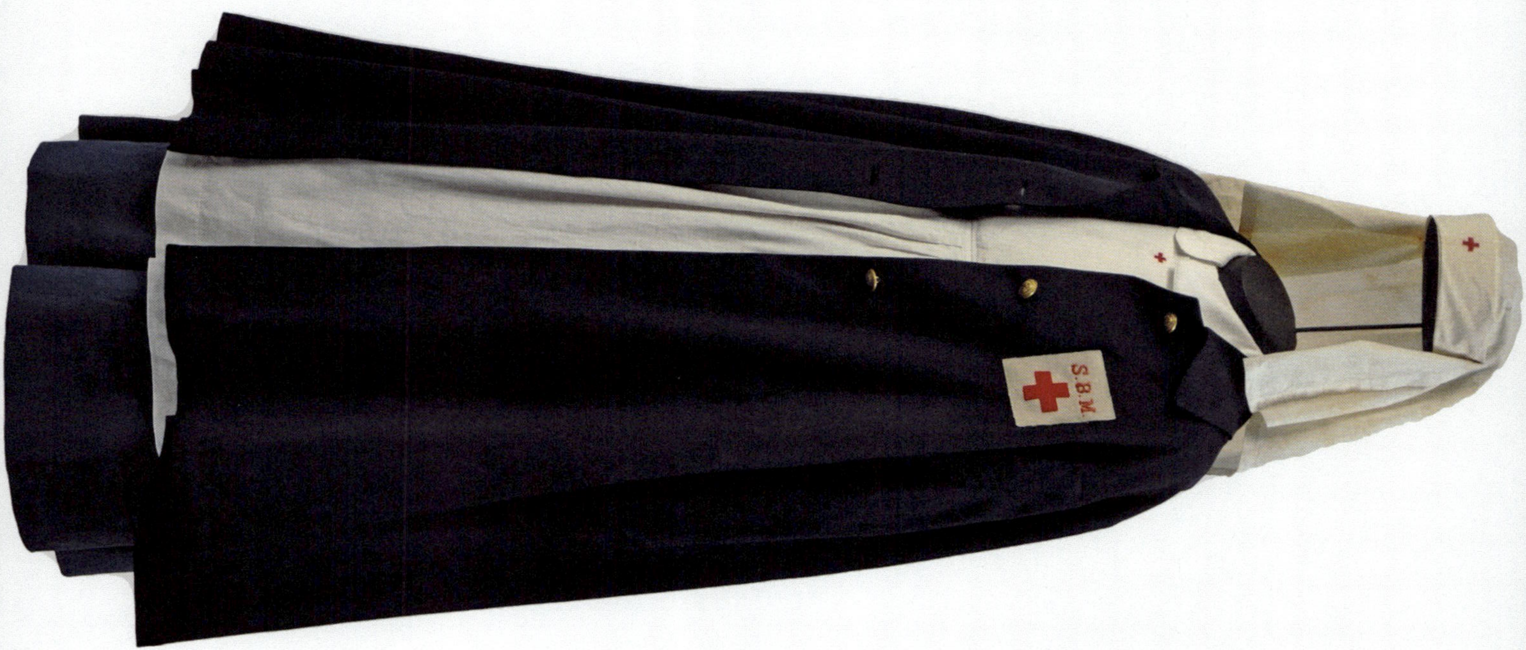

FIG. 1a.10 Nurse's uniform belonging to Sidonie Pocquet. Musée de la Grande Guerre du Pays de Meaux, CAPM.2006.1.7925, CAPM.2006.7937, CAPM.2006.1.12088, and CAPM.2006.1.12089, CAPM.2006.1.12093 to 96, CAPM.2006.1.12101.

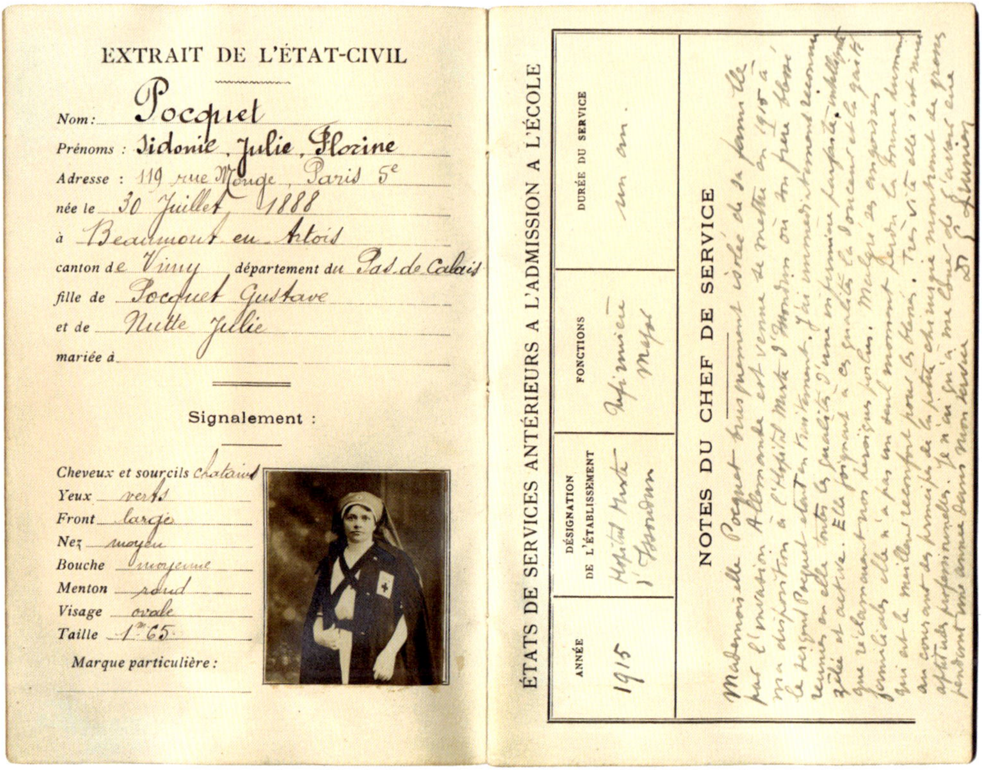

EXTRAIT DE L'ÉTAT-CIVIL

Nom: Pocquet
Prénoms: Sidonie, Julie, Florine
Adresse: 119 rue Monge, Paris 5e
née le 30 Juillet 1888
à Beaumont en Artois
canton de Vimy département du Pas-de-Calais
fille de Pocquet Gustave
et de Nutte Julie
mariée à

Signalement:

Cheveux et sourcils chatains
Yeux verts
Front large
Nez moyen
Bouche moyenne
Menton rond
Visage ovale
Taille 1m65
Marque particulière:

ÉTATS DE SERVICES ANTÉRIEURS A L'ADMISSION A L'ÉCOLE

ANNÉE	DÉSIGNATION DE L'ÉTABLISSEMENT	FONCTIONS	DURÉE DU SERVICE
1915	Hôpital Mixte d'Issoudun	Infirmière major	un an

NOTES DU CHEF DE SERVICE

FIG. 1a.11 Extract from Sidonie Pocquet's nursing log. Musée de la Grande Guerre du Pays de Meaux, CAPM.2006.1.5811.0.

FIG. 1a.12 Nurses preparing bandages, 1914–18. Silver gelatin print. Musée de la Grande Guerre du Pays de Meaux, CE20019.2.1.

uniform from religious ensembles in dark colors and heavy fabrics to the more practical uniform worn by nurses such as Louise Daniel and Sidonie Pocquet (discussed below) points to the changing social status of women. FIG. 1a.8 The collections at the Musée de la Grande Guerre (Meaux, France) include several uniforms and other items worn by French and British nurses during the First World War. Most of the pieces have been identified, along with the names of the women who wore them and some details about their service. The nurse's uniform belonging to Louise Daniel, who worked in a hospital in Brest, includes a pleated, button-down dress with long sleeves that button at the wrist and a pleated bib apron that ties at the waist, both in white cotton. Also included in the ensemble is a cap, or coif, made of a thinner white cotton.[10] FIG. 1a.9 Each item is embroidered with a small red cross. The apron is typical of those seen in the many photographs of wartime nurses, who wear either bib aprons with shoulder straps that cross in the back or tie around the neck or triangular bib aprons that buttoned to the blouse. Most photographs show aprons with pockets, but Daniel's apron has only one. The uniform belonging to Sidonie Pocquet, whose service record is inscribed in her nursing log, is a complete example from the First World War. FIG. 1a.10 She was born in 1888 in Beaumont-en-Artois (France's Nord-Pas-de-Calais region) but was separated from her family and remained in German-occupied France during the war. In 1915, she enlisted as a caregiver in a joint civilian and military hospital in Issoudun (Indre department) and joined the Heine-Fould teaching hospital in Paris in 1916. Pocquet graduated from the Société des Blessés Militaires, an auxiliary of the French military health service, which she then joined. Pocquet's uniform is reminiscent of a nun's habit, although it is more practical. A very tightly woven white cotton dress was worn over a blue skirt and paired with a white apron embroidered at the breast with a white Red Cross emblem. The dress features a detachable Peter Pan collar attached on both sides of the chest. For traveling to town, Pocquet would have worn a long cape made from a dark blue woolen fabric with two armholes.[11] On the left side of the cape is a white badge embroidered with the letters SBM (Société des Blessés Militaires) above a red cross. The three tombak (a brass alloy) buttons are stamped with a cross and the inscription *Croix-Rouge Française*. In the photograph from her nursing log, Pocquet's cape is secured by two woolen straps of the same color that cross in front. FIG. 1a.11 This practical system allows the cape to be secured to the back of the shoulders and offers the wearer freedom of movement. In the same photograph, Pocquet wears a coif and a shoulder-length veil embroidered with the emblem of the Red Cross. For city wear, French nurses wore dark blue veils with white trim; at work their veils were white with a red cross in the middle of the forehead. The veil could accommodate different hairstyles, and each nurse styled hers as she liked. Some nurses, often the youngest, wore their hair tightly over the brow, hiding the ears, like a nun's headdress; others left the forehead relatively uncovered, and their hair was more clearly visible. FIG. 1a.12

1 Catherine Duboys-Fresney and Georgette Perrin, *Le Métier d'Infirmière en France* (Paris: Presses Universaires, 2009), 7.

2 Leroux Hugon, Véronique, Jacques Poirier, and Philippe Ricou, "L'Histoire de l'École d'Infirmières de la Salpêtrière," in *Histoire des Sciences Médicales* 31 (1997), 189.

3 Elizabeth Fee and Mary Garofalo, "Florence Nightingale and the Crimean War," *American Journal of Public Health* (September 2010), 1591.

4 Yvonne Knibiehler, *Cornettes et blouses blanches, les infirmières dans la société françaises (1880–1980)* (Paris: Hachette, 1984), 53.

5 Charles Charton, *Pour Nos Soldats: Guide du Poilu. Avant, pendant, après* (Paris: H. Charles-Lavauzelle, 1916), 26.

6 M. E. Bertheau, "L'Engagement des Infirmières Laïques pendant la Première Guerre Mondiale: Amorce de Professionnalisation des Soins en Milieu Militaire," *Médecine et Armées* (2016), 397.

7 Circular 38 Ci/7 dated March 8, 1916, with instructions regarding the status of the corps of temporary nurses from military hospitals cited in Bertheau, "L'Engagement des Infirmières Laïques," 398.

8 Bolstered by her research on radioactivity and by her position as head of the Institut du Radium since 1909, Marie Curie became a volunteer in August 1914 and head of the Red Cross's radiology department. Source: article from the Clermont-Ferrand University Library, https://buclermont.hypotheses.org/1932.

9 Françoise Thébaud, *Les femmes au temps de la guerre de 14* (Paris: Stock, 1986), 87.

10 This uniform entered the museum's collections in June 2013. It was a gift of Madame Marie-Edith Quoniam, the nurse's granddaughter. In the second half of the 19th century, Louis Pasteur shook the medical world with his recommendations for hygiene. The clothes of caregivers were to be boiled on a daily basis, and the only fabric that could withstand that was undyed cotton.

11 A shade of blue that is reminiscent of the blue of the French artilleryman uniform in 1914. In letters to her family, nurse Léonie Bonnet speaks of her "artilleryman coat." *Aimer et Travailler: Léonie Bonnet, Une Infirmière dans la Grande Guerre* (Paris: Editions d'Albret, 2008), 92.

2

“Needles En Avant!”: The Militarization of Women’s Sewing and Knitting during the First World War in France, Great Britain, and America

SUSAN R. GRAYZEL

I sit and sew—a useless task it seems, — My hands grown tired, my head weighed down with dreams — The panoply of war, the martial tread of men, — Grim-faced, stern-eyed, gazing beyond the ken — Of lesser souls, whose eyes have not seen Death, — Nor learned to hold their lives but as a breath — But–I must sit and — sew. *I sit and sew –my heart aches with desire — That pageant terrible, that fiercely pouring fire — On wasted fields, and writhing grotesque things — Once men. My soul in pity flings — Appealing cries, yearning only to go — There in that holocaust of hell, those fields of woe — But–I must sit and sew.* *The little useless seam, the idle patch; — Why dream I here beneath my homely thatch, — When there they lie in sodden mud and rain, — Pitifully calling me, the quick ones and the slain? — You need me, Christ! It is no roseate dream — That beckons me—this pretty futile seam, — It stifles me—God, must I sit and sew?*[1]

First published in 1920, Alice Dunbar-Nelson's poem "I Sit and Sew," inspired by the First World War, embodies how the domestic labor of women lies at the heart of their wartime lives. FIG. 2.1 In three stanzas, the feminine voice of the poet traces how she dreams of the terrors of war: the martial tread of grim-faced men, the "writhing grotesque" figures of the wounded, and the "sodden mud and rain" that bury the dead. In contrast, she waits at home where she must "sit and sew—a useless task it seems." The required task of mending, patching the seams, and using her domestic needlework skills at the service of the nation while dreaming of the horrors of war experienced by men she cannot aid oppresses her. Yet while the poem questions why women like her can do no more than sit and sew—suggesting that this labor was insignificant in the face of the harrowing experiences of fighting men—sewing and knitting proved vital to this war.

That Dunbar-Nelson was an African American woman describing what had become a widely voiced sentiment helps us to see that this work crossed a range of borders and evoked a range of feelings, including frustration as well as obligation, that could transcend many otherwise stark differences among women.[2] For there are many truisms about the First World War and the roles and experiences of women therein across participant states. Some relate to more general assumptions about the gendering of war experience: men fight, taking action in harrowing battle fronts, and women wait, offering support and comfort in a home front behind the lines. While waiting, women continue to perform their domestic labors, including knitting, sewing, and weaving. They create items such as clothing, blankets, and bandages necessary for the sustaining of life, while their men are agents of destruction. But such myths were both shaken up and reified by the unprecedented nature of the First World War.

In August 1914, men across Europe marched off to battle in the largest armies ever assembled, including those of France. As the war along the Western Front expanded both in duration and range beyond what many had anticipated, supplies for these troops failed to keep up with demand. This was especially true for other participant nations like Great Britain, where the lack of conscription at the start of the war, in contrast to the militaries of the other great powers, meant a similar absence of the infrastructure required to outfit the large numbers of men who flocked to join up in 1914. Another contributing factor was that the very mobilization of men depleted the available laborers needed to manufacture everything that the military required. Thus, one result of the First World War was the expansion of the range and scope of women's industrial labor, especially in their traditional sector of textiles, as well as in the realms of metal working and munitions manufacturing. This took place across nearly every participant state, becoming one of the frequently commented-upon aspects of women's lives during the Great War.[3]

Women's expanded work for pay in and outside of factories offers one important way to understand what was, and was not, transformative about this war. New kinds of waged labor in industrial, transportation, and public service sectors affected what some women wore, and the visual transformation of women's public appearances—with trousers and elements of uniforms cropping up in women's dress—was broadly commented upon.

FIG. 2.2

Yet this remained an era when women's labor within the home still mattered a great deal. Clothing and linens were often hand constructed and certainly hand repaired. The ability to use a needle—to sew or knit—was something often taught to girls and regarded as an asset across geographic and even class borders, even if the importance and scale of such work varied.

During the First World War, the deployment of these domestic skills, especially of sewing and knitting, became deeply integrated with cultural ideas about how all women could contribute to the waging of modern, total war. An exploration of these ideas reveals how the militarization of women's domestic labor in France, Great Britain, and America—especially sewing and knitting—became one of the more ubiquitous and significant ways in which women contributed to the war and by which the war came home. It did so despite the

FIG. 2.1 "Women workers knit for our soldiers," 1914. Postcard.
© Bibliothèque Marguerite Durand, Collection Carte Postale, CP 1739 a.

FIG. 2.2 Chas (Charles) Laborde. "The Feminine Emancipation." Caricature showing a man wearing a kilt walking arm-in-arm with a woman wearing overalls who says "Yes, but after the war, I'll be the one wearing the pants." *Le Rire Rouge*, May 18, 1918, 12. Private collection.

ambivalence that women and their societies expressed about mobilizing domestic skills and settings in the service of war. Far from being a "useless task," simply sitting and sewing or knitting could symbolize feminine commitment to individual soldiers and to their nations. This held true across national borders, with particular challenges in certain areas, including the Central Powers, where wool itself came in short supply. Thus, the following discussion shows how women's domestic labor became part of the war effort in the three allied states. Here, instead of taking up arms, women's arms took up needles and utilized them to support their war-torn nations.

Sewing and Knitting for the Poilus in France

This is how one of the first histories of everyday life in France during the Great War described the significance of the items of clothing—especially woolens—sent in the first parcels to poilus, the popular wartime term for French infantrymen:

> *In each family . . . the mother and the wife make room for balls of yarn and needles. The war has dispersed the hearths (foyers), but knitting has brought together those who are left. Around the lamp, women are making nose coverings (cache-nez), balaclavas (passe-montagne), gloves, socks. Those who will receive this clothing, fabricated with such fervor, will not have the impression of finding an anonymous and cold present (cadeau).*[4]

More than the warmth provided by these personal woolen goods, this assessment emphasizes that the items convey the essence of the hearth, the heart of the home. Constructed with "fervor" and also, implicitly, with other emotions, such as love and concern, the production of knitted items provides its own emotional support, not only for the soldiers who receive these presents, but also for the wives and mothers, and presumably sisters and daughters, of mobilized men.

Evidence of organized knitting and sewing for the war effort can be found throughout France and its wartime media. Such efforts could encompass the traditional aims of feminine needlework charities—creating garments and home linens for the indigent—and add to this aid the specific plight of refugees, many fleeing the invaded and occupied zones of northern France. Yet a new focus on providing items created deliberately for soldiers emerged, especially as the war continued, such as supplying woolen items to enable them to withstand the often brutal conditions of the Western Front—rain, wind, snow, cold. Diseases such as trench foot emerged from the conditions facing men on the Western Front, such as standing in freezing water and mud. Having a pair of clean, woolen socks could make the difference between succumbing to this limb-threatening ailment or not.

Much of the production of knitting for soldiers in France was coordinated under the auspices of its national branch of the Red Cross but took place in localities large and small. As a brief article in *L'Ouest Éclair* of March 1915 explained, since the start of the war, a section of the Red Cross created in Châtelaudran (a small town in Brittany) had responded to the official call for knitting for soldiers by sending "to our soldiers at the front 340 pairs of socks, 349 nose coverings, 35 woolen vests, 200 underpants, 23 balaclava."[5] By December 1915, Parisiennes from the most elegant salons were being praised for the "ardor" of their knitting, in "blue wool, color of the horizon, gray wool . . . khaki wool, brown wool . . . with all the nose coverings that they had thus woven, one could put a band all around the earth."[6] From small communities to the capital, women were knitting for France.

A variety of preexisting charitable organizations for religious women of all denominations also turned their attention to such tasks. In addition to the larger Catholic organizations, both Jewish and Protestant women's groups collected and fabricated clothing and linens for "*orphelins de guerre*" (children whose fathers had died in the war), refugees, and soldiers, as well as producing material such as sheets for ambulances and military hospitals.[7] In addition, locales ranging from municipalities to villages created committees to oversee the production and collection of knitted garments. In west-central France for example, a departmental committee to aid the wounded, soldiers at the front, refugees, and those permanently disabled by the war oversaw knitters producing garments for all these groups.[8]

Knitting became part of the ways in which schoolgirls could contribute to the war. The monthly journal for the secondary education of girls reported on such activities across France; as early as January 1915 it noted that at the Lycée Victor-Hugo in Paris, "knitting was the sole occupation during the hours dedicated to manual work . . . [so that] a considerable quantity of woolen objects had been produced."[9] Reports from various departments also highlight the mobilization of schoolchildren, particularly but not exclusively girls, in the knitting of items for soldiers. Another departmental report in 1915 recorded the work of students in knitting for soldiers: "in girls' schools and mixed schools, directed by female teachers, work desks have been opened to the creation of warm clothing destined for the army: socks, sweaters, nose coverings, balaclavas have been knit in great numbers and sent to the trenches."[10] Elsewhere, this activity seemed more contained to girls, as in the department of Hautes-Alpes, where students in girls' schools were praised for knitting for soldiers during their hours of manual work and where many classes had "imposed on themselves a permanent commitment by adopting one or more "*filleuls*." This term, meaning godson, became used during the war to refer to military men adopted by a *marraine de guerre* (godmother of war) who took special responsibility for sending their filleul letters and packages of comforts.[11] SEE CHAPTER 1 As the war continued into its third year, brief sections on "schools and the war" still appear in departmental reports, such as the Prefect's Report from the Department of Vaucluse in 1917 noting students' ongoing creation of socks and sweaters for soldiers.[12]

Representations of Women Knitting on Postcards and in Song

Images of women of all ages knitting and sewing appeared throughout French wartime media. Parcels offered one way to connect the fronts, as did other forms of mail, especially the postcard. The images on these cards could enhance the written messages and also serve as a shorthand to show what women at home were thinking or meant to be thinking as they supported the war effort. A number of colorful French postcards depicted women knitting, and while these images reinforced expected gender roles, they now also connected them intimately with the national war effort.

Representations of this feminine task feature women of all ages, including young girls. One such postcard uses muted colors with vivid pops of red to depict young girls in an idyllic rural setting or park knitting socks. FIG. 2.3 Two sit together on a bench, focused on their task, while a younger girl peers at an older one as she knits. Only the label, "le tricot du combattant" (knitting for the soldier), suggests the underlying military context for this peaceful scene. Another photographic postcard shows a young girl beside a knitting basket; the interior light shines on her beribboned hair as she gazes at the soldier, presumably her father, who wears a winter coat and helmet. FIG. 2.4 A rhyming couplet below explains her thoughts: "I made a sweater, a balaclava/That will keep you warm during the campaign."[13] The caption "Tricot National" (National Knitting) makes it clear that this is no ordinary domestic task but an embodiment of her service for the nation, now personified by her soldier father.[14] In a particularly dramatic postcard, a daughter and her mother are shown knitting together in an interior setting that dominates the foreground, but across the top, the photograph shows a line of soldiers with the barrels of their guns extended in a trench. FIG. 2.5

Captioned “Le Tricot du Soldat” (Knitting for the Soldier), the card connects two diametrically opposed settings. The needles busy at home will yield knitted items to aid their soldier, and, moreover, “our heart will follow our modest package.” The extended knitting needles in the mother’s hand visually mimics the extended bayonet of the rifles pictured above, equating the two as weapons of war.[15] Three generations of women are featured in a postcard adapted from an illustrated magazine that shows a grandmother teaching her granddaughter how to knit, while the mother works across the room, beside a basket filled with completed garments. FIG. 2.6 In the top left corner, barely visible soldiers covered in snow suggest the need for these warm items and the motivation for the industrious domestic scene. Again, the caption for the image makes clear not only that this knitting is done for beloved combatants (“Le Tricot du Combattant” [Knitting for the Soldier]), but that “all French families work for our soldiers.” This particular family thus stands in for those across France, implying that not to participate is somehow to fail being part of the national family. Underscoring the need for all ages to contribute, the illustration for the postcard “Pour l’Absent” (For the Absent One), shows an older woman in shawl and cap with her knitting as a small child offers a coin. FIG. 2.7 The message underneath reads: “The knitting of the elder and the offering of the child for the one whom duty keeps far from the hearth.” The absent one’s duty is fighting, while the duty of old and young is material and emotional support.[16] Even the most fashionable of French women could contribute to the war effort in this way, or so suggests this postcard from the series Women and the War. In this version of “Le Tricot du Combattant,” a clearly upper-class woman, with a carefully coiffed hairstyle and a tailored crinoline-style suit, holds yarn in her outstretched arms. Unlike the other images in these postcards, she is not shown actively engaged in the task. FIG. 2.8

Indeed, her pose suggests that she might as well be modeling her outfit for an article on fashion. Yet the caption again repurposes a scene seemingly unconnected with military endeavors into being part of what women should do for the war effort.[17]

One postcard celebrates both knitters and nurses, equating them, in a poem attributed to poilu André Soriac, as “Chères Mobilisées” (Dear Mobilized Women). FIG. 2.9 The drawing in the top left corner shows three generations of women illuminated by

FIG. 2.3 Henriette Delalain. "Knitting for the Soldier." Postcard showing young girls knitting outdoors, Paris: Ch. Ramel & Cie, 1918. © Bibliothèque Marguerite Durand, Collection Carte Postale, CP 1725a.

FIG. 2.4 "National Knitwear." Postcard featuring a young girl at home with her knitting basket and a uniformed soldier at the front captioned "I made a sweater, a balaclava, that will keep you warm during the campaign," Paris: M. Boulanger, ca.1914–18. © Bibliothèque Marguerite Durand, Collection Carte Postale, CP 1728a.

FIG. 2.5 "Knitting for the Soldier." Postcard captioned "Our heart will follow our modest parcel," ca. 1914-18. © Bibliothèque Marguerite Durand, Collection Carte Postale, CP 1731 a.

FIG. 2.6 "Knitting for the Soldier." Postcard captioned "All the French families work for our soldiers," Paris: Ad. Welck, ca. 1914–18. © Bibliothèque Marguerite Durand, Collection Carte Postale, CP 1735 a.

FIG. 2.7 “For the Absent One.” Postcard captioned “The knitting of the elder and the offering of the child for the one whom duty keeps far from the hearth,” Paris: AN Paris, ca. 1914-18. © Bibliothèque Marguerite Durand, Collection Carte Postale, CP 1751 a.

FIG. 2.8 Leroy. "Woman and the War." Postcard captioned "Knitting for the Soldier," Paris: P. J. Gallais, 1914–18. © Bibliothèque Marguerite Durand, Collection Carte Postale, CP 1322a.

A ma grande amie, Hortense Jacob.
Très affectueusement.

A Nos Chères Mobilisées

Femmes de France, ô Vous, Sœurs, Epouses et Meres,
O Vous qui loin de nous, vos grands cœurs angoisses.
Endurez vaillamment des tortures ameres
Et souffrez... doublement, nous sachant menaces !

Femmes, qu'avez-vous fait, malgré vos deuils, vos larmes,
Malgré vos noirs soucis, vos cauchemars fiévreux,
Malgré le Foyer vide et malgré vos alarmes,
Vos frissons d'epouvante et vos tourments affreux ?

Vous avez tricoté pour nous des nuits entières,
Vous avez revêtu des robes d'infirmières
Vous penchant sur nos corps tout sanglants et meurtris !...

Et le soir, en veillant un blessé qui délire,
Tremblant pour vos absents, vous vous pressez d'écrire
Une lettre d'amour à vos Poilus chéris !...

ANDRÉ SORIAC
Poilu terrassier-troglodyte,
Gourbi de la Revanche,
Route de la Victoire.

Nº 12 Série des Cartes-Sonnets illustrées de la guerre
Tous droits réservés — Edition Cigalia, 8, Rue de Condé - Paris 6e

FIG. 2.9 Herman, illustrator; André Soriac, author. "To Our Dear Mobilized Women." Postcard with a poem celebrating French women who contribute to the war effort, Paris: Edition Cigalia, 1915–18. © Bibliothèque Marguerite Durand, Collection Carte Postale, CP 1738a.

For my dear friend, Hortense Jacob.
With love.

To Our Mobilized Women

Women of France, O You, Sisters, Wives, and Mothers,
O You who are far from us, your large hearts anguished.
Enduring bitter travails
And suffering... doubly, for knowing our peril!

Women, what have you done, despite your sorrows, your tears,
Despite your dark worries, your feverish nightmares,
despite the empty Hearth and your alarm,
Your chills of terror and your frightful torments?

You have knitted for us entire nights,
You have made nurse's uniforms,
You have stood over our bloody and lifeless bodies!...

And in the evening, watching over a feverish patient,
Trembling for your distant loved ones, you hasten to write
A love letter to your dear Poilu! ...

André Soriac
troglodyte trench-digging Poilu,
Camp Revenge,
Victory Road.

a table lamp and is accompanied by a poem that begins: "Women of France, O You, Sisters, Wives and Mothers / O You who are far from us, your large hearts anguished." The poet then extolls what you—the collective "vous" of all French women—have done, "despite your sorrows, your tears, despite your dark worries, your feverish nightmares, despite the empty Hearth . . . and your frightful torments." The list of what women have contributed begins with their needles: "you have knitted for us for entire nights." Soriac then describes women's roles in nursing and caring for the wounded, and by calling those engaged in the simple task of knitting "mobilized" and by equating these tasks with other more direct aid, such as tending the injured bodies of fighting men, he incorporates this cheerful domestic scene and its labor into the war.[18] Another poetic postcard calls for women to unite not only across generations but also across classes and regions. In the drawing that accompanies "La Chanson des Aiguilles" (The Song of the Needles), three women are busy knitting, but one is clearly a fashionable, modern woman of leisure and the other is attired in more traditional peasant garb.

FIG. 2.10 The female poet calls to them both:

Knit, needles of France — Winter is coming . . . — Knit all in cadence — For the heroes, the sons of France — Who are fighting and dying there — The Peasant or good Chatelaine — In the salon as in the hovel — Will knit the same wool — Without knowing for whom are the stockings. According to this verse, a woman of the highest social status and a peasant woman in her hovel become united in their common task and their desire to provide for a universal poilu. They do not need to know who will benefit from their labor. As the poem continues, it stresses that such "duty exempts no one." The ultimate purpose of such a mundane task is made clear in the final stanza: *— Inch by inch and stitch by stitch — We will repel Germany — To each one her field of battle — Needles of France: en avant!*

By applying a military command to the needles, the purpose of this domestic labor is made clear. French women wielding their needles are engaging in their own battleground, helping to defeat the enemy not only by producing knitted items but also by partaking in the spirit of wartime solidarity despite their differences in rank or location.[19] Like these postcards, songs also extolled the work of all the women who knitted for the nation. The song "Les Tricoteuses de 1915" (The Female Knitters of 1915) resembles the postcards just discussed, as its sheet-music cover shows three generations of women knitting by lamplight around a table. Its verses start in the war zone, where "the trench is cold and the winter is slow," and quickly turn to the schoolroom, where charming fingers forage amidst the wool "to make warm clothing" as its chorus commands: *Knit, Young Girls of France (Fillettes de France) — Nose covers, gloves, stockings — So that you lessen the suffering — Of our Heroes struggling there. — You send hope — When you direct to the Front — All the woolens that will make — Winter warmer for the poilus of France.* As the song continues, its chorus issues the command to knit to women of all ages, beginning with *fillettes*, followed by *femmes* (women) and then by *grand'mères*. In the verse about women, the lyrics praise them for turning from frivolous needlework—embroidery in elegant salons—to a task that alleviates ennui, as "your hand shapes a cozy knitted item." When shifting the call to the grandmothers of France, it suggests that their "knotted" and "shivering" fingers can make their needles play "as if they were the fingers of a twenty-year-old."

In its concluding verse, "Les Tricoteuses de 1915" calls to all women to transform "bourgeois interiors" and "peasant hearths" into "human hives" filled with knitters so that "wherever there lives the heart of a French woman" and "wherever our soil is ours," they will see that their "brave [soldiers] winter at ease."[20] This reference to soil belonging to French women evokes both the territories of Alsace and Lorraine, whose full reintegration into France formed one of the rallying cries of the war, and the ten departments in France's north and east currently occupied by the enemy. Yet it is the heart of the French woman that redeems the nation through her industry, her transformation of her needles into instruments with which to wage war.

Knitting and Sewing among the Allies: The United Kingdom and the United States

In Britain, where men were issued only two pairs of socks with their official uniforms, the ability to make up deficiencies in clothing became the province of women. Having gloves, mittens, scarves, balaclavas, and caps could help safeguard soldiers from ailments, but because of trench foot, socks were absolutely crucial. The entire enterprise of creating these knitted garments received the highest form of official sanction: appeals directly from Queen Mary, who assisted with an official call to provide 30,000 socks to troops.[21] She also lent her name to the Queen Mary's Needlework Guild (QMNG), rechristened in 1914 precisely to honor as well as encourage this type of war work, which claims in its official history to have produced "hundreds

La Chanson des Aiguilles

Il n'est pas une fille de France qui ne filât une quenouillée pour ma rançon.
Bertrand Duguesclin.

Tricotez, aiguilles de France,
L'hiver vient, ils ont froid nos gas;
Tricotez toutes en cadence,
Pour les héros, les fils de France
Qui luttent et meurent là-bas!

Paysanne ou bien châtelaine,
Au salon comme au galetas
Tricoteront la même laine
Sans savoir pour qui sont les bas.

C'en est fait des vieilles entraves!
Savant ou non, noble ou vilain
Devant l'ennemi sont des braves,
Comme messire Duguesclin.

Et notre cœur qui pour eux tremble
D'un émoi si vrai, si profond,
Sous un même nom les rassemble,
Dans un même amour les confond!

Le devoir n'exempte personne,
Donnons notre âme sans compter;
Voici qu'à tous les clochers sonne
L'heure de la fraternité!

Pouce à pouce et maille après maille
Nous repousserons l'Allemand
A chacun son champ de bataille,
Aiguilles de France: en avant!

Amélie DE NÉRY.

Marylie Markovitch

FIG. 2.10 Marylie Markovitch. "The Song of the Needles." Postcard encouraging women of all classes to unite in the fight against Germany, Lausanne: Perrochet and David, La Chaux-de-Fonds, 1915. © Bibliothèque Marguerite Durand, Collection Carte Postale, CP 1737a.

The Song of the Needles

There was not one girl in France who wasn't loading a distaff for my ransom.
Bertrand Duguesclin

Knit, needles of France,
Winter is coming, and our men are cold;
Knit, all in cadence,
For the sons of France, the heroes
Who are fighting and dying there!

The Peasant or good Chatelaine,
In the salon as in the hovel
Will knit the same wool
Without knowing for whom are the stockings.

Enough with old divisions!
Scholar or pauper, saint or scoundrel
Brave are the men who stand before the enemy,
As did sir Duguesclin.

And our heart beats for them
With an emotion so true, so deep,
We call them by the same name,
Bestow upon them the same love!

Duty exempts no man,
So let us wholly devote ourselves;
For all the bells are ringing in
This hour of brotherhood!

Inch by inch and stitch by stitch,
We will repel Germany
To each one her field of battle
Needles of France: en avant!

Amélie de Néry
Marylie Markovitch

of thousands of garments" that were sent to combatants serving overseas. A recent account suggests that the Guild fabricated an estimated 15.5 million separate items during the entire war.[22] Originating in the late nineteenth century as a charitable group to supply linens to the poor, the Guild in its wartime role focused on supplying the military and encouraging all women to turn their needlework into patriotic war work. Initially, there was some criticism of having well-off women doing tasks that working women typically earned a living producing, but Guild members with means were also encouraged to purchase garments from those who relied on fabricating them for their livelihood. Branches of the QMNG spread out across Britain and its empire, with chapters in Canada, Jamaica, and India. Active volunteer members of the Guild could even receive a badge to wear featuring a crown with M.R. above a Tudor rose, suspended from a white enameled bar with the letters QMNG. Local branches of this organization and of many other charitable groups in villages, towns, and cities across Britain sewed and knitted for soldiers and sailors generally on behalf of specific regiments. These often took the form of "comfort funds," organized to coordinate the making and sending of knitted items.[23] As the *Times* suggested in March 1915, war had revived this art, and knitting had usurped reading as the main activity of women riding in railway cars, an "essentially feminine and gracious" task now focused on "the welfare of our brothers-in-arms."[24] It was also evident that those who could not or chose not to knit were willing to hire those who could. In March 1916, Lady Murray, president of one of the comfort funds, the Mediterranean Expeditionary Force Fund, offered to supply wool to "ladies having knitting machines" in order for them to produce socks.[25] This seemingly ubiquitous knitting by women found its way into British wartime media, including a volume of comical drawing and humorous verse, *Our Girls in Wartime*. FIGS. 2.11a,b Here praise is doled out to Pansy and her knitting party: *Oh! The things they knat — Pansy's meetings never ended — And results were simply splendid. — I can swear to that, — Since for weeks we used the socks she sent — To take the place of wire entanglement.*[26]

The mockery of well-meant but misplaced efforts to produce knitted items for soldiers appeared across different media. A cartoon in the *The Tattler* in December 1915, captioned the "Story of the Knitted Scarf," showed how soldiers took the misshapen scarf and stretched it sufficiently to repurpose as a hammock.[27] Yet there were also more sentimental evocations of wartime knitting.

Postcards similar to the ones produced in France showed women knitting in a domestic interior while a photographic representation of a soldier hovers above them, as in the postcard entitled "Absent—yet Near." FIG. 2.12 Another simply portrayed a woman knitting with the caption "Active Service," again overtly suggesting the equivalence between this feminine use of needles and the military work of fighting men.[28] FIG. 2.13 Among the most patriotic versions of British women's knitting for the war can be found in the poems of Jessie Pope. In "Socks," as in Dunbar-Nelson's "I Sit and Sew," the poet combines the homey task of knitting for a soldier with anxious worrying about his safety and well-being. Unlike Dunbar-Nelson, Pope shies away from listing the horrors of war. Instead the focus is on the knitter's efforts as she knits to avoid the "thoughts" of what he faces: *Shining pins that dart and click — In the fireside's sheltered peace — Check the thoughts the cluster thick — 20 plain and then decrease . . . — Never used to living rough, — Lots of things he's got to learn; — Wonder if he's warm enough.* As the poem continues, the knitter keeps up her count of stitches against the backdrop of the paper boy's cries, which only adds to her strain. Her meandering thoughts about the soldier never coalesce into any specific images of danger or battle, and the conclusion that "he'll come out on top somehow" can be read as either willfully naïve or purely jingoistic. Pope also wrote "The Knitting Girls" in 1915, where she invites the "soldier lad on the sodden ground" and the "sailor lad on the seas" to listen for the clacking needles, the sound of the united women of Britain knitting for them. That this is a task that brings women together regardless of their economic status or age is made clear in such lines as "the busy hands may be rough or white, the fingers gouty or slim . . . Lady and workgirl, young and old / They've all got one end in view." In addition to the production of "warm comforts against the cold," something special goes into this wartime task, for all of these women are "knitting love and luck in every row."[29] Beyond the practicality of such items comes something more important still, women's emotional labor and concrete support of war via this basic domestic art.

Despite the late entry of the United States into the conflict, women there soon joined in the production of woolen garments for soldiers. As one of the more popular posters exhorted them: "Our Boys Need Sox. Knit Your Bit."[30] FIG. 2.14 Under the auspices largely of the American Red Cross, a call went out in the summer of 1917 urging women to produce knitted garments,

PANSY RAN A KNITTING PARTY.
OH! THE THINGS THEY KNAT.
PANSY'S MEETINGS NEVER ENDED
AND RESULTS WERE SIMPLY SPLENDID,
I CAN SWEAR TO THAT,
SINCE FOR WEEKS WE USED THE SOCKS SHE SENT
TO TAKE THE PLACE OF WIRE ENTANGLEMENT.

FIG. 2.11a,b Joyce Dennys. "Pansy ran a Knitting-Party." Illustration in Hampden Gordon, *Our Girls in Wartime*, London: John Lane, n.d. University of Toronto, Thomas Fisher Library, Archive.org.

FIG. 2.12 "Absent—Yet Near." Postcard of a woman knitting, ca. 1915. © Mary Evans Picture Library, 10806304.

FIG. 2.13 Harold Copping. “Active Service.” Postcard of a woman knitting, ca. 1915. © Mary Evans Picture Library, 10698716.

including mufflers, sweaters, woolen helmets, vests, and, above all, socks. Facing similar conditions to French and British soldiers—namely the need to change into warm socks to try to stave off trench foot—American soldiers also urgently needed socks. Given the scale of the U.S. Army, the demand was enormous. Many American women could knit before 1917 but, of course, many could not. Since the basic garments needed by servicemen required relatively little skill to make, knitting became a way to express patriotism, and the appeal to women emphasized its seriousness and its fashionableness.[31]

In a case study of the knitting community of women in Seattle, Washington, Paula Becker found groups of knitters organizing across the city in churches, associations, schools, and workplaces. Those who could not knit themselves were encouraged to purchase wool for those who could. Women's participation in this aspect of the war effort cut across significant divides among them. For instance, Seattle's African American Self-Improvement Club was formed specifically to provide comfort packages for African American troops, including hand-knit garments. Naokichi Matsunaga, who was married to the imperial Japanese consul in Seattle, created a Japanese Ladies Auxiliary of the Red Cross, the first civic organization in the city for Japanese women in 1917, and one of its tasks was knitting for soldiers.[32]

As was the case in France and the United Kingdom, American popular culture quickly reflected the new craze for sewing and knitting for men in arms. It did so even before America's official entry into the war, when Al Jolson had a hit in 1915 with "Sister Susie's Sewing Shirts for Soldiers."[33] Its chorus, not unusually, mocks the end result, as the soldiers state their preference for thistles over her garments, but underneath the humor, it also suggests the important reciprocal relationship between this simple task at home and the fighting men:

Sister Susie's sewing shirts for soldiers — Such skill at sewing shirts our shy young sister Susie shows — Some soldiers send epistles — Say they'd sooner sleep in thistles — Than the saucy, soft, short shirts — For soldiers sister Susie sews. FIG. 2.15

In addition to the Red Cross posters illustrated with women knitting, which bluntly told all women "you can help," the illustrations on sheet music for songs such as "We'll Do Our Share" featured women with needles at work.[34] Other wartime songs were more explicit, such as "I Wonder Who's Knitting For Me," with its sheet music cover showing a row of knitting women behind a single doughboy.[35] FIG. 2.16

Behind every man in uniform, such representations imply, should be a woman or two or three deploying their needles to ensure the well-being of the nation's warriors.

Using Domestic Skills Against Weapons of Modern War

What happened when such needlework turned from producing personal items for soldiers to manufacturing war material itself? On April 29, 1915, about a week after the Second Battle of Ypres launched the modern age of chemical warfare, the British government invited such help from its civilian population, especially its women. The War Office mounted an appeal in the national press with instructions and a pattern that showed how civilians could transform ordinary household materials, such as bleached cotton wool and three layers of bleached cotton gauze, into a respirator or a primitive gas mask to safeguard men against this terrifying new weapon. FIG. 2.17 It urged volunteers to send these home-made respirators in packages of no less than one hundred to the Chief Ordinance Officer of the Royal Army Clothing Depot.[36]

The *Daily Mail* instantly framed the call as singling out the women of the nation as the ones to produce these objects: "Rush Job for Women." FIG. 2.18 Others soon followed suit. The *Birmingham Post* described the initiative as "An Opportunity for Women," while the *Daily Express* called attention to this as "Women's Response to War Office Appeal" in a subheading to the lead, "Rush to Make Respirators." Several papers, including the *Express*, published accounts of women who eagerly and enthusiastically took on board this new civic task. The manager of the Royal Army Clothing Depot in Pimlico (the destination for finished respirators listed in the War Office appeal) described himself as having "done nothing all day except willingly answer questions . . . the first lady called as soon as the offices were open, and promised to send 5,000 respirators a day." By early evening, the basic supplies—cotton wool, cotton gauze, and elastic—were running low, and the *Daily Express* took it upon itself to assure readers that "black elastic" would work as well as the white elastic listed in descriptions. The *Express* also took credit for suggesting to Messieurs Selfridge, proprietors of one of London's larger department stores, "for the convenience of those who would like to see the process in detail . . . to give a practical demonstration at their Oxford Street premises throughout the day." It advertised that a female demonstrator would be "in attendance in the surgical instrument department on the ground floor from 10 a.m. onwards." In the meantime, in the workrooms of Selfridge's "rows of expert women were making respirator pads."[37] Not to be outdone, the competing West End department store Harrod's placed

FIG. 2.14 “Our Boys Need Sox.” American Red Cross poster encouraging women to produce knitted garments, 1918. Library of Congress, Prints and Photographs Division Washington, D.C.

FIG. 2.15 Wladyslaw Theodore Benda. "You can help." American Red Cross poster, 1918. Library of Congress, Prints and Photographs Division Washington, D.C.

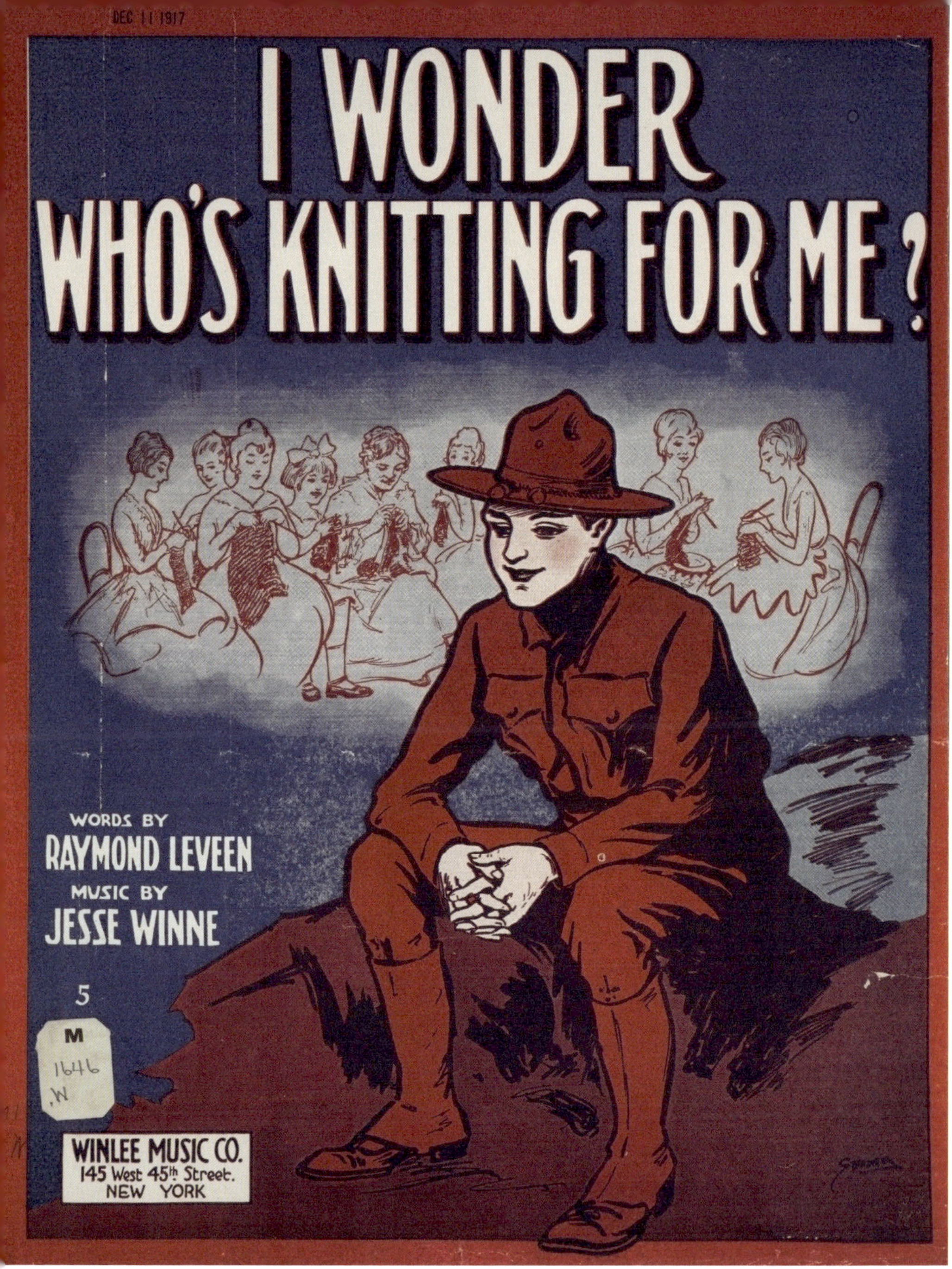

FIG. 2.16 Raymond Leveen, words; Jesse Winne, music. "I Wonder Who's Knitting for Me?" Illustrated sheet music cover featuring a uniformed soldier and women knitting, New York: Winlee Music Co., 1917. Library of Congress, Washington, DC.

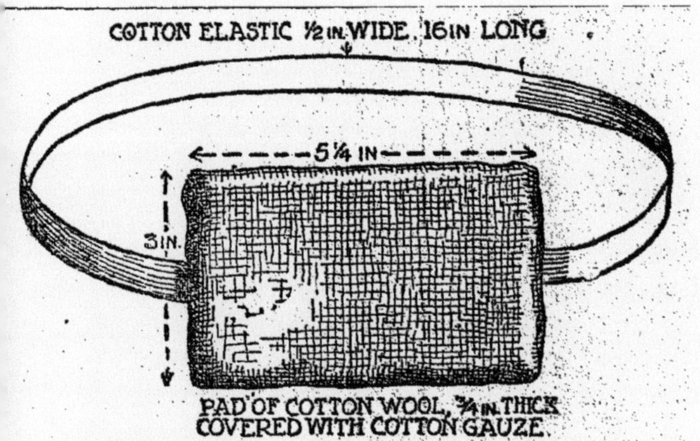

Diagram of respirator needed for our troops at the front.

FIG. 2.17 Pattern for Respirator. *Daily Mail* (London), April 29, 1915. Daily Mail Historical Archive.

RUSH JOB FOR WOMEN.

RESPIRATORS FOR OUR TROOPS.

ALL HOMES CAN HELP.

There is quick work to be done by our women. To protect our soldiers from the effects of German gas attacks, respirators are wanted without a minute's delay. The War Office at midnight last night issued the following appeal:—

Supplies of one or both of the following types of respirator are required by the troops at the front. Either can be made easily in any household.

First.—A face piece (to cover mouth and nostrils) formed of an oblong pad of bleached absorbent cotton wool, about 5¼in. x 3in. x ¾in., covered with three layers of bleached cotton gauze and fitted with a band to fit round the head and keep the pad in position, the band to consist of a piece of half-inch cotton elastic 16in. long attached to the narrow end of the face-pad so as to form a loop with the pad.

Second.—A piece of double stockingette, 9½in. long, 3¼in. in width, in the centre gradually diminishing in width to 2¼in. at each end, with a piece of thick plaited worsted about 5in. long attached at each end so as to form a loop to pass over the ear.

These respirators should be sent in packages of not less than 100 to the *Chief Ordnance Officer, Royal Army Clothing Department, Pimlico.*

FIG. 2.18 "Respirators for our Troops." *Daily Mail* (London), April 28, 1915. Daily Mail Historical Archive.

several samples of homemade gas masks in its Knightsbridge windows and publicized that its drug department could supply cotton wool, gauze, and elastic, while its wool department could provide "scoured wool for knitting respirators" (although there was no such official demand for them).[38] The women responded so successfully that on April 30 (approximately eight days after the battle), newspapers across Britain were filled with notifications that the War Office had "withdrawn" its appeal 24 hours after issuing it. The triumphant headline in the *Daily Mail* proclaimed "Women Foil the Poisoners," suggesting that the "magnificent" response of women throughout the nation had directly affected the war.[39] The appeal had called upon the women of Britain to redirect their domestic skills toward the service of military. It asked them to use ordinary household materials to fabricate a military object that would protect a soldier in the face of modern industrial warfare. Such a directive went far beyond the call for the knitting of socks, balaclavas, and mufflers. This involved women in creating personal, handcrafted items of protection against modern military technology.

This rather remarkable undertaking, speedily carried out by the women of Britain, led to some tens of thousands of such basic masks being sent to the Western Front in the late spring of 1915. The official postwar account recorded that "A cotton wool respirator in a gauze envelope on the pattern of the naval smoke respirator was also issued. 1,000,000 of these respirators were made in a single day by the women of ENGLAND." It was this sentence that formed the basis for how the story of these early respirators then appeared in most historical accounts of chemical warfare on the Western Front, where the episode underlines the futility and waste of the war. For this rudimentary design proved a danger: when the cotton pads were dry, they could not block out chlorine, and when they were wet, it was impossible to breathe.[40] What we can perhaps assume is that the official record helped to set up a myth of resourceful and patriotic women contributing to the military with their needles at home but without acknowledging that it proved a useless effort.

Nor was Britain alone in having women produce hand-crafted gas masks. In France, evidence of women fabricating gas masks appeared in such popular media as *La Vie Parisienne*, where its anecdotal section of news of the week, "On dit" (It Is Said), recorded the new craze among women in June 1915, nearly two months after the introduction of lethal poison gas at Ypres. After praising the "pretty knitters of last January," the report noted that they had found something to occupy them during the summer months, gathering to create "Masks . . . to cover the mouths of our poilus, with a buffer of cotton balls soaked in a solution of hyposulfite of soda that will allow them to brave without danger the terrible effects of asphyxiating gases."[41] Thus instead of *thés-tricots* (knitting teas), gentlewomen were now frequenting *thés-cataplasmes* (poultice teas) when they met in the hostess's salon to create gas masks. Participating in these events had "seduced" the time of Red Cross volunteers so that already a good number of them have mastered "the art of mounting muslin strips" to finish off the masks. However, what had also ensued, according to this article, is a competition among the creators, where "these ladies seek to innovate, to create models, to launch fashions," in short to outdo one another with their masks. Unfortunately, this led to one young woman, "a faithful worker of the "thés-cataplasmes de la Rue de la Bienfaisance," to fabricate a mask more "elegant than practical," something that would be sure to endanger the poilu who wore it. Her response to such criticism is a sigh of regret, because "it is so decorative."

Like the masks produced so efficiently and ineffectively by British women, the elite French women creating these masks were meant to be fabricating objects destined for a vital military purpose. And while the public tone in this light-hearted Parisian weekly finds the misguided efforts of their producers charming, both sets of women ultimately produced gas masks that proved useless. What is worth our attention is not the utility of such efforts, but that they existed at all. For the distance between encouraging women to knit a pair of socks and to sew together the textile components that form a gas mask is substantial. Both may deploy feminine domestic skills in service of the soldier, but the gas mask has no civilian purpose. To have women at home constructing such an object demonstrates how fully their domestic skills and the items that they could produce with them had been militarized.

As this essay began with a poem, it seems fitting to close with lines from one of the more infamous poetic depictions of women during the First World War. In "The Glory of Women," a scathing critique of the divide between the women at home and the soldiers in the field, the celebrated English soldier-poet Siegfried Sassoon contrasts the women, especially mothers, who sit at home ignorant of the horrors faced by their soldier sons. He concludes the sonnet with these lines:

O German mother dreaming by the fire — While you are knitting socks to send your son — His face is trodden deeper in the mud.

These lines powerfully evoke what knitting—and by extension the needlework and handcrafting of garments—had come to mean over the course of the Great War. It demonstrates the ways in which the task of using their needles united women across enemy lines, giving them a common way to try to alleviate the suffering of their beloved men in arms. Yet for Sassoon it also marked the fundamental divide between home and war front, as he calls out the futility of this feminine task of making something for a man already dead.

The warm socks stitched with "love and luck," as Jessie Pope put it, mean nothing to the combatant sunk into mud. Given the enormous death tolls and horrors of the First World War, it has largely been Sassoon's vision of such feminine, domestic labor for the war that has endured. Yet the millions of women across every country during this conflict who took up needles and yarn or thread deserve our attention, not only as dupes of patriotic propaganda, but also as laborers, sources of material and emotional support for their loved ones, and figures who, however ambivalently, answered the call to be vital contributors to their nations.

1 My thanks to Margaret Higonnet and Emily Machen for sources and advice; and to members of the Works-In-Progress Group of the Department of History at Utah State University for helpful feedback on an earlier draft. I am grateful to Maude Bass-Krueger and Sophie Kurdkjian for inviting me to contribute this essay and for their comments. Alice Ruth Dunbar-Nelson, "I Sit and Sew," in *The Dunbar Speaker and Entertainer*, ed. Alice Dunbar-Nelson (Napierville, IL: Nichols, 1920) and also reproduced in Margaret R. Higonnet, ed., *Lines of Fire: Women Writers of World War I* (New York: Plume, 1999), 536–37.

2 For some key works on the experiences of African American troops in the segregated U.S. military, see Jennifer Keene, *Doughboys, the Great War and the Remaking of America* (Baltimore, MD: Johns Hopkins University Press, 2006) and *World War I: The American Soldier Experience* (Lincoln, NE: University of Nebraska Press, 2011); Adrienne Lentz-Smith, *Freedom Struggles: African Americans and World War I* (Cambridge, MA: Harvard University Press, 2011); Jeffrey T. Sammons and John H. Morrow, Jr. *Harlem's Rattlers and the Great War: The Undaunted 369th Regiment and the African American Quest for Equality* (Lawrence, KS: University of Kansas Press, 2014); and especially, Chad L. Williams, *Torchbearers of Democracy: African American Soldiers in the World War I Era* (Chapel Hill, NC: University of North Carolina Press, 2010).

3 Information summarized here and below from Susan R. Grayzel, *The First World War: A Brief History with Documents* (Boston: Bedford/St Martins, 2012) and *Women and the First World War* (Harlow, UK: Longmans, 2002).

4 Gabriel Perreux, *La Vie Quotidienne des Civils en France pendant la Grande Guerre* (Paris: Hachette, 1964), 27. Unless otherwise noted, all translations in the text from the French are my own. The full poems "À Nos Chères Mobilisées" Fig. 2.9 and "La Chanson des Aiguilles" Fig. 2.10 were translated by Tristan Bass-Krueger.
5 "Pour Nos Soldats," *L'Ouest-Éclair*, March 23, 1915.
6 "Pendant la Guerre: Les Parisiennes," *Les Modes*, December 1915.
7 See "Les Ligueuses et la Guerre," *Petit Echo de la LPDF [Ligue Patriotique des Françaises]*, November 1915; "Les Oeuvroirs Israelite: L'Assistance par le Travail," *L'Univers Israélite*, March 1915, 247–48; "Aid Fraternelle aux soldats," *L'Univers Israélite*, January 1915, 202–3; "Crease," *Echo de la LPDF*, 191; "Les Orphelins de la Guerre," *Journal de la Jeune Fille*, September–October 1916. My thanks to Emily Machen for sharing these references with me. For more information on related work, see Emily Machen, "Soldiers of Faith behind the Lines: religious women and community patriotism during the First World War," *Women's History Review* 22, no. 1 (2013), 31–50.
8 Fernand Tardif, *La Vendée deux ans de guerre 1914–1916* (La Roche-sur-Yon: Hamonnet, 1916), 53.
9 "Les Lycées et Collèges de jeunes filles et Les Victimes de la Guerre," *L'Enseignement secondaire des jeunes filles: revue mensuelle,"* January 15, 1915, 100.
10 "Rapports . . .Délibérations du Conseil Général de L'Allier" (Moulins: Fudez Frères, 1915), 148.
11 "Rapports et délibérations—Conseil général des Hautes-Alpes" (Gap: Eds. Vollaire, 1916), 180. For more on the complicated status of the Marraine de Guerre, see Susan R. Grayzel, "Mothers, Marraines and Prostitutes: Morale and Morality in First World War France." *International History Revie* 19, no. 1 (February 1997), 66–82.
12 "Rapport du Préfet," Conseil Generale de Vaucluse (Avignon: H. Auzac, 1917), 421.
13 "J'ai fait un chandail, un passe-montagne / Qui te teindront chaud pendant la campagne."
14 Bibliothèque Marguerite Durand [BMD], Collection Cartes Postales, [CP] 1725a and BMD CP 1728a.
15 BMD CP 1731a.
16 BMD CP 17351 and BMD CP 1751a.
17 BMD CP 1322a.
18 BMD CP 1738a.
19 BMD CP 1737a.
20 "Les Tricoteuses de 1915," words by Léon Hiélard, music by Louis Jacquet (Paris: Cavel, 1915).
21 Joyce Meader, *Knitskrieg: A Call to Yarns* (London: Unicorn, 2016), 43–47.
22 See http://qmcg.org.uk/history/. Lucinda Gosling, *Knitting for Tommy: Keeping the Great War Soldier Warm* (Stroud: History Press, 2014), 14.
23 Meader, *Knitskrieg*, 59.
24 "The Knitters," *Times,* March 2, 1915.
25 "News in Brief," *Times,* March 24, 1916.
26 Hampden Gordon, *Our Girls in Wartime,* with illustrations by Joyce Dennys (London: John Lane, n.d.).
27 "Story of the Knitted Scarf," *The Tatler,* December 22, 1915. Reprinted in Gosling, *Knitting for Tommy,* 81.
28 "Absent—Yet Near," and "Active Service," Postcard reprinted in Gosling, *Knitting for Tommy*, 67.
29 Jessie Pope, "Socks," *War Poems* (London: Grant Richards, 1915), and in Gosling, *Knitting for Tommy*, 22–23; see p. 106 for reproduction of this poem as appearing in *The Needle Worker*, March 1915.
30 "Our Boys Need Sox," Red Cross poster, 1918, Library of Congress [LOC]: POS – US. .R43, See also /lccn.loc.gov/89710295.
31 See Donna Ghelerter, "Knitting in America During the First World War," MA thesis, Fashion Institute of Technology, 1989. UMI Proquest: EP 72108, for insights on why women knit rather than crocheted and the multiple ways in which this activity was constructed and marketed.
32 Paula Becker, "Knitting for Victory—World War I" (2006), http://www.historylink.org/File/5721
33 "Sister Susie's Sewing Shirts for Soldiers," sheet music, words R.P. Weston, music by Hermann E. Durewski, LOC 19/1291; https://www.loc.gov/resource/ihas.100005395.0/?sp=2.
34 We'll Do Our Share," sheet music, Library of Congress (LOC 2013562330); and "You Can Help," LOC POS - US.B45 and https://lccn.loc.gov/2002708897.
35 "I Wonder Who's Knitting for Me," sheet music, words by Raymond Leveen, music by Jesse Winne, LOC M1646.W and https://lccn.loc.gov/2014564406.
36 Just as a sampling, see appeals in *Western Times*, April 29, 1915; *Hull Daily Mail*, April 19, 1915; *Manchester Evening News*, April 28, 1915; the most frequently cited source for the appeal is *Daily Mail*, April 28, 1915.
37 "Rush to Respirators: Women's Response to War Office Appeal," *Daily Express*, April 29, 1915; see also *Birmingham Post*, April 29, 1915, and *Daily Mirror*, April 29, 1915.
38 Lynn Macdonald, *1915: The Death of Innocence* (reprint, Baltimore, MD: Johns Hopkins Press, 2000), 231–32.
39 "Women Foil the Poisoner," *Daily Mail*, April 30, 1915.
40 See the summation of this in Susan R. Grayzel, "Defence Against the Indefensible: The Gas Mask, The State and British Culture during and after the First World War," *Twentieth Century British History* 25, no. 3 (2014), 418–34.
41 "On dit . . . On dit," *La Vie Parisienne*, June 26, 1915. All references in this paragraph are to this article.

3

Fashion, Gender, and Anxiety

MAUDE BASS-KRUEGER

A woman preens in her new crinoline-style dress while her husband, a uniformed officer with a bandaged head, wonders if there is still room in the car for him to come along. FIG. 3.1a,b A soldier returning home on leave, his coat and shoes still muddy from the trenches, asks his girlfriend if "she's happy?" The woman responds that she's very happy indeed—on her way over, she spotted a darling little blue dress in the windows of the Galeries Lafayette department store. FIG. 3.2 These humorous cartoons, published in the satirical magazine *La Baïonnette*, used clothing to unmask deep-seated anxiety about what was perceived as a widening rift between men and women over the course of the war. Caricatures published in popular satirical magazines, articles published in the daily press, diaries written by soldiers and their loved ones, and postcards sent back and forth from the home to the trenches reveal a range of attitudes around fashion and war. Fashion was an ongoing topic of conversation throughout the war and a barometer of social tension. For some, fashion had a crucial role to play in the reunion of men and women during a soldier's leave, while for others clothing choices drove a wedge between the sexes and reinforced the growing divide between the front and the home. For both men and women, wartime fashion represented something greater than its material and aesthetic aspects—it symbolized the changes and challenges of new wartime realities.

The Problem of Fashion in Wartime France

Despite the war we still get dressed? Amidst the blood spilled over the earth and the howls of pain unleashed into the thin air, fashion continues to evolve with the most surprising silhouettes of its imagination! To the horror of the most recent massacres, fashion opposes the grace of its latest creations. The women compete with coquetry while the men do battle with heroism![1] —GUSTAVE GUICHE, 1917

The sheer horror of trench warfare exacerbated soldiers' reactions to domestic life when they returned home on leave. FIGS. 3.3–3.5

Men were alarmed to see that life continued on as normal and that women were buying new clothes. A soldier's letter published by the trench journal *Le Cri du Boyau* (The Cry of the Gut) tells the story of an infantryman "finally returning home . . . and finding his country-women. Ah! But how they've changed! No more clogs, no more aprons: shiny boots and jewels! The soldier asks himself: Are there still men behind the lines who can pay for all these pretty things?"[2] The shock of the new betrayed the soldier's larger fear of being forgotten or replaced by men whose wartime conditions were better than his own. And while his unease appeared to focus on non-combatant men—wartime profiteers perhaps—the "shiny boots and jewels" could also have been purchased by the women themselves.

Battle-scarred, traumatized, dirty, and bone-tired, male soldiers lived a different life from women, who were largely kept away from the front lines in France. While weary and anxious in their own right, women were told that their work contributed valiantly to the national war effort. They were praised for their collective spirit and selfless sacrifice. And although male soldiers were portrayed as valiant and heroic, daily life in the trenches felt terrifying, deadly, and, as the years dragged on, increasingly inhumane. As one soldier from the front in Verdun wrote:

My dear Edith, Life here is very hard. The smell of death reigns over us in the trenches. Rats attack us and parasites eat away at our skin; we live in the mud, they invade us, slow us down, and eat away at our shoes. The cold adds to our suffering. This glacial cold that chills our bones and pursues us every day. At night, it's impossible for us to sleep. At the ready, at every moment, ready to attack, ready to kill. Killing, that is at the heart of our story. They repeat to us that we must kill to survive, but I would say that we live to kill. This is how I live every minute in this hell. Without hygiene. Without rest. Without joy. Without life . . . [3]

—PIERRE, SEPTEMBER 22, 1916, VERDUN

The perceived normalcy of the home front, compounded with the visible changes taking place in the female sphere—women working men's jobs, changing fashions, increased female salaries—magnified the tensions produced by the dragging war and the staggering death toll. In 1916, the journalist Louis Latzarus published an article on the front page of the newspaper *Le Figaro* (he would later become editor-in-chief) in which he attempted to reconcile gender disputes. Men and women were increasingly divided over issues such as luxury and fashion:

I was told that a soldier, returning home on leave, was surprised to find, on his own table, an embroidered tablecloth. He looked at it, then turned to his wife with hostility: Well, he said, you deprive yourself of nothing here! She could have responded in any number of ways, but she couldn't think clearly and began to cry. I wasn't told if her heroic husband was moved by her tears, and, to tell the truth, I don't think he considered himself to have behaved badly. What had he done, except for formulating one of the countless tropes of the great quarrel between the front and the home front, quarrel that has won over the half-front and the half-home front and has finished by dividing the home front itself? [4]

For Latzarus, women were not to be blamed for their "frivolities" but

FIG. 3.1a Louis Icart. Caricature showing a woman trying on a new dress while her soldier husband yawns in the background: "How long the war is." "Oh! . . . much shorter than a fitting." *La Baïonnette*, April 20, 1916, 252. Private collection.

LA BAÏONNETTE

(Dessin de Touraine.)

— Votre robe est exquise, chère amie ; mais, dites-moi, quand vous êtes en voiture, y a-t-il encore une petite place pour votre mari?

— 253 —

FIG. 3.1b Edouard Tourraine, pseudonym of André Bonnafond. A uniformed soldier with a bandaged head looks on as a woman models a crinoline-style dress, noting: "Your dress is exquisite, dear lover; but, tell me, when you are in the car, is there still a small space for your husband?" *La Baïonnette*, April 20, 1916, 253. Private collection.

FIG. 3.2 George-Alfred Pavis. Upon returning from the front, a uniformed soldier asks his fashionably dressed sweetheart: "So, are you happy?" and she replies, "Oh! Yes! You know, on the way over, I saw at the Galeries [Lafayette] a love of a little dress in horizon blue taffeta." "The Arrival of the Soldier on Leave," *Le Rire Rouge*, March 24, 1917. Private collection.

FIG. 3.3 Charles Lansiaux. "Gare de Lyon. Last Kisses Before Departure," Paris, August 10–20, 1914. Silver gelatin print.
© Charles Lansiaux / BHVP / Roger-Viollet, RV-73719-17.

FIG. 3.4 Charles Lansiaux. "At the Tuilleries. The convalescent father walks with his wife and baby," Paris, April 1915. Silver gelatin print. © Charles Lansiaux / BHVP / Roger-Viollet, RV-73732-30.

FIG. 3.5 Charles Lansiaux. "A soldier on leave visiting his family," Paris, June 1915. Silver gelatin print. © Charles Lansiaux / BHVP / Roger-Viollet RV-73732-28.

rather to be commended for their relative restraint: “rarely have we seen fashions as modest and moderate as during this war,” Latzarus declared, while noting that displays of finery had not lost France its battles of the past. Everyday matters such as the choice of tablecloths, shoes, or clothes, when refracted through the lens of war, were fraught with tension.

Yet women were caught between two irreconcilable imperatives: while being condemned by the society at large for wartime “frivolity,” they were also actively encouraged to consume fashion as part of economic nationalism and for the pleasure of the war-weary men. “I believe,” wrote the female fashion journalist Camille Duguet in 1917, “that we must dress even better now, if not only for the joyful eyes of the soldiers on leave who, home from the front, relish seeing pretty things; wherever glorious uniforms are worn, there should be pretty dresses to augment them.”[5] Women, the “reverse image of the war,” in the words of historian Stéphane Audoin-Rouzeau, were expected to maintain a certain elegance as part of their patriotic and female duty. In other words, fashionability was good for the economy and good for natality rates. FIGS. 3.6, 3.7

In fashion magazines, newspapers, and public discourse, the argument was the same: war or no war, a French woman must remain elegant for her country and for her countrymen. Fashion exacerbated what the historian Pierre Darmon has called the “great misunderstanding” between soldiers and civilians.[6] The rhetoric provided in fashion magazines about the need for women to dress up for the pleasure of the men on leave was received by the female readership as heartfelt, but perceived by the soldiers as treasonous.

Social rhetoric around inappropriate frivolity and wartime fashion was fierce and prevalent. The feminist weekly *La Française* railed against the “silliness” of fashion, a “folly” and a “shame” for France.[7] “The Orgy Continues” exclaimed the Catholic monthly *La Libre Parole* as theaters, cabarets, and playhouses reopened their doors in the early months of 1915.[8] As events reappeared on the society calendar and women ordered new dresses to attend them, public anger rose steadily. A ministerial decree imposed in the first days of the war banned evening theatrical shows, so theaters began showing matinées instead. These daytime performances proved so popular that two of the main boulevard theaters, the Olympia and the Petit Casino, began to open daily.[9] Women’s magazines documented popular social activities, such as afternoon teas and ice skating. “Paris is going through a singular time,” the writer Maurice Donnay wrote in his wartime journal in February 1916, *Someone who had fallen from the sky could ask: Is this peace? Is this war? There is theater, concert-cafés, cinema; restaurants and teas; but everywhere there are soldiers in blue, helmeted soldiers on leave; we see more than one wounded soldier in the streets, on the boulevards, and the city is very dark at night.*[10] FIG. 3.8

By 1917, with mutinies on the front, revolution in Russia, and strikes threatening to halt the war effort, the government felt forced to intervene in sartorial matters in order to bring the damning social rhetoric under control: low-cut dresses were banned at the Opéra, which had reopened in November 1915.[11] "Frivolity" and seemingly scandalous dresses may have raised eyebrows and drawn occasional criticism before the war, but during the war, these problems took on serious overtones: fashion had the potential to endanger morale and disturb social order. Men blamed women for being inappropriately attentive to fashion. Gendered concerns about bad female behavior and male demoralization simmered beneath the surface of the caustic public rhetoric.

The Parisienne and the Poilu: Two Archetypes Divided by War

A reoccurring visual trope during the war was that of the bedraggled foot soldier, or poilu, staring wide-eyed at an elegant Parisienne. The joke lay in the disconnect between their two worlds, made deeper by the soldier's naive incomprehension over the new fashions of the day. A caricature by Louis Icart for *Le Rire Rouge* in 1916 depicts two elegantly dressed women walking down the street, completely unaware of the effect that they have on two beleaguered poilus, who stutter in bewilderment. FIG. 3.9 The gulf between the Parisiennes and the poilus was too great to be bridged, and misunderstandings prevailed on both sides. Initially, women commended the poilus for their bravery and heroism, but this positive image deteriorated over the four years of the war.

The poilu is the person that everyone admires but pulls away from when they see him boarding a train, entering a café a restaurant, or a store, for fear that that his boots will sully pretty shoes, that his sleeves will brush up against stylish jackets, that his hands will touch bell-shaped skirts, and that his words will be too crude, a soldier wrote from the trenches.[12] Feeling as if he had lost his status as the symbol of French resistance, the poilu felt increasingly out of touch with women on the home front as the war progressed. *L'Argonnaute,* an internal trench magazine created by the soldiers of the 25th infantry division, captured this sentiment well: *As the war*

FIG. 3.6 "The Soldier on Leave." Postcard featuring scenes of a soldier and his lover: The Departure; The Arrival; Ardent Love; Crazy Love; Calm Love; Temperate Love; Love of Yesteryear; Love Finished. Correspondence dated April 13, 1917. Paris: E.M.; Boulogne-sur-Seine: G. Piprot, 1917. © Bibliothèque Marguerite Durand, Collection Carte Postale, CP 1811 a.

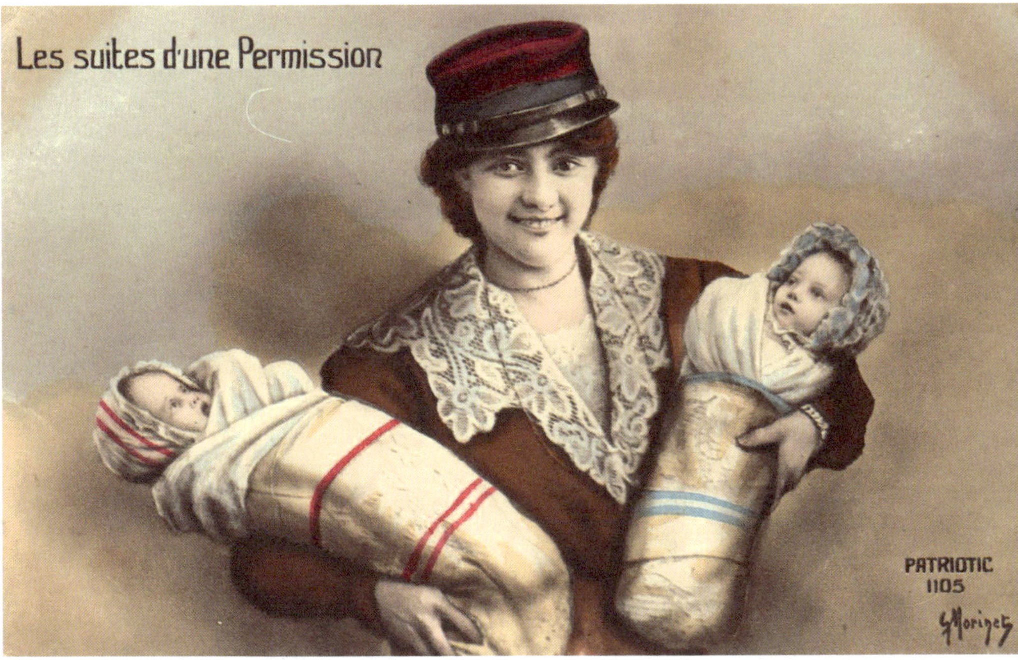

FIG. 3.7 Postcard of a woman holding two children entitled "The Results of a Soldier's Leave," ca. 1914–18. Paris: Patriotic–G.Morinet [A. Noyer], 1914. © Bibliothèque Marguerite Durand, Collection Carte Postale, CP 1813 a.

FIG. 3.8 Charles Lansiaux. Street scene of Paris, September 20, 1914. "The appearance of our Grand Boulevards has suddenly changed, Parisians have regained their confidence." Silver gelatin print. © Charles Lansiaux / BHVP / Roger-Viollet, RV-73738-30.

FIG. 3.9 Louis Icart. In this caricature, "Soldiers on Leave," two soldiers stutter and stare wide-eyed as two fashionable women walk down the street. *Le Rire Rouge*, March 11, 1916. Private collection.

drags on, the kindness granted to the poilu by women for his lack of clothing has decreased miserably. After the [battle of] Labyrinthe, a woman would rush up to a shaggy, filthy poilu and call him "my hero." After the Argonne, she kindly welcomed and empathized with all her heart. Now, the gentleman who presents himself to her in trench garb only hears: Ugh! How dirty they are![13]

The tropes of the Parisienne and the poilu were powerful indicators of society at large. That the two genders and social classes could no longer engage with each other was not a negligible state of affairs. "We'll get them!" a poilu claims in an illustrated postcard, repeating the classic battle cry about winning over the Germans, as he attempts, in vain, to win over an elegant Parisienne.[14] "Sometimes you have to walk a long time before arriving at your goal," a lone poilu states hopefully as he walks behind a fashionable woman on another postcard.[15] But on both postcards, the upper-class Parisiennes have their back turned and they are completely oblivious to the soldiers' presence. The message behind these caricatures is far from trivial—the poilu's despair was a threat to wartime order and national morale.

When social contact was made, as in a scene between two soldiers and an elegant woman from *Le Feu,* a novel by the soldier and writer Henri Barbusse, the interaction between the two worlds was filled with vapid curiosity on one side, and shame on the other:

Now a very elegant lady, who rustles and glows in purple and black silk and is enveloped in perfume, catches sight of our group and, extending her small gloved hand, she touches Volpatte's sleeve and then Blaire's shoulder. They immediately freeze, dumbfounded by this contact with such a vision. "Tell me, sirs, you who are true soldiers on the front line, you have seen such things in the trenches, have you not? . . . Even so, it is a terrible existence and the suffering," she murmurs as she leafs through an illustrated magazine that contains a few sinister views of devastated terrain. "Such things should not be published, Adolphe . . . The filth, the lice, the fatigues . . . As brave as you are, you must be unhappy!" Volpatte, whom she was addressing, turns red. He is ashamed of the misery from which he comes and to which he will return. He lowers his head and he lies, without perhaps realizing the extent of his lie: "No, after all, we are not so unhappy. It is not as terrible as that."[16]

Military Fashion

Reinforcing the diminished status of the poilu, female fashions were often inspired by the military trappings of foreign officers and soldiers rather than those of the common French foot soldier. FIG. 3.10 The dashing aviator, the exotic Scot or American, the elegant officer—these were the heroes the Parisienne eagerly sought out, and whose uniforms she copied. FIG. 3.11 In a series of articles about life on the home front, the theater critic Gustave Fréjaville wrote of the "aviator insignia," "braids," and "officer's coat" popular among the "little Amazons" at home: *The greatest success was shared between the silk pompom beret of the Dixmude riflemen and the soft beret of the alpine hunter . . . The round cap of our English friends, finally the dented felt hat from across the Atlantic had their turn. As soon as the first American contingents arrived, many of Paris' prettiest girls enthusiastically adopted the flat-rimmed hat of the 'Sammies.'*[17] Yet wearing fashions that were too closely linked to the military style of French soldiers was problematic in more ways than one. According to Fréjaville, the fad for wearing police caps went out of style as soon as it became part of the uniform for female tram ticket takers—fashionable women did not want to be linked to working women any more than they wanted to be associated with common foot soldiers. In truth, creating a fashion out of the foot soldier's uniform may have been too great a challenge to wartime decency. There was a brief vogue for the poilu's metal helmet, a *casque Adrian*—a few cartoons and images in fashion magazines feature women wearing the helmet—but the protective covering was too symbolic of heroic sacrifice to be appropriated for "frivolous" use: "This was understood from the very first tries and the attempt not renewed," Fréjaville wrote.[18] FIG. 3.12, 3.13 On July 4, 1915 the *New York Times* reported back from Paris that "Military Models Rule Paris Styles." Hats were inspired by those worn by the Italian army, the correspondent noted, recent allies to the French in the war, while "outside coats are all military in style, with high, close-buttoned neck[s] and buttoned down the front."[19] In *Le Temps Retrouvé*, Proust writes of wartime women who *wore thonged footwear recalling the buskin as worn by Talma, or else long gaiters recalling those of our dear boys at the front; it was, so they said, because they did not forget that it was their duty to rejoice the eyes of these 'boys at the front,' that they still decked themselves of an evening not only in flowing dresses, but also in jewelry which suggested the army by its choice of decorative themes . . . rings or bracelets made out of fragments of exploded shells or copper bands from 75 millimeter ammunition.*[20] The tradition of prewar female fashion—particularly female riding habits, tailored suits, and buttoned jackets—taking its cues from men's tailoring was made more visible and political by the war. As the fashionable wartime female wardrobe began to adopt military features such as

FIG. 3.10 Fabien Fabiano. Caricature showing a woman dressed in a tailored suit and soldier's helmet walking by two uniformed officers, who say "Well! Don't we salute any more, my lieutenant?" *Le Rire Rouge*, April 8, 1916. Private collection.

FIG. 3.11 Albert Jarach. In this caricature, "At the Bar," two women admire a foreign officer's uniform, exclaiming, "Damn, he's chic, he's got little wings!" "My God yes, just like Love . . ." *La Baïonnette*, December 16, 1915. Private collection.

FIG. 3.12 SAT. The woman in this illustration, "The Helmet," wears a poilu's metal helmet and admires herself in the mirror. *Fantasio*, March, 1, 1916. Private collection.

Femina

58

(Phot. Reutlinger).

UNE HÉROÏNE, Mlle YOLANDE DE BAYE

Mlle Yolande de Baye, chevalier de la Légion d'honneur, à titre militaire, deux fois décorée de la Croix de guerre, est un vivant exemple de la bravoure et du dévouement dont sont capables les jeunes filles de France. Cette charmante héroïne, blessée au front où elle est infirmière, porte le casque avec une crânerie et une élégance dont nous offrons l'image à nos lectrices. Quel est le chapeau qui aurait cette allure ?...

FIG. 3.13 Reutlinger. "Une héroine, Mlle. Yolande de Baye," Femina, December 1917. Bibliothèque Forney / Roger-Viollet.

front pockets, neckties, and tricorn hats, men became increasingly anxious about women playing "dress-up" as soldiers.

FIGS. 3.14, 3.15 A caricature by Marco de Gastyone, published in September 1915 in *La Baïonnette* features two women wearing military-inspired tailored suits talking about the war strategy: "In the place of Joffre, I would have . . . " FIG. 3.16 The joke plays on the women's naivete—played up by the elegant fashions—in the face of the gravity of war. A journalist writing for the magazine *La Femme de France* understood that women "admired" the "glorious uniforms" of French soldiers but reprimanded them for "wearing a general's jacket in order to go play dominos."[21] Women in militarized dress had the potential to undermine the seriousness of war.

Postcards and Representations of the Feminine Ideal

A caricature by Raymond de la Nezière, published in *La Baïonnette*, shows four "parakeets," the name given to women who gossiped about wartime secrets, dressed in the latest war crinoline styles and military-inspired hats whispering to each other about wartime confidences "of the highest importance." FIG. 3.17 Behind them, a soldier strolls arm in arm with his young daughter and wife, who is dressed in a simple skirt suit and small cap. The image plays on the opposition between the two groups: the elegant women betray France by gossiping about important war tactics while the common soldier and his family—the true heroes—stroll innocently in the background. The face-off between two opposing worlds pits the fashionable, treasonous women in the foreground against the patriotically and simply garbed model wartime family in the back.

Postcards sent back and forth from the home front to the trenches heightened the contrast between the two worlds. FIGS. 3.18–3.35 Unlike the caricatures discussed above, which contrast the fashionability of women at home against the misery of the poilu, one of the most popular genres of postcards sent between the trenches and the home depicted a very different kind of woman: simply dressed and patiently waiting for her soldier to arrive, the "good" woman wrote letters and dreamt about her absent husband. These postcards, sent by the thousands, flooded the market. Today, they abound in archives and online. Hundreds of different editors, recognized by the initials stamped on the postcards (ELP, REX, WD, JK) printed these *fantaisies patriotiques*, or patriotic fantasy postcards, which had print runs of as many as 100,000 per image.[22] FIG. 3.36

The messages written on the back of these cards reveal messages about friendship, love, and wartime anxiety.

Presented as the opposite of the fashionable Parisienne, these "fantasy" women are all represented inside their homes in pretty but modest day dresses which are hand colored on the cards in pale shades of pastel green, pink, and yellow. They do not wear the latest bell silhouette or the barrel-skirt; in fact, their dresses are hard to date, since the silhouette that appears on the postcards remained constant over the four years of the war. The unchanging dresses the women wear signify their steadfastness and the fact that they were impervious to the whims of fashion. Soldiers were perhaps reassured by the unchanging women on the postcards, but one wonders if these images only served to make the shock of reality more pronounced when the soldier returned home?

Magazines, aiming to spur consumption, informed women that it was their patriotic duty to appear fashionable and attractive to soldiers on leave. Hoping to please their loved ones, many women dressed in their best outfits to celebrate the soldiers' return. A vast majority of French women probably bought some new clothes, or at least ribbons or accessories, with the money they earned at work or from military pensions over the course of the war years. While some soldiers may have been heartened to see women attractively dressed after life in the trenches, others read these garments as an example of the disjunction between the priorities of the front and home front and as evidence of a growing gap between the sexes.

Moreover, the fashion for the insignia of foreign officers or soldiers did nothing to elevate the status of common soldiers within the sartorial and visual culture of the home front. Drawings and postcards caricatured the ease with which foreign aviators and soldiers courted women while depicting the poilu as a pariah in vain pursuit of the object of his desire. Yet the thousands of postcards sent between the trenches and the home depicted a very different kind of reunion. In the saccharine "fantasy" postcards, the soldiers and the women long for each other; in the caricatures, the desire is unrequited and impossible. Young and nicely dressed, the "ideal" woman depicted on the postcards was not fashionable: her chest may have been slightly uncovered, but she did not show her ankles; her clothes were nice but certainly not in the latest styles; she chose patriotic trimmings but never wore any military-inspired garments; her shoes were practical. Yet, like the flighty Parisienne, she too was a fiction invented by postcard publishers—an exaggerated representation of a demure and devoted woman.

The relationship between the war front and the home front was complex and multiform. It is easy to want

FIG. 3.14 Woman wearing a tricorne hat and tailored suit in Nantes, July 1918. Silver gelatin print. Private collection.

FIG. 3.15 Madame l'Hermitte. Tricorne hat, 1914–17. Silk satin, velvet. Paris, Musée des Arts Décoratifs, 70 45 22.

A NOS LECTEURS

Comme nous le disions la semaine dernière, le succès remporté par nos numéros spéciaux nous a décidé à conserver cette formule.

Nos deux prochains numéros étudieront deux des faces éternelles de l'âme humaine, Jean qui pleure et Jean qui rit. Le premier, qui sera mis en vente le 28 septembre, sera réservé aux **PESSIMISTES** *— il en reste encore quelques-uns comprendra, sous une saisissante couverture de* Weiluc, *une double page de* Léandre *qui a traité de main de maître, d'une main cruelle, tous ces broyeurs de noir, des planches en couleur de* Falké, Cheval, Robida, *des dessins de* Huard, Benjamin Rabier, Gallo, Henriot, Hautôt, etc.

Le second glorifiera comme il convient les **OPTIMISTES**, *ces braves gens, chez qui les coups mêmes de la fortune adverse augmentent la confiance en la victoire inéluctable. Le joyeux humoriste* Widhopff *le présente au public. On y trouvera des planches en couleurs d'*Albert Guillaume, Métivet, Legrain, Gerda Wegener, *des dessins en noir de* Huard, Maurice Neumotn, Henriot, Weal, Leroy, etc., *soit seize pages pleines de dessins, dont six en couleurs.*

Quelques-uns de nos numéros antérieurs ayant été épuisés, nous avons fait procéder à un second tirage et nous sommes en mesure de fournir dès à présent notre collection complète : **1, Le Kaiser Rouge, 2, Têtes de Turcs; 3, Le Clown-Prince; 4, Bouillon de Kultur; 5, Impérial Gaga; 6, Élégances Berlinoises; 7, Leurs Espions; 8, Nos Poilus; 9, Nos Civils; 10, Les Naturalisés.**

Adresser les demandes, accompagnées de 20 centimes *par exemplaire, à l'Édition Française Illustrée, 8, Boulevard des Capucines, Paris (Tél. Gut. 04.58.)*

AU BOIS, PAR MARCO DE GASTYNE.

— Moi, à la place de Joffre, j'aurais...

— 162 —

FIG. 3.16 Marco de Gastyne. Caricature of two women in crinolines discussing war strategy: "In the place of Joffre, I would have . . ." *La Baïonnette,* September 16, 1915. © Bibliothèque nationale de France.

FIG. 3.17 Raymond de la Nézière. Caricature entitled "Is the secret well kept?" showing fashionable women gossiping about treasonous secrets while a uniformed soldier and his family stroll in the background: "Of the utmost importance; and above all, do not repeat it to anyone! . . . " *La Baïonnette*, September 16, 1915. Private collection.

FIG. 3.18 "Nothing beats a leave to exalt love / On which the soul feeds both night and day." Hand-colored photographic postcard. Private collection.

FIG. 3.19 "For you our beautiful flowers / We give them to you with our heart." Hand-colored photographic postcard. Private collection.

FIG. 3.20 "The barometer is a beautiful device / Only one kiss brings the sun!" Hand-colored photographic postcard. Private collection.

FIG. 3.21 "Your lips have such sweet flavors for me / That I can only love them and our three [French] colors." Hand-colored photographic postcard. Private collection.

FIG. 3.22 "Two hearts united." Hand-colored photographic postcard. Private collection.

FIG. 3.23 "Vision of love: It's not too expensive to pay with a heart / The gift of love that comes with a flower." Hand-colored photographic postcard. Private collection.

FIG. 3.24 "We were separated! We are reunited! / We will be one for eternity." Hand-colored photographic postcard. Private collection.

FIG. 3.25 "Festival of Love: Champagne and flowers, warm and floating shade, experience the thrill of our singing soul!" Hand-colored photographic postcard. Private collection.

FIG. 3.26 "Happy Easter: A cry of love rises from the bronze bell / Whose flight passes in a dream, among the serene sky!" Hand-colored photographic postcard. Private collection.

FIG. 3.27 "Promise to love me always!" Hand-colored photographic postcard. Private collection.

FIG. 3.28 "The dawn of love by lighting our eyes / A thousand radiant hopes arise." Hand-colored photographic postcard. Private collection.

FIG. 3.29 "My heart is always with you." Hand-colored photographic postcard. Private collection.

FIG. 3.30 "From the dear home, the sweet image / Is engraved on the heart when the gun rages." Hand-colored photographic postcard. Private collection.

FIG. 3.31 "This kiss will give me the strength to win." Hand-colored photographic postcard. Private collection.

FIG. 3.32 "Do you love me? Everything makes me believe in this hope, your confusion, your eyes, even your silence!" Hand-colored photographic postcard. Private collection.

FIG. 3.33 "The gift of a flower is a precious pledge, but know what it entails." Hand-colored photographic postcard. Private collection.

FIG. 3.34 "Stay hopeful: France first! It is our duty; to be cherished brings hope!" Hand-colored photographic postcard. Private collection.

FIG. 3.35 "Who cares about the sad hour / Only our love exists!" Hand-colored photographic postcard. Private collection.

FIG. 3.36 Charles Lansiaux. "Avenue d'Orléans." A young woman selling patriotic images under the protection of her faithful companion, Paris, September 16, 1914. Silver gelatin print. © Charles Lansiaux / BHVP / Roger-Viollet, RV-73736-20.

to see them as dichotomous spheres, where gender differences were polarized and amplified by wartime propaganda: men were represented as masculine and heroic warriors on the front, while discourse about motherhood, devotion, and love was emphasized for women at home.[23] The postcards of the "ideal" woman, lovingly writing and waiting for her husband to return to the hearth, seem to reaffirm this structure. However, the anxiety and tension that women's fashion generated for men during the war shows that there was fear that the separation between the two spheres could too easily be dissolved. Profoundly shaken by their experiences at war, men were all the more afraid of feeling fragilized in their masculinity. Wartime fashion was a topic that helped men vocalize this fear: satirical cartoons drawn by men denounced frivolous women who "forgot" or did not properly address the brave men in their lives; the same cartoonists also condemned the stylish Parisienne for her admiration of the foreign soldier and disdain of the poilu and mocked the working woman whose attire was deemed too "masculine." As violent as these cartoons were toward women, they may have been cathartic for the soldiers in the trenches. By observing and commenting on fashion during the war, men were able to vocalize the fear they felt over shifting wartime norms.

1 Gustave Guiche, *Les deux soldats* (Paris: Faquelle, 1917), 277–79.
2 *Le Cri du boyau* (September–October 1916) cited in Stephane Audoin-Rouzeau, *A travers leurs journaux: 14–18 les combattants des tranchées* (Paris: Armand Colin, 1986), 149.
3 Letter from Pierre to Edith, September 22, 1916, Verdun. Online at: http://www2.ac-lyon.fr/etab/colleges/col-01/jean-moulin/IMG/pdf/Lettres_de_poilus.pdf.
4 "On m'a raconté qu'un soldat, venant l'autre jour en permission, s'étonna de voir, sur sa propre table, une nappe brodée. Il la regarda, et puis tourna vers sa femme un visage hostile: —Eh ! bien, dit-il, vous ne vous privez de rien, ici ! Elle eût pu lui répondre bien des choses, mais elle n'y pensa point, et se contenta de pleurer. On ne m'a pas dit si son héroïque époux en fut touché, et, pour dire vrai, je ne crois pas qu'il se soit attribué le moindre tort. Qu'avail-il fait, sinon formuler une des innombrables répliques de la grande querelle entre l'avant et l'arrière, querelle qui a gagné le demi-avant et le demi-arrière, et a fini par diviser l'arrière même ?" Louis Latzarus, "Frivolités," *Le Figaro*, May 22, 1917.
5 Camille Duguet, "Visons Élégantes," *Chiffons*, November 5, 1917.
6 Pierre Darmon, *Vivre à Paris pendant la Grande Guerre* (Paris: Fayard, 2002).
7 "Les bêtises recommencent," *La Française* (March 20, 1915), cited in Jean-Yves Le Naour, *Misères et tourments de la chair durant la Grande Guerre* (Paris: Aubier, 2002), 64.
8 Cited in Yves Pourcher, *Les jours de guerre: la vie des Français au jour le jour entre 1914 et 1918* (Paris: Plon, 1995), 170.
9 Ibid., 169.
10 Maurice Donnay, *Lettre à une Dame Blanche* (Paris: Société Littéraire de France, 1917), 121.
11 Françoise Thébaud, *Les femmes au temps de la guerre de 14* (Paris: Éditions de la Seine, 1986), 228.
12 Jean-Pierre Gueno, *Paroles de poilus: Lettres et carnets du front (1914–1918)* (Paris: J'ai Lu, 2013), 120.
13 *L'Argonnaute*, June 1917, cited in Audoin-Rouzeau, *À travers leurs journaux*, 150.
14 Postcard archived at the Centre historial de la Grande Guerre in Peronne. The front features two poilus walking behind two elegant women. The text states: "Nos Poilus. Tu parles si all'gazent! T'en fais pas... on les aura!"
15 Postcard archived at the Bibliothèque historique de la Ville de Paris. The front features a soldier walking behind a very fashionable woman wearing a red hat, red jacket, war crinoline, purple stockings, and red high heels. The text states: "Il faut quelquefois marcher assez longtemps pour arriver à son but, mais bah! quand on est sûr du succès de la campagne on n'hésite pas, et d'ailleurs comme acompte, on a le plaisir de reluquer la cheville fine, et ça fait patienter pour… Le reste."
16 "Or, une dame très élégante, qui froufroute, rayonne de soie violette et noire, et est enveloppée de parfums, avise notre groupe et, avançât sa petite main gantée, elle touche la manche de Volpatte puis l'épaule de Blaire. Ceux-ci s'immobilisent instantanément, médusés par le contact de cette fée. -- Dites-moi, vous, messieurs, qui êtes de vrais soldats du front, vous avez vu cela dans les tranchées, n'est-ce pas ?... -- C'est tout de même une existence terrible et des souffrances, murmure la dame en feuilletant un journal illustré qui contient quelques sinistres vues de terrains bouleversés. On ne devrait pas publier ces choses-là, Adolphe… Il y a la saleté, les poux, les corvées... Si braves que vous soyez, vous devez être malheureux ! Volpatte, à qui elle s'adresse, rougit. Il a honte de la misère d'où il sort et où il va rentrer. Il baisse la tête et il ment, sans peut-être se rendre compte de tout son mensonge: -- Non, après tout, on n'est pas si malheureux. C'est pas si terrible que ça." Henri Barbusse, *Le Feu* (Paris: Flammarion, 1916), 215–17.
17 Gustave Fréjaville, "Les petites amazones," *L'Opinion: Journal de la Semaine*, September 8, 1917.
18 Ibid.
19 "Military Models Rule Paris Style," *New York Times,* July 4, 1915.
20 "[...] chaussaient des lanières rappelant le cothurne selon Talma, ou de hautes guêtres rappelant celles de nos chers combattants ; c'est, disaient-elles, parce qu'elles ne devaient pas oublier qu'elles devaient réjouir les yeux de ces combattants, qu'elles se paraient encore, non seulement de toilettes 'floues' mais aussi de bijoux évoquant les armées... Bagues ou bracelets faits avec des fragments d'obus ou des ceintures de 75." Marcel Proust, *Le Temps Retrouvé*, vol. 14 (Paris: Gallimard, 1927), 41–42.
21 J. Colines, "Élégances Parisiennes," *La Femme de France*, December 24, 1917.
22 Marie-Monique Huss, *Histoires de famille 1914/1918: cartes postales et culture de guerre* (Paris: Noesis, 2000), 72. Huss notes 147 different editors for the unique genre of "patriotic fantasy" postcards.
23 The influential theory of the "double helix" advanced by Margaret and Patrice Higonnet promotes the notion that women were always subordinate to men within this polarized system. Margaret R. Higonnet and Patrice L.R. Higonnet, "The Double Helix," in *Behind the Lines: Gender and the Two World Wars*, ed. Higonnet, Jenson, Michel, and Weitz (New Haven: Yale University Press, 1987), 34.

3a Mourning

MAUDE BASS-KRUEGER

In France, 1.3 million men lost their lives on the battlefield during the First World War: 301,000 died between August and December 1914; 349,000 in 1915; 252,000 in 1916; 164,000 in 1917; and 235,000 in 1918.[1] In all at least 600,000 French women were made wartime widows. The scale of loss was unprecedented in French history. The entire nation grieved, but gender roles were assigned differently within the cultural practice of mourning. Public discourse emphasized women as mourners and men as warriors, stereotypes reinforced through fashion as sartorial displays of bereavement were chiefly assumed by women. FIG. 3a.1 Although the experience and reality of mourning challenged these gender codes in private—men deeply grieved the deceased and women endured great pain with remarkable stoicism—women were the "public embodiment" of wartime grief.[2] FIG. 3a.2 Fashion played a central role in how women were seen as enacting public mourning practices and rituals during the war. Female mourning came with its own complex sets of codes: periods of mourning were marked by changes in colors, fabrics, and accessories. Each sartorial mourning period corresponded to sets of rules concerning social life that regulated how soon after a death a woman could suitably resume her activities outside of the home. In addition to signaling grief, female mourning garments marked a family's social status, economic standing, and level of respectability.

The correspondence between mourning practices and mourning fashion was dictated by societal norms. Women were expected to signal their bereavement through their clothing, and they were vilified by the press if they disregarded the rules; however, they were also criticized if they gave the appearance of treating their mourning wardrobe as yet another fashionable folly. Mourning garments followed the silhouette of fashionable garments closely and were subject to the same life cycle of trends and conspicuous consumption as high fashion. Fashion magazines included fashion plates for mourning dresses alongside those for daywear, blurring the line between the two. FIG. 3a.3

Women who disregarded sartorial mourning practices or, to the contrary, paid too much attention to them, were scorned as "bad widows" or "merry widows"—epitaphs that hid the anxiety of men who feared being forgotten or replaced. The war exacerbated these underlying tensions, which came to the fore in discussions of simplified mourning codes that were adopted during the war.

The Simplification of Wartime Mourning Practices

The streamlining of mourning practices was already under way at the turn of the century, but the mass mourning imposed by the war greatly accelerated the process. Nineteenth-century mourning adhered to three strictly prescribed periods: full mourning, mourning, and half mourning. Specific fabrics, colorways, and accessories were prescribed for each period. As the century progressed, the etiquette around mourning became more complex, the social pitfalls more numerous, the mourning periods longer, and the circle of mourning wider.[3] Fashion magazines and etiquette advisors offered rigid advice about "correct" mourning, and women were expected to adhere to the guidelines.[4] Yet, however strict the rules for mourning wear appeared on paper, in practice individuals adapted and interpreted the rules to suit their needs and circumstances. Those who could not afford new clothes for each stage of mourning dyed their old dresses black or else found other ways to incorporate black into their wardrobes; working women went back to their jobs as needed, regardless of the imposed time frame. As the twentieth century dawned, mourning etiquette slowly relaxed, particularly for working middle-class women who needed to combine the constraints imposed by mourning with their employment. The First World War hastened this changing dynamic; upper-class women began to adopt the same exceptions previously limited to middle-class women. The sheer number of deaths—and the deep mourning that the previous century's strict mourning rituals would have required for half of the French population—made lavish displays of bereavement seem ostentatious and inappropriate. For such large-scale social mourning, it seemed more appropriate to mourn simply so as not to hamper the war effort. FIG. 3a.4

Mourning codes have never been as strictly disregarded as during this time of anguish when even the most pained women cannot always manifest by external signs, by the way in which she dresses or by the life that she leads, the pain that constricts her and her detachment from all things,

a journalist wrote in the middle-class women's magazine *La Mode Illustrée* in 1916. The magazine reassured its female readers that they would not be judged for wearing a simple black armband or basic black crepe. Women should not impoverish themselves by buying costly and fragile mourning fabrics, the article warned, as this would be deemed ostentatious in a time of war. Here, the most widely read fashion magazine in France reassured women that returning to work was a way for them to "make abstraction from their pain" and find "the only consolation that they might have in this world."[5]

FIG. 3a.1 A widow wearing a mourning veil stands in front of posters on the base of the Lion of Belfort statue, place Denfert-Rocherau, Paris, 1914–18. Silver gelatin print. © BHVP / Roger-Viollet, RV-77106-24.

FIG. 3a.2 Charles Lansiaux. Young communicant whose father died at the front escorted by her grandfather and her widowed mother, Paris, May 1915. © Charles Lansiaux / BHVP / Roger-Viollet, RV-73739-30.

FIG. 3a.3 Fashion plate showing mourning and half-mourning ensembles. "Deuil et demi-deuil," *Les Élégances Parisiennes*, February 1917, n°11, plate XX. © Bibliothèque Forney / Roger-Viollet, RV-157622-24.

FIG. 3a.4 Cover illustration showing three women in mourning dress. The two women on the left wear nurse's armbands and simplified mourning garments without veils. *Le Petit Écho de la Mode*, October 25, 1914. © Bibliothèque Forney / Roger-Viollet, RV-157622-2.

The Complexities of "Fashionable" Mourning

Nevertheless, certain mourning rules still applied, and it was the fashion magazine's job to inform women what they were. According to the 1916 *La Mode Illustrée* article, wartime bereavement lasted two years: during the deep mourning of the first year, women could wear black wool and crêpe fabrics, followed by six months in textured black wool and silk, three months in black and white, and the last three months in gray, mauve, purple, and mixed-black fabrics. The rules were different for women mourning their parents, stepparents, or a husband. In these cases, the strictest mourning applied: eighteen months of bereavement were required in total, beginning with six months of deep mourning in black wool and crêpe, followed by six months of regular mourning in lustrous black wool and silk, and six months of half-mourning.[6] FIG. 3a.5 A mourning dress made from artificial silk was worn by a woman who lost her two sons in battle, the first in May 1915 and the second in August of the same year. FIG. 3a.6 Uneven hand stitches reveal the homemade quality of the dress, which features a shawl collar and black lace cuffs that may have been added during the half-mourning phase. Likewise, the simple white lace collar adorning the mourning dress from the Musée de la Grande Guerre in Meaux may also be a later addition, following the half-mourning phase. FIG.3a.7 The slim tubular cut, fashionable in the early 1920s, dates this dress as an example of postwar mourning practices. However, the large silk crepe mourning veil was typical of wartime mourning for women of all ages, as can be seen in photographs from the period. FIG. 3a.8

Mourning clothes, like everyday fashion, followed trends, and certain practices that may have not been acceptable before the war became permissible because of the special circumstances. *La Mode Illustrée* informed its readership that mourning shawls were no longer worn in Paris and in the big cities because they prevented movement and did not look fetching with the new short skirts; old shawls could be turned into tailored suits or mourning coats; short skirts were acceptable for mourning as long as boots covered the calf; mourning veils were to be pushed to the side instead of being "thrown back as before"; boots with patent-leather tips were now acceptable for mourning, but full patent- leather boots worn over black chiffon stockings were in "the worst taste"; women could purchase black fabric gloves instead of the more expensive leather suede gloves, which were easily damaged. For *Femina,* a tonier fashion magazine, "proper mourning" required that women purchase mourning garb that was "correct but nevertheless in fashion."[7] FIG. 3a.9

While *Femina* assured its readers that touches of white could be worn even in the deepest mourning, *La Mode Illustrée* declared that this was "incompatible with deep mourning"; on this issue, the journalist wrote, the magazine "sided with our readers against fashion."[8] The profusion of articles about mourning, fashion plates for mourning dresses, advertisements for specialized mourning boutiques, and patterns for mourning clothing in wartime fashion magazines was a change from the light tone the prewar fashion magazines had adopted. FIG. 3a.10 The mix between fashion and mourning could be jarring. An article from *La Femme de France* titled "Frivolities: Mourning jewelry [*fantaisies*]," in which "naturally elegant widows" were "seduced by a thousand pretty things," played into the hands of public criticism that women were desacralizing the mourning process.[9] Fashionable mourners ran the risk of being perceived as less grief-stricken than their peers, particularly if the widows were young and attractive. FIG. 3a.11 "No, these are not our widows," exclaimed the *Écho de Paris* in response to women who wore tight black dresses, silk stockings, and patent-leather shoes.[10] Fashion-conscious women were decried as "fake widows" or "bad widows," or, even worse, prostitutes. Young widows were particularly susceptible to this misogynistic portrayal of the emotionally fragile, economically vulnerable, and sexually experienced mourner: "These women are young and wear austere black mourning crepe from head to foot . . . and for a louis [coin]—wartime pricing— they let their veils drop: black is not always dressed."[11]

Femina's June 1917 article "Can A War Widow Remarry?" reflected deep-seated unease around mourning and remarriage.[12] Article 228 of the French Civil Code mandated a period of widowhood of ten months, after which a woman was legally free to remarry. However, the laws of morality were not always those of the law, the magazine warned its female readers. *Femina* reassured a fictional young widow who "doubted her moral right" to remarry—not for love, the character assured the reader, but to ensure a better life for her children—that a second marriage was "advisable." The article, written as a debate between the writer and the young widow, concludes when they both agree that a second marriage could reinforce and honor the memory of the dead husband while also paving the way for a future with another "fundamentally good" man. "I encourage you to do it," the columnist wrote, "Remarry! It's life, as they say . . . and life will always be right against death." The First World War had a profound impact on changing mourning practices in France. The sheer volume of loss sustained during the war, as well as the horrifying way in which soldiers were killed—death by artillery meant dismembered bodies that were unrecognizable—exacerbated grief and deeply affected societal views toward bereavement. Private mourning took many forms, including prayer, displaying photographs and reliquaries, and collecting objects related to the deceased; public mourning was practiced through commemorative sites and community rituals, one of which was the display of mourning through clothing. Because black-clad widows played such an integral role in the public display of mourning, their clothes and etiquette were all the more commented on. The tension between the fashionable aspects of mourning dress and the expected behavior of women in mourning was aggravated by the war.

In the postwar period, as the black dress evolved into a fashion statement in its own right, the seductive undertones of the widow's dress, which had been remarked on and vehemently criticized by the wartime press, became its main selling point. By the mid-twenties the fashion world appeared ready to divest the color black of its wartime connotations of mourning and reintegrate it into the world of stylish dress. In 1926, less than eight years after the end of the conflict, American *Vogue* marketed a black crêpe de chine dress designed by Gabrielle Chanel as "the Chanel 'Ford' dress, the frock that all the world will wear"—in other words, a standard garment for every elegant woman's wardrobe.[13] "It is paradoxical that in the most colourful of all seasons, black should predominate," *Vogue* wrote, yet "it is extremely chic." Indeed, it was this very contradiction, picked up by the magazine and by postwar designers, that lies at the heart of the complexities of wartime attitudes toward female mourners and their clothing.

1 Françoise Thébaud, *Les femmes au temps de la guerre de 14* (Paris: Stock, 1986), 201.

2 See "Gender and Mourning," in Susan R. Grayzel and Tammy M. Proctor, ed., *Gender and the Great War* (Oxford: Oxford University Press, 2017), 212.

3 Lou Taylor's seminal work on mourning dress outlines the changes in mourning practice from its origins in the Middle Ages until 1980. Lou Taylor, *Mourning Dress: A Costume and Social History* (London: George Allen and Unwin, 1983), 133.

4 Taylor briefly covers the First World War, noting that "it was the terrible slaughter of the First World War that undoubtedly caused the major breakdown in funeral and mourning etiquette." Taylor, *Mourning Dress: A Costume and Social History*, 266.

5 "À travers la mode: le deuil," *La Mode Illustrée*, October 29, 1916.

6 Ibid.

7 "Le Deuil Correct," *Femina*, March 1917.

8 M. Thevenot, "À travers la mode," *La Mode Illustrée*, August 22, 1915.

9 "Frivolités: les fantaisies du deuil," *La Femme de France*, September 12, 1915.

10 Frédéric Masson, "À l'arrière," *Écho de Paris*, April 12, 1915, cited in Jean-Yves Le Naour, *Misères et tourments de la chair durant la Grande Guerre* (Paris: Aubier, 2002), 81.

11 "Eros en deuil," *Le Cri de Paris*, November 22, 1914, cited in Le Naour, *Misères et tourments de la chair*, 82.

12 Maurice de Waleffe, "Une veuve de la guerre peut-elle se remarier?," *Femina*, June 1917.

13 "The Début of the Winter Mode," *Vogue*, October 1, 1926, 69.

FIG. 3a.5 Twin sisters in mourning, Saint-Lizier, Ariège, ca. 1915. © Roger-Viollet, RV-5509-16.

FIG. 3a.6 Mourning dress, 1915. Artificial silk. Private collection.

FIG. 3a.7 Mourning dress, ca. 1920. Musée de la Grande Guerre du Pays de Meaux, 2006.1.12099.

FIG. 3a.8 Charles Lansiaux. Women, mostly in mourning dress, meet to discuss their wartime experiences in front of the restaurant Marguery, Paris, September 23, 1915. The woman in the center wears a crepe mourning veil that was typical for widows of all ages. Silver gelatin print. © Charles Lansiaux / BHVP / Roger-Viollet, RV-73734-29.

Femina

41

LE DEUIL CORRECT

UNE NOTE BLANCHE AU CHAPEAU, A L'ENCOLURE OU AUX POIGNETS, EST PERMISE PENDANT TOUTE LA DURÉE DU DEUIL

Sur la petite toque on pose le voile de différentes manières; celle-ci, dont les côtés tombent droits, rappelle la coiffe de certains ordres religieux. Le voile est posé en travers; la toque à petit bord de crêpe blanc est brodée de perles mates en bandeau et piquée de deux épingles également en perles.

Sur une toque de crêpe blanc est enroulé une sorte de turban. Le voile, d'une originalité nouvelle, est froncé et croisé derrière. Devant, il semble descendre du chapeau pour laisser apercevoir le visage et esquisser un mouvement drapé. Un ourlet de crêpe blanc borde cette partie du voile.

ELLES sont nombreuses hélas, les femmes, les mères, les sœurs, les filles dont la toilette de deuil est le sombre uniforme. Il est parfaitement odieux, alors que le chagrin vous anéantit, de s'occuper de puériles questions de vêtements, mais le deuil obéit à certains rites auxquels il faut se plier. Quant à sa durée, elle varie suivant les villes et les milieux. Si le costume de deuil a le souci avant tout d'être correct il doit cependant être à la mode et la suivre dans ses grandes lignes. Les tissus sont toujours à peu près les mêmes. La gabardine, la serge fine, la vigogne, le cachemire, les voiles et les grenadines sont les lainages les plus généralement adoptés et comme tissus de soie le crêpe de Chine mat, le poult de soie, le satin grenadine, la faille, la mousseline de soie et le crêpe Georgette. On n'emploie pas actuellement la grenadine comme voile, mais le crêpe français et les crépons remplacent le crêpe anglais après la première période de deuil; très mats et très souples ils ont l'avantage d'être très légers. Les voiles se posent en général en travers, recouvrant le plus souvent la calotte du chapeau et quelquefois le chapeau tout entier. Ils sont bordés d'un ourlet de dix centimètres de haut et parfois, pour les deuils moins stricts, d'un picot de jais ou de broderie ou d'un biais de tulle. Les encolures de linon ou de crêpe blanc sont permises durant toutes les périodes du deuil même le plus sérieux.

Blouse russe en crêpe et cachemire de soie. L'empiècement, découpé en pattes carrées, est bordé d'une grosse piqûre. Les longues manches bouffantes sont resserrées dans un haut poignet ajusté et ourlé d'un biais de crêpe blanc comme celui qui rabat sur le col. Le corps de la blouse et la basque sont faits séparément et réunis sous une double-ceinture en cachemire.

Robe de grenadine de laine dont la jupe froncée s'ouvre sur deux panneaux de crêpe. Le corsage se découpe en longues pointes qui remontent jusqu'au col également en grenadine; il laisse apercevoir une blouse tout unie en crêpe. La ceinture, serrée dans une boucle de passementerie mate, se termine par un gland de même passementerie. Petit rabat de crêpe lisse au bord du col.

Ce grand manteau de vigogne remplace le châle pour la période de grand deuil, il est bordé d'un grand biais qui arrive en diminuant jusqu'au bord des manches. Le devant est resserré par une ceinture de crêpe. Le grand col est en crêpe, ainsi que la bande qui entoure les épaules et semble fixer l'effet de châle. La toque avec voile la couvrant presque complètement reste le chapeau du grand deuil.

Deux parapluies pour le deuil, l'un avec manche en ébonite et ivoire, l'autre en perles de jais, et un sac en soie brodé de perles de jais.

FIG. 3a.9 Article instructing women on how to remain fashionable while grieving. "Proper Mourning," *Femina*, March 1917. © Bibliothèque Forney / Roger-Viollet, RV-157622-7.

FIG. 3a.10 Pol de Czernichowski. Advertising poster for Maison Debray where women could purchase mourning garments, "À la religieuse," 1896. © Bibliothèque Forney / Roger-Viollet, RV-86435-8.

FIG. 3a.11 Two widows in mourning dress at the zoo in the Jardin des Plantes, Toulouse, Upper Garonne. © Roger-Viollet, RV-5509-4.

4

Photographing the Working Woman: The Excelsior Archives at Roger-Viollet

SOPHIE KURKDJIAN

Among the 20,000 glass plates in the archives of the newspaper *Excelsior* devoted to the First World War, many depict the home front and feature women. An exceptional series showcases *remplaçantes*, or women who replaced men in traditionally male jobs.[1] FIGS. 4.1a–j

Founded in 1910 by Pierre Lafitte, *Excelsior* had a circulation of 100,000 and was the first French newspaper to give prime space to photography.[2] From the beginning, the newspaper featured about twenty photographs in each issue.[3] During the war, thanks to advances in photojournalism, photographers were sent into the field to cover combat as closely as possible. Because of the official censorship restrictions, the photographs taken on the front lines of the war show neither bodies nor battles. Those of the "rear," or home front, show none of the difficulties of everyday life.[4] The motivation for focusing on women's work, which to some extent served as a response to Prime Minister René Viviani's call to action for French women on August 6, 1914, was to promote and support women in the work force.[5] FIG. 4.2 Yet the photographs largely ignore the harsh reality of the working conditions that could be difficult and might dissuade women from participating.

On June 24, 1917, *Excelsior* featured fifteen photographs from a series about women workers under the headline "The new jobs for women since the war."[6] FIG. 4.3 They showed a *munitionnette* (munitions factory worker), delivery woman, motorist, telegram messenger, mail woman, signal woman, station manager, tramway conductor, trolley conductor, state rail crew, longshorewoman, collection clerk for the gas company (known as collection "boy" in French), bicycle messenger, monitor for a gas lamp company, and gardener.[7] The caption explained that women were now doing more difficult jobs that had previously only been held by men.[8] These fifteen photographs also provide detailed evidence of what working women wore during the war. The munitionnette, the signalwoman at the Gare du Nord, and the longshorewoman on the Bordeaux docks are the only ones wearing overalls; the cyclist has on a shirt and tie, and the other women are dressed in tailored suits. As the *Excelsior* cover shows, there was no work-specific attire for each of these jobs. The turmoil during the first months of the war explains why women did not have special uniforms for the new jobs and instead wore clothes they had at home. This frequently consisted of a tailored suit and a blouse. The suit jacket usually had large pockets that were practical for carrying telegrams, letters, or tools. Other details included collars featuring the initials of the woman's employer as seen on the blouses of the female workers for the gas and postal services (GAZ and PTT [French postal service]). FIGS. 4.1a, 4.1b Delivery women from the department stores such as Le Printemps and Le Bon Marché wore bags and badges stamped with the name or logo of the store. With buttons down the middle and a half-belt, the suit jackets resembled soldier's uniforms. The skirts worn with these suits were quite simple. FIG. 4.1c Some of the women who worked in factories and at the train stations initially had to borrow men's suits, a combination of a jacket and pants, or overalls. The situation changed in 1917 when the Comité du travail féminin (Women's Labor Committee), established a year earlier, asked manufacturers to provide protective clothing made especially for women working with machines. This decision was implemented in some factories with the introduction of specific uniforms created by French designers such as the "Françoise" culotte-skirt by Madame Commard, which aimed to reconcile job practicality and style. A photograph of a longshorewoman wearing this outfit appears on the bottom left of the front page of the June 24 issue of *Excelsior.* The signalwoman in the Gare du Nord train station also seems to be wearing this outfit.[9] FIG. 4.1d

The Feminization of the Remplaçantes

Ten minutes before noon! Greasy hands are carefully cleaned with solvent, big sexless blouses fall off, revealing a subtle waist, a neck emerging from a fresh little lace collar. With quick dabs of the powder puff, faces are made up again. And high heels beat against skirts, shoe buckles shine, attracting one's eye to a thin ankle, to the perfection of a silk stocking. Out of those black smocks come sweethearts, beings who, now that their job is done, seek to please, and think of nothing other than pleasing.[10]

During the war, women's work could be grueling. Therefore, what is immediately striking about the images of women at work in *Excelsior* is that they are not shown working. Most pose in front of the photographer's lens; some even hint at a smile. The high-heeled shoes worn by the munitionnette in the arms factory further substantiates the impression of a staged photograph. Arguably, *Excelsior*'s goal in publishing these contrived photographic images was to promote a positive image of women's work in order to encourage others to contribute to the war effort. In all likelihood the poses were meant to reassure men that the women who had taken over their jobs still adhered to traditional feminine appearances.

Like the quote from French poet Paul Géraldy discussed above about women who, after leaving work, "think of nothing other than pleasing," the

FIG. 4.1a Gas company collection clerk, Paris. "The new professions for women since the war," *Excelsior*, June 24, 1917. Silver gelatin print. © Excelsior–L'Équipe / Roger-Viollet, RV-72189-25.

FIG. 4.1b Postwoman, Paris. "The new professions for women since the war," *Excelsior*, June 24, 1917. Silver gelatin print. © Excelsior–L'Équipe / Roger-Viollet, RV-72189-44.

FIG. 4.1c Delivery woman for Printemps department store, Paris. "The new professions for women since the war," *Excelsior,* June 24, 1917. Silver gelatin print. © Excelsior–L'Équipe / Roger-Viollet, RV-72195-59.

FIG. 4.1d Signalwoman at Gare du Nord, Paris. "The new professions for women since the war," *Excelsior*, June 24, 1917. Silver gelatin print. © Excelsior–L'Équipe / Roger-Viollet, RV-72195-53.

FIG. 4.1e Conductor for a trolley company, Paris. "The new professions for women since the war," *Excelsior*, June 24, 1917. Silver gelatin print. © Excelsior–L'Équipe / Roger-Viollet, RV-72194-56..

FIG. 4.1f Station manager of the Compagnie du Métropolitain, Paris. "The new professions for women since the war," *Excelsior*, June 24, 1917. Silver gelatin print. © Excelsior–L'Équipe / Roger-Viollet, RV-72195-52.

FIG. 4.1g Cyclist newspaper carrier, Paris. "The new professions for women since the war," *Excelsior*, June 24, 1917. Silver gelatin print. © Excelsior–L'Équipe / Roger-Viollet, RV-72189-26.

FIG. 4.1h Motorist, Paris. "The new professions for women since the war," *Excelsior*, June 24, 1917. Silver gelatin print. © Excelsior–L'Équipe / Roger-Viollet, RV-72195-58.

FIG. 4.1i Station manager of the Compagnie du Métropolitain, Paris. "The new professions for women since the war," *Excelsior*, June 24, 1917. SIlver gelatin print. © Excelsior–L'Équipe / Roger-Viollet, RV-72189-43.

FIG. 4.1j Chimney sweeps, Paris. "The new professions for women since the war," *Excelsior*, November 1917. Silver gelatin print. © Excelsior–L'Équipe / Roger-Viollet, RV-72342-58.

République française.

PROCLAMATION DE M. LE PRÉSIDENT DU CONSEIL

Aux Femmes de France !

La guerre a été déchaînée par l'Allemagne, malgré les efforts de la France, de la Russie et de l'Angleterre pour maintenir la paix.

A l'appel de la Patrie, vos pères, vos fils et vos maris se sont levés, et, demain, ils auront relevé le défi.

Le départ pour l'Armée de tous ceux qui peuvent porter les armes laisse les travaux des champs interrompus, la moisson est inachevée, le temps des vendanges est proche.

Au nom du Gouvernement de la République, au nom de la Nation tout entière groupée derrière lui, je fais appel à votre vaillance, à celle des enfants que leur âge seul et non leur courage dérobe au combat ; je vous demande de maintenir l'activité des campagnes, de terminer les récoltes de l'année et de préparer celles de l'année prochaine. Vous ne pouvez pas rendre à la Patrie un plus grand service. Ce n'est pas pour vous, c'est pour elle que je m'adresse à votre cœur. Il faut sauvegarder votre subsistance, l'approvisionnement des populations urbaines et surtout l'approvisionnement de ceux qui défendent à la frontière, avec l'indépendance du Pays, la Civilisation et le Droit.

Debout donc, femmes françaises, jeunes enfants, filles et fils de la Patrie ! Remplacez sur le champ du travail ceux qui sont sur les champs de bataille ; préparez-vous à leur montrer demain la terre cultivée, les récoltes rentrées, les champs ensemencés.

Il n'y a pas dans ces heures graves de labeur infime, tout est grand qui sert le Pays. Debout : à l'action ! au labeur !

Il y aura demain de la gloire pour tout le monde.

VIVE LA RÉPUBLIQUE ! VIVE LA FRANCE !

Pour le Gouvernement de la République :
Le Président du Conseil des Ministres,
René VIVIANI.

38802. — Mâcon, imprimerie X. PERROUX & FILS.

FIG. 4.2 René Viviani. "To French Women," poster urging French women to replace men in the workforce who have been called to war, August 6, 1914. Archives départementales 71, R guerre 14-18/286.

French Republic

Proclamation of the President of the Council of Ministers

To the Women of France!

War has been initiated by Germany, despite efforts to maintain the peace from France, Russia, and England.

Your fathers, your sons, and your husbands have met our country's call, and tomorrow they will face its greatest challenge.

With all who can bear arms departing for Germany, the field work is left interrupted, the crops are unharvested, and the grape harvest is approaching.

In the name of the Government of the French Republic, in the name of the entire country that stands behind it, I call for your courage, and for that of the children whose age—and not their bravery—keeps them from combat. I ask you to continue working in the fields, to harvest this year's crop, and to prepare next year's. There is no greater service you can lend to your country. It is for her that I appeal to your heart. You will need to provide for your own subsistence, for those in the cities, and most of all, for the men fighting at the front.

Stand then, women of France, young children, sons and daughters of the nation! Take to the fields to replace those on the battlefield; be ready to show them the tilled earth, the harvested crop, the sowed seeds.

There is no unimportant work in this hour of need, all that serves the country is essential.

At the ready, women; Arise! To work!

Tomorrow there will be glory for the world entire.

Long live the Republic! Long live France!

For the Government of the Republic:
President of the Council of Ministers
Réné Viviani

Excelsior photographs further reinforce the staged nature of these work scenes with an emphasis on the subjects' femininity. The trolley conductor wears a simple suit embellished with a wide white collar. FIG. 4.1e The station manager for the Compagnie du Métropolitain wears a blouse adorned with a Peter Pan collar and buttons down the front, complemented by a hat bearing the company logo, and a necklace. FIG. 4.1f The monitor for a gas lamp company wears a white sailor collar, a belted waist, a cap with the words *Bec Auer* embroidered on it, and her pose highlights the ring displayed prominently on her left hand. Moreover, these photographs call attention to the jewelry worn by these working women, and accessories that may seem unusual for a factory job. However, in wartime, rings, small chains, and brooches were clearly part of a working woman's wardrobe. These decorative details frequently evoked patriotic symbols or served as mementos of loved ones who had gone to the front or died. FIG. 4.1g These *Excelsior* photographs reveal a sharp contrast between the simplicity of the clothing and the distinctly feminine elements of the garments. This contrast, which also appeared in texts that accompanied photographs in other French daily newspapers, suggests that this was more than coincidental. On January 10, 1917, *Le Figaro* mentions a small glazier wearing a simple "*cotillon* skirt and flat shoes," and a year later, on May 11, 1918, in an article entitled "L'Ève Future," two "wartime tramway" mechanics are described as wearing "a leather belt over the black dress, a small collar, and a cap stamped with the silver embroidered O of the Compagnie Générale des Omnibus . . ."[11] On September 1, 1916, *L'Intransigeant* mentions women bus conductors who were "wearing police caps" and then goes on to explain how women continued to have strong opinions about what they were being asked to wear, noting that "beyond coquetry, some women who disliked wearing caps vehemently protested, asking for something more flattering and prettier, such as the Basque beret worn by tramway employees in Toulon."[12] Were these tropes so prevalent because the press, wanting to dismiss the idea of women's emancipation through work, published staged photographs of working women that showed that accepted standards of beauty and femininity continued during the war? Or was this yet another strategy for reassuring French men—the primary readers of the newspapers—who might have perceived this "masculinization" of working women as a threat? These types of images appeared in French cinema as well, including the 1918

La Femme française pendant la guerre, a propaganda film by Alexandre Devarennes that reinforces the idea that work neutralized any form of women's emancipation.[13] In the opening scene, a man shown leaving for the front describes how French women contributed to the war effort for four years by working at various jobs. They had supported the nation throughout the conflict. In both wide-angle shots and close-ups, the camera shows working women who resemble the remplaçantes featured on the cover of the June 1917 issue of *Excelsior*. Similarly, these women appear on camera smiling pleasantly, elegantly dressed in lace collars, and wearing jewelry. They appear happy at work. Some women stop what they are doing to pose in front of the camera. In another scene, a female worker appears next to a woman breastfeeding a baby in a nursing room. Here, Devarennes accentuates women's double role as worker and mother. The subtitles of this silent film promote an image of women at work that is both feminine and maternal. Describing the French women who bring "tenderness," "well-being," "hope," "joy," and "aid and consolation" to soldiers and the wounded, Devarennes' film promotes the ideal woman, heroic in fulfilling her wartime duty.

In 1910, Pierre Lafitte, writing about the editorial vision of the recently launched *Excelsior* newspaper, remarked how the public who reads it will "see everything!"[14] A year later, Napoleon Bonaparte's nineteenth-century axiom "a good sketch is better than a long speech" appeared as a banner on the cover of each issue. Henceforth, French newspaper publishers relied increasingly on the photographic image to tell stories. The photographs of working women that appeared in *Excelsior* were part of this movement that recognized the power of the image. Strategically placed on the cover of the newspaper, photographs of working women showed the reader how the workforce in France had been reorganized. The clothing and accessories worn by the women in these images underscored the conflicts and tensions they experienced when they responded to the call to work. These photographs emphasize the prominence of women in the French war effort and the implications these changes had on French society as a whole.

EN PAGE 6 : UN CONTE ILLUSTRÉ POUR LES PETITS

EXCELSIOR

Dimanche 24 JUIN 1917

RÉDACTION : 20, rue d'Enghien, Paris
Téléphone : Gutenberg 02.73 - 02.75 - 15.00
ADMINISTRATION : 88, av. des Champs-Élysées
Téléphone : Wagram 57.44 et 57.45
Adresse télégraphique : EXCEL-PARIS
TARIF DES ABONNEMENTS :
France..... 3 mois, 10 fr.; 6 mois, 18 fr.; 1 an, 35 fr.
Étranger... 3 mois, 20 fr.; 6 mois, 36 fr.; 1 an, 70 fr.
PUBLICITÉ : 11, Bd des Italiens. - Tél. : Cent. 80-88
PIERRE LAFITTE, FONDATEUR

Huitième année. — N° 2,413. — 10 centimes.

« Le plus court croquis m'en dit plus long qu'un long rapport. » — NAPOLÉON

LES NOUVEAUX MÉTIERS DES FEMMES DEPUIS LA GUERRE

MUNITIONNETTE AU TRAVAIL AVEC UN MASQUE

LIVREUSE D'UN DES GRANDS MAGASINS

AUTOMOBILISTE DE NOS CAMIONS MILITAIRES

PORTEUSE DE TÉLÉGRAMMES DANS PARIS

FACTRICE DU SERVICE DES POSTES

GARDE-VOIE DE LA GARE DU NORD A PARIS

CHEF DE GARE DE LA Cie DU MÉTROPOLITAIN

WATTWOMAN DES TRAMWAYS PARISIENS

RECEVEUSE DE LA COMPAGNIE DES OMNIBUS

FEMME D'ÉQUIPE DES CHEMINS DE FER DE L'ÉTAT

DÉBARDEUSE SUR LES QUAIS DE BORDEAUX

" GARÇON " DE RECETTES DE LA COMPAGNIE DU GAZ

CYCLISTE PORTEUSE DE JOURNAUX

VÉRIFICATRICE D'UNE Cie DE MANCHONS A GAZ

JARDINIÈRE DANS UN SQUARE PARISIEN

LE DÉFAUT DE MAIN-D'ŒUVRE A OFFERT AUX FEMMES DES EMPLOIS INATTENDUS : EN VOICI QUELQUES-UNS

La guerre aura fait faire un grand pas au féminisme et ce ne sera pas l'une de ses conséquences les moins imprévues. Beaucoup de femmes qui s'employaient à des travaux purement féminins jouent aujourd'hui le rôle d'employés dans des bureaux, des administrations, etc... Mais à côté de celles-là, il y en a d'autres qui ont adopté des métiers tout à fait nouveaux, des métiers d'homme, souvent très pénibles. Elles s'y montrent courageuses et beaucoup plus résistantes à la fatigue qu'on ne l'aurait supposé

FIG. 4.3 Cover of the newspaper *Excelsior*, featuring photographs of women workers, "The new professions for women since the war," June 24, 1917. Private collection.

1 The *Excelsior* archives are housed by the newspaper *L'Équipe* and are managed by the Roger-Viollet agency. The archives include 170,000 images in all. See also Joëlle Beurier, *Images et violence, 1914–1918. Quand le Miroir racontait la Grande Guerre* (Paris: Éditions Nouveau Monde, 2007), 150.

2 In 1917 the newspaper was transferred to Paul Dupuy, who was then running *Le Petit Parisien*. It was bought in 1918 by the owners of the newspaper *Auto*. It closed in 1940, and its thousands of photographs were acquired by Roger-Viollet before becoming part of the Parisienne de Photographie.

3 *L'Illustration* and *Le Miroir* also published photographs on the front page. Jean-Noël Jeanneney, *Jours de guerre, 1914–1918. Les trésors des archives photographiques du journal Excelsior* (Paris: Éditions Les Arènes, 2013), 500.

4 André Gunthert and Emmanuelle Toulet, *Paris 14–18: La guerre au quotidien* (Paris: Bibliothèques, 2014), 240. While the images glossed over harsh realities, they show little "brainwashing," to use the term of the historian Jean-Noël Jeanneney. Jeanneney, *Jours de guerre*, 500. *Les trésors des archives photographiques du journal Excelsior* (Paris: Editions Les Arènes, 2013), 500.

5 "In these grave hours, there is no lowly work. That which serves the country is all great. Arise! To action! To work! Tomorrow there will be glory for all." René Viviani, *Le Figaro*, August 7, 1914.

6 This front page is quite different from the other issues that *Excelsior* published during the war. In addition to the unprecedented subject matter, the primary innovation was the layout with fifteen images tightly organized in a grid. With the exception of the captions, there was no other text, a device that together with the density of images heightened the overall visual impact of the working women. The layout of images on the cover of the June issue was a unique portrayal of this unprecedented moment in the history of women in France.

7 The photograph of the woman telegrapher had already been published in the March 18, 1917, issue of *Excelsior* with this description: "The mailman's letterbox proved to be too heavy for the feeble shoulders of French women, but the sack used by young female telegraphers was just a bit heavier than a handbag and there was even room for a small mirror, a powder puff, and lip liner." See also "Les factrices de Paris ont commencé leur service hier," *Excelsior*, May 31, 1917.

8 Generally speaking, French newspapers were divided when it came to women's work. Some ignored the question, including *Le Petit Journal*, *Le Petit Parisien*, *Le Journal*, and *Le Matin*; others published cultural criticism as a means of removing any hints of feminism, while others actively celebrated women's work. See Françoise Thébaud, *Les femmes au temps de la guerre de 14* (Paris: Payot, 2013), 223–24, 478.

9 Advertisement for the "Françoise," by Madame Commard, 1916, cited by Jérémie Brucker, "Le vêtement professionnel en France des années 1880 à nos jours," forthcoming doctoral thesis supervised by Christine Bard, Université d'Angers.

10 Paul Géraldy, *Les femmes et la guerre* (Paris: Devambez, 1920), preface. This book contains twelve lithographs by Étienne Drian of women working. "Munitionnette, mailwoman, lamppost employee, train ticket manager, train conductor, department store deliverywoman, Drian's women at work cultivate grace and elegance. Their hair falls from their caps, their jewelry is promoted, their shoes are from another century, and their dresses, which are puffy at times, help emphasize their femininity."

11 *Le Figaro*, January 10, 1917, and "L'Ève future," *Le Figaro*, May 11, 1918.

12 *L'Intransigeant*, September 1, 1916.

13 Alexandre Devarennes, *La femme française pendant la guerre*. Documentary film, 1917–18. © Établissement de Communication et de Production Audiovisuelle de la Défense (ECPAD), 14.18 A 975.

14 Pierre Lafitte, "Notre programme," *Excelsior*, November 16, 1910, 2.

4a Overalls

JÉRÉMIE BRUCKER

Throughout the war, photographers captured images of women working in overalls. In one such photograph, a woman working at a factory wears button-down overalls with two pockets on the chest. FIG. 4a.1 The garment is too big for her body—she is clearly wearing overalls made for a man. Although men's overalls had the benefit of being easy to put on and remove, they were ill fitted for women's bodies. Despite this fact, they were worn by women at the start of the war for the simple reason that female overalls had not yet been designed. This image of a woman in work overalls, her hair pulled back from her face, reflects a certain ambiguity in the traditional way in which women were perceived. The photograph reconciles work-safety norms, which prohibit leaving long hair loose near machines, with the social norms of femininity, emphasized by the incongruous presence of a white ruffled blouse collar, heeled shoes, and a necklace. The image, produced and published in the newspaper *Excelsior* in 1917, reinforced a representation of femininity that was compatible with the new status of women workers during the war. In a way, such images helped make the idea of women working more acceptable to those who were still unprepared for the redistribution of roles in the workplace.

At the front and at home, there was increasing anxiety about the so-called masculinization of women at work that was impeding on traditional norms of femininity.[1] Satirists and illustrators who published in a censored press regularly drew on these anxieties in their work. FIG. 4a.2 In order to assuage public concerns and to preserve the image of women as mothers and wives, representations of female workers adhered to gender stereotypes and often feminized and even sexualized the work overall. FIGS. 4a.3, 4a.4 As press photography developed during this period, staged photographs of women looking elegant and feminine in work clothing were often published in the popular press. These images reassured both men and women that women were not losing their traditional feminine identities in their new roles. The question of objectivity arose since the women photographed were often not working and usually wore accessories and makeup that would not have been acceptable on the job. This issue became so relevant that journalists and publishers struggled to respond to it clearly. In *La Baïonnette*, Paul Iribe's female worker wears makeup and overalls with an open neckline that is in no way appropriate for factory work. In the background, another female worker wears high heel shoes. In 1917, a *munitionnette* in overalls was featured on the cover of the French magazine *Les Modes*—the first time that the fashion magazine depicted a working woman on its inside cover, thereby conferring an aura of fashionability on the working girl archetype. FIG. 4a.5

Although there were more than seven million women workers in France during the early 1910s, when French women were already largely integrated into the professional world from field to factory and workshop, they were rarely dressed in clothing intended specifically for work.[2] After the start of the First World War in France, women were granted access to work sites that had been almost exclusively reserved for men and where women had, until then, only very limited roles and responsibilities. The new economic and social reality caused by the war made the question of work clothes for women more relevant: exposed to messy and often dangerous activities in their new jobs, they needed suitable clothing to protect them.

The protection of male workers and the question of whether they should receive free compulsory clothing was the subject of much debate in France between the end of the nineteenth century and the 1910s. As a result, men working in the most dangerous jobs were required to wear work clothing capable of covering all parts of the body.[3] The overall, or *combinaison* (from the English word combination), was adopted for such jobs, and some aspects of the "designs," including positioning of pockets or zippers, were protected by American patents that had been registered in France. The "clothing overall" (*vêtement-combinaison*) by the Olus Manufacturing Company, for example, was licensed in Paris in 1908, as was the version called "combination" made in 1913 by the American Innovation Shirt Company.[4]

Even though women were considered to be substitute workers for the men away at war, they were not protected by the same rules. Dresses for everyday wear and aprons intended for domestic use were clearly not adapted to cover the body in hazardous conditions, but existing protective overalls designed for men ran the risk of masculinizing women's bodies. This fact elicited a dilemma that was at once moral, cultural, political, economic, and social. The problem of women's work clothing was a concern from the start of the war even as many assumed the conflict would be short lived. However, given the circumstances and the urgent wartime needs, women continued to wear their own clothing to work or, when absolutely necessary,

FIG. 4a.1 A woman in work clothes, Paris. "The new professions for women since the war," *Excelsior*, June 24, 1917. © Excelsior–L'Équipe / Roger-Viollet, RV-72194-51.

LA BAIONNETTE

(Dessin de Villemot.)

— Et ton homme, qu'est-ce qu'il fait, pendant ce temps là ?
— Mon homme ? Il s'occupe à la maison. Il remmaille mes bas de soie...

Imp. CRÉTÉ, Corbeil (S.-et-O.) *Le gérant :* F. TINESSE.

★

FIG. 4a.2 Jean Villemot. Caricature of a man and woman in a bar wearing work overalls: "And your man, what's he doing, meanwhile? / My man? He's busy at home. He's darning my silk stockings . . ." *La Baïonnette,* October 4, 1917. Private collection.

FIG. 4a.3 Paul Iribe. Illustration of a woman working in a factory captioned "Not all of them are in Biarritz or Deauville." *La Baïonnette*, October 4, 1917. Private collection.

FIG. 4a.4 Jean Villemot. Illustration of a woman working in a factory. *La Baïonnette*, October 4, 1917. Private collection.

N° 168 **LES MODES** 1917

DIRECTION
15, rue de la Ville-l'Evêque, Paris

ABONNEMENT ET VENTE
24, boulevard des Capucines, Paris

RÉDACTION ET ADMINISTRATION
15, rue de la Ville-l'Evêque, Paris

PARIS — LONDRES — NEW-YORK

SOMMAIRE DU NUMÉRO

LES « MUNITIONNETTES » DANS NOS USINES DE GUERRE
AUX USINES DE LYON. — LE DÉCOLLETAGE SUR TOUR GRIDLEY

FIG. 4a.5 Inside front cover featuring a woman in overalls. "Munitionettes in our war factories." *Les Modes*, 1917, no. 168. © Françoise Cochennec / Galliera / Roger-Viollet, RV-157097-3.

FIG. 4a.6 Factory workers on the rue de Tolbiac, Paris, March 1915. Silver gelatin print.

purchased men's overalls from department stores from the late nineteenth century onward.[5] Despite shortages in fabric, new forms of clothing were devised to dress women at work and to adapt men's overalls to the female body. In a 1916 advertisement, the designer Madame G. Commard promoted attire specially designed for women in the workplace: *With the war calling women into the workplace, a suit for the tasks they are to perform has become necessary. To say nothing of having her wear men's pants, which have no aesthetic value, a woman can, in the clothing we recommend, retain the inherent stylishness of her sex. The "LA FRANÇOISE" suit, all in one piece, is complemented by a culotte skirt, and the bottom part of the skirt cinches around the ankle boot like a bodice, held in place by a buttonhole and a button. The apron sleeve circles tightly around the wrist and is held in place by buttons.*[6] The "La Françoise" suit, which can be found in certain photographs in 1917, kept the body clean and also opened in back to make it easier for women to use the bathroom.[7] FIG. 4a.6 It was perhaps inspired by the culottes-skirt presented by the couture house Béchoff-David & Cie in 1910–11 at the Auteuil race track.[8] Clothing and body language had to correspond to what was expected of women in a male-dominated society. How could one reconcile the demands on workers asked to serve the war effort with the social attitudes that supported a clear distinction between the sexes and their appearance? At the Compagnie du Tramway de Bordeaux, women substitute conductors were given "dresses, which served as a kind of uniform."[9] The matter of work attire seemed to have been important, as it was mentioned several times in letters that were sent between members of the family and the son who had left for the front line. Whether it took the form of a dress, a uniform, or a loose piece of clothing that male and female workers wore over their clothes, work wear had to transform the remplaçantes into a full-fledged worker. The sister of the soldier condemned "those ladies . . . who liked to dress up" at work, as well as "a certain number of women [who took] advantage of the start of winter to don glaringly colored coats." To ensure that "they would no longer coif themselves in hats such as *polos*, *boléros*, *marchandes de pommes*, or other objects that at times were grotesque," the wife and daughter of the head of Bordeaux tramways designed a suitable hat so that the substitute workers would be able to reconcile the performance of their jobs with their status as women in society.[10] FIG. 4a.7 More than the actual uniforms, it was these accessories that signaled women's work during

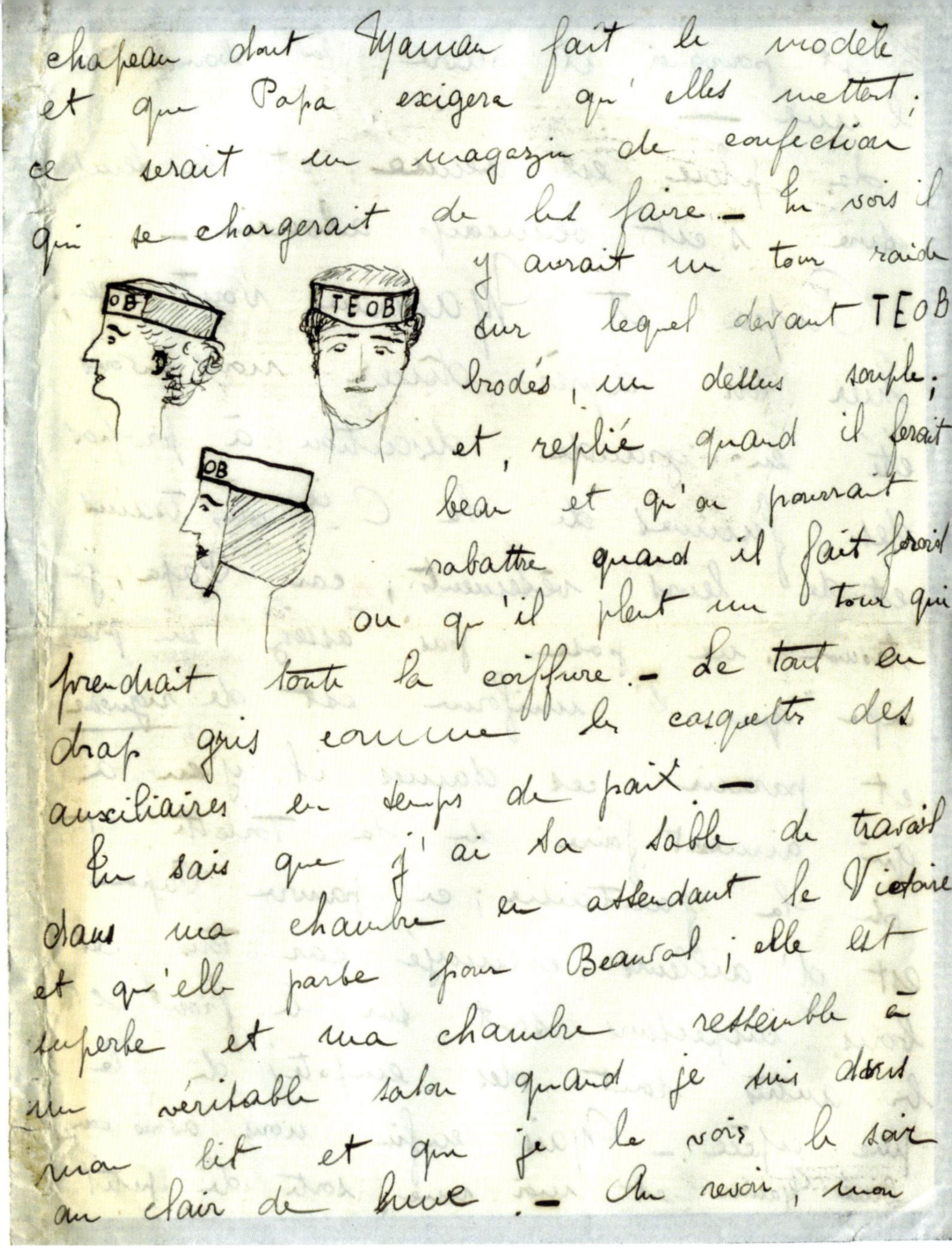
chapeau dont Maman fait le modèle
et que Papa exigera qu'elles mettent;
ce serait un magazin de confection
qui se chargerait de les faire. — Tu vois il
y aurait un tour raide
sur lequel devant TEOB
brodés, un dessus souple;
et, replié quand il ferait
beau et qu'on pourrait
rabattre quand il fait froid
ou qu'il pleut un tour qui
prendrait toute la coiffure. — Le tout en
drap gris comme les casquettes des
auxiliaires en temps de paix —
Tu sais que j'ai sa table de travail
dans ma chambre en attendant la Victoire
et qu'elle parte pour Beauval; elle est
superbe et ma chambre ressemble à
un véritable salon quand je suis dans
mon lit et que je la vois le soir
au clair de lune. — Au revoir, mon

FIG. 4a.7 Letter from Cherifa Résal to her brother Salem Résal describing the hats worn by the women tram drivers in Bordeaux, November 30, 1915. © Jacques Résal.

the war. In many cases, the adoption of overalls by French women did little to actually affirm their roles. More often they were worn because there were no other options. The war was an exceptional period for women's work in France. With full knowledge that it was temporary, it could be argued that men delayed the development of full and proper professional uniforms for women.

1 Christine Bard, *Une histoire politique du pantalon* (Paris: Le Seuil, 2010).

2 Françoise Thébaud, *Les femmes au temps de la guerre de 14* (Paris: Payard, 2013).

3 Jérémie Brucker, "Le vêtement professionnel et l'inspection du travail, entre normes et pratiques," *Modes pratiques. Revue d'histoire du vêtement et de la mode,* vol. 1 (Paris : IRHIS-École Duperré, 2015), 308–27.

4 Patents no. 396.731 and no. 454.469, Office national de la propriété industrielle, Archives de l'Institut National de la Propriété Industrielle, Paris. Jérémie Brucker, "Le vêtement professionnel en France des années 1880 à nos jours," forthcoming PhD thesis supervised by Christine Bard, Université d'Angers.

5 For example, *La Belle Jardinière,* seasonal catalogue 1910, file 66 AQ 30, Archives Nationales du Monde du Travail, Roubaix, France.

6 Madame G. Commard was the widow of a reserve officer who had died in 1915. Advertisement for la Françoise, Madame Commard, 1916.

7 Photos from the Delahaye Automobile Society photo album, *Collaboration des femmes à la Défense nationale.* Jérémie Brucker, "Le front de l'arrière en 1914–1918: des femmes mobilisées par—et pour—l'habit?," in Maude Bass-Krueger et al., *Fashion, Society, and the First World War* (London: Bloomsbury, forthcoming), 2019.

8 Béchoff-David was founded by Émile Béchoff (born ca. 1868), Siegfried David (dates unknown), and Philippe Hecht (born ca. 1874).

9 Letter from Julie Résal to her son Salem Résal, October 21,1914, Plateforme 1418, http://www.plateforme1418.com/ressources/de-julie-resal-a-salem-resal-21101914_497

10 The *polo* was a round hat that looked like the polo cap worn for sports; the *bolero* a Spanish hat with raised edges. The *marchandes de pommes* refers to a mockery of the merchants' hats worn by "ladies" at work. Letter from Cherifa to her brother Salem Résal, November 30, 1915, and letter from Eugène Résal to his son Salem Résal, December 2,1915, Plateforme 1418, http://www.plateforme1418.com/ressources/de-cherifa-resal-a-salem-resal-30111915_1228 and http://www.plateforme1418.com/ressources/de-eugene-resal-a-salem-resal-02121915_123

5

The Wartime Fashion Industry

MAUDE BASS-KRUEGER

On August 2, 1914, as church bells rang to signal the start of general mobilization, the French government mandated the closure of all theaters, cinemas, and music halls. In Paris alone, 75,000 people were out of work.[1] The timing could not have been worse for the fashion industry. Parisian couturiers had begun to show their collections during the last week of July, and foreign buyers were already in Paris, ready to place their orders. The cables sent from Paris on July 26 bear no hint of the impending war: a journalist for the *New York Times* observed that French designers had changed the style from last season, adding metallic embellishments and lowering the waistline. American women were urged to buy new dresses to keep up with the ever-changing Parisian fashions.[2] Six days later, on July 31, the even tenor of the fashion reporting had dramatically shifted: "TOURISTS IN PARIS ARE IN A WAR PANIC / Flock There by Thousands, Fearing That They Won't Get Ships Home. / HARD PRESSED FOR FUNDS / Steamship Agent Reassuring—Sobbing Women in Need of Funds Besiege our Consulate" ran the *New York Times* headline, along with news that "the fashion openings have been abandoned, and that inasmuch as all business is at a standstill many houses are likely to close."[3] FIG. 5.1 Despite the dire predictions, most of the major Paris fashion houses maintained their viewings throughout the month of August. Couture was business, not entertainment, and the couture houses were not subject to the mandated closures. The financial stakes for the fashion industry were too high and had a direct impact on the French economy on the whole. The Parisian couture industry was the luxurious face of France's second largest economic sector: the garment and textile industries employed more than a third of the country's active work population and generated a third of all exports.[4] In 1913, the couture industry exported over 160 million francs' worth of dresses and coats; the confection, or ready-made clothing, industry also exported 160 million francs' worth of ready-made clothes.[5] On the eve of the war, 75 percent of all French silk production was exported abroad and to the French colonies.[6] The government needed the garment and textile industries to thrive, not only because it had new, urgent demands for uniforms and other textile-based war supplies, but also because a healthy fashion industry stabilized the national economy and galvanized public morale. Both industries relied on exports for revenue, but domestic consumption was of critical symbolic importance. What French women purchased had a direct impact on the orders submitted by foreign buyers.

The month of August 1914 was chaotic for the couture and confection industries. Foreign buyers were not sure whether they should stay in Paris to preview the collections or take the first boat home. Those who chose to remain had to pay for their orders in cash, an unprecedented requirement that may have cost the industry thousands of francs in revenue. FIG. 5.2 The couture houses that had taken orders suddenly found themselves at a loss for materials to fulfill their sales. Male couturiers Paul Poiret, Jacques Doucet, and Jean-Philippe Worth were all mobilized for war and closed their houses during the first weeks of their duty.[7] FIG. 5.3 Although the closures were provisional, couturiers such as Poiret designed, oversaw production, and managed business from the front for the duration of the war.[8] Maison Worth transformed its delivery garage into a Red Cross ambulance center. FIG. 5.4 Couture houses led by women, however, largely stayed open. Callot Sœurs put 1,500 of its employees to work making hospital supplies.[9] Department stores draped their storefronts in patriotic flags and stocked the shelves with ready-made uniforms and war supplies. FIGS. 5.5, 5.6 When clients made themselves scarce, department store vendors took to sewing necessities for life in the trenches. FIGS. 5.7, 5.8 Seamstresses agreed to be paid half wages, called *salaires de misère* or "war wages," in order to help the fashion houses remain financially solvent. Couturiers, seamstresses, tailors, models, and vendors worked together to finish the August designs, show the garments, and sell the new styles to buyers. French clients placed their orders, demonstrating to foreign buyers that the new styles would prevail on the streets of wartime Paris.

Meanwhile, the American press, sensing that the situation in France was unsteady, seized the opportunity to promote American designers: "Paris May See End of Style Control, Designs Predict our Emancipation from French Modes as Result," the *New York Times* exulted on August 6, 1914. In September, the newspaper predicted that Parisian couture houses would not be able to "lay down the law at the beginning of the [January] season," and called on American designers to create new fashions to take their place. In October, the newspaper published a series of articles on new American designers and fashions coming out of New York.[10] By December, the rumors across the Atlantic had grown to such an extent that the French Chambre Syndicale de la Couture Parisienne (Trade Association of Paris Couture) felt obliged to remind foreign buyers that the winter collections would be shown "at the same date

FIG. 5.1 Charles Lansiaux. Infantry patrol in front of the shop of designer Mme. Pouyanne at 4, rue de la Paix, October 1914. Silver gelatin print. © Préfecture de Police, Service de l'Identité judiciaire / BHVP / Roger-Viollet, RV- 76435-3.

FIG. 5.2 Louis Rémy Sabattier. Illustration of mobilized British buyers viewing spring designs including a collared coat over a blouse and tailored skirt (center). *L'Illustration,* February 13, 1915. Private collection.

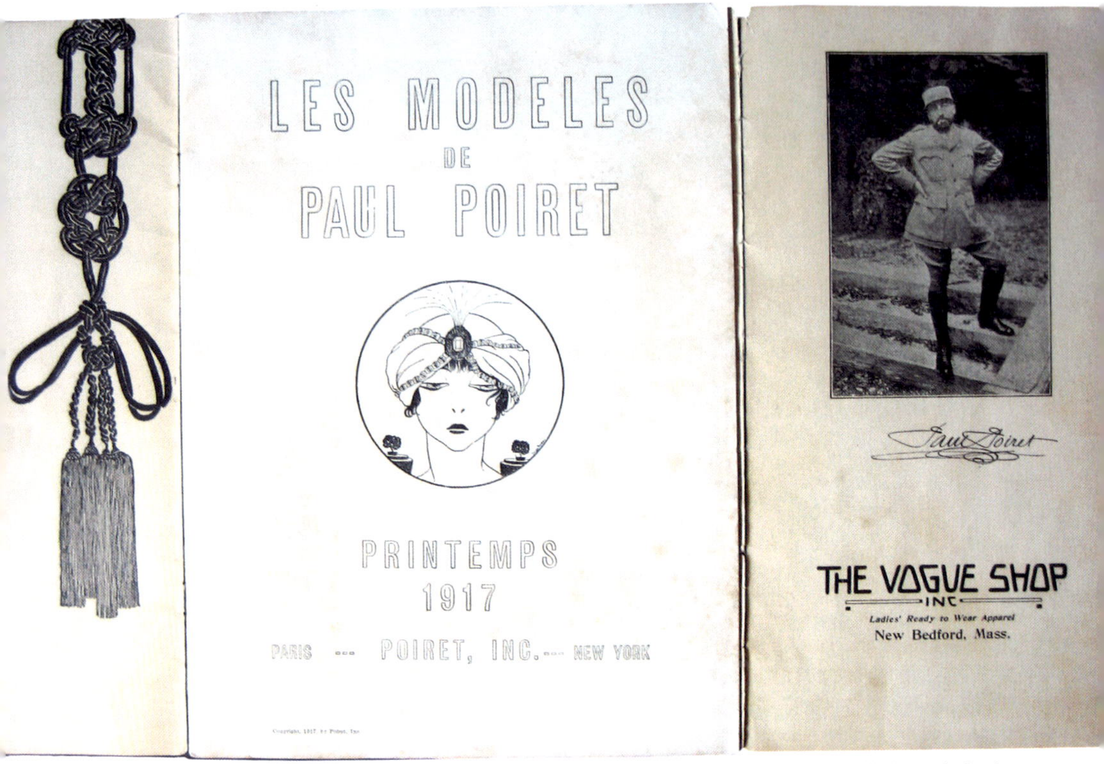

FIG. 5.3 Photograph of Paul Poiret in uniform included in a catalogue called *Les Modèles de Paul Poiret, Printemps 1917* (The Designs of Paul Poiret, Spring 1917.) Paris and New York: Paul Poiret, Inc., 1917. Diktats bookstore.

FIG. 5.4 Charles Lansiaux. Worth delivery garage at 7, rue de la Paix transformed into ambulance center no. 152 of the Red Cross of France, Union of French Women, October 1914. Silver gelatin print. © Préfecture de Police, Service de l'Identité judiciaire / BHVP / Roger-Viollet, RV-76435-1.

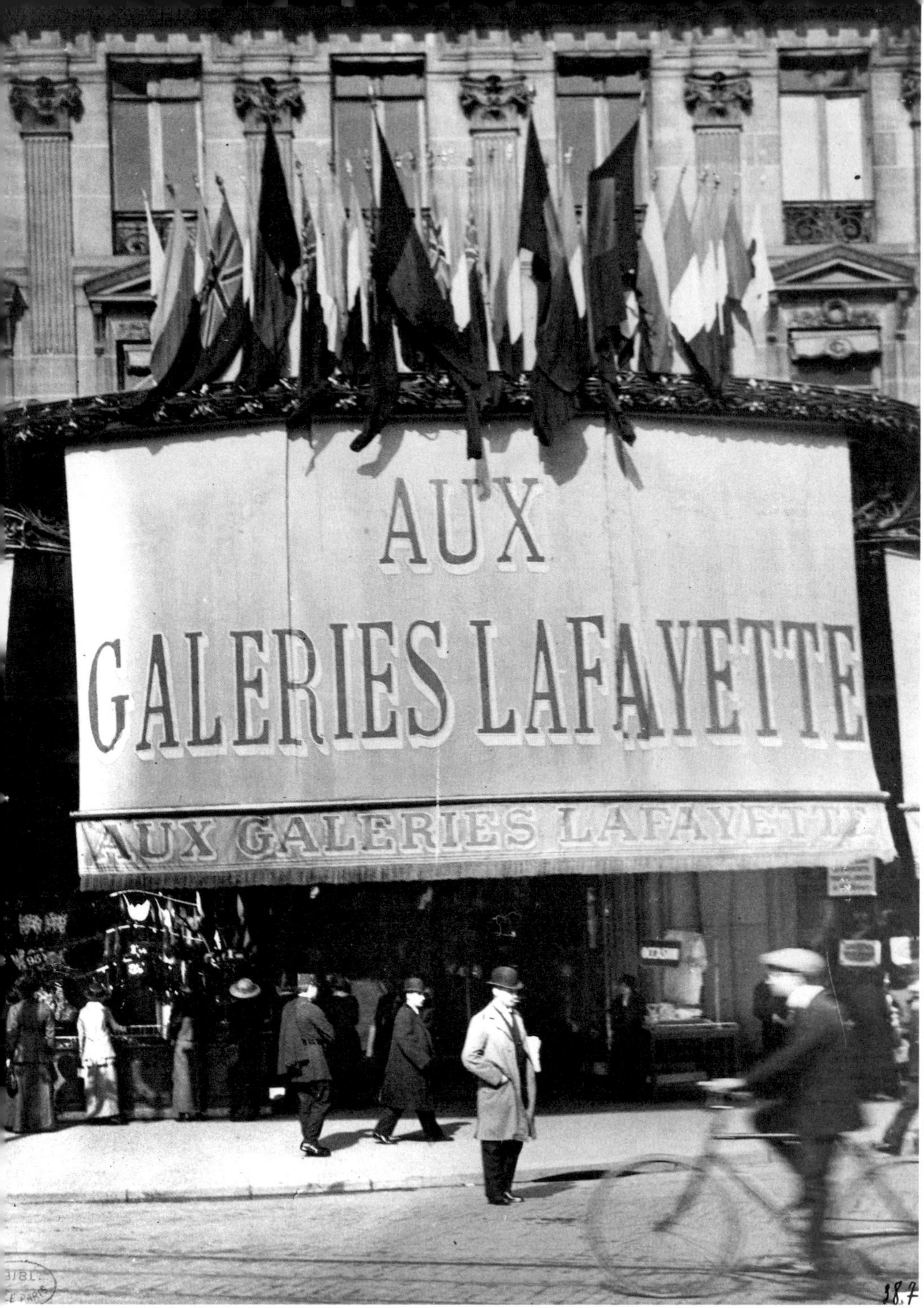

FIG. 5.5 Charles Lansiaux. Façade of Galeries Lafayette department store at 38, Boulevard Haussmann heavily decorated with flags of French allies, September 23, 1914. Silver gelatin print. © BHVP / Roger Viollet, RV-73734-18.

FIG. 5.6 Charles Lansiaux. Belle Jardinière department store where French soldiers' cars stock up on equipment and supplies, Paris, September 25, 1914. Silver gelatin print. © Charles Lansiaux / BHVP / Roger-Viollet, RV- 73723-21.

FIG. 5.7 Charles Lansiaux. Workers at Galeries Lafayette who, without clients, join together to sew military outfits, Paris, August 1914. Silver gelatin print. © Préfecture de Police, Service de l'Identité judiciaire / BHVP / Roger-Viollet, RV-76464-3.

FIG. 5.8 Charles Lansiaux. Unemployed milliners and dressmakers at Galeries Lafayette working at their counters to help wounded soldiers, Paris, August 1914. Silver gelatin print. © Préfecture de Police, Service de l'Identité judiciaire / BHVP / Roger-Viollet, RV- 76464-4.

and in the same condition as the previous seasons" and demanded excuses from the American press for invoking the contrary.[11]

SEE CHAPTER 6 The verdict was delivered in January 1915, following the winter showings of the newest Paris collections: "French Silhouette Wins, Proving Fashion Still Bows to Paris."[12] The American press declared defeat. Parisian couture had made it through the first six months of the war.

Wartime Silhouettes: The "war crinoline" and the "barrel silhouette"

Two new silhouettes were introduced during the war. The first, a shorter, bell-shaped silhouette was shown by leading Parisian designers in August 1914. According to the historian Florence Brachet-Champsaur, the launch of this style was determined by wartime conditions and responded to the new wartime needs of French women.[13] The "bell skirt" silhouette (*robe* or *jupe cloche*), a full skirt that used between four and eight meters of textile and was consequently dubbed the "war crinoline" (*crinoline de guerre*), supposedly liberated the stride and allowed women to move about freely in their new wartime roles. FIG. 5.9

"While patriotic representations of women enclosed them within stereotypes," writes Bachet-Champsaur, "fashion freed them."[14] However, fashion's emancipatory power has been questioned by fashion historians such as Valerie Steele, among others.[15] For Steele, fashion evolves according to an internal logic unrelated to practical function or sexual liberation. The war was no exception: the two wartime silhouettes were not created in response to the war but rather evolved within the mechanism of the fashion cycle, where impulse was driven by novelty, desire, and prestige.

Moreover, the bell silhouette was designed before the war broke out, not after it began. First presented in the collections of late July and early August 1914, the style was rebranded as the war crinoline in August and September—a savvy tactic meant to reassure buyers of its longevity as the fashion of the Parisian fall and winter season. Furthermore, its voluminous use of textiles made the style heavy and impractical. Women complained about the tall, tight boots they wore in order to compensate for the style's shorter hemline.[16] FIG. 5.10 "Probably the most unwelcome piece of news to the majority of women is the fact that the skirts for the street are cut circular, and coats are so long and full that they are exactly three times as heavy as those we have worn for three years," lamented the correspondent for the *New York Times* in an article filed on September 1 and published on September 13, 1914.[17]

Fashion illustrations make the war crinoline look light and supple, but photographs tell a different story: Lanvin's "Arianne" black faille skirt lined in fur may have been warm, but it was also heavy and cumbersome. SEE CHAPTER 5 AND FIG. 5c.32 In other words, the war crinoline was adapted for the war in name only.

In January 1917, French couturiers collectively introduced the "barrel" silhouette (*robe* or *jupe tonneau*). FIG. 5.11 "Will Barrel Silhouette Provide New Silhouette?," the *New York Times* asked on January 7, 1917: "If So, World of Dress will be Turned Topsy-Turvy and Every Woman Will Have to Buy New Spring Gowns." The newspaper described the new silhouette to its readers:

"The skirt is a bit high-waisted and ends just above the ankles. It gradually flares out into its broadest circumference above the knees, shaping downward until it reaches the narrowest hem we have had in years. There are no hoops, no crinoline. The barrel shape bulge is provided by cutting the material."[18] FIG. 5.12

Brachet-Champsaur writes that the style was designed to respond to the difficulty of acquiring raw materials during the war: the barrel silhouette used half as much fabric as the bell silhouette, easing the burden on French consumers at a time of economic crisis.[19] FIG. 5.13 Yet costs for silk fabric were falling during this time, and there seems to be no indication from French designers that they were responding to the wartime economic crisis. Rather, it appears that the primary purpose of the new style was to spur consumption. FIG. 5.14 After three years of bell-shaped fashions, French designers created a fresh silhouette that demanded women purchase anew. "There is no way of transforming a one-piece medieval tunic robe into a barrel-shaped, melonshaped, gored frock," the *New York Times* declared—women would have to update their wardrobes.[20] While this might have caused financial hardship for French clients who were in the midst of serious economic and morale strain in the spring of 1917, foreign clients had no other choice but to oblige and place new orders—welcome news for the couture industry. SEE CHAPTER 8

In other words, couturiers did not respond to the war by changing the silhouettes of their garments; this dynamic was caused by the natural tendency of the fashion industry to move from one style to the next in order to spur consumption. Yet choices in textiles, color palette, and overall style or trimmings—many of which were militaristic or patriotic in nature—were directly influenced by wartime conditions.

FIG. 5.9 Fashion plate showing bell-shaped traveling coats and car coats by designers Premet, Beer, and Martial and Armand. *Les Élégances Parisiennes*, no. 5, 1916, pl. VIII-IX. Image provided by The Metropolitan Museum of Art, New York, Thomas J. Watson Library, 233.4 E12 Q 1916:1-6.

LES ÉLÉGANCES PARISIENNES

MANTEAUX DE SPORT ET DE VOYAGE

Modèles de MARTIAL et ARMAND (*fig. 208 et 209*)

FIG. 5.10 Fashion plate showing coats for sport and traveling by designer Martial and Armand. The outfit on the left pairs a shorter skirt with tall boots. *Les Élégances Parisiennes*, no. 7, 1917, pl. XVIII. © Bibliothèque Forney / Roger-Viollet, RV-157622-21.

Les Elégances Parisiennes

433 434 435

LA LIGNE NOUVELLE

Modèles de Jenny (fig. 433), Premet (fig. 435), Worth (fig. 434).

L'étroitesse des jupes fera ressortir le peu d'ampleur que possède encore les basques des jaquettes, soit qu'elles soient coupées en forme, ou bien composées de plusieurs tuniques superposées, de différentes longueurs. —

Fig. 433. Serge marine soutachée garnie de vison. — Fig. 434. Jaquette en "Burella" garnie de kolinsky; jupe en même tissu quadrillé de vert. — Fig. 435. Serge marine avec cravate et dépassant à la manche en hermine.

Planche XI. — Supplément des "Élégances Parisiennes" N° 7.

IMP. BUTTNER-THIERRY
PARIS

Le Gérant : H. Bernard.

FIG. 5.11 Three models of the barrel silhouette by Jenny, Premet, and Worth illustrated in a plate called "The New Line." *Les Élégances Parisiennes*, no. 7, 1917, pl. XI. © Bibliothèque Forney / Roger Viollet, RV-157622-22.

FIG. 5.12 Barrel silhouettes in fabrics by Labbey & Co. The new barrel silhouette required half the fabric of the bell silhouette. *Les Élégances Parisiennes*, no. 9, December 1917, pl. VIII-IX. Image provided by The Metropolitan Museum of Art, New York, Thomas J. Watson Library, 233.4 E12 Q 1916-1917:7-12.

FIG 5.13 Au Printemps department store catalogue showing selection of barrel silhouettes, March 1918. © Bibliothèque Forney / Roger Viollet, RV-203791-6.

FIG. 5.14 A woman in the town of Vorey (Haute Loire) wearing a barrel silhouette, September 1917. Silver gelatin print. Private collection.

The Destruction of the Northern Textile Industries

With mobilization came an urgent demand for domestically produced textiles, particularly wool, linen, and cotton for uniforms, socks, blankets, tents, and other military stuffs. The fibers for these textiles were traditionally grown, spun, and woven in France's northern regions, particularly around Lille, Roubaix, and Tourcoing, cities that had grown prosperous from textile manufacturing during the Industrial Revolution. Two-fifths of the entire French garment and textile manufacturers were situated in this narrow department, or political region, called the Nord, near the Belgian border.

On August 2, 1914, the Germans marched into Belgium, violating its neutrality and forcing Belgian families to flee on foot to France. From there, the German army pushed toward France. Bombs rained down on French border cities throughout August. On September 9, 1914, the French government called on all mobilized men in the region to leave and find refuge safe from enemy fire. The city of Lille—one of the largest cities in France with a population of half a million in 1914—fell to enemy fire on October 13. FIG. 5.15

The next day, the Germans reached Tourcoing and Roubaix, parading triumphantly into the city centers. The six northern departments of the Aisne, Ardennes, Marne, the Nord, Pas-de-Calais, and the Somme remained under German occupation for the entirety of the war. Textile manufacturing ground to a halt. Nearly half of the entire French textile industry was either in a battle zone or under German occupation by the end of 1914.[21] The wool industry, the hardest hit of all, lost almost two-thirds of its total manufacturing power during the war.[22] French textile factories were requisitioned for German use, forced labor was imposed, and deportations were frequent.[23] What did the German occupation of French textile factories look like? The "Report on the Condition of Textile Industries in the Invaded Districts of France," commissioned by the English government and printed in 1919, detailed the devastation encountered by English inspectors.[24] German soldiers emptied the textile factories and requisitioned all of the metals, as well as tools, raw materials, finished cloth, and machinery. An inspector noted that soldiers had even stripped unfinished cloth from the looms and punched holes in the jacquard cards to render them unusable. Soldiers dismantled these machines to recover the metals or else removed them, sending them back to Germany to be put to use. The fabric left behind was unusable or destroyed. FIG. 5.16 "It gives a funny impression," David

Hirsch, a shop owner from Roubaix, wrote in his journal in 1917, "to see a great nation like Germany remove all pipes from a small factory like the Desbonnets . . . There must be a shortage of metal in Germany; [they removed] locks, storefront signage, dressing hooks, hangers, door knobs, coffee grinders, etc."[25] John Reed, an American journalist and socialist activist who traveled to the northern factories in 1915, described how "a vibrant world has been struck dead in an instance . . . One wonders what happened to the millions of people working in the kilometers of dead man's land."[26] Maurice Delmotte, a private citizen, noted in his diary: "the Germans have requisitioned all the cloth, cotton, linen, and silk. We will soon not be able to dress ourselves, nor eat, as it is forbidden to have butter, wine, alcohol, flour, grain beer, or grain at home."[27] The devastation of northern France was both material and psychological. The French resisted as well as they could. Hirsch noted proudly in his journal that he closed his shop on Sunday "as the Germans usually buy on Sunday. We help the blockade in our own small ways."[28] Delmotte gave false numbers for his chickens and hid objects of value from the Germans. French acts of sabotage, obstruction to stock, or misadministration have been chronicled by historians.[29] FIG. 5.17 Yet despite these small acts of civic resistance, the damage done to the northern French textile factories was devastating to the region and to the French economy. Even if factories operating at 20 percent capacity could potentially repair the German destruction, they still had the impossible task of finding materials, coal, and workers.[30] As many as 312,000 people—one third of all French textile workers—were employed in the textile factories in northeastern France. Almost all of them lost their jobs during the First World War.[31]

From Wool to Silk: Lyon and the Silk Textile Trade

With half of its textile manufacturing under German occupation, an urgent solution was needed to find textiles to supply the army, domestic consumers, and the export market. FIG. 5.18 The answer was found in Lyon, a city located in the center of France, far from the front lines. Famous for its silk production since the sixteenth century, Lyon became the foremost manufacturer of silk textiles in the eighteenth century and maintained this position throughout the nineteenth and twentieth centuries. In 1913, the Lyonnais silk industry employed 300,000 people and had a textile production estimated at 467 million francs, 370 million francs of which were accounted for by exports. Lyon, as well as the neighboring towns

FIG. 5.15 Street in Lille shortly before the city fell to German troops, October 12, 1914. Silver gelatin print. © Ullstein Bild / Roger-Viollet, RV-75258-8.

FIG. 5.16 A textile factory in Roubaix destroyed by German soldiers, late October–early November 1918. Published in *Excelsior* November 5, 1918. Silver gelatin print. © Excelsior – L'Equipe / Roger-Viollet RV-74130-1.

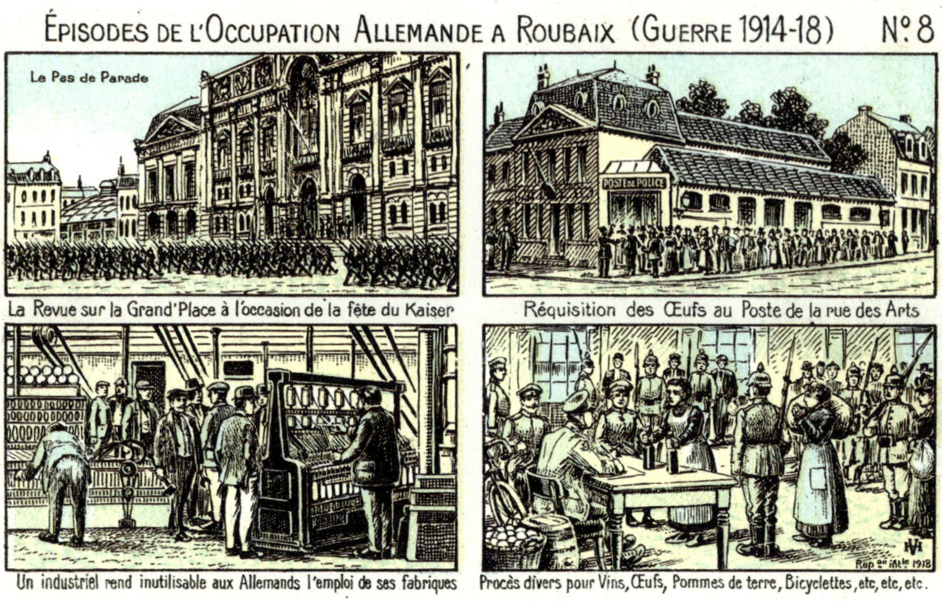

FIG. 5.17 Postcard showing life in Roubaix under the German occupation, after 1918. No. 8 in a series of 12. © Bibliothèque numérique de Roubaix, CP_A25_L01_S1_006.

LE STYLE PARISIEN

ETOFFES A LA MODE

1. Taffetas pékiné noir et blanc : COUDURIER, FRUCTUS et DESCHER n° 1 486 (le même, violet coloris b). — 2. Taffetas rayé marine et blanc : BIANCHINI et FÉRIER n° 18795. 3. Foulard bleu pékiné blanc : MOULY et SCHULZ n° 9015. — 4. Taffetas noir broché blanc : COUDURIER, FRUCTUS et DESCHER n° 10 332 (coloris H). — 5. Faille pékinée noir et vieil or : COUDURIER, FRUCTUS et DESCHER n° 1 469 (coloris 5). — 6. Batiste quadrillée « Linetta » RODIER n° 5602 (toutes teintes). — 7. Crêpe de Chine Albion : MOULY et SCHULZ n° 23040. — 8. Voile pékin MOULY et SCHULZ n° 23004. — 9. Twill damier MOULY et SCHULZ n° 27026. — 10. Twill pointillé MOULY et SCHULZ n° 9021. — 11. Taffetas bleu corbeau pékin broché : BIANCHINI 18857. — 12. Faille rayée grisaille BIANCHINI n° 18798 Dⁿᵉ V.

FIG. 5.18 Plate showing "Fashionable Fabrics" intended to stimulate the French silk economy after the destruction of northern textile factories. *Le Style Parisien*, no. 1, supplement of "Style Parisien," September 1915, pl. XXI. © Bibliothèque nationale de France.

of Saint-Etienne and Saint-Chamond, which specialized in silk ribbon production, constituted the largest silk market in all of Europe. However, the shift from the northern textile-producing region to Lyon was not simple. Wartime mobilization cost Lyon 50 percent of its work force. Women stepped in to replace the absent men, but some women were drawn away from the silk looms into the metal factories, where the pay was higher.[32] There were other hardships as well: regulations imposed throughout the war made it difficult to export silk to England, the industry's biggest buyer; Turkey's declaration of war and subsequent submarine warfare made it difficult to obtain silk fibers from the Middle East; the dying and printing industries also struggled, provoking a domino-chain reaction with Lyon, which relied on them to produce finished silk textiles. Lyonnais silk manufacturers found solutions to these problems. Silk factories raised their wages to compete with the munitions factories, and production remained steady. Manufacturers turned to Japan for raw silk. Companies began to experiment with wool and wool blends and learned how to make textiles for combat. Lyonnais silk production, valued at 467 million francs in 1913, dropped to 324 million in 1914. Yet by 1916 export values were equal to those in 1913. By 1917, production had risen to 608 million, surpassing prewar levels.[33] The north was devastated by the war, but Lyon survived and profited. The price for a meter of wool soared from 1.95 francs in the summer of 1915 to 7.50 francs in the summer of 1918. Woolen gabardine, a popular textile for daily wear, tripled over the same period. Yet the cost of silk dropped dramatically: radzimir, a luxurious, heavy silk fabric used for formal wear, decreased by half, from 8.75 francs in 1915 to 4 francs in 1918. Taffeta decreased from 5.90 to 2.95 francs. Over the course of the war, silk became cheaper than wool.[34] Parisian couturiers willingly incorporated more silk into their collections. The fabric helped shape wartime silhouettes. The fashion press reported on the new "supple," "draped," and "fluid" silhouettes, which were much appreciated by customers.[35] In turn, manufacturers sought to create new textile hybrids to keep up with the demand for light, pliant fabrics by adding silk to woolen weaves. Pure wool gabardine was reworked with silk to create *djersette*, a fabric with a silk warp and wool weft.[36] New techniques such as *moiré ciré* were also marketed in an effort to use silk as a replacement for other hard-to-come-by fabrics, such as leather.[37]

The Rise of Jersey and the Case of Chanel

One of the most pervasive narratives about the First World War and fashion is that of Gabrielle Chanel's dramatic rise in the midst of the war—a success credited to her use of jersey fabric from the manufacturer Rodier to make elegant daywear garments for the new modern woman. Like many long-accepted narratives, it merits nuancing. In the late nineteenth and early twentieth centuries, jersey was mainly used for underwear, sweaters, and sportswear.[38] During the war, manufacturers such as Rodier began to experiment, combining wool, silk, and even cashmere to create jersey blends.[39] Designers such as Chanel, but also Lanvin and Worth, began to experiment with the fabric for dresses and tailored suits as early as 1915. Known to fashionable women for her hats since 1910, when she opened her first millinery store at 21, rue Cambon (a second store would follow in Deauville in 1913), Chanel began designing garments during the war, first for herself and then for a few select clients. She opened her first dress shop in Biarritz in 1915 and quickly became known for her silk jersey marine blouses and wool jersey suit ensembles. SEE CHAPTER 5c A photograph of Gabrielle Chanel in 1913 on the northern beaches of Étretat shows her wearing a skirt and sweater jacket made from thick wool jersey. FIG. 5.19 Her hand, enclosed in the pocket, shows off the material's elasticity. Chanel wool jersey ensembles were featured in *Les Élégances Parisiennes* in May 1916, the first-ever promotion for her garments. Still unknown as a designer of clothes, her name was misspelled as "Channel"—an error that the magazine corrected two months later when it published three more "Chanel" jersey suits. Chanel became known for her jersey clothing, but she was not the first or the only designer to design such pieces during the war. In April 1917, the *New York Times* described their surprise "when the packers opened the enormous boxes which came over on the French steamers from Bordeaux and lifted gown after gown, suit after suit, and coat after coat of jersey."[40] The fabric hadn't been taken seriously at first, the journalist admitted, but it now appeared that jersey would be as ubiquitous as blue serge. The colors, mainly beige and gray, were "sad" and not particularly becoming to the American skin tone; the silhouettes were "shapeless" and needed to be belted or girdled to provide any shape. Regardless, the journalist was forced to admit that jersey had by that point become "the standard fabric" and that elegant women had all integrated such ensembles into their wardrobes by 1917.

FIG. 5.19 Gabrielle Chanel on the beach in Étretat wearing a wool jersey skirt and sweater jacket, ca. 1913. Silver gelatin print. © DR/CHANEL, © All rights reserved/CHANEL.

Colors and Dyes

Dyes and colorants posed another problem for the French textile industry during the war. Before the outbreak of hostilities, the French couture industry had relied on dyes imported from Germany. These imports were formally prohibited following the declaration of war. The small quantities of domestically-produced dyes were immediately requisitioned by the French government to make gunpowder and explosives.[41] Textile manufacturers began experimenting with new kinds of dyes but could not guarantee their color fastness. As Brachet-Champsaur has observed, labels affixed to the inside of garments informed customers of potential problems: "The Chambre Syndicale des Teintures et Apprêts (Union of Dyers and Finishers) informs us that colorants have been requisitioned to make explosives and dyers have had to replace them with products whose outcome cannot be guaranteed."[42] By July 1916, *Les Élégances Parisiennes* reported that suitable replacements had been found for the color taupe.[43] The couture industry did what it could to promote the most widely available colors—chiefly blues, reds, greens, and pale beiges and gray—by marketing them as "patriotic" and "discreet". In order to cater to Americans, who preferred bright colors, Parisian couturiers used bright pink and purple fabrics for couture designs exported abroad. SEE CHAPTER 5b The stark contrast between the bright fabrics used for export and the sober ones for the domestic market underline the extent to which the Parisian couture houses catered explicitly to foreign buyers, while trying to appeal to French customers with different needs.

Shifting Export Markets

The war changed the composition of the couture industry's international clientele, shifting it from Europe to North and South America. In 1913, the French couture industry exported 35 percent of its production to Great Britain, 21.5 percent to Argentina, 8.4 percent to Germany, 8 percent to Belgium, 6.8 percent to Switzerland, 5.7 percent to the United States, and 5 percent to Austria. Yet these numbers represent only the legal exports declared at customs and do not take into account "the great number of dresses that were stowed in voyager's trunks."[44] In reality, the numbers must have been much higher. Great Britain declared war on Germany on August 4, 1914; Austria-Hungary declared war on Belgium on August 28. Not surprisingly, these declarations had immediate and drastic repercussions for sales of couture garments into Great Britain, Germany, Belgium, and Austria, countries that, combined, represented more than half of

France's export clientele. In order to make up for lost revenue, the industry transferred its attention to Argentina, Switzerland, and the United States. Buyers from Argentina and the United States had to be persuaded to sail to France despite the danger of submarine attacks. Throughout the war, problems with transportation, customs taxes, credit, and rules regulating the export of certain textiles made exporting couture garments particularly challenging, even to neutral countries. For instance, new wartime regulations slowed the export of clothing to Switzerland to such an extent that the Swiss Society for Economic Surveillance lamented that women's fashions "would already have changed by the time they arrived." French train companies were confused about the textile prohibitions, the Swiss Society complained, and flatly refused to transport any items at all. By 1916, the export of all textiles except for linen and silk had been banned. Not even "embroidered corset-covers" got over the border.[45]

Yet despite these problems, the French couture industry did not collapse. Indeed, the wartime couture industry lost no more than one third of its prewar revenue—losses due primarily to the ban on exports to Germany and Bulgaria, the reduction of Belgian clients, and fewer orders from Great Britain, which had reduced 50 million francs worth of garments purchases in 1913 to only 8 million in 1915.[46] These deficits were largely offset by silk garment exports, which rose exponentially during the war, as well as new clients in Australia, Italy, Portugal, and Japan. Brazil and Argentina bought ten times more silk garments during the war than they had before the war began. The Parisian couturiers also concentrated their effort on the United States, sending new garments regularly overseas to be shown in department stores, special fashion shows, and international exhibitions. SEE CHAPTER 5 AND 6

The fashion and textile industries averted financial collapse during the war by imposing various policies. From the very beginning, and perhaps most crucially, the government did not intervene to regulate the fashion industry or curb the activities of Parisian couturiers during the very first weeks of the war, when collections were being shown in Paris. Savvy rebranding of the new bell-shaped silhouette as a war crinoline helped market the fashion at home and abroad. French fashion magazines sold the design's wide circumference as adapted to French women's new wartime activities, reassuring foreign buyers that the silhouette would prevail throughout the war. International success depended on the style being first adopted at home. Photographs from 1914 and 1915 show that French women adopted the flared war crinoline skirt for day and evening wear and the style quickly sold overseas. The devastation wrought by the German occupation of northeastern France and the large-scale destruction of the textile manufacturing of these regions were mitigated by the strength of the Lyon-based silk industry. Prices for wool soared, while those for silk dropped. By 1916 the couture industry had regained half of its lost revenue, and the launch of the 1917 barrel silhouette gave designers a much-needed increase in sales during the darkest year of the war. The couture industry survived the First World War, thanks to its resilience and determination. Indeed, the war helped to cement the position of France as the world leader of fashion, a position it strives to maintain today.

1 Françoise Thébaud, *Les femmes au temps de la guerre de 14* (Paris: Éditions de la Seine, 1986), 226–29.

2 "Changes in Styles Every June and December Due to Fact That Frenchwomen Insist on Having Something New," *New York Times,* July 26, 1914.

3 "Tourists In Paris Are In War Panic," *New York Times,* filed July 31,1914; printed August 1, 1914.

4 The total for exported sewn textiles, lingerie, and male and female confection (ready-made) equaled 41.1% of all manufacturer goods. If we add raw materials to sewn goods, the textile industry represented 30.9% of total French exports. These figures were drawn from three sources: Albert Aftalion, *L'industrie textile en France pendant la guerre, Publication de la Dotation Carnegie pour la paix internationale* (Paris: P.U.F., 1924); Henri Hauser and Henri Hitier, *Enquête sur la Production Française et la Concurrence Etrangère,* 6 vols. (Paris: Association national d'expansion économique, 1917); *Union des Syndicats patronaux des industries textiles de France. Rapport présenté à MM. les Ministres du Commerce et du Travail sur les industries textiles en France leur importance avant la guerre, leur situation pendant la guerre, ce qu'elles désirent pour après la guerre. 10 décembre 1915* (Paris: rue du Louvre, 1918).

5 *Rapport Général sur l'Industrie Française, sa situation, son avenir, Ministre du Commerce, de l'Industrie, des Postes et Télégraphes, des Transports maritimes et de la Marine marchande,* 3 vols. (Paris: Imprimerie Nationale, 1919), 687; Hauser and Hitier, *Enquête sur la Production Française*, 126.

6 Mary Lynn Stewart, *Dressing Modern Frenchwomen: Marketing Haute Couture, 1919–1939* (Baltimore, MD: Johns Hopkins University Press, 2008), 73.

7 Poiret remained closed throughout the remainder of the war. The houses of Doucet and Worth opened in November and December 1914.

8 At the start of the war, Poiret closed his couture house but maintained production for the Atelier Martine. He was stationed first in Lisieux and then, in 1915, in Bordeaux, where he was integrated into the Army's tailoring unit. In 1915 he was transferred to a wartime job in the Archives of the Ministry of Defense, but by 1917 had been re-appointed head tailor of his Army regiment, stationed in the heavily bombarded commune of Epernay, near Reims in the north of France. In August 1918 he was transferred one last time to Clermont-Ferrand. Although he designed fashions for domestic and international sale, as well as for the theater throughout the war, by 1918 he was broke and began selling off his family car and real estate. Poiret's wartime activities and designs are treated in depth by Guillaume Garnier in *Paul Poiret et Nicole Groult : maîtres de la mode art deco* (Paris: Musée de la mode et du costume, 1986), 184–85.

9 "Paris Fashions—In Spite of War's Alarms, Dressmakers at French Capital Have Set New Modes Which Will Doubtless Be Adopted Here," *New York*

Times, August 16, 1914.

10 "Now Is The Time for Americans to Design New Fashions," *New York Times,* September 27, 1914; "The War Brings Unique Opportunity to American Designers," *New York Times,* October 4, 1914; "Society Asks New York Designers to Create Fashions," *New York Times,* October 25, 1914.

11 Archives of the Chambre Syndicale de la Couture Parisienne, located at the FHCM, Register 21/12/1914.

12 "French Silhouette Wins, Proving Fashion Still Bows To Paris," *New York Times,* December 27, 1914.

13 Florence Brachet-Champsaur, "De l'odalisque de Poiret à la femme nouvelle de Chanel: une victoire de la Femme," in Evelyne Morin-Rotureau, *1914–1918: Combats de Femmes* (Paris: Éditions Autrement, 2004), 200.

14 Brachet-Champsaur, "De l'odalisque de Poiret à la femme nouvelle de Chanel," 200.

15 Valerie Steele, *The Corset: A Cultural* History (New Haven: Yale University Press, 2001), 157.

16 Germaine Daudet was a medical student at the University of Bordeaux during the war. Her thesis on female dress castigated the high, leather wartime shoes for imprisoning and deforming the feet. Germaine Daudet, *Le costume féminin et ses dangers,* thesis for medical school, Bordeaux, 1919, 113. Cited in Jean-Yves Le Naour, *Misères et tourments de la chair durant la Grande Guerre* (Paris: Aubier, 2002), 65.

17 "Sweeping Changes In Garments Decreed By Paris," *New York Times*, September 13, 1914.

18 "Will Barrel Skirt Provide New Silhouette?," *New York Times,* January 7, 1917.

19 Brachet-Champsaur, "De l'odalisque de Poiret a le femme nouvelle de Chanel," 205.

20 "Will Barrel Skirt Provide New Silhouette?," *New York Times,* January 7, 1917.

21 Only the Ardennes was under total German occupation; the Vosges and Meurthe-et-Moselle were semi-occupied and do not figure into the account. Reports in the National Archives suggest that even these regions suffered badly under the occupation. *Report on the Condition of Textile Industries in the Invaded Districts of France,* Archives Nationales, F/12/7686.

22 Aftalion, *L'industrie textile en France pendant la guerre*, 21.

23 See Annette Becker, *Oubliés de la Grande Guerre: Humanitaire et culture de guerre* (Paris: Noesis, 1998), introduction; John Horne and Alan Kramer, *German Atrocities, 1914–1997* (London: Cambridge University Press, 1998); Helen McPhail, *The Long Silence: Civilian Life Under the German Occupation of Northern France, 1914–1918* (London: I. B.Tauris, 1999).

24 *Report on the Condition of Textile Industries in the Invaded Districts of France,* Archives Nationales, F/12/7686.

25 David Hirsch, diary entry from July 1917, cited in Annette Becker, *Oubliés de la Grande Guerre,* 46.

26 John Reed, "German France," *Metropolitan Magazine,* New York, March 1915, cited in Annette Becker, *Oubliés de la Grande Guerre,* 46.

27 Maurice Delmotte, diary entry from May 4, 1917, cited in Nathalie Philippe, *Vie quotidienne en France occupée: journaux de Maurice Delmotte, 1914–1918* (Paris: L'Harmattan, 2007), 39.

28 David Hirsch, diary entry from December 29, 1917, cited in in Becker, *Oubliés de la Grande Guerre,* 38.

29 See McPhail, *The Long Silence,* and Becker, *Oubliés de la Grande Guerre.*

30 *Report on the Condition of Textile Industries in the Invaded Districts of France,* Archives Nationales, F/12/7686, 37. An estimation given by the cotton factory Thiriez Pere et Fils, based in Lille. The factory employed 32,500 workers before the war.

31 203,000 people were employed in textile industries of the Nord; 109,000 people were employed in the Ardennes, Pas-de-Calais, Somme, Aisne, and Marne. Taken together, the six departments employed a third of all French textile employees (312,000 people out of 914,000). Aftalion, *L'industrie textile en France pendant la guerre,* 8–9.

32 Raoul Blanchard, "L'effort industriel de Lyon pendant la guerre," *Revue de Géographie Alpine* (1919), 593–600.

33 Ibid., 595.

34 Prices gleaned from commercial catalogues for department stores archived at the Bibliothèque Forney.

35 See, for example, "Mouvement nouveau," *Chiffons,* January 20, 1917.

36 "Nouvelles de la mode," *Les Élégances Parisiennes,* April 1916.

37 "Moire Cire the French Novelty in Fabrics," *New York Times*, April 16, 1916.

38 Jersey, a plain-knit, elastic, ribbed fabric, usually made from wool, originated on the island of Jersey in the Middle Ages.

39 The manufacturer Rodier deposited a copyright in 1916 on a particular jersey made from wool and cashmere, which they called "Kasha."

40 "Jersey Cloth Among Ruling Fabrics," *New York Times*, April 8, 1917.

41 Aftalion, *L'industrie textile en France pendant la guerre,* 17.

42 Label dated October 4, 1915, sewn into a child's vest sold by the Belle Jardinière department store. Archived at the Palais Galliera. Cited in Brachet-Champsaur, "De l'odalisque de Poiret à la femme nouvelle de Chanel," 217.

43 "Quelques industriels et la guerre," *Les Élégances Parisiennes,* July 1916.

44 Hauser and Hitier, *Enquête sur la Production Française et la Concurrence Étrangère,* 312 ; *Rapport Général sur l'Industrie Française, sa situation, son avenir,* 682.

45 M. Vars, *Association générale du commerce et de l'industrie des tissus et des matières textiles. Conférence faite par M. Vars sur la Société suisse de surveillance économique (S.S.S.), 4 mars 1916* (Paris: Imprimerie de Levé), 13–16.

46 Hauser and Hitier, *Enquête sur la Production Française et la Concurrence Étrangère,* 312–15.

5a The Evolution of the Fashionable Silhouette, 1911–19

MAUDE BASS-KRUEGER

The "S-shape" silhouette gradually gave way to a softer, more natural silhouette in the early 1910s. FIG. 5a.1 Styles were still bust-heavy, but fabric fell loosely from the waistline instead of being pulled tight around the hips. The waistline rose during this period, with a revival of the Empire line; skirts began to taper around the bottom in the style of the "hobble skirt" popularized by Paul Poiret. By August 1914, Parisian designers were ready to launch a new, fuller silhouette, which they dubbed the "war crinoline." This dress by Callot Sœurs shows the evolution of this style during the first years of the war: the waistline had returned to its natural position, designs were simplified on top, and skirts were made full through the gathering of fabric. FIG. 5a.2a,b Hemlines rose to ankle or even calf-length. The silhouette changed again with the launch of the "barrel" line in 1917. A rare example of a "barrel" dress, this example by Weeks features the narrow hemline, higher waistline, and fullness around the hips typified by the style. FIG. 5a.3 By 1918, dresses had begun to draw away from the body, presaging the tubular style of the postwar period. FIGS. 5a.4–5a.8

FIG. 5a.1 Prewar woman's dress, 1911. Silk mousseline with silk embroidery, lace, metallic thread passementerie. Palais Galliera – musée de la Mode de la Ville de Paris, GAL 1971.61.1.

FIG. 5a.2a, b Callot Sœurs. Bell silhouette day dress, summer 1917. Silk charmeuse, filet lace, metallic flower.
The Museum at the Fashion Institute of Technology, Gift of Rosalie Davidson.

FIG. 5a.3 Weeks. Barrel silhouette evening dress, ca. 1918. Silk georgette, metallic beads, black seed beads. The Museum at the Fashion Institute of Technology, Gift of the Barnard College Theatre Co.

FIG. 5a.4 House of Worth. Postwar evening dress, 1918. Silk, metal, glass.
Chisholm Halle Costume Wing, Western Reserve Historical Society, Cleveland, Ohio, 83.19.7.

FIG. 5a.5 Madeleine Vionnet. Postwar dress, 1918. Crêpe de chine, velvet. Paris, Musée des Arts Décoratifs – collection UFAC, UF 52 18 19.

FIG. 5a.6 Madeleine Vionnet. Postwar evening dress, June 1918.
Silk satin, silk embroidery, mousseline de sole. Paris, Musée des Arts Décoratifs – collection UFAC, UF 52 18 9.

FIG. 5a.7 Callot Sœurs. Postwar evening dress, ca. 1919. Silk. The Museum at the Fashion Institute of Technology, Museum purchase.

FIG. 5a.8 Jeanne Lanvin. "Résurrection" dress, winter 1919-1920. Crêpe, velvet, glass beads. © Patrimoine Lanvin, Paris.

5b Selected Designs Registered for Copyright, 1917–19

MAUDE BASS-KRUEGER

These fashions designs and textile samples were deposited during the war for copyright purposes at the Prud'hommes de Paris, or Parisian Labor Court. The illustrations, swatches, and descriptions were supposed to protect the designers in case of copyright disputes. Housed in the Archives de Paris, these swatches provide valuable information about the nature and color of the textiles used by Parisian designers during the war. FIGS. 5b.1–5b.10

FIG. 5b.1 House of Worth. "Horizon" tailored suit in wool with silk trim and wooden buttons with textile sample for copyright deposit, February 14, 1918. Paper, ink, wool swatch. Archives de Paris, D12U10398 dépôt n° 4684 du 14 février 1918, n°8959. © Carole Rabourdin / Archives de Paris / Roger-Viollet, RV- 157094-3.

FIG. 5b.2 House of Worth. "Mobolisé" *(sic)* tailored suit in wool with textile sample for copyright deposit, March 26, 1917. Paper, ink, wool swatch. Archives de Paris, D12U10397 dépôt n° 4439 du 26 mars 1917, n°6337. © Carole Rabourdin / Archives de Paris / Roger-Viollet, RV-157094-1.

FIG. 5b.3 House of Worth. "Trotteur" coat in wool with wooden buttons and leather belt with textile sample for copyright deposit, February 14, 1918. Paper, ink, wool swatch. Archives de Paris, D12U10398 dépôt n° 4684 du 14 février 1918, n°8852. © Carole Rabourdin / Archives de Paris / Roger-Viollet, RV-157094-2.

FIG. 5b.4 House of Worth. "Panam" afternoon dress in silk with silk piping with textile sample for copyright deposit, February 21, 1918. Paper, ink, silk swatch. Archives de Paris, D12U10398 dépôt n° 4694 du 21 février 1918, n°1409. © Carole Rabourdin / Archives de Paris / Roger-Viollet, RV-157094-5.

FIG. 5b.5 House of Worth. "Camargo" evening dress in jersey silk with jet embroidery with textile sample for copyright deposit, February 10, 1919. Paper, ink, jersey swatch. Archives de Paris, D12U10399 dépôt n° 4850 du 10 février 1919. © Carole Rabourdin / Archives de Paris / Roger-Viollet, RV-157094-6.

FIG. 5b.6 House of Worth. "Footing" dress in jersey with textile sample for copyright deposit, February 10, 1919. Paper, ink, jersey swatch. Archives de Paris, D12U10399 dépôt n° 4850 du 10 février 1919. © Carole Rabourdin / Archives de Paris / Roger-Viollet, RV-157094-7.

FIG. 5b.7 House of Worth. "Rosinette" coat with textile sample for copyright deposit, February 14, 1918. Archives de Paris: *Modèle Rosinette* (dépôt n°4684, 14 février 1918, n° de modèle dans la collection : A0256, n° de modèle dans le dépôt : 44) D12U10 398. © Archives de Paris / Roger-Viollet, RV 203794-15.

FIG. 5b.8 House of Worth. "Vauban" coat with textile sample for copyright deposit, February 14, 1918. Archives de Paris: Modèle *Vauban* (dépôt n°4684, 14 février 1918, n° de modèle dans la collection : 8961, n° de modèle dans le dépôt : 40) D12U10 398. © Archives de Paris / Roger-Viollet, RV-203794-16.

FIG. 5b.9 House of Worth. "Kiri" ensemble with textile sample for copyright deposit, February 14, 1918. Archives de Paris: Modèle *Kiri* (dépôt n°4684, 14 février 1918, n° de modèle dans la collection : 6367, n° de modèle dans le dépôt : 24) D12U10 398. © Archives de Paris / Roger-Viollet, RV-203794-12.

FIG. 5b.10 House of Worth. "Madelon" ensemble with textile sample for copyright deposit, February 14, 1918. Archives de Paris: *Modèle Madelon* (dépôt n°4684, 14 février 1918, n° de modèle dans la collection : 6369, n° de modèle dans le dépôt : 25) D12U10 398. © Archives de Paris / Roger-Viollet, RV-203794-11.

5c Jeanne Paquin, Jeanne Lanvin, Jenny, and Gabrielle Chanel, 1914–18

SOPHIE KURKDJIAN

The calls for mobilization at the start of the war did not spare Parisian couturiers. Paul Poiret, Jean Patou, and the Maison Worth all shut their doors at the start of the war as their designers were called to serve their nation.[1] Although the houses eventually reopened after a few months—the designers continued to serve while overseeing their businesses from the front—their departure initially left a vacuum. Mobilization raises several questions about the status of the couture industry during the war. Most importantly, did women designers step back in to take the lead in the Parisian fashion scene during this time? What impact did the war have specifically on women designers? It would be facile to assume that the war allowed women designers to replace the men, much as the *remplaçantes* replaced their male counterparts in other sectors. The reality is more complicated. Aside from Gabrielle Chanel, who rose to prominence as a fashion designer during the war, the leading Parisian female couturiers were all well-established designers before the war, some of them as early as the turn of the century.[2] Jeanne Lanvin, Jeanne Paquin, Jenny Sacerdote (whose real name was Jeanne Bernard and whose couture house was called Jenny), the Boué Sœurs (Sylvie Montegut and Baronne Jeanne d'Etreillis), Jeanne Margaine-Lacroix, Callot Sœurs (Marie Callot-Gerber, Marthe Callot-Bertrand, Regina Callot-Tennyson-Chantrell, and Joséphine Callot Crimont), and Louise Chéruit were all heads of large international businesses. It would be naïve to think that the war had no impact on the way these women ran their businesses or on the way that female designers were covered by the press during the conflict. Focusing on Jeanne Paquin, Jeanne Lanvin, Jenny, and Gabrielle Chanel provides an overview of the wartime activities and designs of four of the leading French women couturiers. This summary reveals how the war shaped their professional identities and the specific contributions they made to the critical issue of protecting the rights of Parisian couturiers.

At the beginning of the war, in the November 1914 issue, *Vogue* depicts accurately the prominence of women designers in Paris in an article by Anne Rittenhouse entitled "The Women Who Create the Mode in Paris." French women "govern the fashion destinies of many continents that they have never seen."[3] Although Rittenhouse gave more attention to the lives and personalities of these women rather than to what they were creating, their importance in the profession before the war in France was made clear.[4] Many of them who had begun their careers modeling clothes were now the heads of major fashion houses that were helping the French economy as they earned millions of francs of revenue. Furthermore, they guided the fashion choices of thousands of women.[5] *Vogue* praised Jeanne Paquin for having both a man's will and "masculine business knowhow" and noted that as a "genius of business organization," men did not dare challenge her.[6] Louise Chéruit, who was as influential as Paquin, was described as an astute judge of style and business and as a good money manager. The "legendary" Callot Sœurs were in a class of their own: wealthy and hardworking, they managed more than fifteen hundred employees and maintained strict standards. The *Vogue* article also briefly described Jeanne Lanvin as an established couturier, and the up-and-coming designer Jenny Sacerdote, who was a promising businesswoman.[7]

Jeanne Paquin, Jeanne Lanvin, and Jenny Sacerdote emerged from the war as well-established designers and experienced businesswomen, and Gabrielle Chanel was beginning a promising career. All four continued to develop their respective activities after the war, although Paquin stopped managing her company in 1920 (she died in 1936) and Sacerdote left her role in 1938, after being awarded the Légion d'Honneur in 1926. At the height of Lanvin's career between the world wars, she developed different departments devoted to sportswear, interior decoration, perfume, and menswear. Gabrielle Chanel's practical style and sportswear, emblematic of feminine modernity, defined the interwar period.

Jeanne Paquin

Founded as Paquin, Lalanne et Cie in 1889, and renamed Paquin in 1891, Jeanne Paquin's couture business, located at 3, rue de la Paix in Paris (in addition to a registered office located in London starting in 1896), had already been open for twenty-three years at the outbreak of war in 1914.[8] She became director of the company in 1907 after the death of her husband, Isidore Paquin, and contributed substantially to its success while developing her own artistic and commercial interests.[9] FIG. 5c.1

Indicative of her rather remarkable rise to fame, the 1915 book *Makers of New France* by Charles Dawbarn called her one of the most important people in France alongside the prime ministers Raymond Poincaré and Georges Clémenceau.[10] In 1911 Paquin collaborated with the artists George Barbier, Paul Iribe, and Georges Lepape on an exclusive fashion album called *L'Éventail et la*

MME. PAQUIN.

FIG. 5c.1 Portrait of Jeanne Paquin from *Makers of New France* by Charles Dawbarn. (London: Mills & Boon, limited, 1915), 208. Archive.org.

FIG. 5c.2 Paul Iribe. Plate from *L'Éventail et la Fourrure chez Paquin* (*The Fan and Furs by Paquin*) (Paris: Maquet, 1911). Pochoir over lithograph. Fashion Institute of Technology SUNY, FIT Library Special Collections and College Archives, New York.

Fourrure chez Paquin (The Fan and Furs by Paquin).[11] FIG. 5c.2

An accomplished costume designer for theater, Paquin worked with Léon Bakst and the Ballets Russes in 1912. During this prewar moment of considerable prosperity, she expanded the couture business abroad and opened a boutique in Buenos Aires in 1911 and a fur boutique in 1912 on Fifth Avenue in New York City. In 1913, she was awarded the Légion d'Honneur for her artistry and business acumen in the field of fashion design.[12] The following year, Paquin established a new shop in Madrid.[13] In the years before the outbreak of the First World War, both the French and American fashion press, especially *Vogue* and *Women's Wear Daily*, covered Jeanne Paquin both as a business woman and designer.[14] Paquin entered the war fully aware of the international commercial and economic stakes, and like many Parisian couturiers she focused on the American market. In 1915, Paquin signed a contract with *Women's Wear Daily* that gave the publication exclusive rights to preview her collections.[15] She also participated in the 1915 Panama–Pacific International Exposition in San Francisco where she showed a tailored suit and a *tilleul* (pale yellow-green) French crêpe dress with veiled draping across the chest and metallic roses dotting the skirt. FIG. 5c.3 According to *La Gazette du Bon Ton*, the lush ensemble was complemented by a dark taffeta bolero "barely covering the bust" and a supple hat.[16] While the war raged on in France, *La Gazette du Bon Ton* extolled Paquin's originality, claiming that she had reinvented fashion for the "postwar" woman. The dresses in her 1915 collection were slightly gathered at the hips, unstructured at the waist, and loose around the ankles, allowing women to "run" and "closely attend to those suffering and offer consolation."[17] Among the other designs shown in San Francisco were another dress, an evening coat, two dresses for young women, and a ballgown in silver lace that was embroidered in shades of "bleu de France" and had required the work of twelve seamstresses.[18] The San Francisco Exposition of Paquin's work evoked two sides of her creativity. She both understood the changing needs of women during the war while nurturing the French tradition of luxury that appealed to upper-class women in the United States.

Then in the fall of 1915, Paquin exhibited a collection that included two evening gowns, three morning dresses, and two afternoon dresses at the Fête Parisienne in New York. Similar to San Francisco, the event featured highly elaborate designs meant to appeal to the foreign clientele. FIG. 5c.4 Roses adorned the hem of the pleated skirt of a navy-blue taffeta afternoon dress by Paquin, called "Séduction." The pink muslin guimpe, or blouse, fell from a wide standing collar and square neckline.[19] Paquin utilized luxurious materials on her evening gowns: the one called "Loin du Bal" (Far from the Ball) was made of pink taffeta. Another even more elaborate dress, called "Manon," had luxurious silver lace with green and pink wool embroidery on pink and a corsage of crystal and sapphire. Paquin's interest in fur seen earlier in the drawings she made for *L'Éventail et la Fourrure chez Paquin* was evident in the use of blue-dyed fox trim on the pink-tinted ivory velvet "small visiting suit" that was shown with a matching muff.[20]

At the height of the war in 1917, Paquin continued to show her new collections abroad while serving the war effort. In Madrid that year, luxury prevailed in the black satin crêpe dress embroidered with bright red beads and a navy blue silk dress embroidered with Japanese motifs.[21] Photographs of Paquin's designs deposited in August 1917 and February 1918 for copyright purposes at the Prud'hommes de Paris, or Paris Labor Office, show that Paquin's designs had incorporated many of the most typical silhouettes of wartime fashions: ankle-length tailored suits, apron-front dresses, sailor-style collars, and smart vests and coats with military-like features and prominent pockets.[22]

FIGS. 5c.5–5c.13

Paquin also retooled her factory to make uniforms for the American army. The workers were initially skeptical but they soon adapted to producing clothing on a mass scale. According to *Women's Wear Daily*, Paquin's decision to adopt American manufacturing techniques would bring "revolutionary changes to the French clothing industry." Specifically, seamstresses would use the faster methods needed to produce mass-produced designs instead of the couture sewing methods.

During the war, Jeanne Paquin was active in two couture trade organizations. She was a member of the Syndicat de Défense de la Grande Couture Française as early as 1914 and became president of the Chambre Syndicale de la Couture Parisienne in July 1917.[23] Paquin directed the Chambre Syndicale at a moment of considerable strife. During the strike of the *midinettes* (couture seamstresses), she replaced Jean Aine-Montaillé, who had resigned two months earlier.

SEE CHAPTER 6

Les Élégances Parisiennes welcomed the news, stressing that Paquin was the most qualified person for the job of representing Parisian couture both in France and abroad. *Women's Wear Daily* wrote that the election of a woman to the head of the Chambre was an acknowledgment of Paquin's "genius,"

IL PLEUT ENCORE...

Tailleurs de Paquin, Lanvin, Dœuillet, Manteau de Paquin

FIG. 5c.3 "It's still raining: tailored suits by Paquin, Lanvin, Dœuillet, coat by Paquin," *La Gazette du Bon Ton*, Summer 1915. © Bibliothèque Forney / Roger Viollet, RV-2154-3.

LE STYLE PARISIEN

WORTH (Fig. 307). *CHÉRUIT (Fig. 308).* *PAQUIN (Fig. 309).* *CHÉRUIT (Fig. 310).*

LA "FÊTE PARISIENNE" A NEW-YORK

FIG. 5c.4 Dartey, pseudonym of Anette Osterlind. Dresses by Worth, Chéruit, and Paquin for "La Fête Parisienne à New-York," *Le Style Parisien,* July 1916, pl. XI. © Bibliothèque nationale de France, UMP-12465.

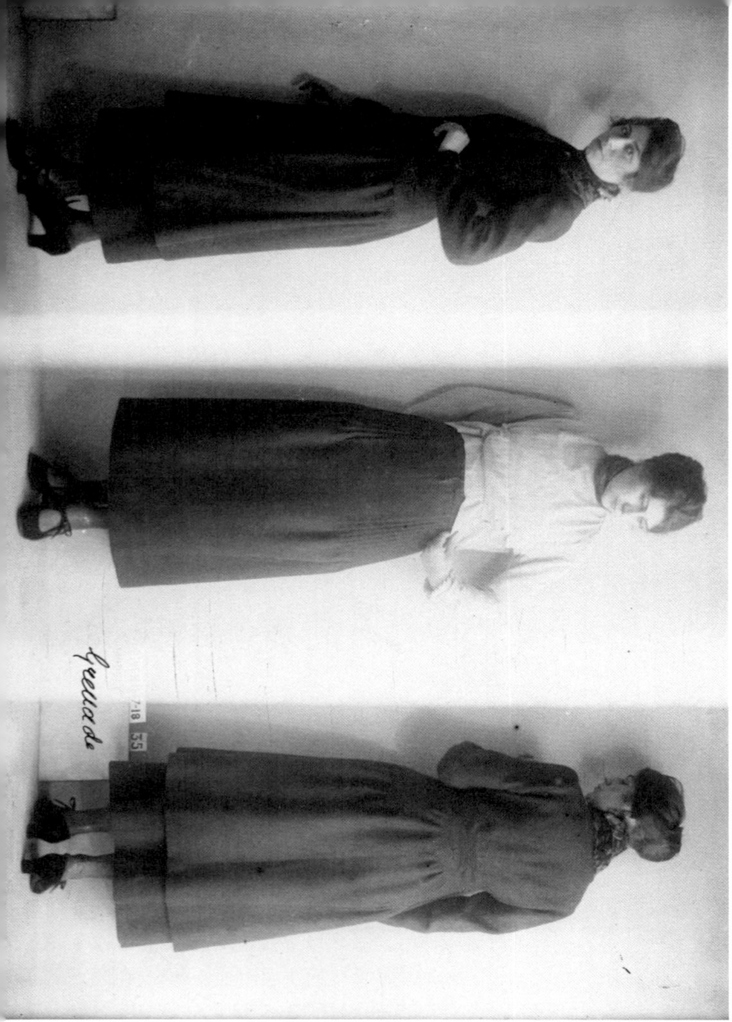

FIG. 5c.6 Jeanne Paquin. "Grenade" tailored suit in cheviot wool and crêpe de chine blouse for copyright deposit, August 13, 1917. Silver gelatin print. © Archives de Paris / Roger-Viollet, RV-101321-28.

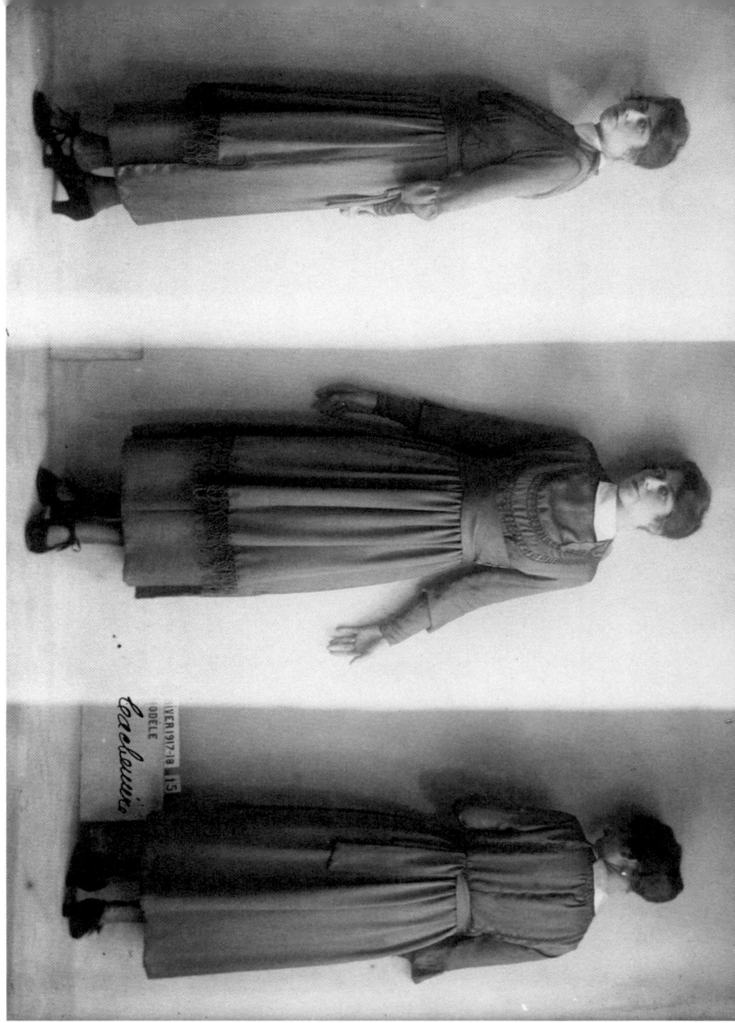

FIG. 5c.5 Jeanne Paquin. "Cachemire" afternoon dress in crêpe de chine, silk braids, cashmere fringes, and silk for copyright deposit, February 14, 1917. Silver gelatin print. © Archives de Paris / Roger-Viollet, RV-101320-25.

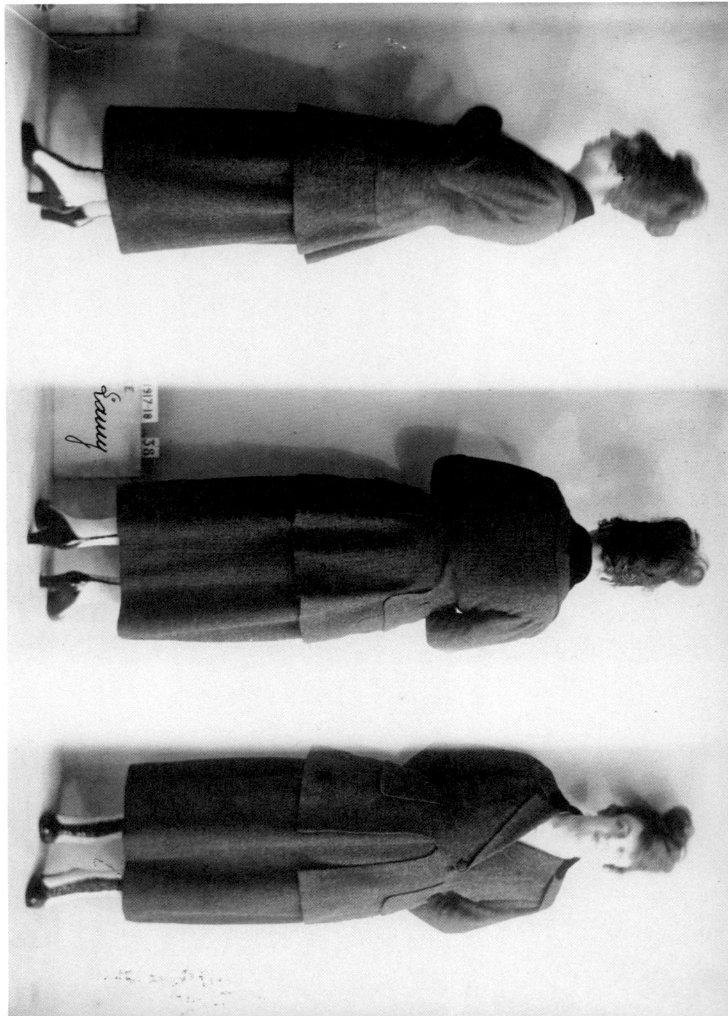

FIG. 5c.7 Jeanne Paquin. "Lamy" tailored suit in wool for copyright deposit, August 13, 1917. Silver gelatin print. © Archives de Paris / Roger-Viollet, RV-101322-1.

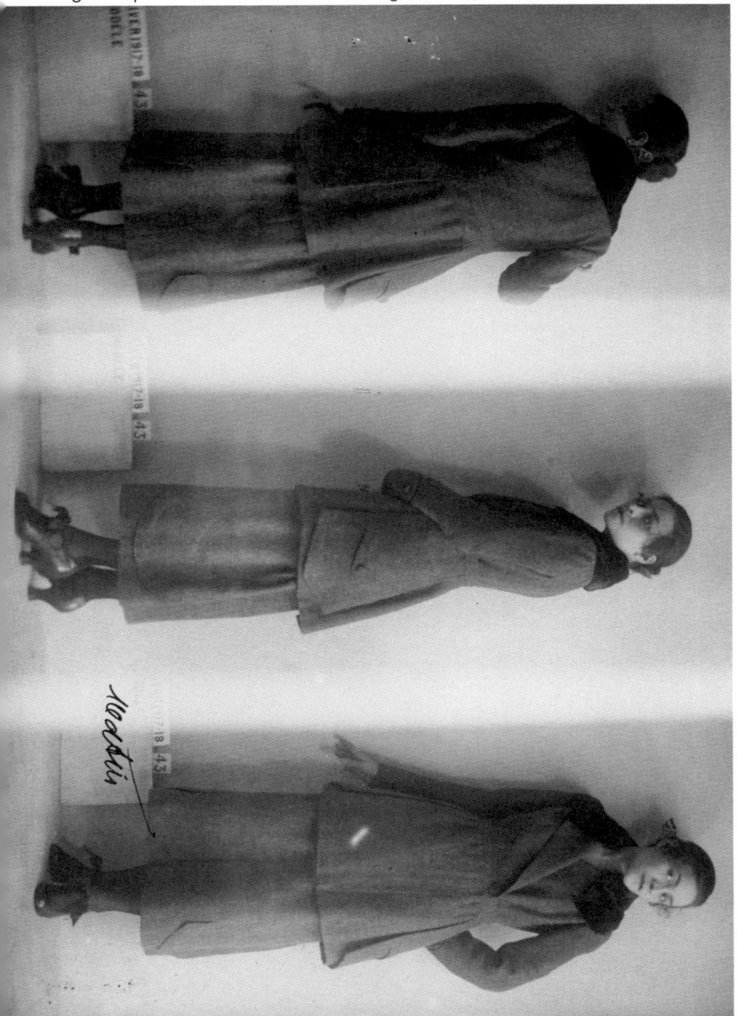

FIG. 5c.8 Jeanne Paquin. "Matin" tailored suit in wool with beaver and otter fur collar for copyright deposit, August 13, 1917. Silver gelatin print. © Archives de Paris / Roger-Viollet, RV-101322-7.

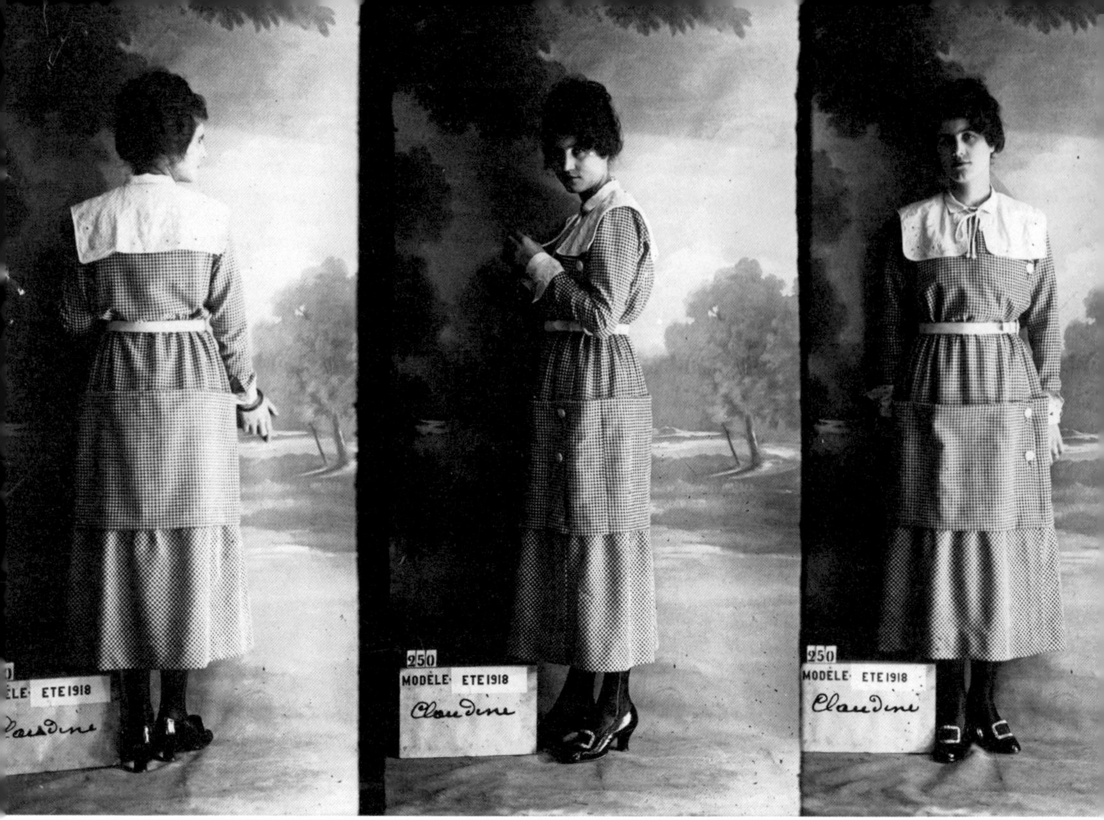

FIG. 5c.9 Jeanne Paquin. "Claudine" dress for copyright deposit, February 21 1918. Silver gelatin print. © Archives de Paris / Roger-Viollet, RV-101330-21.

FIG. 5c.10 Jeanne Paquin. "Kiki" tailored suit for copyright deposit, February 21, 1918. Silver gelatin print. © Archives de Paris / Roger-Viollet, RV-101327-30.

FIG. 5c.11 Jeanne Paquin. Photograph of "Matelassé" tailored suit for copyright deposit, August 13, 1917. Silver gelatin print. © Archives de Paris / Roger-Viollet, RV-101321-2.

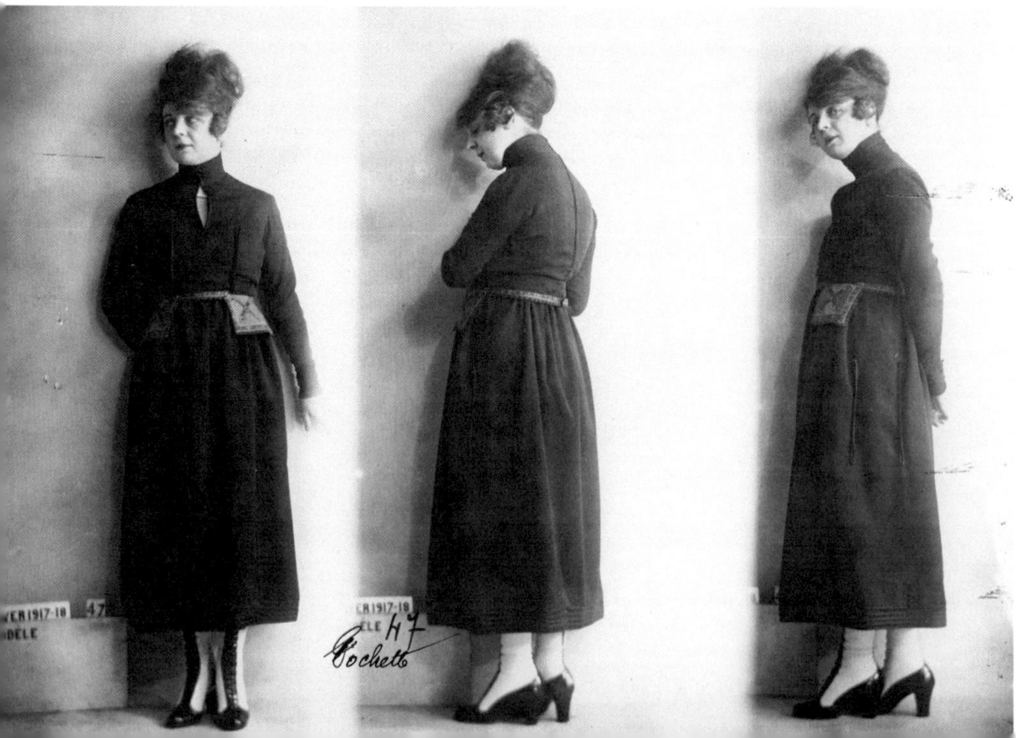

FIG. 5c.12 Jeanne Paquin. Photograph of "Pochette" dress for copyright deposit, August 13, 1917. Silver gelatin print. © Archives de Paris / Roger-Viollet, RV-101322-13.

FIG. I-10 Paquin. "Marmouset" afternoon dress in blue poplin for copyright deposit, August 13, 1917. Silver gelatin print. © Archives de Paris / Roger-Viollet, RV-101320-1.

FIG. 5c.13 Jeanne Paquin. Photograph of "Prélat" tailored suit for copyright deposit, August 13, 1917. Silver gelatin print. © Archives de Paris / Roger-Viollet, RV-101323-4.

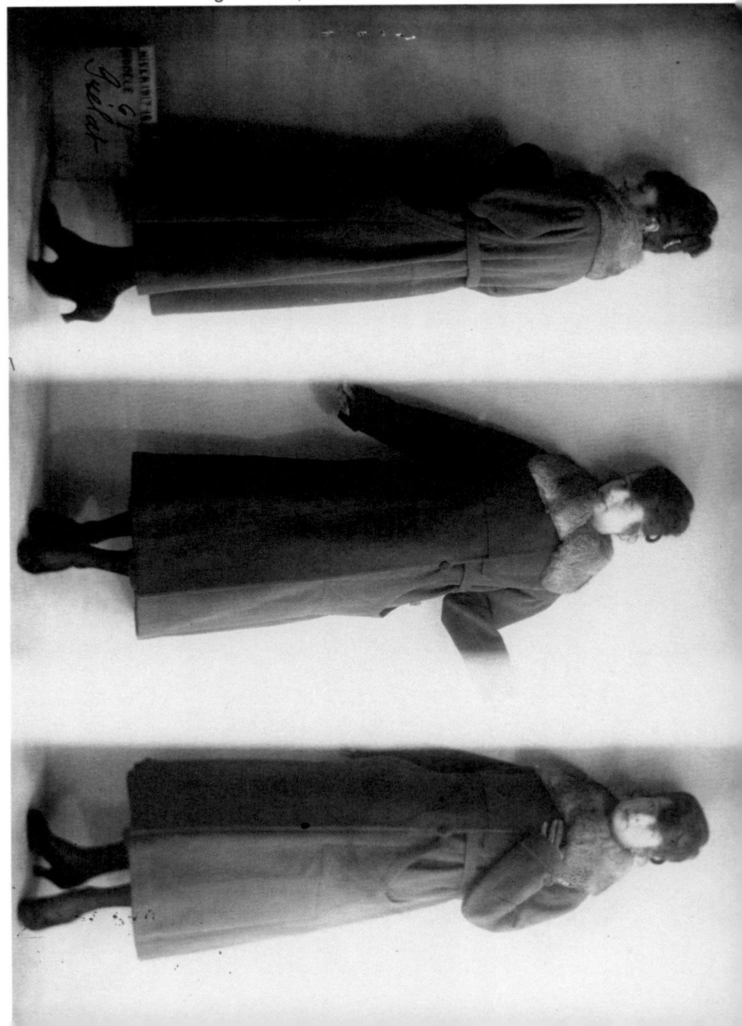

and *Les Modes* also applauded the Chambre's homage to Paris couture and this "great step toward feminism."[24] The motivation behind the nomination was not only that a woman was more capable of helping the women who constituted the majority of the organization's membership, but also that Paquin in particular, who had worked as both a seamstress and a model, understood the plight of fashion workers. Her first actions as president of the Chambre confirmed this idea: she supported the demands of the strike and hailed the actions of the seamstresses as those of "free women."[25] When the strike ended, she founded the Caisse de Défense Patronale and the Commission Permanente des Conflits (Employer's Defense Fund and the Standing Committee on Conflicts).[26] However, even Paquin soon understood the complexities of her position as the strikers' demands expanded, from the issue of termination notification in November 1917, a call for an increased cost-of-living allowance in January 1918, and overtime compensation in March 1918. She also endured personal attacks by some of the strikers who were suspicious of her ascent through the ranks of the couture industry, claiming that she must have made too many compromises or have been dishonest to have reached her position.[27] Although Paquin had previously been praised by workers, public opinion turned against her after the war. When claims were made that she had been responsible for the death of one of her employees, Paquin resigned from the Chambre presidency on July 17, 1920.

Jeanne Lanvin Jeanne Lanvin's fashion career began in 1885 when she opened a store called "Lanvin (Mlle Jeanne) Modes" on the Faubourg Saint-Honoré in Paris where she sold hats. Four years later, in 1889, she expanded and opened a fashion house at 16, rue Boissy d'Anglas. FIGS. 5c.14 Initially Lanvin designed clothes for children, but her real success as a fashion designer came in 1909, when she launched her first collection for girls and women.[28] It was then that she joined the Chambre Syndicale.[29] Recognized for their fine craftsmanship and rich color palette, her collections were frequently covered by the French and American press. In 1915, *Vogue* described her as a "couture artist" and a "creative genius."[30] Another French journalist in *Le Figaro* described her work as distinctly "Parisian" and acknowledged that the most renowned women abroad and in France wanted Jeanne Lanvin to dress them.[31] In 1918 *Le Figaro* asked: "Who does not know that intense and warm blue that bears her name?"[32] Following a difficult transition when war broke out in August 1914, the Lanvin fashion house was one of the most ambitious and well-equipped in Paris during the conflict.[33] There were nine ateliers—five dedicated to couture, two to embroidery, one to hats, and another to drawing—and a large staff that included seven models and several hundred workers (as many as 370 in 1917). FIGS. 5c.15, 5c.16 Problems meeting demand meant that Lanvin had to postpone the launch of her collection for American buyers to January 1915 with a promise to have them ready for export in September that year.[34] Recognizing that there would be a delay, she encouraged her American clients to visit the Lanvin shop on the rue Faubourg Saint-Honoré. Ultimately, the spring 1915 Lanvin collection was a success: *Women's Wear Daily* called it the best Parisian collection and the best the designer had made to date.[35] Like other couturiers, Lanvin drew inspiration from military uniforms and other prevalent wartime dress, such as nurses' uniforms.[36] She adopted the "war crinoline" silhouette in the summer of 1914 to what she later called the "robe de style," an emblematic outfit of the 1920s.[37] FIG. 5c.17 Her 1916 "Bersaglière" suit in green mouflon (wild sheep's wool) with stitched piping, double collar, red woolen jacket and cuffs, and gold buttons was based on the uniform of an Italian infantryman.[38] Her "Gouraud" coat paid homage to the Dardanelles campaign commander Henri Joseph Eugène Gouraud, and she named the "vieux bleu" dress from 1917–18 "Loin du Front" (Far from the Front). In 1916, Lanvin created a special ensemble for a wealthy client that combined ivory silk twill typical of couture ensembles with a knotted sky-blue sailor collar of a nurse's uniform, and a buckled armband and badge reminiscent of the air force with two bird wings and an airplane propeller. FIG. 5c.18a, b These designs diluted the reality of wartime.[39] Allusions to wartime patriotism are also evident in other Lanvin designs such as her "Madame" day dress introduced in 1917, and in the way she developed the embroidery techniques that became characteristic of her work.[40] FIG. 5c.19 Made of night-blue silk georgette crêpe, the "Madame" dress is embellished with Cornelli machine embroidery in the colors of the French flag. The lush Lanvin blue and interplay between opacity and transparency on the back highlights the geometric embroidery. A simply cut dress with pockets, this design represents the simplification of women's silhouettes during the war that still retained aspects of luxury, particularly the embroidery, that were associated with Parisian couture. The label

FIG. 5c.14 Jeanne Lanvin, ca. 1934. Silver gelatin print. © Harcourt Studio / Patrimoine Lanvin, Paris.

FIG. 5c.15 Jeanne Lanvin. "Feuille Morte" dress, summer 1914. Silk. © Patrimoine Lanvin, Paris.

FIG. 5c.16 Jeanne Lanvin. "Feuille Morte" dress, summer 1914. Graphite with ink and gouache. © Patrimoine Lanvin, Paris.

FIG. 5c.17 Jeanne Lanvin. "Greuze" Robe de Style, 1919. Graphite with ink and gouache. © Patrimoine Lanvin, Paris.

FIG. 5c.18a, b Jeanne Lanvin. Nurse ensemble dress in two parts created for a wealthy client, summer 1916. Ivory silk twill. © Paris, Musée des Arts décoratifs, UF-88-60.

FIG. 5c.19 Jeanne Lanvin. "Madame" dress in French national colors, perhaps designed for Lanvin herself, 1916. Crêpe, crêpe georgette, Cornely machine embroidery. © Patrimoine Lanvin, Paris.

FIG. 5c.20 Jeanne Lanvin. Simplified label in "Madame" dress, 1917.
© Patrimoine Lanvin, Paris.

and the size, forty-four, suggest that Lanvin likely designed the "Madame" dress for herself. FIG. 5c.20 Other examples of Lanvin embroidery are similarly patriotic, with the colors and symbols of France, such as a French rooster. FIGS. 5c.21, 5c.22 Beaded embroidery on the front, on the collar, and on shoulders was a feature of many wartime designs by Lanvin.[41] FIGS. 5c.23–5c.25

The press regularly discussed the numerous variations she created using embroidery and color that transformed even the simplest designs, such as shirtwaist dresses.[42] FIG. 5c.26

In addition to the Chambre Syndicale, Jeanne Lanvin also joined the Syndicat to fight against copying. A victim of counterfeiting, she registered her designs with the Conseil des Prud'hommes as early as 1916 to protect them from being copied.

As the copyright did not protect her models from either unfair competition or foreign competition, Lanvin joined the Syndicat with the hope of helping establish a copyright system for fashion. From the start of the war, the Syndicat had sought to establish a copyright system to protect Parisian couture. SEE CHAPTER 6 After discussion with American buyers, the organization considered implementing "the official authentication of models and the management of reproduction rights for the members of the SDGC," namely "the adaptation of current reproduction rights to Grande Couture," like those in effect for literature, music, design, painting, and sculpture.[43] In concrete terms, every copy of a model sold to an individual client would be marked with the "original label of the fashion house that designed it and an indication that the reproduction of that design had been authorized by the Syndicat." Very few archives document this initiative or allow for research into its enforcement, but two of the original designs by Lanvin for the summer of 1917 and the winter of 1918 have a special tag with the Jeanne Lanvin label stamped alongside the seal of the SDGCF, its letters interlaced, which suggests that the system was enforced and put to the test by designers.[44] FIG. 5c.27 During the war, because many aristocrats and families of soldiers had taken refuge in Deauville, Jeanne Lanvin opened a boutique there on rue Gontaut-Biron; she also opened one in Biarritz at 7, place de la Liberté in June 1918. On June 18, 1918, *Le Figaro* remarked that the dresses, garments, and hats sold in Lanvin's Deauville store were far more beautiful than fashions being sold by other couture houses in Paris.[45] An album of designs from the store in Biarritz, a resort town on the Atlantic coast reveals that all of the stores sold the same clothes.[46] FIG. 5c.28

Lanvin participated in the promotion of French couture abroad by exhibiting in fairs and fashion salons throughout the war. In 1917, she sent about one hundred hats to the Foire de Lyon and to an exhibition in Madrid.[47] She also continued to build a clientele in the United States. Together with other Parisian couturiers, she sent several designs to the San Francisco Panama–Pacific International Exposition in 1915 and displayed several others ("Buffalo," "Musette," "Velazquez," "Escurial," "Peau-d'âne") at the Fête Parisienne in New York that same year. *Le Style Parisien* photographed the designs and reported on what was exhibited and sold there.[48] One journalist covering the exhibition asked,

And what about the very stylish two dresses by Lanvin? . . . Flat in front and back so as to appear very wide when facing forward and very narrow when in profile, their line is entirely new and unexpected. I am very fond of the combination of black tulle trimmed with ribbon and silver embroidery; and I'm mad about the transparent sleeves![49]

FIG. 5c.29

Among the designs Lanvin sent to New York were garments that integrated the different influences that emerged from the war with characteristics that had become typical of the "Lanvin style." A blue twill dress in Rodier fabric, with two large pleats in front and three in back, featured cherry, gray, and blue wool stitching embroidery with silver thread. The dress combines embroidery (the Jeanne Lanvin trademark), patriotism (through the use of blue, white, and red), and Lanvin blue.[50] FIG. 5c.30 Her "Ariane" suit, made of black faille, trimmed with gray beaver and embellished with taffeta frog closures at the bottom of the skirt, is at once a war crinoline silhouette and a tailored suit—two of the most popular wartime designs. The details, notably the trim, convey the influence that the military uniform had on women's civilian clothing.[51] FIGS. 5c.31, 5c.32

Jenny

The less well-known fashion house Jenny was also founded before the war, in 1909, by Jenny Sacerdote, née Jeanne Bernard, who was a saleswoman at the couture house Béchoff-David & Cie before she opened her own company.[52] FIG. 5c.33 Her first store, located on the rue Castiglione in Paris, moved to the Avenue des Champs-Élysées in 1915. FIG. 5c.34 That year *Vogue* called Jenny a "new star in the Parisian constellation of fashion houses.[53] The young company became a member of the Syndicat de Défense de la Grande Couture Française in 1915.[54] During the war, Jenny received considerable press attention. Fashion journalists often described her clothes as "simple" and adapted to wartime.[55]

FIG. 5c.21 Jeanne Lanvin. Embroidery sample of the Gallic rooster (an unofficial symbol of France) in national colors, 1918. Beaded and rhinestone sequins on silk. © Patrimoine Lanvin, Paris.

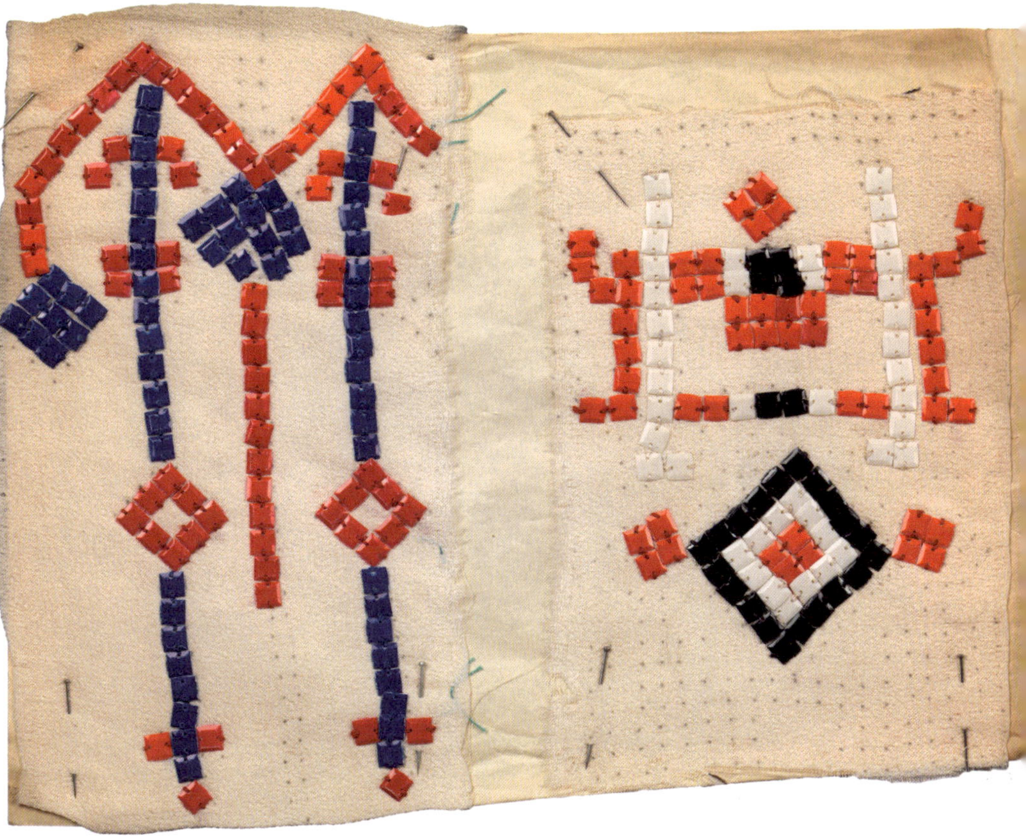

FIG. 5c.22 Jeanne Lanvin. Embroidery as in this sample often embellished the collars and shoulders of Lanvin's wartime designs. Colored metal or cellulose acetate on crepe, 1918. © Patrimoine Lanvin, Paris.

FIG. 5c.23 Jeanne Lanvin. "Saxe" dress with embroidery around the sleeves, tie, and skirt, summer 1917. Crêpe. © Patrimoine Lanvin, Paris, JL n°269.

FIG. 5c.24 Jeanne Lanvin. Dress with elaborate beadwork on the bodice, skirt, and hem, winter 1917. Crêpe, satin. © Patrimoine Lanvin, Paris, JL N°377.

FIG. 5c.25 Lanvin tailored suit in navy serge trimmed with red, blue, and gold stitching and satin dress with lapel embroidery in black pearls. "Robes Simples, Lanvin," *Les Élégances Parisiennes*, October 1916, pl. V. © Bibliothèque nationale de France.

MME. LANVIN IN BUSINESS HOURS

A Couturière to Whom Work-time Is Play-time, So Natural Is Her Liking for the Designing of Tempting Models

Photograph by Talbot.

Mme. Jeanne Lanvin, designer first for children's frocks and now designer for the world, is herself of irrepressible youth and charm

IN the old rue du Faubourg Saint Honoré, not more than a stone's throw from the rue Royale, Mme. Jeanne Lanvin began, about twenty-two years ago, to create fashions for young girls and children. And so marvelously did she succeed that for years now the Maison Lanvin has been one of the leading dressmaking houses of Paris.

Mme. Lanvin chose for her salons an old hotel and remodeled it to suit her needs, which are manifold. Her salons she made gray, with large mirrors effectively placed. There are gray carpets and gray chairs, and the walls are hung with quaint fashion-plates from the *Journaux des Modes* of years ago. Clad in tight bodice and crinoline, these pictured ladies simper and smile at each other across the rooms. And it is evident that these old engravings have often inspired Mme. Lanvin in the creation of new fashions for the younger generation.

FASHION "COMME IL FAUT"

"Never," says Mme. Lanvin, "have the fashions been so pretty, so becoming to the young, and so *comme il faut*."

It is Mme. Lanvin's idea to continue to frock girls and young women in skirts short and very wide. Just now her skirts are very short, but a trifle less wide at the hem than they were early in the season. She prefers linon to organdy, and borders her frocks of white, pink, and pale blue linon with narrow bands of fur.

"And the petticoat?" one asks. Mme. Lanvin employs the petticoat, but not the voluminous fluffy affair worn by our grandmothers. The Lanvin petticoat is of small dimensions, and is made of very thin and dainty fabrics—silk, linon, or *voile de soie*.

The autumn frocks from the Maison Lanvin will be made of serge and gabardine—principally serge. Owing to the war, these stuffs are difficult to procure, but fortunately Mme. Lanvin has secured a plentiful supply of both.

A THOUSAND ARTISTIC TRIFLES

The creative genius of Mme. Lanvin does not find sufficient outlet in the making of frocks, but overflows into all kinds of bibelots—bags, fans, dolls, lace table-covers, lamp- and candle-shades, and a hundred pretty trifles of silk and embroidery. In her embroideries Mme. Lanvin uses many beads; her shelves are filled with odd bits of beadwork which she introduces into her smartest frocks.

The separate bead motifs now so popular for hat trimmings and motifs on collars and sleeves first appeared in Mme. Lanvin's pretty shop. And every one should have a bead bag from the Maison Lanvin. One of the most effective bags of the entire season is her bag on this page. The foundation is of *drap de fantaisie* and the embroidery is in beads, mostly black and emerald green; the bead tassel is black.

Mme. Lanvin possesses the rare gift of stamping her models with an intangible bit of her own personality. Nothing banal ever appears in her establishment. The lamp-shade sketched below, with its encompassing, crystal-tipped yellow drapery, is an example of her artistic trifles. The base is painted white.

The première of the Maison Lanvin herself posed in this frock, for it was designed for Vogue. In it dark blue taffeta is banded with blue "voile de soie." Collar and cuffs are of light blue muslin

Mme. Lanvin uses such bits of beadwork as this in beige with pink and green roses, as belts on linen and serge frocks—a fashion to be heeded, as Mme. Lanvin initiated the bead-motif fashion

A treasure to hold treasures is this bead bag of emerald and black with pink roses. Bag and handle are lined with green silk

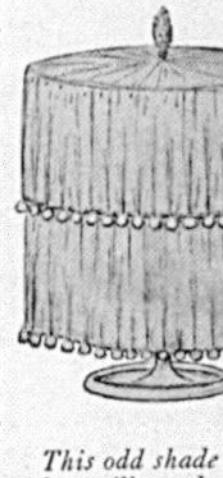

This odd shade of yellow silk and crystal drops glows friendlily

Salons of gray has Mme. Lanvin, delicate settings for the old prints on the walls, for the manikins, and for the dainty bits of laces and beads and embroidery such as appear on the shelves of this second-floor salon. The manikin is frocked in a dark blue taffeta gown embroidered in white

FIG. 5c.26 Article about Mme. Jeanne Lanvin's salon on the rue de Faubourg Saint Honoré, where shelves are filled with bits of beadwork that she incorporates into her designs. "Mme. Lanvin in Business Hours," *Vogue*, July 15, 1915, 45. © Condé Nast.

FIG. 5c.27 Jeanne Lanvin. SDGCF label in cotton dress, summer 1917. Brooklyn Museum Costume Collection at The Metropolitan Museum of Art, Gift of the Brooklyn Museum, 2009; Gift of Jill Failey, 1985, 2009.300.8110a, b.

FIG. 5c.28 Jeanne Lanvin. "Voyageuse" cloak pattern, 1918. Graphite with ink and gouache. © Diktats bookstore.

FIG. 5c.29 Francine. "Buffalo" and "Musette" dresses by Jeanne Lanvin exhibited and sold during La Fête Parisienne in New York. "Lettres d'une Parisienne," *Le Style Parisien*, November 1915, 25. © Bibliothèque Forney / Roger-Viollet, RV-157813-12.

LE STYLE PARISIEN

CHÉRUIT (Fig. 274). *LANVIN (Fig. 275).* *CHÉRUIT (Fig. 276).*

LA "FÊTE PARISIENNE" A NEW-YORK

FIG. 5c.30 Illustration of models by Lanvin entitled "A Celebration of Paris in New York." *Le Style Parisien*, November 1915, pl. III. © Bibliothèque nationale de France, NUMP-12465.

LE STYLE PARISIEN

LANVIN (Fig. 183). CHÉRUIT (Fig. 184). PAQUIN (Fig. 185).

LA "FÊTE PARISIENNE" A NEW-YORK

FIG. 5c.31 Dartey, pseudonym of Anette Osterlind. Illustration of models by Lanvin, Chéruit, and Paquin entitled "A Celebration of Paris in New York." *Le Style Parisien*, November 1915, pl. V. © Diktats bookstore.

FIG. 5c.32 Philippe Ortiz (Bain News Service). Model wearing Lanvin "Ariane" dress a black silk faille, 1915. Silver gelatin print. © Diktats bookstore.

FIG. 5c.33 Henri Gervex. Portrait of Jenny Sacerdote, 1921. Oil on canvas. Tajan Auction.

WHERE MME. JENNY KEEPS OPEN HOUSE

Photograph by H. C. Ellis

The "maison Jenny," the first building erected in Paris purely as a dressmaking establishment (all the others are housed in fine old mansions), presents a wonderfully arranged series of gray-carpeted salons, with gray velvet chairs edged with gold braid, and with gray-toned walls as a background for the pretty manikins

THE flurry and excitement of the openings and the hurried departure of the buyers is succeeded always by a great calm; and the *grandes dames* and actresses may order their new frocks in all the peace and quiet of orderly salons.

This season we have the true French taste, to the entire exclusion of all chicanery, which, it is to be hoped, has disappeared forever; for this year, thanks to the war, all but the genuinely French houses have been closed.

A NEW STAR IN THE CONSTELLATION

Among the salons which have been established for years, a new salon of such importance has arisen it may well be called a new star in the Parisian constellation. This establishment is *la maison Jenny*. It is owned by Mme. Jenny and her associate, Mme. Le Corre, and is beautifully situated in l'avenue des Champs Elysées. Having been especially constructed for the business—the first house in Paris built for the purpose—everything about the building has been arranged with the view of securing the greatest convenience.

Everywhere in these salons the gray tone dominates. The carpets are light gray, the wall-paper is gray, and the armchairs and sofas are of gray velvet with a touch of narrow gold braid. There is a bit of white introduced into the wall decoration, which is repeated in the crystal of the chandeliers and candelabra. Everything is simple, in good taste, and planned to form a most becoming background for the manikins.

Although the *maison Jenny* is comparatively new, it is already classed among the most important houses in Paris. The taste of Mme. Jenny, so sure and so delicate, soon forced its way in the city, and her clientele is chiefly composed of Parisians who appreciate refinement and conservatism.

Mme. Jenny herself is dark and surprisingly young. Her face, with its regular features, has an expression of great firmness, but when she smiles her eyes soften amazingly. Dressed in black—as she almost always is—she is good to look at, and she meets the patrons of her establishment with charming talk of frocks, frills, her salons, and herself.

The story of the creation and building of her business is interesting. When she was quite young, she determined to be independent in her own way. She chose the affairs of fashion, although prepared by education for so-called "better" things. With energy she combated all the foolish extravagances of the last two or three seasons, and opposed to every fancy of bad taste the simple and graceful lines of her own models.

THE BUSINESS OF THE SEASON

Pretty and charming afternoon gowns seem to be her specialty. Her tailored skirts are short and wide, but with no exaggeration. To wear with them, she favors high boots in soft Russian leather, which give a most charming effect, for, the skirt being short, the silhouette is not "cut," as she expresses it. A military coat of the new soldier blue cloth christened "Généralissime" is one of her great successes.

In spite of the present difficulties, Mme. Jenny is very busy. While the buyers were in Paris, she sent out about one hundred and twenty-five dresses a day. Many of them were sent to Russia, England, and America. Her house has never been closed and all her staff has been employed since the beginning of the war. Just now she is preparing a small collection of models which will be sent to the San Francisco Exposition.

Two photographs copyrighted by Reutlinger

It is one of Mme. Jenny's professional maxims that models must not be created only to be admired in a glass case, but to be worn as well

Simple in every line, as good taste prescribes this season, is this Jenny model with old-time flutings of the material used for trimming

FIG. 5c.34 Article discussing Mme Jenny and her salon on the Avenue des Champs-Elysées, which remained open throughout the war. "Where Mme. Jenny Keeps Open House," *Vogue*, May 1915, 51.

FIG. 5c.35 For example, according to *Le Style Parisien* in 1916, Jenny suits for women were made for "the active life most women lead. No more automobiles . . . but now the democratic Métro; no more meetings over tea or tea tangos, but now visits to every corner of France."[56] The company was known for its dresses, sold with fitted jackets, and tailored suits. According to *Le Style Parisien,* the latter were ideal for starting the day, walking in the woods, going on errands, or visiting the ambulance centers.[57]
Jenny's early war models were cut in the popular "war crinoline" silhouette, which featured a full, flared skirt. In an article that accompanied a photograph of a tailored suit by Jenny from the first wartime issue of *Le Style Parisien*, the journalist noted that in regards to the trend of the popular suit,

A woman can finally walk freely, step up onto a sidewalk, and reach an automobile's running board without running the risk of breaking her neck, and she can show her legs up to her knee! No more hindrances! Movement is now supple and graceful, the folds of dresses flare naturally with lightness![58]

FIG. 5c.36 In reality, however, tailored suits, particularly those in the crinoline style which required up to eight yards of fabric, may not have been as light and supple as the journalist suggested. Some were lined in heavy fabrics, such as velvet. At the end of 1917, following new trends, Jenny produced barrel line suits, with narrower skirts that embodied the "new line."[59]

Jenny's fashions were often based on wartime uniforms. For example, a military-like coat called "Généralissime" from 1915 was made in the same shade of blue worn by troops (*bleu horizon*), and a 1916 tailored suit with a crinoline skirt named "France" had a collar made from red, white, and blue patterned fabric. FIG. 5c.37 The "Serbie" (Serbia) dress from 1917 was cut from a banana-colored woolen fabric and featured a bell-shaped skirt and a bodice adorned with three inverted pleats tapering to the neckline. Like most Parisian couturiers, Jenny focused on exporting her designs, mainly to the United States, Russia, and Great Britain, as she worked to remain visible abroad. For the 1915 Fête Parisienne in New York, she created models specifically for an American clientele that were more colorful and elaborate than those she sold in France to Parisian women. As *Le Style Parisien* emphasized, "Gold and silver everywhere! Let's hope American women get the hint!"[60] A silver and pink lamé coat, brocaded in blue, green, and violet (and cut from pink satin made by Coudurier, Fructus et Descher) and complemented by three bands of sable on pink tulle, stood out for its "magnificent appearance."[61] FIGS. 5c.38 Moreover, three afternoon dresses—"so 1830," according to the same magazine—delighted clients, the first for its dark green Lyon velvet (Bianchini-Férier) and its gold braiding; the second for its blue-black velvet (Bianchini-Férier); and the third for its cyclamen-pink velvet.[62] Two years later, alongside Beer, Callot, Chéruit, Lanvin, Paquin, Premet, and Poiret, Jenny exhibited several designs at the Palacio Real in Madrid, notably a black satin dress embroidered with chimera and tarnished gold Japanese leaves, along with a number of suits.[63] One of them, a "bishop veloutine suit," consisted of a narrow skirt covered by a large jacket with godet pleats and large pockets.[64] The Jenny suit featured a fringed scarf, which *Le Style Parisien* called a convenience "at a time when life must be made easier . . . when the drafty Métro has, for many, come to replace the comfortable automobile, where one can wear a tulle blouse but remain warm in a fur coat."[65] Although the Jenny fashion house adapted to the conditions of war, a decision made in coordination with Paquin, Chéruit, Dœuillet, Lanvin, Poiret, Premet, and Worth to close their ateliers on Saturday afternoons for two months that cut worker salaries ignited one of the largest strikes of the early twentieth century. Jenny's 180 workers were the first to take to the streets, when a letter of demands left on her desk went unanswered. SEE CHAPTER 9 Jenny proposed opening a dining hall at the company to compensate for lower wages, but the midinettes on strike rejected the offer. Nonetheless, the Jenny fashion house prevailed through the war and eventually closed in 1940.

Chanel

Gabrielle "Coco" Chanel opened her first hat shop, Chanel Modes, in 1910 at 21, rue Cambon in Paris.[66] FIGS. 5c.39, 5c.40 She was known for the simplicity and elegance of her designs, as exemplified by a 1917 hat that seems to be made of straw but is in fact luxuriously embroidered in chains of khaki-colored silk and adorned with a brown satin ribbon.[67] FIG. 5c.41 Chanel's trademark style is already present in this design. In 1913, Chanel opened a branch of her hat shop in Deauville, a seaside resort for elegant women.[68] FIG. 5c.42 It was at this time that she designed the first clothing for her Deauville clients who wanted garments that imitated her own personal style—simple, straight skirts, blouses with sailor collars, shirts, sport jackets, and plain hats.[69] Chanel told French writer

FIG. 5c.35 Three designs by Jenny: brown and white checkered suit, wool jersey sweater with green and blue checkered skirt, and jacket with high soft collar in green and blue checkered fabric. "Simple Tailored Suits: Models by Jenny," *Les Élégances Parisiennes*, October 1916, pl. XII. © Bibliothèque nationale de France.

le Style parisien

LETTRE D'UNE PARISIENNE

Vous m'avez demandé, ma chère amie, de vous parler de Paris et de vous décrire minutieusement les modes nouvelles, les créations que j'ai vues, dans la rue, dans le Monde et chez les couturiers.

C'est une tâche charmante pour moi que d'essayer de vous satisfaire et de vous donner un aperçu de toutes les élégances de cette saison.

Les événements terribles que traverse la France ont rendu la vie journalière plus grave; et il est évident qu'en ce moment les femmes ne pensent pas à la toilette avec beaucoup d'entrain; elles s'habillent pourtant, et elles le font en mettant dans leurs recherches leur goût habituel.

Nos fabricants et nos couturiers, malgré les difficultés de l'heure présente, ont fait un effort considérable cette année et ont créé des modèles tout à fait réussis et plus parisiens que jamais.

D'ailleurs pour vous en donner une idée, je joins à ma lettre un nouveau journal qui rendra ma tâche plus facile. Il me paraît être exactement ce qu'il vous faut, car il contient à la fois des modèles choisis de nos principales maisons de couture et de mode; d'autres inventés par le *Style Parisien* avec les tissus, dentelles, rubans et garnitures de fabricants français très connus, et beaucoup de renseignements sur tout ce qui concerne la mode.

Si vous le voulez bien, je m'occuperai d'abord des tailleurs, costumes avec lesquels nous commençons notre journée, pour faire une promenade au bois, pour nos courses, ou pour nous rendre à l'ambulance.

Je ne vous apprendrai pas que nos trotteurs ont de l'ampleur; vous avez pu constater cette nouveauté vous-même et vous en réjouir. Les femmes peuvent enfin marcher librement, monter sur un trottoir, atteindre le marchepied d'une auto sans risquer de se casser le cou ou de montrer ses jambes jusqu'aux genoux! Plus d'entraves! Les mouvements deviennent souples et gracieux, les plis des robes s'évasent avec légèreté et naturel!

Je ne saurai vous dire la joie que j'en ai, la marche est redevenue un plaisir en même temps qu'une nécessité, puisque toutes nos autos sont au front.

Le bas des jupes peut atteindre jusqu'à quatre ou cinq mètres de tour; on obtient cette ampleur de bien des manières. On voit des jupes avec des plis plats, d'autres avec des fronces, beaucoup avec des godets; quelquefois, les plis partent d'une ceinture étroite et sont très serrés les uns contre les autres ou, au contraire, très espacés; d'autres fois les plis crevés forment cônes; certaines jupes ont des tabliers devant et derrière, avec les côtés coupés en forme; d'autres sont faites d'une façon absolument différente, c'est-à-dire que le tablier et le dos taillés en biais prennent toute la hauteur de la jupe, tandis que de côté descend un empiècement d'une hauteur de dix centimètres environ. Dans les étoffes à carreaux, ces deux dernières coupes produisent des effets tout à fait amusants.

Cl. Félix

Mlle Yvonne DARTEIX. — Trotteur de JENNY

Vous qui aimez toutes vos aises et la commodité dans chaque détail de votre toilette, sachez que les poches que l'on commençait à voir apparaître dans les jupes des tailleurs sont presque indispensables maintenant. On les fait très apparentes et on les souligne même quelquefois d'une passementerie, d'un galon, ou du même liseré qui accompagne la jupe ou la jaquette. On peut dire que, d'une façon générale, la forme des jaquettes n'a pas beaucoup changé depuis la dernière saison; elles ont cependant, comme les jupes, des poches et beaucoup plus d'ampleur du bas.

Notons que l'on voit quelques jaquettes très courtes, avec une toute petite basque et quelques autres très longues dans le genre des redingotes amazones que l'on met pour monter à cheval. J'ai vu des jaquette-redingotes

1

FIG. 5c.36 Article discussing the merits of the tailored suit featuring a photograph of a suit by Jenny. *Le Style Parisien*, July 1915. © Bibliothèque nationale de France.

FIG. 5c.37 Dartey, pseudonym of Anette Osterlind. "France" ensemble of tailored overcoat in khaki with red, white, and blue collar by Jenny. *Les Élégances Parisiennes*, August 1916, pl. V. © Bibliothèque Forney / Roger-Viollet, RV-157622-23.

FIG. 5c.38 Evening coats by Premet, Chéruit, and Jenny. *Le Style Parisien*, November 1915, pl. XIX. © Bibliothèque Forney / Roger-Viollet, RV-203791-1.

FIG. 5c.39 Gabrielle Chanel in *Comœdia Illustre*, October 1, 1910. © Diktats bookstore.

Modèle de GABRIELLE CHANEL, *21, Rue Cambon*

Grand CHAPEAU velours violet évêque, fond souple ; une garniture de ruban violet évêque semé de petits motifs argentés garnit les bords ; nœud du même ruban.

FIG. 5c.40 Louis Strimpl. *Modes d'Hiver*, 1914–15. Colored lithograph.

FIG. 5c.41 Gabrielle Chanel. Hat, spring–summer 1917. Satin, silk embroidery, satin ribbon. © Patrimoine Chanel. © All rights reserved.

FIG. 5c.42 Gabrielle Chanel in front of her boutique in Deauville, 1913. Silver gelatin print. © Patrimoine Chanel.

FIG. 5c.43 Navy blue jersey suit with light blue chenille underlay, white cotton jersey suit embroidered with navy blue silk, and sand jersey suit with dark jacket. "Jersey Suits: Designs by Gabrielle Channel" (*sic*), *Les Élégances Parisiennes*, July 1916, pl. XI. © Bibliothèque Forney / Roger-Viollet, RV-157622-20.

FIG. 5c.44 Gabrielle Chanel. Blouse, 1915. Silk.

Paul Morand, "I used to cut them [the women in Deauville] stable boy sweaters in jersey and riding knits similar to what I was wearing myself . . . There was a need for simplicity, comfort, and clean lines."[70] According to Edmonde Charles-Roux, French writer and later editor-in-chief of French *Vogue,* Chanel's first garments were inspired by the outfits worn by Arthur (Boy) Capel, an English polo player and Chanel's lover. Based on the knit from one of his sweaters and the flannel from one of his blazers, she made a blouse that looked like a cross between a marinière and a "stable boy's pullover."[71] Her clothes were as successful as her hats, and in 1915, with Capel's backing, she opened her first couture boutique in Biarritz.

Chanel began creating jersey suits during the war with fabric she had bought from the textile manufacturer Rodier.[72] Jersey was not an invention of the war; wealthy, elegant women were already wearing it before 1914 for sports and travel and as undergarments (nightgowns, bathing suits, and the like).

SEE CHAPTER 5

However, the fabric was deemed too rough, too pale in color, and too reminiscent of work clothing for everyday wear. During the war, Chanel began using jersey as an everyday fabric, counting on the appeal of its simple quality. According to *Women's Wear Daily*, Chanel wanted to introduce her new jersey designs in August 1914, but the war pushed the presentation back to February 1915 in Monte Carlo (although apparently the designs were never unpacked). Chanel then sent a few designs to Deauville in 1915, and by December the jersey trend seems to have reached Paris.[73] Her friend Madame Geneviève Vix helped to popularize the style when she wore a Nattier blue jersey sports coat to the Hôtel de Paris.[74]

The American press was quick to pick up on the new fashion, and in 1916 the Chanel jersey suit became a success.[75] As *Women's Wear Daily* wrote, "It would be difficult to cite a fashion or a fabric which has taken such a hold on the public as jersey . . . Chanel has become the craze and jersey the rage."[76] The paper reported on the growing success of the suit as certain clients bought three or four of them in different colors. The jersey coat became popular for travel and for "general day wear."[77] Within a single year, Paris had given jersey its stamp of approval for everything from simple sport jackets to entire suits, evidenced by the now iconic plate published in the fashion magazine *Les Élégances Parisiennes* in July 1916. FIG. 5c.43

Although Chanel's use of jersey is part of the company's legend, it is important to note that she was not the only designer to use the fabric—Worth, Paquin, and even Lanvin used it for their designs as well.[78] Another of Chanel's significant innovations was the trademark simplicity and minimalism of her designs, which prefigured postwar modernity in fashion. One of her most "iconic" creations, which embodies the "simplicity" of her style, is the 1915 silk ivory blouse with a sailor collar. FIG. 5c.44

The demand for Chanel's suits and dresses from clients in Madrid, San Sebastián, and Bilbao was so strong that the Chanel atelier hired almost sixty workers in 1915 and more than three hundred workers before the end of the war. She was even able to reimburse Arthur Capel and become financially independent for the first time in her life.[79] In 1918, at her first fashion house in Paris, on the rue Cambon, where the ground floor served as offices for management and inventory, *Women's Wear Daily* commented on the "pretty staircase" leading to the second-floor salons that would later become a signature of the Chanel store.[80] Although the young designer did not receive a great deal of attention from the press during the war (her name was even misspelled in *Les Élégances Parisiennes* in 1916), she became a force to be reckoned with in the interwar period as the embodiment of a new kind of modern femininity.

1 However present these female designers were in the wartime years, it should be noted that the leading male couturiers Paul Poiret and Jean Patou also continued designing during the war, despite being mobilized and actively enrolled. Paul Poiret became a tailor in the 119th infantry regiment. He developed a new overcoat that required sixty centimeters less than the model being used, which saved four hours of work. He was then promoted to administrative officer third class and was assigned to the general store in Vanves. In 1917, he was in Clermont-Ferrand, where he headed the large workshops for the cut and manufacture of uniforms. While stationed in various cities throughout France, Poiret nevertheless kept up with his business in Paris: in 1915 he designed several dresses to be sent to the Panama-Pacific International Exposition in San Francisco and the Fête Parisienne, a display of French imports at the Ritz-Carlton Hotel in New York; in 1916 he edited a single issue of *L'Almanach des lettres et des Arts*; in 1917 he sent models to an exhibition of French fashion in Madrid and opened a branch of his boutique "Poiret Incorporated" in New York. He also served as the powerful head of the Syndicat de Défense de la Grande Couture Française (Syndicate for the Defense of French Haute Couture). In his autobiography, Poiret regrets the time he lost during the war. Paul Poiret, *En Habilant l'Époque* (Paris: Grasset, 1986), 155. Jean Patou was assigned to the 269th infantry regiment and began serving as an army lieutenant; he was first a munitions supply officer, then a liaison officer. Given sick leave on January 1, 1915, Patou did not return to his regiment until the summer of 1915. He was then appointed head of the section before he was accused of deserting. On August 13, 1915, Patou's rank was revoked. A soldier second class again, he was assigned to the 404th infantry regiment and positioned on the Aisne front until April 1916. Cleared of all charges, he was reestablished as lieutenant in March 1916 and joined an expedition corps to the East, the 148th infantry regiment. See Johanna Zanon, "De la Baïonnette aux Ciseaux: Les Premières Années de Jean Patou," in Maude Bass-Krueger et al., *Fashion, Society, and the First World War* (London: Bloomsbury, forthcoming), 2019.

2 Sophie Grossiord, *Roman d'une Garde-Robe: Le Chic d'une Parisienne de la Belle Époque aux Années 30* (Paris: Paris Musées, 2013), 226. In 1915,

Vogue describes Louise Chéruit as one of "of the most famous designers in the world" and talks about the "magic name Chéruit." Louise Chéruit, "At the Sign of the Maison Chéruit," *Vogue* 4 (August 15, 1915), 24.

3 Anne Rittenhouse. "The Women Who Create the Mode in Paris," *Vogue* 10 (November 15, 1914), 52.

4 The author's analysis reveals a certain gendered conception of women's couture, describing the designer firstly by her physique and attributing her success to masculine attributes.

5 Ibid.

6 Ibid.

7 Ibid. The only major female designer not mentioned is Gabrielle Chanel, who emerged as a couturier two years later. Chanel's success during the war cannot be ascribed to the fact that she took advantage of new roles granted to women, but because the simple and innovative clothes she was proposing were influential.

8 In November 1896, a branch of The House of Paquin was opened in London, and the business became a limited company. See Waleria Dorogova and Veronique Pouillard, "Couture Ltd. French Fashion's Debut in London's West End," *Business History*, 1–20 (forthcoming).

9 Dominique Sirop, *Paquin* (Paris: Éditions Adam Biro, 1989). See also Dominique Sirop, *Paquin, 1891–1956* (Tokyo: Fondation de la Mode, 1990).

10 Charles Dawbarn, *Makers of New France* (London: Mills & Boon, 1915).

11 Paquin collaborated twice with Leon Bakst: first she commissioned Bakst for a capsule collection, and secondly, her workshop executed costumes by Bakst for the Ballets Russes. See *Comoedia illustré*, April 5, 1913.

12 "L'Haute Couture," *Women's Wear Daily*, June 15, 1914, 1, 6.

13 "Mme. Paquin Has No Idea of Quitting Paquin, Ltd; Is Elected A Director: Mme, Paquin to Continue as Director," *Women's Wear Daily*, May 7, 1915, 10, 31.

14 The company was also the subject of caricatures, paintings, and songs. In 1913 Paquin was awarded the Légion d'Honneur for excellence and for her contribution to the development of both the art and the economy in the field of fashion design. On the eve of the war, the caricaturist Georges Goursat (known as Sem) included her along with Chéruit, Worth, and Dœuillet, as the embodiment of "true chic." For example, see especially "La Rue de la Paix," *Excelsior*, January 22, 1912; "Figures Contemporaines," *Le Journal, Supplément Illustré*, January 1912, 14; "Créations Paquin," *Comoedia illustré*, March 15, 1910, 356–57; Leonetto Cappiello, "Les Célébrités de la Mode," *Femina et la Mode*, supplement to *Femina*, January 1903; "Jeanne Paquin," column "Tête de Turc," *Fantasio*, March 1, 1913, 534.

15 "Paquin Designs For Women's Wear," *Women's Wear Daily*, December 18, 1914, 1.

16 "Atours Simples," *La Gazette du Bon Ton*, Summer 1915, 22.

17 Ibid.

18 De Lange, "The Paquin Models For San Francisco," *Women's Wear Daily*, March 16, 1915, 1, 6.

19 "Paris at the Panama-Pacific Exposition," *Women's Wear Daily*, June 5, 1915, 1, 6.

20 "Lettre à une Parisienne," *Le Style Parisien*, p.28.

21 "Paris Models Are Shown At Madrid Exhibit," *Women's Wear Daily*, May 18, 1917, 1, 12.

22 "Paquin Would Make American Uniforms to Keep Help at Work," *Women's Wear Daily*, May 20, 1918, 2.

23 Paquin was involved on different levels, as president of the Syndicat and a member of the Chambre Syndicale. In 1914, like many other designers, she became a member of the Syndicat (see Chapter 6) and hoped to find in it a place to share ideas on how to fight against the copying of her prototypes. But in 1916, barely two years after joining, she left the organization, explaining that she had realized that the Syndicat was prioritizing the interests of certain individual designers over the collective interest of French couture. She criticized the Syndicat's lack of justice, vision, and quietude and its lack of diplomacy with foreign clients and buyers, who had become suspect simply because of their names. She also took issue with Paul Poiret, president of the Syndicat, for focusing only on the copies of his and his company's designs instead of fighting against the copying of all designer prototypes. "La Haute Couture," *Women's Wear Daily* 35, August 11, 1916, 24; "Paquin's Withdrawal From Syndicat Rumored," *Women's Wear Daily*, December 10, 1915, 25.

24 "Mme. Paquin Named Head of Paris Syndicate," *Women's Wear Daily*, July 7, 1917, 1; "Les Élections à la Chambre Syndicale de la Couture Parisienne," *Les Élégances Parisiennes*, August 1917, 262; "Une Grande Manifestation de Charité du Syndicat de la Presse Parisienne en Faveur des Éprouvés de la Guerre," *Les Modes*, 1917, 9.

25 Paquin archives cited in Sirop, *Paquin*, 42.

26 See *Bulletin Bimensuel / Association Générale du Commerce et de l'Industrie des Tissus et des Matières Textiles*, Paris, May 1917.

27 Archives of the Préfecture de Police de Paris, "Habillement, 1917–1918," BA 1376, September 23, 1918, cited by Maude Bass-Krueger, "La Mode en France Durant la Première Guerre Mondiale: Approches d'Histoire Culturelle," MA thesis, Institut d'Études Politiques de Paris, 2008, 91.

28 Lanvin, "Mme. Lanvin in Business Hours," *Vogue* 2 (July 15, 1915), 45.

29 "Jeanne Lanvin," *La Renaissance de l'Art Français et des Industries de Luxe*, January 1924, 7.

30 Lanvin, "Mme. Lanvin in Business Hours," 45.

31 Ghenya, "La Mode au Théâtre," *Le Figaro*, December 26, 1916, 3. See also E. Ainé, "La Couture Parisienne Depuis la Guerre," *Le Monde Illustré*, December 23, 1916, 425;

32 Rosine, "Propos Féminins," *Le Figaro*, June 18, 1918, 3.

33 APP, F7/13272, 13/05/1917, cited by Bass-Krueger, "La Mode en France," 82.

34 Lanvin's designs, later described by *Women's Wear Daily* as "always unique and different from anything else coming out of the other houses," were not all ready, which explains why some of them as a result were not presented to American buyers until the end of January 1915 for distribution in September 1915. "The Doucet and Lanvin opening," *Women's Wear Daily*, December 26, 1914, cover; "Couturiers Will Remain in Paris," *Women's Wear Daily*, December 4, 1914, 2

35 "The Lanvin Collection," *Women's Wear Daily*, April 1, 1915, 1.

36 See "Lettre d'une Parisienne," *Le Style Parisien*, October 15, 1915, 20. This influence is not new because in the nineteenth century, and especially during the Franco-Prussian war, the military uniform was already inspiring women's clothing; nevertheless, the war would exacerbate the movement.

37 This model generally belongs to a historical tradition and owes a great deal to panniers and to crinolines in the 18th century and the Second Empire. Palais Galliera, *Jeanne Lanvin*, exh. cat. (Paris: Paris Musées, 2015), 83.

38 Jérôme Picon, *Jeanne Lanvin* (Paris: Flammarion, 2002), 123.

39 See Chapter 1a.

40 "Mme. Lanvin in Business Hours," *Vogue*, July 1915, 45.

41 Ibid.

42 *Les Élégances Parisiennes*, June 1917, 219.

43 "Pour Défendre Nos Industries," *Les Élégances Parisiennes* (August 1916), 70.

44 See Jeanne Lanvin dress, summer 1917, Brooklyn Museum, 85.2.1a, MET; and Jeanne Lanvin dress no. 383 RJ, Lanvin archives.

45 Rosine, "Propos Féminins," *Le Figaro*, June 18, 1918, 3.

46 "Échos," *Le Journal*, June 4, 1918. Thanks to Antoine Bucher of Diktats for sending the portfolio.

47 "L'Exportateur Français," *Le Temps*, March 24, 1917, 4; "Manifestation de la Couture Parisienne à la Foire de Lyon," *Les Élégances Parisiennes*, March 1917, 184. "Fashion: Paris Sends its Representatives to Madrid," *Vogue*, June 15, 1917, 44, and "Fashion: Paris Builds Fashions in Spain," *Vogue*, July 1, 1917, 27.

48 "The Lanvin Collection," *Women's Wear Daily*, April 1, 1915, cover; Roger Boutet de Monvel, "La Fête Parisienne à New York," *Le Style Parisien*, November 1915.

49 "Lettre à une Parisienne," *Le Style Parisien*, November 1915, 25.

50 Ibid., pl. 3.

51 *Le Style Parisien*, December 1915, 23, pl. I.

52 "Jenny: Society: Where Mme. Jenny Keeps Open House," *Vogue*, May 1, 1915, 51.

53 Ibid; "Le Syndicat de Défense de la Grande Couture Française et Ses Industries s'y Rattachant," *Le Style Parisien*, November 1915, 1.

54 "Le Syndicat de Défense de la Grande Couture Française et Ses Industries s'y Rattachant," *Le Style Parisien*, November 1915, p.1.

55 "La Mode Simple," *Les Élégances Parisiennes*, April 1916, 2.

56 "Les Dernières Créations de la Mode," *Les Élégances Parisiennes*, April 1916, 2.

57 "Lettre d'une Parisienne," *Le Style Parisien*, July 1915, 1.

58 Ibid.

59 "La Ligne Nouvelle," *Les Élégances Parisiennes*, October 1917, pl. XI.

60 "Francine: Lettre d'une Parisienne," *Le Style Parisien*, November 1915, 26.

61 Ibid.

62 Ibid.

63 "La Maison de France à Madrid," *Les Élégances Parisiennes*, January 1917, 198; "La Maison de France à Madrid," *Les Élégances Parisiennes*, May 1917, pls. VIII, IX.

64 "Les Dernières Créations de la Mode," *Les Élégances Parisiennes*, July 1917, 233.

65 Ibid.

66 Fashion: The Fashions of Paris Lead the Simple Life," *Vogue*, August 1, 1917, 29.

67 "La Mode Actuelle au Théâtre," *Comoedia Illustré*, September 15, 1910, 730; "Nos Chapeaux Chics," *La Mode du Temps*, December 15, 1912; "La Mode et les Modes," *Les Modes*, May 1912, 8; Winter catalogue 1915, ed. Lucien Vogel.

68 "Les Commerçants," *Les Echos de Deauville*, March 1, 1912; and "Chanel's Rapid Rise Result of Jersey Vogue," *Women's Wear Daily*, November 14, 1918.

69 Paul Morand, *L'Allure Chanel* (Paris: Gallimard, 2014), 61. See also Edmonde Charles-Roux, *L'Irrégulière. L'itinéraire de Coco Chanel* (Paris: Grasset, 2016), 236. See also de Lange, "Chanel's Rapid Rise Result of Jersey Vogue," *Women's Wear Daily*, November 14, 1918, 1.

70 Paul Morand, *L'Allure Chanel* (Paris: Gallimard, 2014), 61.

71 Charles-Roux, *L'Irrégulière*, 227–28.

72 "It was Gabrielle Chanel, the foremost creator of sports raiment who revived jersey and who is responsible for its success today," De Lange, "Paris Finds New Ideas and Combinations for Continued Use of Jersey," *Women's Wear Daily*, June 23, 1916, 27.

73 "Jersey Craze Is Watchword From Paris For Spring," *Women's Wear Daily*, December 6, 1915.

74 "Chanel's Rapid Rise Result of Jersey Vogue," *Women's Wear Daily*, November 14, 1918.

75 De Lange, "Paris Finds New Ideas," 27, 32.

76 Ibid.

77 "Chanel's Sport Costumes Increasing in Popularity Daily on The Riviera," *Women's Wear Daily*, February 28, 1916, 1.

78 See *Les Élégances Parisiennes*, May 1916, 23; "Les Dernières Créations de la Mode," *Les Élégances Parisiennes*, July 1916, 58.

79 Charles-Roux, *L'Irrégulière*, 259.

80 "Maison Chanel Now Located in New Building," *Women's Wear Daily*, June 29, 1918, 1, 14.

5d The Costume Tailleur

MICHELE MAJER

The Christmas 1915 cover of the high-end fashion magazine *Les Modes* presents the actress Yvonne de Bray wearing a deep blue velvet tailored suit, trimmed with dark gray fox and secured at the waist with a large, gold plaque, designed by the well-known couturiere Jeanne Paquin.[1] FIG. 5d.1 Accessorized with a close-fitting matching velvet hat topped with a standing bow knot, black high-heeled boots, and a delicate, furled umbrella, de Bray's *costume tailleur*—called tailored suits or suits in English—constituted a mainstay of French women's wardrobes during the First World War. Not only does her ensemble demonstrate the popularity of such suits between 1914 and 1918, but it also attests to the determination of the Parisian couture industry to maintain its dominance as the trendsetting capital for women's fashion, despite multiple hardships, and to retain clients both in France and abroad by introducing style changes. SEE CHAPTER 5 De Bray's long, flared jacket with its deep folds, accentuated at the hem by a wide band of fox, displays the bell-shaped silhouette that came into vogue late in the summer of 1914 and was dubbed the *crinoline de guerre*, or "war crinoline," after the outbreak of the war.[2] Notwithstanding their often-touted practicality for women coping with wartime conditions, these suits were fashionable garments that kept pace with seasonal developments. In addition to day and evening dresses from prominent couture houses that appeared regularly in *Les Modes*, *L'Art et la Mode*, *Femina*, *Le Style Parisien*, *Les Élégances Parisiennes*, and *Les Modes de la Femme de France*—magazines aimed at an upper- and middle-class readership—costumes tailleurs were extensively illustrated and reported on.[3] An English import in the latter decades of the nineteenth century, the tailored wool suit for day wear became fashionable in France among both elite women, who were increasingly participating in public life, and working women, whose numbers rose dramatically at the turn of the century. The former purchased expensive, custom-made suits from top couturiers, while the latter bought ready-to-wear versions from large department stores. By the outbreak of the First World War in August 1914, two distinct forms of the costume tailleur, or tailored suit, were well established.[4] The classic suit, or *tailleur classique* (also referred to as the *tailleur pratique* and the *tailleur simple*), retained the discreet simplicity of the English "tailor made" in its understated construction, subdued fabrics, and minimal trimming, while the *tailleur couturier* or *tailleur fantaisiste* exhibited a more visually complex cut, richer fabrics, and more applied decoration.

The prewar designation of the two types of suits for different functions and occasions continued during the war years. In January 1915, Sybil de Lancey, fashion editor of *Les Modes*, noted that either a fur coat worn over an afternoon dress or a tailleur couturier was suitable for late day visits.[5] She distinguished at length between the "flou," or softness, of the "tailleur couturier" and "le vrai tailleur classique," with its note of severe simplicity indebted to its English origins, that was made in a variety of wools with fur trim and now worn exclusively in the morning.[6] In October 1918, just before the end of the war, de Lancey once again reported on the two "camps" of costumes tailleur—the "classique" and the "fantaisiste."[7] She deemed the former appropriate for the country and the seaside, while the latter was intended for town wear. Interestingly, de Lancey observed that many of the new tailleurs fantaisiste were of taffeta, since high-quality wools were both rare and expensive.[8] SEE CHAPTER 5 As noted above, French fashion magazines regularly offered images of and information on both types of suits. Generously illustrated, *Le Style Parisien*, founded in July 1915, contains numerous colored and monochromatic plates showing a wide range of costumes tailleur with the war crinoline silhouette that was at its height of popularity at the time. The September issue alone includes "Costumes Tailleur d'Après-midi" by Martial et Armand in black velvet trimmed with mohair and blue serge trimmed with astrakhan; fur-trimmed tailleurs in wine-colored *poult de soie*, raven-breast-colored velvet, and "Britannia" blue faille; two "Tailleurs Couturier" in blue serge, one embroidered with red silk and trimmed with imitation astrakhan, the other trimmed with embroidered green and black wool bands; FIG 5d.2 "Tailleurs Classiques" in rust-colored tweed, blue serge, gray wool edged with black velvet, and black-and-white checkered wool with black satin trim; "Tailleurs Simples" by Paquin, one in deep yellow checkered wool and the other in blue serge, and by Redfern in "covercoat" (a twilled wool or wool blend) trimmed with mink; FIG. 5d.3 "Tailleurs Fantaisie" in black duvetine (a napped wool or silk) and steel-gray, striped, and blue-and-green plaid wools; and "Tailleurs en Lainage" by Worth, Chéruit, and Premet.[9] Although both the "Tailleurs Couturier" and the "Tailleurs

FIG. 5d. 1 Mlle. Yvonne de Bray in a fur-trimmed velvet tailleur by Jeanne Paquin. *Les Modes*, Christmas 1915. © Bibliothèque nationale de France.

LE STYLE PARISIEN

Fig. 122. *Fig. 123.* *Fig. 124.* *Fig. 125.*

TAILLEURS COUTURIER

Modèles du " Style Parisien "

d'après les tissus et garnitures de RODIER

FIG. 5d.2 Fashion plate showing couture suits after fabrics and trimmings by Rodier. *Le Style Parisien*, September 1915, plate XV. © Bibliothèque nationale de France.

LE STYLE PARISIEN

PAQUIN (*Fig. 130*) REDFERN (*Fig. 131*) PAQUIN (*Fig. 132*)

TAILLEURS SIMPLES

FIG. 5d.3 Fashion plate showing "Simple Suits" by Paquin and Redfern. *Le Style Parisien*, September 1915, plate XVII. © Bibliothèque nationale de France.

FIG. 5d.4 Illustration of a "Little English suit in covercoat. Pocket jacket with pleated skirt. Matching straw police hat, with a black background and taffeta cockade. Spring Fashions. Drawing by Dick." *L'Art et la Mode,* March 6, 1915. Image provided by The Metropolitan Museum of Art, New York, Thomas J. Watson Library.

Simples" feature full-skirted, flared silhouettes, long fitted sleeves, and hip- and thigh-length jackets, the "brandenbourg" passementerie fastening (on the figure second from the left), applied decoration, and tiered jackets and skirts of the former create a "dressier" look, while the latter are more streamlined and devoid of trimming.[10] Functional pockets were an important aspect of the practicality of wartime suits. Prewar tailored suits often included discreet pockets that did not interfere with the smooth-fitting silhouette. During the war, however, fashion editors extolled large, visible pockets as both utilitarian and stylish elements. In July 1915, *Le Style Parisien* assured readers who appreciated ease and convenience in their toilettes that pockets in tailleur skirts, now "almost indispensable," were often accentuated with passementerie or galloon.[11] Illustrations and photographs of skirt suits in fashion magazines between 1914 and 1918 show a range of pocket forms that are integral to the design of a particular suit and in keeping with the two styles of tailleurs. In August 1917, Sybil de Lancey differentiated between the pockets "un peu 'Tommy'" of the "tailleur pratique"—a reference to the large, flapped patch pockets of British soldiers' uniforms—and the finely embroidered pockets (that matched the collar) of the latest "tailleur couturier."[12] FIG. 5d.4

The Fashionable Tailleur and Patriotic Dressing

In their stated roles as organs of the couture industry in a time of crisis, *Le Style Parisien* and *Les Élégances Parisiennes* not only cited the many well-known houses whose designs they showcased—Worth, Paquin, Premet, Chéruit, Redfern, Dœuillet, Beer, Jenny, Lanvin, and Martial et Armand, among others—but they also indicated the names of leading textile manufacturers and of their wools, silks, linens, cottons, and blends in illustration captions and fashion columns.[13] In response to wartime shortages and restrictions and in order to stimulate consumption, textile manufacturers introduced new fabrics, particularly knits and silk-and-wool blends. SEE CHAPTER 5 Among the firms identified by the two magazines as suppliers of materials for couture garments, including costumes tailleur, are Bianchini-Férier (renowned for their silks), Rodier (who specialized in innovative knits), Simonnot-Godard (producers of fine cottons and lawns), and Lesur et Cie and Labbey & Cie (manufacturers of wools and silks). In addition to the more familiar prewar fabrics such as taffeta, satin, velvet, serge, and tweed, the newly popular jersey and its many variations appear frequently in the magazines.[14] Although Gabrielle "Coco" Chanel was among the first to promote jersey as a fashionable fabric, particularly for sports and casual dress, many other couturiers also appreciated this soft, supple wool or silk fabric for suits.[15] SEE CHAPTERS 5 AND 5c, FIG. 5c.43 Further, as part of their efforts to actively support and promote the fashion and textile industries, *Le Style Parisien* and *Les Élégances Parisiennes* presented their own "modèles," or designs—including tailleurs—that specified the types of fabrics and their manufacturers, and a scaled pattern selected from among these *modèles* was included at the back of most issues.[16] FIGS 5d.5, 5d.6 Thus, a woman who was unable to afford couture prices could purchase the requisite fabric and pattern and commission a fashionable suit from her local dressmaker. Illustrations of dresses, suits, and coats in *Les Modes de la Femme de France* also indicate the amount of material required for each garment and the magazine similarly offered patterns to its subscribers.[17]

During the war, the French fashion industry encouraged the consumption of new styles as a form of patriotism for women. On the one hand, women were expected to present an appropriately subdued appearance, particularly when they were out in public and for daytime activities that involved charitable and other war-effort related work. On the other hand, it was incumbent upon them to keep up with changes in fashion to support this all-important sector of the national economy and to maintain their superior feminine allure as French women, especially in the face of the rival German fashion industry and the fledgling American industry.[18] SEE CHAPTER 5 Couturiers and textile manufacturers dubbed their latest offerings with topical names that, by evoking patriotic colors and military heroes, conveyed both novelty and support for the Allied cause. In the latter months of 1915, *L'Art et la Mode* illustrated several suits in "serge moscovite" in blue, purple, and "vert russe" (Russian green).[19] In April and June 1916, respectively, *Les Élégances Parisiennes* illustrated tailleurs in "Joffrette vert canadien" (Canadian green Joffrette—a silk gabardine) and "bleu-soldat" (soldier blue) wool taffeta.[20] In October of the same year, the magazine illustrated "Mail Coach," a tailleur in "bleu Marne" silk faille by Worth (commemorating the Allied victory at the Battle of the Marne in September 1914) and in November, a green wool tailleur named "Galliéni," in honor of the former Military Governor of Paris and Minister of War, General Joseph Simon Galliéni, who died in May 1916.[21] FIG. 5d.7 In November 1917, a few months after the United States joined the Allies, Sybil de Lancey detailed a black-and-white suit "baptized" with the name of "the brilliant American general

FIG. 5d.5 Fashion plate showing "Morning Suits" in fabrics by Labbey & Co. *Les Élégances Parisiennes*, June 1916, plate XIV. Image provided by The Metropolitan Museum of Art, New York, Thomas J. Watson Library.

LES ÉLÉGANCES PARISIENNES

LA MODE ET LA COUPE

Le costume (planche XIV, fig. 193), dont nous donnons ci-joint le patron, est en ce nouveau tissu de la maison Labbey intitulé " grain de lime ", patron N° 84358. Souple et légère, c'est l'étoffe par excellence pour les costumes d'été. Toutefois, inutile d'ajouter que l'on peut à volonté choisir tout autre genre de lainage, à l'exception cependant des tissus trop secs et trop cassants.

La jupe est montée un peu au-dessus de la taille sur un gros grain, avec quelques fronces, mais très légères seulement, afin d'éviter toute pince. Le devant est droit fil et sans couture, comme l'indique le patron ci-contre (taille 44). De chaque côté sont rapportés deux soufflets fournissant l'ampleur nécessaire. La coupe en est calculée sur une largeur d'étoffe de 140 centimètres. Toutefois, avec quelques petites modifications, on peut adapter cette façon à des tissus de moindre largeur. Si l'on dispose de 120 centimètres, il faut mettre la couture au deuxième soufflet; dans ce cas, couper le dos sans pointe ajoutée, ce qui donnerait un très vilain mouvement. Si l'étoffe est encore plus étroite, on peut à la rigueur placer une couture à chaque soufflet; mais ce ne peut être que dans un cas de force majeure, car cela donne comme résultat une jupe à petits lés, par conséquent moins dernier cri.

Pour la jaquette, il est absolument nécessaire de placer le droit fil rigoureusement selon les indications données sur le patron. Ceci est absolument indispensable si l'on veut obtenir une jaquette sans défaut, la coupe en étant assez compliquée. Elle est composée d'une sorte d'empiècement tombant très bas tout autour et d'un paletot sac de forme toute droite. L'empiècement, qui ne fait qu'un avec le col légèrement rabattu et très évasé, est composé de six parties séparées les unes des autres par un liseré. On peut, au besoin, remplacer ce liseré par des piqûres de grosses soies.

Le gilet peut se faire en schantung ou en taffetas. D'une coupe très simple, il est seulement très légèrement soutenu à l'endroit de la taille; la fermeture en est invisible.

La manche, de forme pagode, est également très facile à couper et à monter.

Signé : La Première.

N.-B. — La Rédaction se met à l'entière disposition de ses lectrices pour leur donner tous les renseignements désirés sur les modèles des " ÉLÉGANCES PARISIENNES " et, sur demande, est prête à en fournir les patrons avec explications détaillées.

Patron au 1/10e
d'un Costume Tailleur (figure 193)

... de tissu quadrillé blanc et bleu, col formant capuchon à volonté (Martial et Armand).

Fig. 209. Manteau de velours de laine gris-fer, ceinture de galon rebrodé dans les tons rouge, bleu et vert (Martial et Armand).

Fig. 210. Chapeau de sport en tresse " poilu " vieux rose, garni d'un ruban amaranthe.

Fig. 211. Tricorne de paille " liseré " garni de ruban picot. Voilette " five o'clock ".

Fig. 212. Haute toque à quatre coins en tagal tête de nègre, garnie d'une " voilette-bandeau ". Cette dernière est bordée dans le haut d'un grand scarabée or et bleu, dans le bas d'une guirlande de soie.

Fig. 213. Marin de tagal noir. Voilette carrée en tulle hexagone brodé de soie.

Fig. 214. Marin de paille " liseré " aux bords très relevés, gros cabochon et tresse de paille autour de la calotte.

Fig. 215. Chapeau de paille " liseré " bleu-marine, croqué sur le côté à l'aide de deux grosses épingles de paille.

Fig. 216. Robe de fillette en crêpe Georgette bleu garni de cerises bleu foncé; corsage banc, collerette d'organdi (Paquin).

Fig. 217. Robe de mousseline anglaise blanche, brodée de roses bleu-nattier (Paquin).

Fig. 218. Robe de tulle brodé de coton, recouverte de deux volants de même broderie, garnie d'une bande de broderies rococo au haut du corsage et descendant le long de la robe (Paquin).

Fig. 219. Petit paletot en tricotine fraise formant deux pèlerines. Ceinture avec plaque de cuir d'un ton plus foncé (Paquin).

Fig. 220. Costume de toile champagne, jaquette vague garnie d'une pochette brodée de laines multicolores (Paquin).

Fig. 221. Grande jaquette de drap bleu-soldat garnie d'une encolure de linon tuyauté.

Fig. 222. Robe de taffetas fleuri bordé d'un velours noir gansé. Petite veste de faille rose à revers de taffetas (Weeks).

Fig. 223. Robe de drap bleu-soldat, petits volants bordés de ganse de soie du même ton (Margaine-Lacroix).

Fig. 224. Robe de tussor, soulignée de grosse ganse. Cravate de ruban picot noir (Laferrière).

Fig. 225. Costume de gabardine banane orné d'une ceinture en tresses de soie et de passementerie du même ton (Laferrière).

Fig. 226. Robe de foulard blanc à pois noirs, corselet de faille.

Fig. 227. Robe de foulard pékiné noir et blanc avec ourlet et corsage de taffetas noir.

Fig. 228. Costume de quadrillé noir et blanc, large ourlet et ceinture de faille noire.

36

FIG. 5d.6 Patterns for designs included in the back of *Les Élégances Parisiennes.* "Fashion and the Cut," *Les Élégances Parisiennes,* June 1916, 35. Image provided by The Metropolitan Museum of Art, New York, Thomas J. Watson Library.

FIG. 5d.7 "Suits and Tailored Suits," *Les Elégances Parisiennes*, October 1916, plate X. Image provided by The Metropolitan Museum of Art, New York, Thomas J. Watson Library.

FIG. 5d.8 G. Dupon-Emera. Spread showing ensembles by Agnès – Mme Havet including a suit for the city, two suit overcoats, and a morning suit. *Les Modes*, no. 177 (1918), 14–15. © Dupon-Emera / Galliera / Roger-Viollet, RV-157097-7.

Pershing," a description that, as she acknowledged, would probably have surprised the unsuspecting "godfather."[22] Probably the most overtly patriotic suit shown in these periodicals was "France" by the house of Jenny, which appeared in the August 1916 issue of the *Les Élégances Parisiennes*. SEE CHAPTER 5c, FIG. 5c.37 The simple, uniform-inspired suit of khaki-colored covercoat with a plain, gently fitted jacket and full skirt, is enlivened by a turn-down collar in the French national colors of blue, white, and red.

Throughout the last year of the war, the costume tailleur remained a popular and all-important option for women—one that signaled the unadorned simplicity of fashion in the late teens and early 1920s and the radical change in lifestyle following the social and economic upheaval of the conflict. SEE CHAPTER 5, FIG. 5.13 In April 1917, the writer and translator Frédéric Roger-Cornaz published an article in *La Guerre Mondiale* entitled "Le 'Tailleur.'"[23] He discussed the feminine ensemble in the context of men's suits, class, and the perceived democratization that this (ostensibly) standardized, three-piece garment implied. Ultimately, he argued, it was the tailleur's demonstrable appropriateness for modern urban life and its "special elegance to which the word chic is applied so well" that made it the best sartorial choice for French women.[24] In her December 1917 report on the recent shift from the wide-hipped *robe tonneau* (barrel dress) to the *robe droite* (straight dress), Sybil de Lancey noted that the costume tailleur "had not been abandoned"—it was practical, convenient, and clean-lined.[25] Further, this slim-silhouetted tailleur was now "modernized" with newly styled, straight blouses and waistcoats that "independent" women wore outside of the skirt, like a sweater, rather than tucked in as had been customary since the late nineteenth century.[26] FIG. 5d.8 After the declaration of peace in November 1918, the fashionable costume tailleur maintained its prominence—and relevance—in French women's wardrobes. As it had during the war, the tailleur continued to reflect and respond to their changing societal roles.

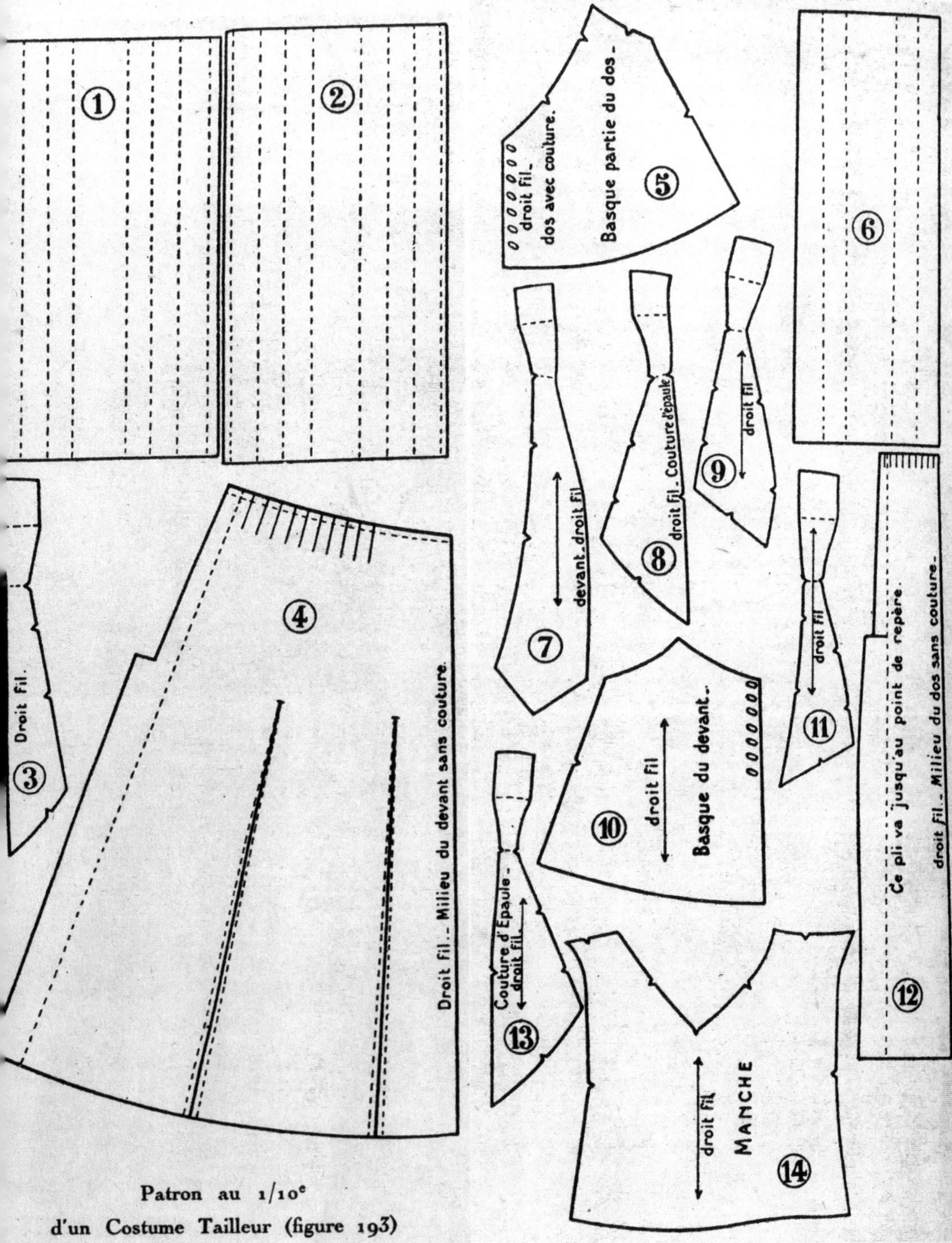

Patron au 1/10e
d'un Costume Tailleur (figure 193)

1 The suit is described as "Costume Tailleur. Paquin. Costume en velours vieux bleu, garni de renard gris; plaque chimère vieil or." *Les Modes, Revue mensuelle des arts décoratifs appliqués à la femme*, Christmas 1915. This description appears on the last page of the issue, *La Mode et les Modes, Nos Gravures*.

2 See Chapter 5 for a discussion of the couture industry and the introduction of new fashions during the war. The magazines reviewed for this essay published many articles addressing both the need to support the couture industry for the sake of the national economy and the importance of clients among the Allies and neutral countries, which, until April 1917, included the Americans.

3 Publication dates for these magazines are as follows: *Les Modes*, 1901–37; *L'Art et la Mode*, 1880–1956; *Femina*, 1901–74; *Le Style Parisien*, 1915–16; *Les Élégances Parisiennes*, 1916–24; *Les Modes de la Femme de France*, 1915–25. Fashion magazines were also impacted by the war. *Les Modes* suspended publication entirely during 1916 and, in June 1917, the editors informed their subscribers that, due to the paper crisis and increase in shipping costs, the magazine was obliged to raise its prices. See "À Nos Abonnés" in *Les Modes* 168 (1917). *L'Art et la Mode* suspended publication between August 1914 and March 1915. *Femina* suspended publication between September 1914 and February 1917; between March 1917 and December 1921, it appeared as *Femina et Vie Heureuse Réunies*. This survey is limited to ensembles specifically described as *tailleurs* (*tailleur classique, tailleur pratique, tailleur simple, tailleur couturier, tailleur fantaisiste* and *tailleur de fantaisie*) in the above-cited periodicals between July 1914 and December 1918. The term "trotteur" was generally used interchangeably with "tailleur." Although I focus on fashionable *tailleurs* for daywear, they were worn for mourning as well, and illustrations and descriptions appear in the magazines under review. See, for example, "L'Art d'être toujours chic: Le Deuil," *Les Modes de la Femme de France*, September 1, 1918. The article advises women on the types of fabrics for mourning suits and suggests that, if necessary, it is acceptable (and even preferable) to dye a well-made suit in one's wardrobe and cover the collar and cuffs with English crepe, rather than purchase a poorly made suit. See also Chapter 3a.

4 In *Les Modes*' March 1912 issue, the fashion editor Sybil de Lancey referred to the *costume tailleur* as "le maître de l'heure" (the master of the hour) and discussed the differences in fabrics and cut between the "tailleur classique," or "tailleur de tailleur," and the "tailleur de fantaisie," or the "tailleur de couturier." See Sybil de Lancy, "La Mode et les Modes," *Les Modes*, March 1912. The American fashion press used both French and English terms. *Women's Wear* included sketches of "Costume Tailleur"; see, for example, September 20, 1913; January 20, 1915; August 2, 1915; and September 20, 1916. *Vogue* frequently used the term "tailored suit;" see, for example, February 15, 1915; March 15, 1915; April 1, 1917; September 15, 1917. Although the time of day and/or occasion for which the suit was intended to be worn was sometimes specified, for the most part, the magazine did not indicate this information. In March 15, 1914, *Vogue* illustrated "Three Suits Varied in Use and Material"; one of these is described as a "semi-tailored type of suit that may do double duty for morning and afternoon wear." In "Eight Ways to Make a Suit,", October 15, 1914, each of the examples is described simply as "suit."

5 Sybil de Lancey, "La Mode et les Modes," *Les Modes*, January 1915.

6 Ibid.

7 Sybil de Lancey, "La Mode et les Modes," *Les Modes* 177 (1918): "Pour les costumes tailleur, toujours partagés en deux camps, le classique et le fantaisiste, nous établirons, nous aussi, une démarcation, laissant les uns pour la rubrique des toilettes de campagne et de plage, tandis que nous verrons maintenant les autres, destinés à nos dernières semaines parisiennes." When *Les Modes* resumed publication in 1917, the month of each issue was no longer indicated. Given that no. 179 is the "Noël" issue, no. 177 is probably October.

8 Ibid.

9 See *Le Style Parisien*, September 1915, pls. V, XIV, XV, XVI, XVII, XIX, and XXI. Full descriptions for each ensemble are listed in the "Explication des Gravures," 15–16. To the 21st-century eye, it is sometimes difficult to distinguish between a *tailleur classique* and a *tailleur simple* in terms of their overall silhouette and fabrics.

10 Both types of *tailleurs* received similar coverage in other issues of *Le Style Parisien* during its nine-month publication. *Les Élégances Parisiennes* regularly covered the latest couture designs, including *costumes tailleur*. See for example, the articles "Les Dernières Créations de la Mode," in the September and October 1916 issues; the latter refers to the diversity of *tailleurs* from the house of Jenny. Regarding military-inspired fashions, including brandenbourgs, due to the war, see Frivoline, "L'Art de la Mode," *L'Art et la Mode*, March 27, 1915.

11 Francine, "Lettre d'une Parisienne," *Le Style Parisien*, July 1915: "Vous qui aimez toutes vos aises et la commodité dans chaque détail de votre toilette, sachez que les poches que l'on commençait à voir apparaître dans les jupes des tailleurs sont presque indispensables maintenant. On les fait très apparentes et on les souligne même quelquefois d'une passementerie, d'un galon, ou du même liseré qui accompagnela jupe ou la jaquette." See also Frivoline, "Impressions de la Semaine," *L'Art et la Mode*, March 15, 1915. The column discusses pockets in the context of the new, simplified lifestyle and visible pockets on skirts in addition to jackets.

12 Sybil de Lancey, "La Mode et les Modes," *Les Modes* 170 (1917). It should be noted that dresses also had pockets; they were not exclusive to *tailleurs*.

13 The full title of the latter magazine is *Les Élégances Parisiennes, Publication officielle des Industries françaises de la mode*. Both were founded during the war (see note 3) and both, in their inaugural and subsequent issues, addressed the need to rally behind the French couture industry.

14 In addition to all-wool or all-silk "jersey," there were many other jersey-weave blends of wool and silk; see Chapter 2. In *L'Art et la Mode*, see, for example, two *tailleurs* in "Djersette," January 22, 1916; a tailleur in "Djersabure 'Suède'," March 24, 1917; and a *tailleur* in "Djersaline grise," April 27, 1918.
15 In August 1916, *Les Élégances Parisiennes* illustrated a "Tailleur en jersey bleu" by Jeanne Lanvin; the colored fashion plate is captioned "Sur la Plage." See also Martine Rénier, "Les Dernières Créations de la Mode," in *Les Élégances Parisiennes*, March 1917. Immediately under the column title, Rénier highlights the use of supple wools and the continued popularity of jersey. In the section "Les Tissus de Laine," she commends Rodier's "Djersabure," which she describes as a thick jersey.
16 As seen in figure 9a.6, brief construction instructions by "La Première" (a reference to the highest-ranking seamstress in the atelier of a couture house) accompanied the pattern as well as the notification that patterns with detailed instructions were available from the Editor. For pattern prices, see, for example, *Les Élégances Parisiennes*, May 1917; these appear on the last page of the issue. Coats, dresses, and suits were all 15 francs; skirts and bodices were 8 francs; sleeves were 2 francs. See also, for example, the November 1915 issue of *Le Style Parisien* for the pattern of a *tailleur* in "Serge Mouflonne," a wool fabric by Rodier (pl. VIII, fig. 196; the pattern appears on page 30 and the description of the suit on page 31).
17 Regarding fabric restrictions during the war that impacted dressmaking, see Chapter 2. Most of the patterns for *tailleurs* indicate four meters, or slightly more.
18 All of the periodicals examined for this essay frequently address one or both of these issues. The French fashion industry was a matter of national and economic pride and magazine editors took seriously the potential competition from both Germany and the U.S. As longstanding buyers of French fashion, however, American clients (private and commercial) were quickly enlisted in the effort to support French couture. See Chapters 2, 3, and 4.
19 For *tailleurs* in "serge moscovite 'marine,'" see *L'Art et la Mode*, August 14, 1915; pl. XXXVI, August 21, 1915; and, September 4, 1915; for the *tailleur* in "serge moscovite 'violine,'" see ibid. October 30, 1915; for the *tailleur* in "serge *Mouflonne* 'vert russe,'" see ibid. October 3, 1915. The color "vert russe" likely refers to the uniform worn by the Russian infantry. The powers of the Triple Entente were France, the United Kingdom, and Russia.
20 "Vert canadien" likely refers to the uniform of Canada's rifle regiments; see *Les Élégances Parisiennes*, April 1916, pl. XII. "Bleu-soldat" refers to the color of the uniform of French *poilus*; see *Les Élégances Parisiennes*, June 1916, pl. XIV. The caption indicates that the fabric for the latter is from Labbey & Cie.
21 See *Les Élégances Parisiennes*, September 1916, fig. 478, and, October 1916, fig. 552.
22 Sybil de Lancey, "La Mode et les Modes," *Les Modes* 173 (1917): " . . . un costume qui se baptise du nom du brillant général américain Pershing—quel étonnement sans doute pour le parrain sans le savoir—est la plus heureuse fantaisie."
23 Frédéric Roger-Cornaz, "Le 'Tailleur,'" *La Guerre Mondiale*, April 28, 1917. https://data.bnf.fr/fr/11922378/frederic_roger-cornaz/ (accessed 1/16/2019). Roger-Cornaz's article is in response to a recent article (or other publication) on the tailleur by Maurice de Waleffe, a contributor to *Les Modes*. As of this date, I have not been able to find Waleffe's article.
24 Ibid. "Le 'tailleur' avait crée en partie cette élégance spéciale à laquelle s'appliquait si bien le mot de chic."
25 Sybil de Lancey, "La Mode et les Modes," *Les Modes*, Christmas 1917: "malgré le succès presque exclusif des robes droites et des grands vêtements, le costume tailleur n'est point abandonné, et ne pourra jamais l'être, tant qu'il nous est pratique, commode, et, dans sa netteté, d'une si parfaite distinction."
26 Ibid. "Mais il [le tailleur] se modernise par les blouses et les gilets qui l'accompagnent . . . Si certaines femmes restent fidèles à la chemisette-chemisier en grosse soie, en gros crêpe de Chine, ou en linon de fil, les indépendantes préfèrent la blouse droite portée *sur* la jupe, un peu à la facon d'un chandail."

6

Restructuring French Couture, 1914–18

SOPHIE KURKDJIAN

In 1868, Parisian couturiers and manufacturers of *confection*, or ready-made women's wear, united under the aegis of one organization that represented and defended their economic and commercial interests: the Chambre Syndicale de la Couture et de la Confection pour Dames et Fillettes (Trade Association of Couture and Readymade Clothing for Women and Girls), which quickly became the Chambre Syndicale des Couturiers, des Confectionneurs et des Tailleurs pour Dames (Trade Association of Couturiers, Dressmakers, and Tailors for Women).[1] In 1911, the association was dissolved in the wake of internal problems, and after removing confection producers and tailors from its membership, became the Chambre Syndicale de la Couture Parisienne (Trade Association of Parisian Couture, henceforth the Chambre Syndicale), which was dedicated exclusively to couturiers.[2] The purpose of the Chambre Syndicale was to protect Paris couture commercially and legally. It also protected workers' salaries and upheld suitable working conditions, guarded against copying and foreign competition, and promoted fashion design in France. The new mission was the first step toward institutionalizing the couture business and establishing Paris as the capital of fashion.[3]

The First World War, which weakened production in France and revealed the determination of foreign competition, accelerated that process. From August 1914 to November 1918, the Chambre Syndicale developed initiatives to protect Parisian couture and its dissemination abroad. Not only did the organization become aware of the need to structure couture more effectively from within the industry so as to better present a united front, but its leaders also understood how important it was to enhance the visibility of the couturiers abroad in order to assert their productivity and creativity in spite of the war. The Chambre Syndicale henceforth waged a war of words and images in the defense of Paris couture.

At the same time, couturiers also united under the aegis of another organization, the Syndicat de Défense de la Grande Couture Française (Syndicate for the Defense of French Haute Couture, SDGC, henceforth the Syndicat), which was founded in 1914 to defend against the copying of Parisian couture designs. Although membership in the Chambre Syndicale included the entire profession of couturiers, the Syndicat was more exclusive. The two organizations were clearly separate but they had complementary missions. The Chambre Syndicale continued after the war and is still in existence today.[4] The Syndicat, however, mired in problems since 1915, seems to have quietly vanished at the end of the war. The archives of the Chambre Syndicale, which are housed at the Fédération de la Haute Couture et de la Mode, notably includes reports on all of the meetings of couturiers from 1911 to today. FIG. 6.1 However, these reports have not been readily accessible to researchers.[5] Drawing on studies of the Chambre Syndicale and on a systematic inventory of its archives between 1917 and 1918, this chapter examines the key role the Chambre Syndicale played for French couturiers both in safeguarding the profession in wartime and in protecting it against competition and copies. Furthermore, it explains how the wartime organizational efforts of the Chambre Syndicale had long-term repercussions for the history of French couture primarily in how it created the economic and commercial structure that remains relatively unchanged today. This method of analysis reveals how the First World War represents a pivotal moment for the Chambre, strengthening its trade-union foundation and developing new strategies to protect the French couturiers from competitors. It is as if the First World War compelled the Chambre Syndicale to assert both the commercial and the cultural importance of Parisian couture. Attacked and threatened by an increased number of foreign competitors as a result of the war, the organization seems to have taken on the considerable challenge of protecting this venerable French industry. Examining the history of Chambre Syndicale in relation to the Syndicat, it becomes clear that the Syndicat's history is also the history of French designers' awareness of foreign competition as well as of their own status and methods of marketing fashion.[6]

Organizing for Better Protection: the Chambre Syndicale de la Couture Parisienne during World War I

Both the economic and social crises that emerged at the start of the war threatened the very existence of French couture at home and abroad. The fashion industry was a key component of the French economy and, thanks to highly successful exports, it brought in several foreign currencies. Moreover, it employed thousands of young women in Paris. During the first chaotic weeks of August 1914, the Chambre had to decide whether the French couture industry should continue when there was uncertainty about whether the leading couturiers, including Gaston and Jean-Philippe Worth and Paul Poiret, could still work while they were at the front. SEE CHAPTER 5

There was also the question of clientele and whether French women would continue to purchase luxury goods and what would happen to exports.[7] Further uncertainty stemmed from the fact that

France was unsure how the leading importers of French fashion—Great Britain, Belgium, and the United States—would react to the political upheaval and whether they would abandon the Parisian market. Reports of the general meetings in which couturiers participated reflect the Chambre's sharpened focus on the impact of the war both in France and abroad. The organization focused on a range of concerns, and beginning in the fall of 1914, the Chambre's mission became international. For example, they remained closely informed about the couturiers' decisions concerning worker morale, about private donations to Parisian seamstresses (who were called "les petites mains de la mode," or "the little hands of fashion"), about government-sponsored "propaganda" events (fairs, salons, exhibitions), as well as about journalists in the United States. Although this global view did not result in a perfect solution that would shelter Parisian couture from outside threats, it enabled the Chambre Syndicale to evaluate the economic, social, and diplomatic parameters of the situation worldwide, so as to better take action to protect both the identity and the dissemination of Paris couture.[8] Fashion thus became an economic imperative (exports) and a social imperative (labor and employment). By 1914, Paris was already facing competition from Germany, Austria, and the United States that manifested in different ways. This amounted to nothing less than ruthless copying of couturiers' designs. Parisian fashion journals and newspapers were also copied at an alarming rate, as foreign countries wanted to develop a fashion industry independent of Paris. The declaration of war not only affirmed this competition; it went so far as to reinforce it. On December 21, the Chambre Syndicale reacted to the launch by the *New York Times*, *Women's Wear Daily*, and *Collier's Weekly* of "a campaign against Paris couture to benefit American fashions."[9] In response, it announced that the next French couture collections would be presented on the same date as in 1913 and under the same conditions.[10] To ensure that the news reached foreign markets, the Chambre even sent out a brochure to French consulates, chambers of commerce abroad, and major newspapers in Italy, Spain, England, and North and South America.[11] Although there was fear at the time that a distinctive American fashion industry would develop, it ultimately proved irrelevant, given that the French couture houses resumed activity very soon after war broke out. Couturiers even congratulated themselves at the end of December 1914, boasting that "[our] industry has made it known that, contrary to certain misleading rumors, our couture houses have remained open."[12] They thwarted the American threat, but the issue persisted in the minds of the Chambre Syndicale, the couturiers, and the French manufacturers who focused on asserting their control over the industry throughout the war, especially in relation to the United States.[13]

Although the couture industry remained active, the Chambre Syndicale sought to "purify" it by eliminating foreign members who, despite having been part of the Parisian fashion industry since the beginning of the century, were from countries that had become "enemies" since the declaration of war. Paul Poiret was the first to ask the Chambre to consider the matter, proposing several ideas concerning the total exclusion of foreigners, the prohibition of sending original designs abroad, the commercial rules for suppliers, and measures that could be taken against Austrian-German workers and German-Americans.[14] Worth, in accordance with Poiret's proposals, called for an "effective agreement in view of the national defense of our industry," and when he even proposed to dissolve the Chambre Syndicale in order to drive out all foreign and suspect designers, the voting members unanimously approved his motion.[15] Once dissolved, the Chambre was then reestablished during a plenary assembly of members on May 5, 1915. The new Chambre Syndicale was reestablished on new grounds "into a large family," the members of which were either French or belonged "to friendly governments, having the same ideas, the same needs, the same missions, and the same aspirations."[16] Before new members were admitted, a verification committee conducted investigations and reviewed the nationality of fashion houses and any foreign capital to which they might have access.[17] Twenty-one members were excluded from the organization, including Redfern (English) and Drecoll—a major couture house before the war.[18] The Chambre intervened in the Drecoll case directly as its president, Jean Aine-Montaillé, implicated German companies that were still open in Paris during a meeting sponsored by the Association des Tissus (Association of Fabrics).[19] He singled Drecoll out as an example, noting that it was "a branch of a Viennese company" with a partner named Mr. Berg and shareholders who were Austrian and German.[20] After the publication of Aine-Montaillé's remarks in the daily press, the director of Drecoll, Mr. de Wagner, sued Aine-Montaillé and the French daily newspaper *Le Figaro*. He argued not only that Drecoll was in fact English, with its headquarters and administration in London, but also that the only German in the firm, Albert Berg, had

FIG. 6.1 Wartime register of the Chambre Syndicale de la Couture Parisienne.

FIG. 6.2 *Exposition Universelle San Francisco, Panama–Pacific International Exposition, Section Française, Catalogue Officiel 1915* belonging to Jeanne Lanvin (Paris: Devambez, 1915). © DR, Patrimoine Lanvin, Paris.

resigned in August 1914. The trade unions supported Aine-Montaillé, hoping that the resulting ruling would set a precedent and "would act as a shield for the French industry menaced by disloyal competitors."[21] In July 1915, Drecoll lost its case against Aine-Montaillé.[22]

The reestablishment of a new Chambre Syndicale was not enough to completely purge French couture of foreigners nor was it enough to counter or prevent copies and remove those who engaged in illicit behavior from Parisian couture houses. In June 1915, the Chambre proposed instituting stricter rules on forgery and encouraged both couturiers and their clients to reflect on the legality of this issue that was at the heart of Parisian couture. At stake was the originality of the couturiers' designs.[23] But how could an idea be protected? Plans were launched to create a trade union seal consisting of a star medallion bearing the inscription "Chambre Syndicale de la Couture Parisienne" accompanied by a numbering system that distinguished original designs from copies.[24] There is no evidence that this was a convincing strategy, as the Chambre Syndicale continued debating and discussing Austrian-German copiers. In 1916, it even agreed to meet with the Chambre Syndicale des Tailleurs et des Couturiers (Trade Association of Tailors and Couturiers) to consider how to fight an economic war against "cosmopolitan copiers" and "fashion houses thought to belong to enemies."[25] In addition to Austrian-German copiers, a primary target of the French couture industry was the United States, where forgeries and copies of original designs were numerous. American designers even copied French design labels, causing the president of the Chambre Syndicale to lament "the lenient American laws."[26] As a result, the Chambre considered launching a wartime advertising campaign in the United States to "better promote the excellence of [our] products."[27] The goal was to strengthen the relationship between the Parisian houses and American newspapers by opening the Paris salons to American journalists and restricting advertisements for French houses in American magazines that might also advertise German houses.[28] At the same time, the Chambre organized a meeting with American buyers in order to develop a defensive alliance against copying.

Paris Couture Houses and the Call to Arms

The patriotic mobilization of the Chambre Syndicale was accompanied by a realization that in order to mount a successful campaign against copying, French couture must present a united front backed by strong internal leadership and administration. However, in 1915, the couture profession was still weakened by the war. As the treasurer of the Chambre explained in the French fashion magazine *Les Élégances Parisiennes*: "Yet, because you are speaking to me about 'organization,' I will respond that the Fashion Industry does not suffer from poor organization . . . it is worse than that; there is no organization at all."[29] He further explained that the Chambre Syndicale, "considering the workforce it must represent, remains very small, and its voice is lost in the deafening noise of associations of greater scope."[30] The new objective that the Chambre then set for itself included engaging more members from mid-size and small companies to thereby rally as many as possible around the couture cause.[31] To have a real impact abroad, the quantity of members was more important than the quality, and the war was given as an example:

Because our era is about mobilization, let us draw inspiration from what we see; in times of peace as well, it will be necessary to organize every sector of our industry, companies both large and small. Does the army consist only of officers? No, it also needs its soldiers, modest military personnel that follow its leaders while lending full support.[32]

The challenge was to establish a "stronger, more active group," a "defensive alliance through size," and a "reflection of [our] fine national industry, its primacy in the world we wish to retain" in the name of the different interests of the fashion houses forming a united front.[33] In 1917, in the midst of the strike of the *midinettes* (couture seamstresses), the Chambre Syndicale reiterated the absolute need for employers to organize, to enlarge its ranks, to increase its sales in order to be stronger in case of attack, and to be more sophisticated and more efficient.[34] The Chambre's treasurer called for expanding membership. Thus, the war served as a catalyst for unity.[35] The Chambre membership began to increase, reaching 97 in 1917, 125 in 1918, and 130 in 1920 (of the 3,500 couturiers in Paris during that period).[36]

The Syndicat de Défense de la Grande Couture Française and the Fight against Copying

As *Le Style Parisien* published in November 1915: "In every place that a battle can be fought, the Syndicat de Défense will strike . . . and will conquer."[37] Clearly, both the Syndicat de Défense de la Grande Couture Française and the Chambre Syndicale took similar actions to protect Paris couture.[38] It was Paul Poiret who established the Syndicat after he discovered during a trip to New York in 1913 that a store was selling copies of his designs using his name at a very low price.[39] Returning to Paris, he was determined to find a way to prevent this phenomenon from happening again.[40] Poiret created an association that would unify all Paris couturiers and protect their interests.[41] French couturiers and fabric manufacturers enthusiastically welcomed the idea because they had already encountered the same problem.[42] And so the Syndicat de Défense de la Grande Couture Française was founded on June 14, 1914.[43] Poiret became the president, Jacques Worth the vice president, Prosper Chéruit the treasurer, and Louis Rodier the secretary. Other members included the fashion houses Paquin, Atuyer, Premet, and Callot Sœurs, as well as the fashion magazine publisher Lucien Vogel and the textile firm Bianchini-Férier. In 1915, Doucet, Lanvin, and Jenny joined the Syndicat, whose priority was to prevent foreign couturiers from copying designs for later sale to private clients. Foreign buyers, especially Americans, were the Syndicat's main targets.[44] There were thirty-two articles in the Syndicat's charter, with a three-fold mission as its objective: "to fight against the invasion of foreign fashion houses in France," "to fight against copying and forgery in all its forms," and "to fight against the invasion of foreigners."[45]

Poiret's methods caused some discontent among those in the profession. Despite a strong start, several couturiers criticized the Syndicat for claiming that it represented the interests of the entire French fashion industry, when indeed certain houses, such as Dœuillet and Boué Sœurs, were not members.[46] The situation worsened in 1915 when Poiret decided to reinforce the Syndicat's regulations, claiming that the rules established in 1914 were not being respected and that copying was becoming more of a problem. From then on, admission to fashion shows became more difficult because it required presenting a document stamped by Poiret himself.[47] This decision was condemned by American buyers and even sparked a controversy between Parisian couturiers and their American clientele at a time when the United States was a much-needed market for Parisian designers.[48] One of the consequences of this incident was the December 1915 decision by Callot Sœurs to leave the Syndicat. Yet even as the organization faced growing criticism, Poiret was able to bring together designers and buyers in order to present the Syndicat's new policy statements.[49] Following a virulent speech against foreign buyers (Germans, Austrians, Turks, Swiss, Americans, and Poles) that equated France's wartime enemies with these couture design "pirates," Poiret reasserted his determination to permanently eradicate copying.[50] The effects were immediate: afraid that the Syndicat would have a negative impact on their business, Premet resigned in January 1916 along with Jenny and Lanvin. In the meantime, rumors spread about the organization's imminent demise. Poiret continued to establish new rules to combat copying, the most consequential of which was the formation of a legal copyright system.[51] In August 1916, he endeavored to establish "the official authentication of original designs and the management of copyrights for the members of the SDGC."[52] In other words, he wanted to institute a copyright system for fashion that was similar to that which existed for publishing, music, and painting.[53] According to art historian Nancy Troy, these efforts against copying should be understood less as a preventative measure than as an opportunity to exploit the American market, which had become essential to Paris designers when the national market crashed at the beginning of the war.[54]

Paris Couture Abroad

Parallel to their efforts to support the fashion industry in France, the couturiers, the Chambre Syndicale, and the Syndicat very quickly became aware of the need to strengthen the position of Paris abroad as the leading international center of fashion. This was clear in December 1914, when the Chambre de Commerce and the Chambre Syndicale asked the Parisian luxury industries to participate in the 1915 Panama–Pacific International Exposition in San Francisco, a world's fair that commemorated the inauguration of the Panama Canal, the construction of the city of San Francisco in 1776, and its rebuilding after the 1906 earthquake.[55] FIG. 6.2 Both organizations later raved about the unprecedented success of the San Francisco International Exposition as "proof of France's vitality and of [our] fine industry at a critical time when Americans may have doubted it."[56]

Beer, Callot, Chéruit, Dœuillet, Doucet, Jenny, Lanvin, Martial et Armand, Paquin, Premet, and Worth all sent several designs to the exhibition. The *Gazette du Bon Ton* explained that these couturiers thus showed to their American friends the persistence of Parisian good taste.[57] Two special issues of *La Gazette du Bon Ton* were published in order to promote the San Francisco International Exposition in France and the United States.[58] Established in 1912 by Lucien Vogel, *La Gazette du Bon Ton* stopped publishing at the outbreak of the war, but was resumed specifically for the exhibition with a special double issue, with editions in both French and English.[59] FIG. 6.3, 6.4 Both editions addressed the ongoing war directly through a series of patriotic fashion images created by Étienne Drian, but only the English edition had

FIG. 6.3 Front cover of the English-language edition of *The 1915 Mode as Shown by Paris, Panama Pacific International Exposition, La Gazette du Bon Ton,* Summer 1915. © BHVP / Roger-Viollet, RV-157095-1.

La Gazette du Bon Ton
et la Guerre

La huitième livraison de la deuxième année de la "*Gazette du Bon Ton*" était sous presse quand éclata la grande Guerre. Ce fut un vide soudain, un arrêt complet de toutes les activités. Nous dûmes subir le sort commun. En quelques heures, la plupart de nos collaborateurs avaient rejoint leurs postes.

1

Copyright June 1915 by Lucien Vogel, Paris.

FIG. 6.4 "The Gazette du Bon Ton and the War." *La Gazette du Bon Ton,* Summer 1915. © Bibliothèque Forney / Roger-Viollet.

photographs.[60] FIGS. 6.5–6.12 The double issue was clearly intended to support "the delicate resurrection" of Paris couture by proclaiming its preeminence: *Although a part of French soil is yet in the hands of the invader, Paris remains as ever the Paris of good taste and fashion. Therefore, in spite of the glorious trials of war, and in order that Paris may retain her accustomed rank in every Exhibition, the following great and justly renowned Dressmakers have sent to San-Francisco their latest and most stylish creations.*[61]

A portfolio with three foldouts representing the sites of fashionable French society—"Vichy" (illustrated by Georges Barbier), "Longchamp" (George Lepape), and the "Côte d'Azur" (Pierre Brissaud)—was intended to demonstrate that Paris "continues to dictate the peaceable decrees of elegance throughout the world, amidst the turmoil of war."[62] FIGS. 6.13, 6.14

After the exhibition in San Francisco, twenty of the sixty dresses traveled to the Panama–California Exposition in San Diego from 1915 to 1917, where they were exhibited against a backdrop image of Monte Carlo.[63] The Chambre Syndicale supported several other initiatives during the war, including fairs in Lyon and exhibitions in Madrid.[64] Moreover, on July 2, 1918, it took over the initiative of the Office Commercial Français in Switzerland to organize an exhibition with the French Ministry of Commerce to be held in Zurich on August 21 and 22, 1918, that would "offset German and Austrian activity."[65] This exhibition, "the national character of which should not escape anyone's notice," according to the couturier Réverdot, consisted of a presentation of dresses.[66] On July 16, 1918, the new president of the Chambre Syndicale, Jeanne Paquin, also invited designers to participate in the Foire de Paris, proclaiming that, "We must show, once again, both to France and to countries abroad, that our couture exists, works, and is thriving. The bulletins of the Foire, sent all over world, are indeed the best publicity." According to Paquin, what was at stake was a matter of national interest. "Couturiers and patriots: they complement one another, and the former grants the latter the luster that is lent by all the great and noble instincts."[67] On October 22, 1919, Paquin agreed to show dresses on live models at an exhibition in Sarrebruck, a city on the French-German border, which she described as "good propaganda for the French trade that is Couture."[68]

The Syndicat developed a plan of action that was similar to that of the Chambre Syndicale. One of its first initiatives outside France was to organize an event that would raise money to help couturiers and other French fashion employees who were faced with "forced unemployment." In November 1915, it organized a Fête Parisienne (Celebration of French Fashion) in New York, sponsored by *Vogue*.[69] FIG. 6.15

It was meant to be "the most beautiful demonstration of French taste and the best evidence for the admirable vitality that too many people, interested in dethroning Paris from its sovereignty, continue to question."[70] The largest French fashion houses, including Worth, Poiret, Paquin, Doucet, Jenny, Chéruit, and Lanvin, sent between ten and twelve garments each, whereas smaller companies sent three or four, depending on their means. Leading American department stores, including Bonwit Teller, B. Altman, John Wanamaker, and Henri Bendel, purchased designs from the collection. One of the dresses displayed during the Fête was designed by Callot Sœurs: pink and gold, it was both photographed by Philip Ortiz and illustrated in *Le Style Parisien*. FIGS. 6.16–6.18

The celebration, which was held at the Ritz Carlton hotel, took the form of a "theatrical performance."[71] With revenue from the sales estimated at a million francs, the event proved to be both a financial and a cultural success for the couture houses.

Still keen on visibility abroad, the two associations paid particular attention to the American press, which had been critical of French fashion in 1914. However, the opinions became increasingly more positive, especially after the United States entered the war in April 1917.[72] *Vogue*, *Harper's Bazaar*, and *Women's Wear Daily* were among the publications that changed their position on Paris couture over the course of the war. *Women's Wear Daily*, notably, sent a telegram to the Chambre Syndicale in the spring of 1917:

The invincible spirit of France has been nowhere else better mobilized than in its brave couture. We are delighted to have become brothers in arms in the pursuit of our common ideals. May our great and inspiring friendship grow even more in time.[73]

In the period immediately following the war, the Chambre Syndicale reasserted how important it was for couturiers to make themselves known to American clients. To that end, the Chambre cited two observations made by the French trade mission that had been sent to the United States: first, Americans who had been unable to travel to France during the war had placed orders with American companies that had sold them "very imperfect reproductions of originals from Paris couture houses." Second, because the anti-French propaganda did everything it could to "turn Americans away from French fashion,"

FIG. 6.5 Étienne Adrien Drian. "French Bouquet." *La Gazette du Bon Ton,* Summer 1915. Pochoir. © Bibliothèque Forney / Roger-Viollet, RV-157813-6.

FIG. 6.6 Étienne Adrien Drian. "Following the Operations." *La Gazette du Bon Ton,* Summer 1915. Pochoir. © Bibliothèque Forney / Roger Viollet, RV-157813-4.

FIG. 6.7 Étienne Adrien Drian. "The Marseillaise." *La Gazette du Bon Ton,* Summer 1915. Pochoir. © Bibliothèque Forney / Roger Viollet, RV-157813-7.

FIG. 6.8 Étienne Adrien Drian. "The Bulletin." *La Gazette du Bon Ton,* Summer 1915. Pochoir. © Bibliothèque Forney / Roger Viollet, RV-157813-8.

FIG. 6.9 Étienne Adrien Drian. "Without her car." *La Gazette du Bon Ton,* Summer 1915. Pochoir. © Bibliothèque Forney / Roger Viollet, RV-157813-5.

FIG. 6.10 Étienne Adrien Drian. "Avenue du Bois." *La Gazette du Bon Ton,* Summer 1915. Pochoir. © Bibliothèque Forney / Roger Viollet, RV-157813-9.

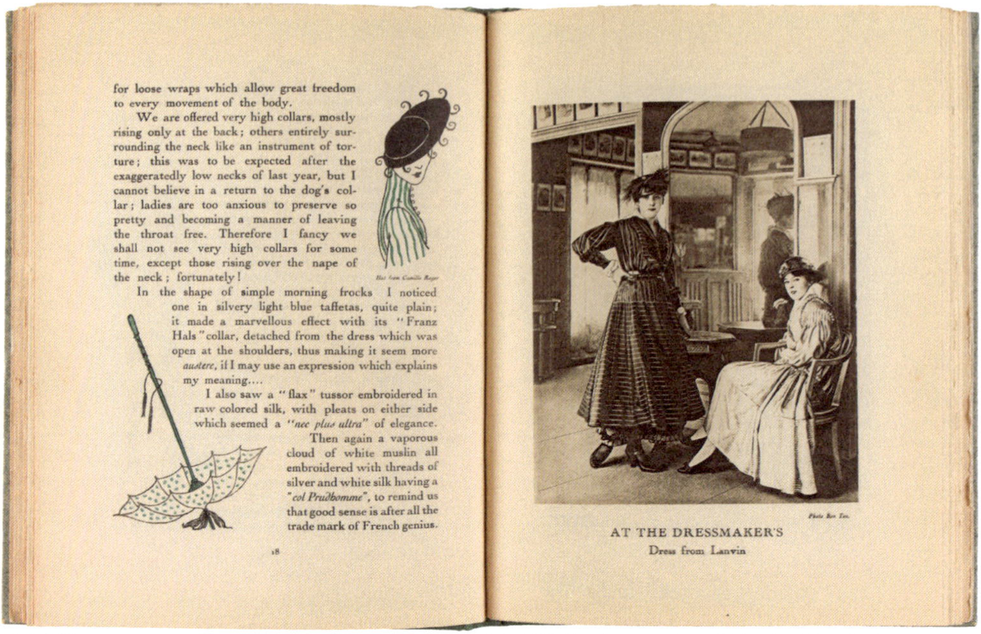

for loose wraps which allow great freedom to every movement of the body.

We are offered very high collars, mostly rising only at the back; others entirely surrounding the neck like an instrument of torture; this was to be expected after the exaggeratedly low necks of last year, but I cannot believe in a return to the dog's collar; ladies are too anxious to preserve so pretty and becoming a manner of leaving the throat free. Therefore I fancy we shall not see very high collars for some time, except those rising over the nape of the neck; fortunately!

Hat from Camille Roger

In the shape of simple morning frocks I noticed one in silvery light blue taffetas, quite plain; it made a marvellous effect with its "Franz Hals" collar, detached from the dress which was open at the shoulders, thus making it seem more *austere*, if I may use an expression which explains my meaning....

I also saw a "flax" tussor embroidered in raw colored silk, with pleats on either side which seemed a "*nec plus ultra*" of elegance.

Then again a vaporous cloud of white muslin all embroidered with threads of silver and white silk having a "*col Prudhomme*", to remind us that good sense is after all the trade mark of French genius.

18

Photo Bon Ton.

AT THE DRESSMAKER'S

Dress from Lanvin

FIG. 6.11 Two women in Lanvin dresses entitled "At the Dressmakers." *The 1915 Mode As Shown by Paris, La Gazette du Bon Ton,* Summer 1915. © BHVP / Roger Viollet, RV-157095-1.

Photo Bon Ton.

PLACE VENDOME

Dress from Premet

FIG. 6.12 "Place Vendome" dress by Premet. *The 1915 Mode As Shown by Paris, La Gazette du Bon Ton*, Summer 1915. © BHVP / Roger Viollet, RV-717446.

FIG. 6.13 Pierre Brissaud. Illustration of evening dresses by Callot Sœurs, Jenny, Dœuillet, Chéruit, Beer, Lanvin, Paquin, Doucet, Premet, Worth, and Martial and Armand entitled "The Côte d'Azur or A Celebration on the Terrace," *La Gazette du Bon Ton*, Summer 1915. Pochoir. © Bibliothèque Forney / Roger Viollet.

E D'AZUR
ou
sur la terrasse
56. Worth. 57. Martial et Armand.
Paquin. 52. Doucel. 53. Paquin.
met. 55. Worth.
58. Martial et Armand. 59. Premet. 60. Callot.
Été 1915. — Pl. 6.

FIG. 6.14 Georges Lepape. Illustration of models by Beer, Lanvin, Paquin, Callot, Doucet, Worth, and Premet entitled "Longchamp (I), or She Won!," *La Gazette du Bon Ton*, Summer 1915. Pochoir. © Bibliothèque Forney / Roger-Viollet, RV-157813-2.

MP (I)

né !

26. Paquin. *27. Doucet.* *28. Worth.* *29. Premet.* *30. Doucet.*

FIG. 6.15 Dartey, pseudonym of Anette Osterlind. "La Fête Parisienne à New York" (A Celebration of Paris in New York). From left to right, dresses by Worth, Paquin, Chéruit, and Premet. *Le Style Parisien*, November 1915, pl. XV. © Diktats bookstore.

FIG. 6.16 Callot Sœurs designs at the "Fête Parisienne" in New York. *Le Style Parisien*, December 1915, pl. XXI. © Diktats bookstore.

FIG. 6.17 Callot Sœurs. Evening dress exhibited at the Panama–Pacific International Exposition in San Francisco, 1915–16. Silk, metallic thread. The Metropolitan Museum of Art, Purchase, Irene Lewisohn Bequest, 1951, C.I.51.97.1a,b.

FIG. 6.18 Philippe Ortiz. Model wearing the “Déesse” dress by Callot Sœurs at the Fête Parisienne in New York, 1915. Silver gelatin print.
© Diktats bookstore.

FIG. 6.19 Helen Dryden. "This Number a Forecast of Autumn Fashions." British *Vogue*, September 1916, cover. © Diktats bookstore.

FIG. 6.20 Helen Dryden. "We'll get them." Continental *Vogue*, July 1918, cover.

FIG. 6.21 Georges Lepape. "The Heart of France," Continental *Vogue*, December 1915, cover. © Diktats bookstore.

FIG. 6.22 Georges Lepape. Continental *Vogue*, August 1918, cover. © Diktats bookstore.

FIG. 6.23 Alice de Warenne Little. Continental *Vogue,* Early July 1918, cover.
© Diktats bookstore.

FIG. 6.24 Georges Lepape. "Long live France!" British *Vogue*, Early November 1917, cover.
© Diktats bookstore.

Americans had been told that "French couture houses had designed nothing or almost nothing at all."[74] And so there was a new call to organize events in the United States: the treasurer of the Chambre Syndicale called on the Parisian couture houses to either establish venues in the United States, together or individually, in New York, Washington, and Chicago or to present collections there every season.[75] The campaign that *Vogue*, Condé Nast, and the American and English press were waging against "the official means of German commercial propaganda" also drew the attention of the Chambre Syndicale.[76] Condé Nast released British *Vogue* on October 15, 1916 and a Continental edition followed the next year in 1917. Distributed in France and published in English, the Continental edition dealt primarily with France and wartime couture, and featured covers by Helen Dryden and Georges Lepape.

FIGS. 6.19–6.24 Members of the Chambre Syndicale expressed their determination to further embed *Vogue* in French fashion culture with a French-language edition of Contintental *Vogue*.[77] This goal was realized four years later on June 15, 1920, when French *Vogue* was released. The Chambre Syndicale de la Couture Parisienne and the Syndicat de Défense de la Grande Couture Française proved to be indispensable in protecting the couture industry during the war by establishing its business practices during a period of immense struggle. They were responsible for the survival of French couture by creating initiatives that were directly related to the French war effort. Breaking away from traditions that had existed since the nineteenth century, they reorganized the fashion houses and the fashion trade unions. In the long history of the Chambre Syndicale, the war represents a pivotal moment in the structural reorganization of Parisian fashion design. Twenty-five years later, there was a similar movement when the Second World War broke out. The Chambre Syndicale once again mobilized to reinforce power and authority in France and abroad, especially in regard to foreign markets and competition, which grew proportionately with the severity of the war.

The only areas the Chambre Syndicale and the Syndicat seem to have ignored during the First World War were the actual designs and issues of style. Frequently citing French couturiers and their plight, whether they were on the front lines (Poiret, Worth), in the midst of the 1917 midinette strike (Jenny), or elected as head of the Chambre Syndicale (Jeanne Paquin), the associations never discussed changes in style or the textile industry—issues that the press often addressed. The press discussed new collections and trends in Parisian couture and offered considerable support to designers and unions even though they also faced their own wartime difficulties. Threatened by German publishers who had been making copies of French fashion magazines for years, the Parisian fashion press had to protect itself by continuing to fight against forgeries while simultaneously promoting French fashion.

1 Trade Association of Couture and Readymade Clothing for Women and Girls; Trade Association of Couturiers, Dressmakers, and Tailors for Women.

2 Both were founded under the aegis of the Association Générale du Commerce et de l'Industrie des Tissus et Matières that partially financed the Chambre Syndicale de la Couture. Session of February 15, 1922, archives of the Fédération de la Haute Couture et de la Mode (FHCM).

3 Véronique Pouillard, "In the Shadow of Paris? French Haute Couture and Belgian Fashion Between the Wars," in Regina Lee Blaszczyk, *Producing Fashion: Commerce, Culture, and Consumers (Hagley Perspectives on Business and Culture*) (Philadelphia: University of Pennsylvania Press, 2007), 65.

4 It merged with the Chambre Syndicale de la Mode Masculine and the Chambre Syndicale du Prêt-à-porter des Couturiers et des Créateurs de Modes, both founded in 1973, under the Fédération de la Haute Couture et de la Mode.

5 Didier Grumbach considered different sources for his book *Histoires de Mode*, whereas Véronique Pouillard has focused on the 1920s to1940s to study the history of the Chambre during the interwar period; and David Zajtmann has turned toward contemporary documents to write his thesis on the history of the Fédération de la Haute Couture et de la Mode, to which the Chambre Syndicale de la Couture Parisienne has belonged since 1973; Didier Grumbach, *Histoires de la mode* (1993, repr. Paris: Editions du Regard, 2008); Véronique Pouillard, "Managing fashion creativity: The history of the Chambre Syndicale de la Couture Parisiennne during the interwar period," *Investigaciones de Historia Económica (Economic History Research)* 12, no. 2 (2016), 76–89; David Zajtmann, *Meta-organisations professionnelles et incitations sélectives. La Fédération de la couture, du prêt-à-porter des couturiers et des créateurs de mode (1973–2011)*, doctoral thesis, Université Panthéon-Sorbonne, 2014. Maude Bass-Krueger used these archives on the First World War to write her Master's thesis on fashion between 1914 and 1918. In envisioning the role of "couture groups," she analyzes the role of the Chambre in supporting dressmaking in wartime. Maude Bass-Krueger, "La mode en France durant la Première Guerre mondiale: Approches d'histoire culturelle," MA thesis, Institut d'Études politiques de Paris, 2008.

6 Nancy Troy has considered the history of the Syndicat from the perspective of the dissemination of fashion and matters of copyright and copying. Nancy Troy, *Couture Culture, A Study in Modern Art and Fashion* (Cambridge, MA: MIT Press, 2002), 450.

7 Extraordinary general assembly of December 21, 1914, FHCM archives. See also Anne Rittenhouse, "Fashion Under Fire," *Vogue*, October 1, 1914, 40, 41, 110.

8 The Chambre Syndicale de la Couture Parisienne even founded a military hospital at the beginning of the war. See "L'hôpital de la couture," *Les Élégances Parisiennes*, August 1916, 71.

9 Extraordinary general assembly of December 21, 1914, FHCM archives. See the numerous articles published in the *New York Times*, including "Paris may see end of style control, designs predict our emancipation from French modes as result," August 6, 1914; "Society asks New York designer to create fashion," October 25, 1914; "Now is the time for Americans to design new fashions," September 27, 1914. See Chapter 5 in this volume.

10 Extraordinary general assembly of December 21, 1914, FHCM archives.
See for example "American Designer Redivivus: Fifth Avenue Designer Gives Reason For Lack Of Prestige— Sees Chance To Get Rid Of Paris Influence," *Women's Wear Daily*, August 13, 1914; "French And American Designers: Contributor Says It Is Useless To Compare American Ready-To-Wear Manufacturer With French Couturier Because They Are In Different Lines Of Business— Urges American Designers To Do Their Best And Says Beauty Will Not Depart From American Clothes If Influence Of Paris Is Cut Off For A Time," *Women's Wear Daily*, August 11, 1914.

11 Extraordinary general assembly of December 21, 1914, FHCM archives.

12 Ibid.

13 "L'Amérique et les industries du vêtement," *Les Élégances Parisiennes*, August 1917, 261.

14 Session of December 21, 1914, FHCM archives.

15 Ibid. In the Register, Worth is only identified by last name, which makes it difficult to determine which of Charles Frederick Worth's descendants made this decision.

16 Session of May 14, 1915, FHCM archives. Naturalized members were also admitted.

17 Ibid.

18 For further information on expelled members, see Bass-Krueger, "La mode en France," 72. See also Adelheid Rasche, "Two Drecoll Houses of Fashion in Paris—A New Discovery," symposium "Les Échanges Franco-Allemands dans la Mode," October 6–7, 2016, in Paris, October 10–11 in Berlin.

19 See Drecoll's proceedings against the Chambre: "L'oncle abandonné," *Le Figaro*, February 11, 1915; "La couture française intervient," *Le Figaro*, February 13, 1915, "Nouvelles judiciaries," *Le Figaro*, October 15, 1916. See also *Le Gaulois*, February 14, 1915, 2.

20 Session of July 21, 1916, FHCM archives. The Swiss-born Wagner, director of Drecoll, bought the design company Ch. Drecoll and Kohlmarchk in Vienna with a German, Albert Berg, as well as with a Mr. Kahn, a French naturalized citizen; he then established a branch of that company in Paris in 1902. See also "Nouvelles Syndicales: Le Procès Aine-Drecoll," *Les Élégances Parisiennes*, September 1916, 88.

21 Ibid.

22 *Bulletin de la Ligue anti-allemande. Organe de défense des intérêts économiques français et coloniaux*, August 1, 1916.

23 Session of June 9, 1915, FHCM archives.

24 Ibid. In April 1916, the idea came about to create an intersyndicate brand, "Unis-France." See "La marque intersyndicale," *Les Élégances Parisiennes*, April 1916, 6; "Unis-France," *Les Elégances Parisiennes*, May 1916, 23; and "Unis-France," *Les Élégances Parisiennes*, September 1916, 86; " La marque Unis-France," *Les Elégances Parisiennes*, October 1917, 187.

25 Plenary session of February 24, 1916, FHCM archives.

26 Extraordinary plenary session of July 7, 1915, FHCM archives.

27 Ibid.

28 Session of December 13, 1916, FHCM archives. "La maison de couture de Paris et les acheteurs de New-York," *Les Elégances Parisiennes*, April 1916, 8.

29 "Ce que devrait faire la mode parisienne," *Les Élégances Parisiennes*, June 1916, 37.

30 Constituent plenary assembly, May 5, 1915, registry of reports on general assemblies, FHCM archives.

31 Treasurer report to the General Assembly of April 19, 1916, FHCM archives.

32 "Ce que devrait faire la mode parisienne," *Les Élégances Parisiennes*, June 1916, 37.

33 General Assembly of July 12, 1917, FHCM archives, and constituent plenary assembly, May 5, 1915.

34 General Assembly of July 12, 1917, FHCM archives.

35 Danièle Fraboulet, Pierre Vernus, *Genèse des organisations patronales en Europe (19è–20è siècles)* (Paris: PUR, 2012), 108.

36 Plenary assembly of December 2, 1918, FHCM archives. The large number of couturiers at this time is due to the fact that in the early twentieth century, "couture" was a much broader field than it is today.

37 "Le Syndicat de Défense de la Grande Couture française et des industries s'y rattachant," *Le Style Parisien*, November 1915, 1.

38 "Pour défendre nos industries," *Les Élégances Parisiennes*, June 1916, 38.

39 "Copyrighting clothes," *Vogue*, February 1915, 17, 100.

40 Caroline Seebohm, *The Man who was Vogue, the Life and the Times of Condé Nast* (London: Weidenfeld and Nicolson, 1982), 84.

41 Edna Woolman Chase, *Always in Vogue* (New York: Doubleday, 1954), 381, 109.

42 See "Les Fausses étiquettes," *Les Élégances Parisiennes*, July 1916, and André de Fouquières, "Du prestige de la mode aux États-Unis," *La Gazette du Bon Ton*, April 1913, 177–78, and Nancy Troy, *Couture Culture: A Study in Modern Art and Fashion* (Cambridge, MA: MIT Press, 2002), 266.

43 Le Syndicat de défense de la grande couture française et des industries s'y rattachant, 3053 3110W44, Archives de Paris. See also "Statutes of French Fashion Syndicate, now published for the first time," *New York Times*, January 23, 1916.

44 "La Grande couture française et quelques-uns de ses clients," *Le Style Parisien*, November 1915, 35.

45 "Le Syndicat de Défense de la Grande couture Française," *Le Style Parisien*, November 1915; "First news of French Fashion syndicate's official plans," *New York Times*, January 23, 1916.

46 *La Renaissance*, June 10, 1916.

47 "Paris dressmakers in protective union," *New York Times*, October 24, 1915; "Paris couturiers' break," *New York Times*, December 1, 1915; "Our buyers indignant," *New York Times*, November 12, 1915; and "First news of French fashion syndicate's official plans," *New York Times*, January 23, 1916.

48 *Le Petit Parisien*, November 21, 1915; "Mrs. Galt's gowns cause Paris row," *New York Times*, November 20, 1915. Troy, *Couture Culture*, 289.

49 "Paul Poiret assails American buyers," *New York Times*, January 23, 1916.

50 "First news of French fashion syndicate's official plans," *New York Times*, January 23, 1916. Nancy Troy speaks of a "national rhetoric" even though Poiret, before the war, was considered a cosmopolitan, taking advantage of foreign influences to create his collections. This explains why Poiret's diatribe seems above all to reflect the weighty ideological climate in France at that time, as well as the designer's personal situation. In fact, during that same period, Poiret was accused by the newspaper *La Renaissance* of promoting German tastes in his dresses. A few weeks later, the paper published a retraction, but it was too late. Poiret had been publicly implicated, and would forever seek to prove his patriotism. See Troy, *Couture Culture*, 278.

51 "Projet d'organisation de la copie et de la reproduction des modèles des grands couturiers," *Les Élégances Parisiennes*, August 1916, 70.

52 Ibid.

53 "First news of French fashion syndicate's official plans," *New York Times*, January 23, 1916.

54 Poiret's measures (copyright, licensing system for copying, renting and exhibiting prototypes) were also a way of retaining control of an industry undergoing upheaval, as well as a way of taking advantage of emerging mass production. In fact, after having failed to eradicate copying, which they learned was impossible, couturiers wanted to benefit from it. Wishing to protect the authenticity of their design from copying, they were simultaneously aware of the need to produce copies of their prototypes themselves so that American clients would continue to be their clients, and would not turn toward illegal copies. To a certain extent, this meant turning the situation to their advantage, even anticipating the post-war period by taking advantage of the mass production of their prototypes. Troy, *Couture Culture*, 273–74.

55 Extraordinary General Assembly of December 21, 1914, FHCM archives.

56 In June 1915 and also in April 1916, Session of April 19, 1916, FHCM archives.

57 Daniel Delis Hill, *As Seen in Vogue: A Century of American Fashion Advertising* (Lubbock, TX: Texas Tech University Press, 2004), and Steele, *Paris Fashion*, 236–37.

58 Postponed when war was declared, the organization of this exhibition began again starting on November 20, 1914, and, less than nine weeks later, the Palais de la France was built. Overcoming problems with customs officials who almost denounced them, luxury fashion houses were able to send their products to San Francisco under the aegis of the Chamber of Commerce. See Exposition Internationale de San Francisco, 1915, general report (Paris: E. Larose, 1915).

59 *La Gazette du Bon Ton* began publishing again in January 1920 with issue 1, third year. The English edition of the 1915 issue was sold in the United States by the American publisher Condé Nast as "The 1915 Mode as shown by Paris," subtitled "Panama Pacific International Exposition: A De Luxe Portfolio of Paris Styles."

60 Although the basic text in both editions was the same, the illustrations were different—the English edition included photographs of fashionable women taken by Bon Ton, Felix, Léopold-Emile Reutlinger, Frédéric Boissonas, and André Taponier that did not appear in the French edition. This highly ambitious initiative, in all likelihood proposed by Condé Nast, was unprecedented. Until then *La Gazette du Bon Ton* had never published photographs.

61 *La Gazette du Bon Ton,* Introduction.

62 *La Gazette du Bon Ton*, Summer 1915. See also Etienne Mascré, "Tissus et Couture: La couture Parisienne," Exposition Internationale de San Francisco, 1915, general report, Paris, *La Gazette du Bon Ton*, Summer 1915, and Etienne Mascré, "Tissus et couture: La couture parisienne," Exposition Internationale de San Francisco, 1915, general report (Paris: E. Larose, 1915), 501–2.

63 Six of the twenty dresses exhibited in San Francisco were sold, which was considered a great success. Session of April 19, 1916, FHCM archives.

64 Session of December 13, 1916, FHCM archives. See also "Le succès de la Foire de Lyon," *Les Élégances Parisiennes*, December 1916, 22, and "Les Foires de France," *Les Élégances Parisiennes,* December 1916, 133, "La Foire de Lyon," *Les Élégances Parisiennes*, May 1917, 213.

65 Report on the committee meeting of Tuesday, July 2, 1918, FHCM archives.

66 Report on the committee meeting of July 8, 1918, FHCM archives.

67 Sessions of July 16 and 23, 1918. The design houses Barotte, Beer, Bourniche, Marie Claverie, Chéruit, Détrois, Dœuillet, Garrigue, Jeanne Hallé, Jenny, Jeanne Lanvin, Martial et Armand, Memessier, Paquin, Redfern, and Réverdot participated. Each designer presented two dresses.

68 Plenary assembly of October 22, 1919, FHCM archives.

69 Before that, in November 1914, Edna Woolman Chase and Condé Nast organized a "fashion event." The sales from that event went toward the French war effort, but the initiative was not well received by the French, who were unhappy about the independence of American fashion. It was then rumored, mostly by *Harper's Bazaar, Vogue*'s rival, that *Vogue* was abandoning French couture in order to devote itself to American fashion. To reassure Parisians, Condé Nast sent envoys to Poiret and to the Syndicat de la Couture to propose a "Fête de la Mode Parisienne" in November 1915.

70 "Le Syndicat de Défense de la Grande couture Française," *Le Style Parisien,* November 1915.

71 The piece was written by Roger Boutet de Monvel. See "Paris dressmakers in protective union," *New York Times,* October 24, 1915.

72 Session of April 19, 1916, FHCM archives.

73 Committee session of Wednesday, May 9, 1917, FHCM archives.

74 Plenary assembly of December 23, 1919, FHCM archives.

75 Ibid.

76 Session of December 13, 1916, FHCM archives.

77 Ibid.

7

“Copying is Stealing!”: The Fashion Press & Counterfeiting

SOPHIE KURKDJIAN

Ever since the French fashion press began in the eighteenth century, French fashion magazines have been counterfeited by foreign publishers.[1] In the nineteenth century, as the French fashion press expanded, illicit copies became even more pervasive. FIG. 7.1

The problem of counterfeit magazines developed in tandem with the actual theft of designs from Parisian fashion designers, to the point that one illegal activity seemed to foster the other. Most of the counterfeit magazines were founded by German, Austrian, and Belgian publishers who specialized in the sale of fashion magazines with French names. They featured the latest collections that had been illegally obtained from the Parisian fashion shows.[2]

On the eve of the First World War in 1914, the number of fake French fashion magazines in Europe had increased considerably: more than forty fashion titles owned by Belgian and Austrian-German publishers were actually illicit copies of French magazines.[3] German editors were particularly active counterfeiters, publishing a wide array of copies with titles such as *Paris-Chic-Parfait*, *La Confection Parisienne*, *Paris-Confection*, *Les Modèles Parisiens*, *L'Idéal Parisien*, *Le Grand Chic*, *La Revue Parisienne*, and *La Toilette Parisienne*.[4] In 1915, the actual French magazine *Le Style Parisien* noted that the French fashion press had been greatly affected by this problem:

Many publications that were very successful in France until last year came to us from Berlin, Vienna, and Frankfurt and poorly concealed their origins by calling themselves 'Parisian.' Despite their cumbersome design and spirit, many people were fooled and sought ideas in those fashion catalogues, which were nothing more than systematic copies of designs by our couturiers.[5]

The First World War revealed the German and Austrian hold on the French publishing market. When war was declared, the copies ceased being available at French newsstands.[6]

Although scholars have studied the subject of stealing original French couture designs, counterfeit fashion magazines have received less attention.[7] These magazines affected the ways in which French fashion circulated internationally at the beginning of the twentieth century and specifically during the First World War. The increase in plagiarized magazines just before the outbreak of the war heightened awareness of the counterfeiting problem and the risk of foreign competition. During the war, editors organized initiatives to attempt to thwart foreign publishers and fashion houses took greater precautions to stem the market for copied couture designs. Through an analysis of the fashion press, newspapers published during the war, archives of the Chambre

Syndicale de la Couture Parisienne (Trade Association of Parisian Couture), as well as the archives of fashion publications, this essay investigates the economic and legal mechanisms behind the counterfeiting of fashion magazines and the reactions of the fashion industry and the French fashion press, and responds to key questions that illuminate the complexity of this issue.[8]

The Problem of Counterfeit Publications

The First World War enhanced the controversy surrounding counterfeit fashion magazines. French publishers, journalists, couturiers, and fashion organizations were all concerned with this national problem. According to the journalist Henri Lapauze, counterfeiters used French titles and copies of original French designs to fool readers. Above all, he explained, "you had to be Parisian in Berlin and in Vienna alike, and lead readers to believe that it all came from Paris, both the writing and the designs."[9] However, although the titles of these publications appeared to be from Paris, there was nothing truly Parisian about them. Lapauze writes about this falsification of French fashion, and the "definite deception regarding the origin of merchandise."[10] The gravity of the problem demanded that French president Raymond Poincaré, in his speech to the Congrès National du Livre at the Sorbonne in June 1917, mention the "problem of German publications:"

Through methodical and incessant propaganda, Germany successfully sold us a growing number of books and periodicals published in Prussia, Saxony, and Bavaria and often printed as though they were actually French. Passing through customs, to monopolize the shelves of obliging bookstores, came hundreds of. . . fashion magazines, which were cynically titled the "Façon Parisienne," the "Modèles Parisiens," and "Idéal Parisien," and which offered lessons on French manners from the banks of the Spree River.[11]

Several initial questions emerge from this discussion: how and why were these counterfeits so easily disseminated? A loophole in custom tariffs seems to explain how counterfeit fashion magazines at the beginning of the twentieth century were distributed. In most other countries, foreign publications were subjected to an elevated customs tax if they were printed in a foreign language. As a protective measure, imports were only granted duty-free access if they were written in the native language.[12] In France, however, laws were more flexible, and any publication that read "printed in France" could pass through customs duty for free. Since French was the prevailing language of these counterfeit publications, they circulated easily.

L'IDÉAL PARISIEN

FEMININA

CLOCHES DE MAI

Avec le soleil et le gai muguet, Mai nous ramène l'époque de la jolie vision qu'est une communiante.

Quoi de plus gracieux que la fillette dans son immaculée robe de mousseline blanche, la couronne de roses blanches ou le fin bonnet sur la tête, enveloppée dans son voile blanc!

Regardez-la passer. Le front penché il semble que, reine d'un jour, car ce jour-là c'est la reine de la famille, elle comprenne mieux que la veille ce que la vie attend d'elle. Elle comprend qu'il lui faudra désormais renoncer à être petite fille. Elle va devenir la compagne de sa mère et sera bientôt la jeune fille qui secondera la maîtresse de maison.

Fille d'ouvrier ou d'artisan, elle quittera l'école pour faire son apprentissage, car elle devra apporter son appoint au budget familial.

Photo Félix

Grand Chapeau noir, ondulé, garni panache de plumes ibis dégradé, posé moitié sur la calotte

Modèle de la Maison Marie-Jeanne, 17, place de la Madeleine

Photo H. Manue

Grand Chapeau Tagal noir, ajouré, doublé Valenciennes, deux grosses roses France et feuillage, Derrière nœud Louis XVI bleu de roi

Modèle de la Maison Marie-Jeanne, 17, place de la Madeleine.

Je vais donc aujourd'hui donner quelques types de robes simples, c'est-à-dire de circonstance, et que les mamans pourront exécuter elles-mêmes si elles le désirent et pour peu qu'elles soient adroites.

D'abord une jupe ornée de trois groupes de sept plis fins espacés.

Le corsage, rappelant la jupe, est composé de groupes de plis également, décolleté sur un empiècement rond fait d'entre-deux réunis par un jour. Bas de manches assortis.

Le deuxième modèle, plus riche, se compose d'une jupe ornée de plis séparés par trois entre-deux en Valenciennes imitation.

Le corsage, entièrement fait de groupes de cinq plis séparés par des entre-deux prend la forme kimono, le haut décolleté en carré sur une guimpe de tulle finement plissé.

Enfin une jupe en broderie anglaise, incrustée de carrés de

186

FIG. 7.1 Example of an article in a counterfeit French publication produced by a German publisher. "Feminina," *L'Idéal Parisien: Magazine illustré universel,* May 1911, 186–87. © Bibliothèque nationale de France.

FIG. 7.2 Fabien Fabiano. Caricature of a woman wearing German fashions. "Élégances Berlinoises," *La Baïonette*, August 12, 1915. © Bibliothèque Marguerite Durand / Roger-Viollet RV-157096-1.

Then there is the question of the publishers: who was printing and distributing these magazines? The journalist Camille Duguet identified the four main publishing houses responsible for the counterfeit magazines in the 1915 article "There Are Still Austro-German Publishers in Paris." These firms included the Bachwitz company, located in Vienna, which published twenty-five counterfeits, including *La Mode Parisienne*, *La Revue Parisienne*, *Le Grand Tailleur*, *Le Carnaval Parisien*, *La Saison Parisienne*, and *Le Goût à Paris*.[13] To make the magazines more French, Bachwitz decorated the covers with the French flag and the coat of arms of the city of Paris. Indicative of the depth of foreign infiltration of the Parisian publishing industry, the Viennese Finkelstein company was represented in Paris by Mr. Gruenwald, a naturalized Austrian. The firm's titles included *Le Grand Chic*, *La Couturière Parisienne*, *Tailor Made*, *La Grande Confection*, and *Le Chic*, but they were discontinued in 1915, during the height of their popularity. The firm also distributed fashion journals in London during the war, including *L'Élégance de Paris*. Another publisher, Gustav Lyon in Berlin, sold *La Toilette Moderne*, *L'Idéal Parisien*, *Albums de Travestis*, *La Mode Artistique*, and *Les Jolies Modes de Paris*. When English authorities seized *Les Jolies Modes de Paris*, Lyon replaced the "Printed in London" label on the cover of the magazine with "Printed in The Hague." This simple gesture disguised it as neutral, thus allowing it to enter France.[14] The fourth publisher Duguet mentions is German counterfeiter G. Martens, located in Frankfurt, who published *Chic de Paris* and *Les Modèles de Paris*.[15]

It is furthermore necessary to consider what the counterfeit fashion magazines reveal about the rivalry between France and Germany. This tension, in the context of increased wartime nationalism, involved all sectors of culture and society, including fashion and design. Even the couturier Paul Poiret was accused of designing clothes that were too "German," while the French fashion publisher Lucien Vogel was suspected of being a foreigner.[16]

From an economic perspective, the copying of French fashion magazines seemed to be part of a larger plan to develop the German fashion industry.[17] In the early twentieth century, when Paris was the international capital of couture, Germany was the leader of a dynamic ready-to-wear industry (Konfektion), though most goods they produced were based on French designs.[18] Although Parisian style was recognized throughout the world for its quality and diversity, exports of fashion were greater in Germany than in France.[19] Many exports that were sold internationally as original

Parisian designs were in fact made in Germany (and exported from Germany) by ready-to-wear manufacturers who had gone to Paris to copy them.[20] Just as Germany greatly profited from the sale of its so-called French Konfektion designs, so too did the country benefit from marketing "French" fashion magazines. In addition to being profitable, the distribution of such magazines allowed Germany greater visibility in the European and American markets. By capitalizing on the reputation of Paris, this practice gradually weakened the French fashion press and interfered with its success.

This problem of German publishers counterfeiting French fashion magazines increasingly concerned French fashion designers and publishers, especially as they noticed that many of the tailors and couturiers working in Paris were German; in other words, they feared that Germans had managed to infiltrate the French fashion industry from the inside. An article written by the journalist Jeanne Bonton in 1916 is revealing: German shopkeepers and manufacturers, unable to unseat Paris as the capital of fashion, "circumvented the problem" by embedding themselves directly into the French fashion industry in Paris. "They slipped into design houses, into specialized magazines, with the result that, on the eve of war, they had become the primary operators and the top beneficiaries of that mine of unfathomable wealth: French Fashion."[21] The author of this article is perhaps alluding to Christoff von Drecoll and Gustave Beer, two Paris-based German designers who were barred from the Chambre Syndicale when it purged foreigners from its membership in 1915.

These different German initiatives had but one goal: to replace Paris on the international commercial stage of fashion. In 1914, the Germans took a major step toward that objective when they decided, in accordance with the resolution by the Deutscher Werkbund, to create German fashion that was independent of Paris.[22] At the beginning of the war, the dominance of French fashion led to renewed opposition in Germany that was "both philosophical and commercial."[23] In aggravating the nationalist rivalries, the war marked "Berlin's renunciation of taking designs from Paris" and even represented, according to *Le Temps*, "a milestone in the aesthetic history of Germany and the world."[24]

FIG. 7.2

From a legal perspective, it should be understood that the German copies of French publications, even if they were not the only copies, were the primary source for the counterfeit designs. During this period, French magazines and newspapers played a critical role in the distribution and marketing of French fashion. Publications promoted fashions and conveyed information regarding the size, prices, and even patterns of the original designs. In other words, they were the main vehicle for the dissemination and commercialization of French fashion. In this capacity, however, these publications facilitated the copying of designs by legally divulging the details needed to make the garments, sometimes even before they were marketed. Once the French fashion magazines were printed, German publishers had only to take the information they needed to make the counterfeit magazines. As early as the 1910s, French couturiers had to reconcile the protection of their designs with their distribution and marketing. It was necessary to disseminate information about the new collections in order to sell them. However, it was this sharing of information that put designers at risk of being copied. Couturiers were concerned with this issue because it affected their businesses.[25] Designers needed to publicize their designs to remain visible, but at what cost?

With the success of counterfeit fashion magazines at the beginning of the twentieth century, this question became increasingly relevant, and the many lawsuits initiated by Paris couturiers are revealing of the backlash. For example, Paquin and Callot Sœurs sued the German publishers Bachwitz and Finkelstein for including their designs in counterfeit magazines even before they were marketed, thereby exposing the originals to piracy. In September 1905 and June 1907, the Paquin fashion house sued G. Martens in Frankfurt, publisher of *Chic* and *Chic Parisien*, magazines that had illustrated two of Paquin's patented designs, which had been obtained from a worker at Paquin.[26] Similarly, in December 1911, Callot Sœurs sued Finkelstein and Gruenwald, the publisher and director of *Le Grand Chic Paris,* for having published Callot Sœurs designs in certain issues of the magazine without authorization.[27]

Putting an End to the Counterfeits

Then there is the question of what efforts were made to prevent the copying of Parisian magazines. Nothing substantial had been attempted before the First World War. One exception much earlier was the establishment of the Société des Journaux de Mode Réunis (United Society of Fashion Magazines) in 1870. They published twelve newspapers in different languages that were all similar in content and layout. Thus, one publisher was in charge of many French fashion periodicals and could disseminate them in many European countries, thereby thwarting the foreign counterfeiters.[28] No other initiatives were undertaken until the outbreak of the war for legal reasons: since the magazines published by Bachwitz and Finkelstein were counterfeit, they could not be considered "illegal," either in France, where they were sold legally, or in Germany, where it seems that no authority could prohibit their production.

The war forced the fashion industry to take action. Two "official" fashion publications, *Le Style Parisien* and *Les Élégances Parisiennes*, were created to replace or compete with the German counterfeits. Lucien Vogel published six monthly issues of *Le Style Parisien* at the Librairie Centrale des Beaux-Arts between July 1915 and February 1916.[29] Initially linked to the Syndicat de Défense de la Grande Couture Française (Syndicate for the Defense of French Haute Couture), the editors of *Le Style Parisien* made it clear "that it is our duty to replace these magazines with a new review that aims to be the true organ of great Parisian couture and the fashion industries".[30] According to Vogel, "the best way to abolish foreign competition is to outdo it."[31] From its start, the magazine made clear its deep commitment to France: "*Le Style Parisien* is supported by French couturiers and manufacturers, designed by French artists, produced by French publishers, and is printed in Paris using French typography."[32] An article entitled "New French Fashion Magazine Started as a Result of the War in Europe," published in the *Washington Herald* on August 8, 1915, declared that the war had "its effect on fashion magazines, lingerie, gowns, and the latest styles in headdress, as well as its effect upon dynastics and the future of nations, and races."[33]

Le Style Parisien was linked from its inception to the French couturiers who wanted to display their designs in a genuine French fashion publication entirely dedicated to Parisian couture. In order to appear impartial, the magazine did not include paid advertisements with the articles or illustrated plates. With the exception of a few pages at the back of each issue that were open to all French designers, it only published the work of the couturiers who were members of the Syndicate. As a political and patriotic enterprise, *Le Style Parisien*, which was available in New York, London, Geneva, and Bologna, wanted to serve the couturiers by disseminating their designs but it also aimed to be useful to the general readers.[34] The magazine specified that readers could draw inspiration from the published designs and copy them, but only if the reproductions were not used for commercial ends. *Le Style Parisien* intended to supplant the German counterfeits by becoming the only official media outlet recognized by Parisian couturiers. The articles it published mentioned "only French or allied design houses and manufacturers" and championed only French articles, products, and designs, while regularly publishing useful trade information. Furthermore, only Paris couturiers who were members of the organizations that constituted the Syndicat could be represented in the magazine. The publication relied on a close partnership between the world of couture and the world of publishing in Paris. The former, which included the industries of dressmaking, silk, lace, wool, trimming, embroidery, and more, agreed to provide images of their designs for the magazine.[35]

FIG. 7.3 A study of *Le Style Parisien* not only shows the close collaboration between designers and the magazine, but it also reveals the "propagandist" elements of the publication in its role as the official showcase for couture during the war.[36] Though it was not the only fashion magazine published during this period, it was the only one dedicated to Parisian couture. As such, *Le Style Parisien* was the first to publicize all events related to couture: fashion shows, new silhouettes, innovative textiles, and information relating to exhibitions, namely the display of Parisian couture at the Panama–Pacific International Exposition in San Francisco, the Fête Parisienne, and the Foire de Lyon trade fair.[37] In articles published in 1915 and 1916, alongside regularly published news about the couture trade unions, the magazine also made it a point to explain the relationships between Parisian couturiers and American buyers and with Germany.

Furthering the Fight: *Les Élégances Parisiennes* and La Librairie Hachette

By the beginning of the war, the Syndicat de Défense de la Grande Couture Française began struggling, and *Le Style Parisien* announced that it was ceasing publication.

FIG. 7.4 As Lucien Vogel explained, protecting couture and the fashion press meant that "first we [must] work together as a group. Companies pursuing the same purpose must agree, join forces, and pool their strengths."[38] Indirectly alluding to internal friction at the Syndicat, he also spoke about the need to publish a magazine that was even larger, using new methods:

We were the first to create, in the midst of war, a vehicle meant to replace Austrian-German publications, but we did not consider that first effort to be sufficient, and it seemed to us that a larger organization than ours was needed to fully carry out the endeavor . . . The Librairie Hachette has this plan and ambition. We therefore believe that both parties should unite their efforts. Consequently, Le Style Parisien *will merge with* Les Élégances Parisiennes, *the official publication of the Délégation des Industries*

Créatrices de la Mode [Delegation of Creative Fashion Industries, a new trade union involving more fashion and textile industries than the Syndicat]."[39] The publishing house Hachette began developing this new collaboration in June 1915. One of the first steps was to publish a fashion magazine for professionals and couturiers "to replace the Austrian-German magazines that, before the war, were the only ones disseminating designs from Parisian fashion houses abroad."[40] At the end of September 1915, Lucien Vogel, who at the time was still managing *Le Style Parisien*, helped outline the editorial objectives of both *Le Style Parisien* and *Les Élégances Parisiennes* so that each would have its own plan of action. Nevertheless, that Vogel was publishing two fashion magazines with the same objective was presumably a conflict of interest, and he therefore proposed a compromise: in exchange for selling *Le Style Parisien* and *La Gazette du Bon Ton* to Hachette, Vogel would work with the company and remain in charge of *Les Élégances Parisiennes*.

Les Élégances Parisiennes was published for the first time in April 1916 and continued monthly until February 1924 under that name, with the subtitle "the official publication of the creative industries of fashion."[41] The editorial in the first issue, "To Our Readers," explained that the magazine "will offer shopkeepers and professional buyers the most reliable information and the most accurate news on the latest trends in French fashion and will enable them in turn to guide the public."[42] Unlike *Le Style Parisien*, the magazine was not sponsored by the Syndicat but rather by the Délégation des Industries Créatrices de la Mode (Delegation of Creative Fashion Industries).[43] Both *Le Style Parisien* and *Les Élégances Parisiennes* were devoted to Parisian couture. Articles promoting French fashion provided information about the latest collections, organization news, the evolution of the fashion industry, and patterns (on spreads entitled "Fashion and the Cut"), as well as color templates and photographs.[44] The magazines published three types of illustrations: mounted engravings by artists including F. Lorenzi, L'Hom, Jan van Brock, and Dartey accompanied articles on the latest fashions; black-and-white engravings by André Soulé with captions about each design appeared at the beginning; and stencil-colored etchings were included at the end of each issue.

This new magazine had great significance in the world of couture and the fight against counterfeiting.[45] The Chambre Syndicale welcomed the new arrival that during wartime functioned as a symbol for the French couture industry and took pride in it, as

PAQUIN
3, Rue de la Paix, 3

Paris, le 29 Mai 1915.

Monsieur,

C'est avec plaisir que nous authentifions la reproduction de nos modèles qui paraîtront dans ce numéro, très heureux de fournir ainsi à un journal Français les documents nécessaires à sa réussite.

Veuillez agréer, Monsieur, nos salutations bien sincères.

G. DŒUILLET
24, Place Vendôme, 24

Paris, le 23 Juin 1915.

Monsieur,

Je suis heureux de pouvoir collaborer à votre nouvelle publication en vous autorisant à reproduire certains de mes modèles, et je suis persuadé que vous saurez en donner une image très fidèle.

Je crois tout à fait que le moment est opportun de créer à Paris une publication entièrement française pour remplacer les journaux de Vienne et de Berlin qui nous envahissaient de plus en plus ces dernières années.

Veuillez agréer, Monsieur, mes salutations distinguées.

G. BEER
7, Place Vendôme, 7

Paris, le 24 Juin 1915.

Monsieur,

Nous sommes heureux de pouvoir vous assurer de notre concours dans votre nouvelle entreprise et nous applaudissons à votre idée de saisir l'occasion actuelle pour remplacer par un journal essentiellement français les publications de modes faussement dénommées parisiennes et entièrement éditées à l'étranger.

Enfin: Paris est redevenu Paris!

Nous vous prions de croire, Monsieur, à l'assurance de notre parfaite considération.

G. BEER Limited.

PREMET
8, Place Vendôme, 8

Paris, le 24 Juin 1915.

Monsieur,

Pour faire suite à la visite au cours de laquelle vous m'avez fait part de votre désir de créer un nouvel organe, Le Style Parisien, *j'ai l'avantage de vous informer que nous apprécions l'effort artistique que vous avez l'intention de faire et suis heureux de vous dire que nous apporterons autant que faire se pourra, le concours que vous voulez bien nous demander pour assurer le succès de ce nouvel organe à qui nous souhaitons bonne réussite et bon succès.*

Veuillez croire, Monsieur, à l'assurance de nos civilités distinguées.

p. Mr Mathaux

MARTIAL & ARMAND
10, Place Vendôme, 10

Paris le 17 Juin 1915.

Cher Monsieur,

Nous applaudissons à votre initiative de faire un journal de modes dont le goût seul guidera la composition, en dehors de toute question de publicité.

Nous serons heureux d'aider à votre entreprise en vous donnant des croquis de nos modèles.

Croyez, cher Monsieur, à nos sentiments distingués.

REDFERN
242, Rue de Rivoli, 242

Paris le 25 Juin 1915.

Monsieur,

Nous avons trop souffert des concurrences Austro-Allemandes sous toutes leurs formes.

Des maisons soit disant Françaises n'étaient au fond que des entreprises commanditées par les Allemands.

Des journaux de Vienne, ne craignaient pas de se donner un titre français.

Je ne peux donc qu'applaudir et vous encourager de tous mes moyens possible dans votre œuvre de créer un journal où il n'y aura que des modèles des maisons vraiment parisiennes et où nous ne verrons pas ces crudités des modes étrangères qui hélas finissaient par s'imposer chez nous.

Je vous envoie mes très cordiales salutations.

WORTH
7, Rue de la Paix, 7

Paris, 28 Juin 1915.

Monsieur le Directeur,

J'ai parcouru avec un vif plaisir le premier numéro du Style Parisien, *auquel je souhaite le plus grand succès étant donné son principe entièrement français et l'intelligence avec laquelle chaque détail de toilette y est présenté.*

Vous pouvez être persuadé que je serai très heureux de faire mon possible pour contribuer à la réussite de votre intéressant journal.

Je vous prie, Monsieur le Directeur, d'agréer l'assurance de mes sentiments distingués.

Jeanne LANVIN
22, Faubourg St-Honoré

Paris, le 28 Juin 1915.

Cher Monsieur,

C'est avec plaisir que nous apprenons la création, à côté de cette délicieuse Gazette du Bon Ton, *d'un nouveau journal de mode plus pratique et qui doit remplacer les publications étrangères dont nous étions les victimes.*

Vous réussirez et vous pouvez compter sur notre appui pour y parvenir.

FIG. 7.3 Page showing written support from French couturiers including Paquin, Martial et Armand, Dœuillet

N° 1 Revue Mensuelle AVRIL 1916

Les
ÉLÉGANCES
PARISIENNES

PUBLICATION
OFFICIELLE
des Industries françaises
DE LA MODE

Paris

HACHETTE ET Cie

LES ÉLÉGANCES PARISIENNES
90, Avenue des Champs-Élysées

FIG. 7.4 Front cover of *Les Élégances Parisiennes,* April 1916. © Bibliothèque nationale de France.

an excerpt from the organization's October 1915 report shows:

After having carefully read Hachette's letter and appreciated its full significance, the Committee accepts the terms, with certain conditions stipulated here, regarding the selection of designs. Les Élégances Parisiennes, *while having the appeal of a fashion magazine, will above all be the voice of the industry, primarily that of couture, as well as those French industries connected to it. In sum, it responds to the desire expressed on many occasions before the war to have a magazine that specifically represents our industries. No entity is better qualified to implement this objective than the emphatically French publishing house Hachette et Cie.*[46]

Beyond the world of couture, the magazine attracted the attention of the general public, as shown in an April 19, 1916 letter from a mother (who seems to have no connection to couture or the clothing industry) to her son on the front line. The letter attests to the French population's awareness that fashion was of great importance to the economy and therefore needed protection:

Now the design houses in Paris have come together to create a magazine called 'Les Élégances Parisiennes,' which will be the official magazine of Paris fashion. It is a monthly magazine published by Hachette. This is to fight against the Germans and Austrians who had little by little taken hold of every fashion magazine and modified them to suit their ideas and especially their industry by trying to pass off their goods as French.[47]

The nationalistic aspect of the magazine did not rally everyone around its cause. For example, a so-called group of patriotic businessmen attacked the magazine's editor, Lucien Vogel, expressing their frustration in a December 20, 1916 letter addressed to the Sûreté Nationale.[48] The letter begins: "We have been told that *Les Élégances Parisiennes* was specially created to replace the many Boche [German] newspapers that were flooding France before the war. We have been deceived."[49] Another group of patriots disapproved of Lucien Vogel as the head of the magazine. They accused him of being a foreigner, even though the regulations, as established by the presidents of the syndicates, stipulated that "contributors to the magazine, in no matter what capacity . . . must be of essentially French origin."[50] The charge was supplanted by many details about Vogel's family, including the fact that his father had been born in Schleswig-Holstein and served in the German army in 1878. Vogel was accused of being the son of a Prussian, of having collaborated as a correspondent with the August Scherl publishing house in Berlin before the First World War, and of writing for the newspaper *Die Woche*, among others. Vogel was, in the eyes of these "patriots," a German spy who had infiltrated the profession in France and could therefore not, under any circumstances, become head of *Les Élégances Parisiennes*.[51] The condemnation was phrased in the following terms:

How is it that the syndicates accept Mr. Lucien Vogel Jr. as the editor of the French magazine that is their official organ? The only organ responsible for defending the interests of the trade, it is published with their support; the latest innovations that will make up the Fashion of tomorrow are received directly from manufacturers and the great fashion houses; how can they agree to entrust him with fabrication secrets, with their samples, their prices, their designs, for him to do as he pleases . . .?[52]

According to the accusers, the Librairie Hachette, in giving control of the magazine to Vogel, a pacifist editor in contact with "Boche" publishers, "thus demonstrates the full extent of its patriotism."[53] The group of patriots then clearly announced its refusal to recognize the role of an individual with German roots at the helm of *Les Élégances Parisiennes* and asked that "the voluntarily blind tolerance of those who had committed to defending their interests" be reconsidered.[54] Reminding Hachette of its commitments to the couture industry and in an attempt to correct the mistake, the detractors went so far as to ask that the trade unions refuse to lend their prestige and authority to the situation. Nevertheless, the publisher ignored the accusations, which were common at the time, and kept Vogel at the head of the magazine.

Within the Librairie Hachette, Vogel was the art director for both *Les Élégances Parisiennes*, which Hachette considered to be a trade magazine, and for specialty publications such as *Les Blouses* (September 1916), *Les Tailleurs de Paris* (October 1916), *Les Élégances du Soir* (in 1917), and *Les Chapeaux des Élégances Parisiennes* (1917). He commissioned all the articles (except for the sections reserved for Syndicat news) and guided the artists and photographers who were employed to showcase the new models from Paris couture and design houses by asking them to produce artistic illustrations that provided practical information to the readers.[55] In July 1917, as Vogel gradually withdrew from the magazine, Hachette recruited the journalist Camille Duguet, who had previously written about counterfeiting to cover all matters relating to couture.[56] At that time, Duguet was already working for a number of other fashion magazines, including *Les Modes, Chiffons*, and *La Revue Mondaine Illustrée*. Her role was primarily to keep in touch with the couturiers and abreast of their new collections so that every month she could share with her readers "the most successful and newest designs in haute couture."[57] The First World War enhanced the negative impact that German counterfeit fashion magazines had on French couture. Designers and fashion publishers and editors mobilized to eradicate copying. The two magazines founded during the war, *Le Style Parisien* and *Les Élégances Parisiennes*, attest to France's efforts to put an end to the problem. Nevertheless, German publishers did not stop. Far from it. After the war, there were many accounts of journalists and publishers complaining about copies of "French" fashion magazines. In 1923, Henri Lapauze again wrote:

Now, here is what I have noticed, during a stay abroad, particularly in Italy: all the bookstores, all the train stations, all the newsstands, in cities both large and small, are inundated with so-called 'Parisian' fashion magazines . . . These publications are printed in French . . . but . . . you would search in vain for the name of the printer and the city where that printer operates . . . The ridiculous headlines of these magazines alone prove that we are dealing with forgery, but it is forgery that dishonors us, because what it contains is absolutely mediocre.[58]

To support his claims, Lapauze gives the names of the "forgeries of our genuine fashion publications" and cites *Excelsior*, *Paris Chic Parfait*, and *Paris-Confection*. When the couturiers Madeleine Vionnet and Louis Dangel founded the Association pour la Protection des Industries Artistiques Saisonnières (Association for the Protection of Seasonal Artistic Businesses) in 1921 to combat the copying of couturiers' designs, Lapauze concluded that there was hope of soon seeing "newsstands throughout the world . . . less invaded by fraudulent Paris fashion."[59] The counterfeiting of French fashion magazines continued until the end of the 1930s. During World War II, Hitler aimed to move the French couture industry to Germany and therefore position Berlin as the fashion capital of the world. When Germans troops invaded France in June 1940, the French press, including the fashion press, was subjected to censorship by both the German authorities in Northern Occupied France and the Vichy government in Southern France. The Germans even created new French fashion magazines promoting the Pétain Révolution Nationale. Although during World War II no counterfeit French fashion magazines were published, controlling the French fashion press remained a great concern for Germany.

1 *Le Cabinet des Modes* was counterfeited in Liege, Belgium, in 1785, in Great Britain in June 1786 under the title *The Fashionable Magazine,* and in Italy between 1786 and 1788 under the title *La Donna Galante Ed Eurudita*: *Giornale Dedicato al bel Sesso.* See Annemarie Kleinert, *Le Journal des dames et des modes, ou la conquête de l'Europe féminine (1797–1839)* (Stuttgart: Thorbecke, 2001), 502; "Original oder Kopie? *Das Journal des Dames et des Modes* und seine zahlreichen Varianten," *Francia* (1993), 99–120.

2 "La Grande couture française et quelques-uns de ses clients," *Le Style Parisien* (December 1915). *Les Élégances Parisiennes* exposed the different kinds of copies: "Copies abroad, copies of certain commissions, department-store copies, devious copies, and unfaithful copies of 'Exhibitors,' scandalous trade of outdoor photographs." "Ce que devrait faire la mode parisienne," *Les Élégances Parisiennes*, June 1916, 37.

3 Chambre Syndicale des Dentelles et Broderies, plenary session of November 19, 1915, bimonthly Bulletin of the Association Générale du Commerce et de l'Industrie des Tissus et des Matières Textiles, 852–53.

4 According to the journalist Camille Duguet, in 1914, out of 90 fashion magazines in Paris at the time, 70 were copies of French magazines from Berlin, Vienna, or Frankfurt. The same information is found in "Les journaux de mode," *L'Ami: Journal Paroissial de Ménilmontant*, February 1916, 12.

5 "A nos lectrices," *Le Style Parisien,* July 1915.

6 "La Mode allemande," *L'Homme Enchaîné: Journal Quotidien du Matin*, December 10, 1915, front page. See also, "Ayons la foi," *Les Élégances Parisiennes*, July 1917, 54.

7 Mary-Lynn Stewart, "Copying and Copyrighting Haute Couture: Democratizing Fashion, 1900–1930s," *French Historical Studies* 28, no. 1 (2005), 103–30; Nancy Troy, *Couture Culture*: *A Study in Modern Art and Fashion* (Cambridge, MA: MIT Press, 2002), 438; Véronique Pouillard, "Design Piracy in the Fashion Industries of Paris and New York in the Interwar Years," *Business History Review* 85 (2011), 319–44.

8 Archives of the Fédération de la Haute Couture et de la Mode (FHCM): primarily the reports on the general assemblies attended by couturiers, and during which several issues concerning the fashion industry were addressed, including worker salaries and conditions, training of the *petites mains*, and the matter of foreign competition. Archives of the Institut Mémoires de l'Edition Contemporaine, Hachette files, HCT (contract between Hachette and Lucien Vogel regarding *Les Élégances Parisiennes* and *Le Style Parisien*, 44HAC).

9 Henri Lapauze, "Dans le Royaume de la Mode," *La Renaissance de l'Art Français et des Industries de Luxe*, November 1923, 1.

10 Ibid.

11 *Femina,* June 1917, 19, cited by Maude Bass-Krueger in "La mode en France durant la Première Guerre Mondiale: Approches d'histoire Culturelle," MA thesis, Institut d'Etudes Politiques de Paris, 2008.

12 *L'Impartial*, June 16, 1915

13 Camille Duguet, "Il y avait encore à Paris des journaux austro-boches," *Le Journal*, June 14, 1915. (There were still Austrian-Boche magazines in Paris.) See also "Dans le Royaume de la Mode: La Camelote Allemande sous un Masque Parisien Concurrence à l'Étranger," *L'Homme Libre*, November 16, 1923.

14 "Les Journaux de Mode Allemands," *Bulletin de la Ligue Anti-Allemande: Organe de Défense des Intérêts Économiques Français et Coloniaux*, December 1, 1915, 5–6.

15 Camille Duguet explains that a complaint against his companies was filed with Mr. Darry, the commissioner of judiciary delegations.

16 Troy, *Couture Culture*, 278.

17 Mila Ganeva, *Women in Weimar Fashion: Discourses and Displays in German Culture* (London, Camden House, 2011), 4.

18 Moreover, Germany provided "trimmings" and raw materials to many countries. According to Lucien Nicot, in fact, other products used to make Paris prototypes were called "French," even though they were manufactured in Germany and imported by the French: "French" silks that were manufactured in Krefeld, in Limbach, and in Fürth; "French" fabrics from Elberfeld and Augsburg; "French" ribbons" from Barmen; "French" woolen fabric from Chemnitz and Schmoeln. Nicot, *L'Allemagne à Paris*, 190. See also "Ce que nous dit la 'Gazette de Francfort,'" *Les Élégances Parisiennes*, November 1916, 117.

19 In the early twentieth century, Germany imported 4 million marks of fashion products, but exported 90 million marks worth of fashion products throughout the world.

20 "La Guerre et la Mode allemande," *La Lanterne: Journal Politique Quotidien*, May 3, 1915.

21 Jeanne Bonton, "La Mode Française et la Contrefaçon Allemande," *La France Universelle*, July 22, 1916, 15.

22 Deutsche Werkbund was an association of artists founded in 1907 in Munich by Hermann Muthesius to promote innovation in Germany in the decorative arts and architecture. After the 1870 war, the Germans wanted to free themselves of the yoke of French fashion, especially since they had just conquered the French. Germans were asked to now follow German fashion, but they preferred Paris. Even the Reformekleid movement was ineffective in the matter, as were the many articles published to that end at the beginning of the century in Germany. "La Mode Allemande," *Le Temps*, May 1, 1915, 3. See also "La Guerre et la Mode allemande," *La Lanterne: Journal Politique Quotidien*, May 3, 1915.

23 An imperial league championing German fashion was formed on August 30, 1914, "Variétés: Femmes de France," *Journal des Débats Politiques et Littéraires*, August 25, 1918.

24 "La Mode Allemande," *Le Temps*, May 1, 1915, 3.

25 Moreover, as Nancy Troy explains in *Couture Culture*, above all, fashion was considered an art form, a unique skill, and the personal inspiration of a designer. Nancy Troy, *Couture Culture, op.cit.*

26 "Bachwitz contre Paquin," in N/A *L'Art et le Droit* (Paris: Marchal & Godde, January 1914), 18 (March 11, 1909; July 29, 1913). *Les Elégances Parisiennes* however notes that those trials were futile, either the Chambre du Tribunal de Commerce sided with forgers, or they were made to pay a modest amount in so-called damages. See "Le Syndicat de Défense de la Grande Couture et des Industries s'y Rattachant Fait la Chasse aux Contrefacteurs," "Pour Défendre Nos Industries," *Les Elégances Parisiennes*, June 1916, 38.

27 "Callot contre Finkelstein and Gruenwald," in N/A *L'Art et le Droit*, 110, 83.

28 See Raymond Gaudriault, *La Gravure de Mode Féminine en France* (Paris: Editions de l'Armateur, 1983), 224, 40; Jean-Claude Poitelon. "À Propos du Catalogue Collectif des Périodiques." *Bulletin des Bibliothèques de France* (BBF), no. 1 (1967), 5–8.

29 Each issue of *Le Style Parisien* was sold for 6 francs. During that period, there was much debate about the status of *Le Style Parisien*. For some, it was the official publication of the Syndicat; for others, it was only sponsored by the organization. See *La Renaissance*, April 1, 1916. In a curriculum vitae that Vogel wrote in 1941, he explains that he founded *Le Style Parisien* "upon the request of officials and the trade," L. Vogel, "La Famille de Lucien Vogel and Son Curriculum Vitae," T. Ginsburger-Vogel archives.

30 *Le Style Parisien*, August 1915, editorial.

31 Ibid. In another handwritten document, Lucien Vogel writes that he founded *Le Style Parisien* to "replace technical fashion publications in all foreign countries and especially in the Americas; during that period, Berlin and Vienna had a near monopoly," Lucien Vogel, "La Famille de Lucien Vogel and Son Curriculum Vitae, May 5, 1941," T. Ginsburger-Vogel archives.

32 *Le Style Parisien*, August 1915.

33 "New French Fashion Magazine Started As a Result of the War in Europe," *Washington Herald*, August 8, 1915.

34 Ibid.

35 See Chambre Syndicale des Dentelles et Broderies, plenary session of November 19, 1915, bimonthly Bulletin / Association Générale du Commerce et de l'Industrie des Tissus et des Matières Textiles, December 15, 1915, 853.

36 See also the second page of the first issue of *Le Style Parisien* with the letters of support that Lucien Vogel received for *Le Style Parisien*. Among the supporting designers are Jeanne Paquin, Martial & Armand, Georges Dœuillet, John Redfern, Gustav Beer, Gaston Worth, Jeanne Lanvin, and Premet. *Le Style Parisien*, July 1915.

37 See "La Fête Parisienne à New York, *Le Style Parisien*, November 1915, 1–11, 25–28, and plates; Francine, "A l'Exposition de San Francisco," *Le Style Parisien*, July 1915, 2–4.

38 "Pour défendre nos industries," *Les Élégances Parisiennes*, June 1916.

39 "A nos lectrices, à nos amies," *Le Style Parisien*, February 1916.

40 Letter from Hachette & Cie to Lucien Vogel, IMEC archives, Hachette files, January 5, 1916.

41 Like *Le Style Parisien, Les Élégances Parisiennes* was available abroad. See Letter from Joël Shweitzer to Hachette, May 24, 1916, Hachette files, IMEC archives; letter dated May 26, 1916, from Mr. de Francheville (The Ehrich Galleries) to Mr. E. Delesalle (Hachette), and Contract between Max Grab and Hachette for the sale of *Les Élégances* Parisiennes in the United States, June 7, 1916, Hachette files. Sold for six francs in France, subscriptions were also available.

42 *Les Élégances Parisiennes,* April 1916.

43 Established at the end of 1915 by the Association des Tissus, it came into effect in March 1916 and was meant to replace the Syndicat. It included several syndicates, including the Chambre Syndicale de la Couture and was bigger than the 1914 Syndicat since it represented the interests of the fashion and dressmaking industries (and not only the couture industries, as was the case with the Syndicat). As with the Syndicat, however, there were denouncements regarding the status of the new association. See *La Renaissance*, June 10, 1916.

44 Other, more specific articles were added on a regular basis, such as "L'Avenir de Nos Industries du Luxe à l'Etranger" in April 1916, or "La Société Suisse de Surveillance Économique" in May 1916.

45 "First of all, a Tribunal for the defense of French Fashion has just been established by this magazine, with Hachette in agreement. The propaganda in support of the Fashion Industries will therefore be organized," "Ce que devrait faire la mode parisienne," *Les Élégances Parisiennes*, June 1916, 38.

46 Session of October 20, 1915, register of La Chambre Syndicale de la Couture Parisienne, FHCM archives.

47 Letter from Julie Résal to Salem Résal, April 19, 1916, platform 14–18, Jacques Résal Collection.

48 The accusations against Vogel were even the subject of an article, which caused the director of the Chambre, Aine-Montaillé, to intervene. See "L'Affaire Vogel," *Bulletin de la Ligue Anti-Allemande: Organe de Défense des Intérêts Économiques Français et Coloniaux,* November 11, 1916, Collection of the Bibliothèque nationale de France.

49 Letter sent to the director of the Sûreté Générale, Palais de Justice, July 29, 1916, Archives Nationales, Moscow files, inv. 940482 art 169, dossier no. 16782.

50 Ibid.

51 This information could not be tallied with archives. There are no records of Lucien Vogel's contribution to those magazines.

52 Letter sent to the Sûreté Générale, Palais de Justice, July 29, 1916.

53 Ibid.

54 Ibid.

55 Contract signed between Lucien Vogel and Hachette, January 6, 1916, IMEC archives, Hachette files.

56 During that same period, Lucien Vogel left France for Morocco to join Hubert Lyautey's army and became the Marshal's secretary. On July 27, 1917, Camille Duguet accepted the Librairie Hachette contract, which would increase her pay to 400 francs per month. Letter from Camille Duguet to Hachette, July 27, 1917, Hachette files. As early as December 21, Madame de Gramont was also in charge of establishing *Les Élégances Parisiennes*. Letter from Hachette to Mme de Gramont, December 21, 1915, Hachette files, IMEC archives. Sophie Kurkdjian, *Lucien Vogel et Michel de Brunhoff: parcours croisés de deux editeurs de presse illustrée au XXe siècle* (Paris: Fondation Varenne, 2013).

57 At the end of 1917, Camille Duguet faced challenges, primarily because of the low productivity of design houses. For further information, see the undated letter from Hachette to Camille Duguet, IMEC archives, Hachette files.

58 Lapauze, "Dans le Royaume de la Mode," 583.

59 Ibid., 587.

8

The Crisis of 1917: "National Fashion" and American Textile Restrictions

MAUDE BASS-KRUEGER

The year 1917 was the hardest of the war for the French. Men and women questioned whether the means of war still justified the end.[1] Raymond Poincaré, French president from 1913 until 1920, later described 1917 as a "dark year" of tactical doubts, bloody battles, economic instability, and mutinies on the front.[2] Much has been written about the mutinies, which were particularly hard on French morale: soldiers began protesting the war in May 1917, and several thousand men deserted the army in the months following—perhaps as many as one in every fifteen or twenty front-line soldiers.[3] Their rebellion was fostered by a number of events, including the failed Nivelle Offensive at the Chemin des Dames (an east-to-west road north of Paris), strikes on the home front, news of a Russian revolution, rumors about an offensive battle plan, and discussion about the Stockholm Peace Conference.[4] Soldiers were confused, angry, deflated, and, above all, tired. The mutinous soldiers weren't pacifists, but they demonstrated a general attitude of having had enough of the terrible war.

And terrible it was: between July and November 1917, 250,000 soldiers under British command, 38,000 Australian soldiers, 15,000 Canadian soldiers, 8,500 French soldiers, 5,300 New Zealanders, and 220,000 Germans were wounded or lost their lives in the battle of Passchendaele, near Ypres in Belgium, in one of the deadliest battles of the war. Depression was rife away from enemy lines as well. Unprecedented loss and mass mourning, rising economic inflation, increasing food prices, and food shortages all contributed to public anger and low morale. The price of daily consumer goods had become prohibitively expensive by 1917, with meat costing nearly double its prewar price and potatoes costing twice as much as meat.[5] A decree to ration bread was enacted on February 9, 1917, and bread cards were distributed the following month; sugar rationing and sugar cards followed shortly after for Parisian citizens; restaurants were ordered to limit courses to two. Further proposals to limit meat and pastries were only partially successful.[6] FIGS. 8.1–8.4

Wealthy industrialists profited from war while the working classes suffered. In Russia, this discontentment led to revolution and the overthrow of the czarist regime. In France, strikes and social movements surged through Paris and the provinces throughout the spring of 1917, threatening to upend a tenuously united political and civil society. SEE CHAPTER 9

The textile industry faced its own hardships as well, despite rising profits in 1916. The price of wool had skyrocketed, and although silk was affordable, wool was badly needed for daily dress. A good wool coat bought before the war had likely become threadbare by 1917. The winter of 1917 was cold, and both civilians and soldiers were desperate for warmth and peace. Afraid that unaffordable textile prices would exacerbate the simmering discontent, the government began planning a fixed-price *mode nationale* (national fashion) to help alleviate the cost of new, sturdy garments, textiles, and shoes for the working classes. FIG. 8.5, FIG. 8.6 This was the government's first, and last, intervention in the business of the textile industry over the course of the Great War.

A National Fashion, 1917–18

Despite the existence of substantial and accessible archives, almost nothing has been written about the short-lived *mode nationale*. According to sources in the National Archives, government officials first discussed a "national fashion" in early 1917. By December 1917, portions of the plan had become public knowledge—notably the idea of fixed-price "national shoes" and ration cards for 3.5 meters of "national fabric." A special edition of the satirical magazine *La Baïonnette* from December 27, 1917, skewered the proposal. The national fashion drawn on the cover of the magazine was subdued—the gray calf-length dress worn by the woman in the center appears drab compared to the colorful fashions that surround her, and her large, brown worker's boots seem inelegant next to the dainty, high-heeled shoes of the two women in front of her. FIG. 8.7 Cartoonists lambasted the idea of selling 3.5 meters of regulatory fabric and drew these new outfits as suggestively small and ridiculous. FIG. 8.8 Soldiers criticized the frivolity of needing new clothing during the war. FIG. 8.9 In short, a national fashion was anathema to the fundamental tenets of French elegance.

However, by September 1918, the French government felt an urgent need to implement the plan. "Our country's situation concerning clothing and textiles destined for our poor classes is becoming increasingly agonizing," a government report noted.[7] Arguing that England and Italy had successfully implemented standardized pricing for a range of textiles and garments, the French government decided to move forward with national fashion for the lower classes, large families, government workers, and families in which the head of the household had been mobilized.[8] Clothing cards would be provided, covering a range of subsidized ready-made goods for men and women including national shoes, shoe soles, a suit for men, a tailored suit for women, and 3.5 meters of national fabric that could be used for shirts, underwear, pants,

FIG. 8.1 Parisians receiving ration cards for bread at the town hall in the 10th arrondisement, Paris, October 9, 1917. Silver gelatin print. © Excelsior–L'Équipe / Roger-Viollet RV-72342-13.

FIG. 8.2 A queue of people in front of the grocery stores waiting to buy sugar before the introduction of a restrictive card, Paris, March 5, 1917. Silver gelatin print. © Excelsior–L'Équipe / Roger-Viollet RV-72694-35.

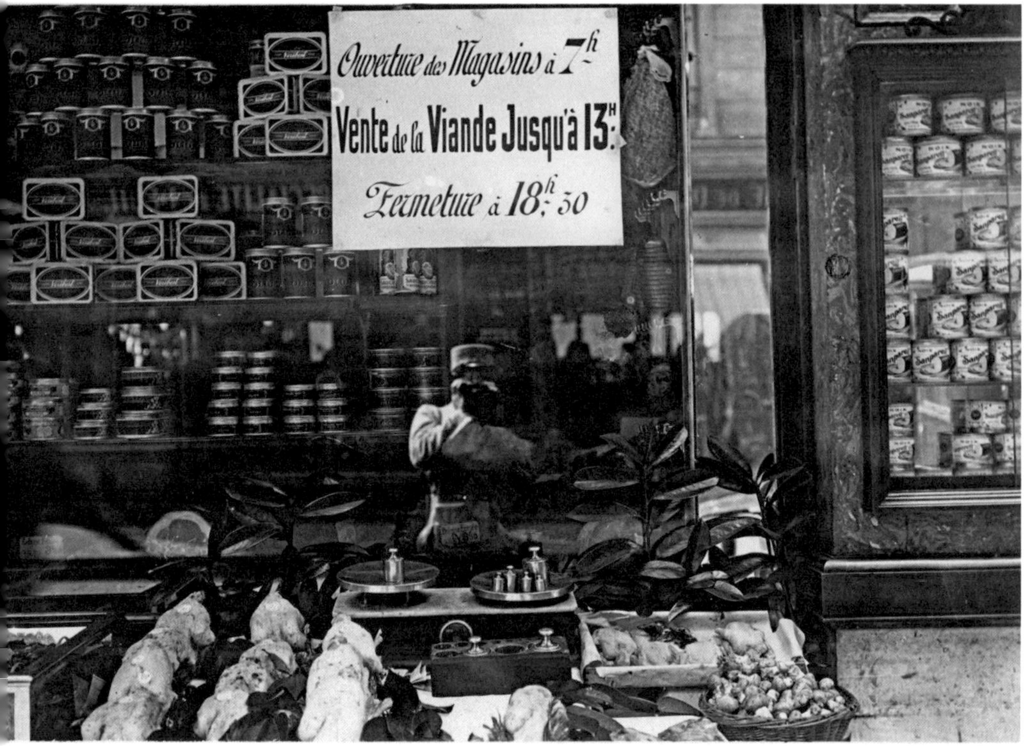

FIG. 8.3 Restriction sign posted at a grocery store on the corner of Rue Drouot and Grange-Batelière in the 9th arrondisement, Paris, June 1917. Silver gelatin print. © Préfecture de Police, Service de l'Identité judiciaire / BHVP / Roger-Viollet, RV-76468-8.

FIG. 8.4 A meal at the Café de Paris following a decree that reduced the number of dishes in a menu to two, February 15, 1917. Silver gelatin print. © Excelsior–L'Équipe / Roger-Viollet, RV-72692-56.

FIG. 8.5 A shop on the Avenue des Gobelins in Paris selling "National Shoes," July 1918. Silver gelatin print. © Préfecture de Police, Service de l'Identité judiciaire / BHVP / Roger-Viollet, RV-76469-12.

FIG. 8.6a,b Woman's boots stamped with "National Shoe" ("Chaussure Nationale") and detail of label on the sole, 1914–18. Leather. Paris, Musée des Arts Décoratifs, 53 730B.

FIG. 8.7 Gerda Wegener. A woman dressed in "national fashion" surrounded by colorful and elaborate Parisian fashions. *La Baïonnette*, December 27, 1917. Private collection.

FIG. 8.8 Henry Fournier. Caricature of the new "national fashion" showing women in suggestively small and ridiculous outfits, including ensembles for nurses and factory workers and for women at the front and walking the boulevards. "The National Fashion? Show your Legs!" *La Baïonnette*, December 27, 1917, 827. Private collection.

FIG. 8.9 Cartoon commentary on the French "national fashion" in which two soldiers in uniform walk behind two fashionably dressed women and exclaim: "We're also wearing national dress and national shoes… I don't think we look that much like them!" "The Soldier's Opinion," *La Baïonnette*, December 27, 1917, 820. Private collection.

socks, stockings, and work wear. In order to make these goods, the government planned on a "friendly requisition" of luxury fabrics imported from England. French textile manufacturers were also solicited to provide samples of potential fabrics. An archival box at the Archives Nationales contains one such sample: the fabric, made from 25 percent cotton waste, 25 percent new wool, and 50 percent reused wool, is thick, stiff, and scratchy to the touch. Its price is noted as 8 francs per meter.[9]

Was the national fashion ever commercialized? Although the garments may never have been produced—there are no extant examples, photographs, or archives of suits or shirts to indicate otherwise—there is sufficient evidence that the national shoes were. A pair of national shoes in the collection of the Musée des Arts Décoratifs, Paris are tall, leather boots for women stamped with the "Chaussure Nationale" label on the bottom of the soles. FIG. 8.6

The production of national shoes was likely delegated by the government to local manufacturers. Jacques Chauvin, who has studied the production of national shoes in the central region of the Cher, found that a local leather tanner and socialist deputy first suggested the production of national shoes in May 1917.[10] By early August, the local newspaper, *L'Avenir de la Vienne*, was advertising the imminent manufacture of 500,000 fixed-price national shoes pending the procurement of leather. A decree published in the *Journal Officiel* in mid-August specified that shoes would be produced for the working classes, their price would be fixed, the leather would be procured from the Army's leather scraps, the shoes would conform to the governmental prototype and bear a stamp labeling them national shoes, and their price would not exceed a certain sum.[11] Expectations may have been too high, Chauvin concludes; by the end of 1917, only 250,000 pairs of national shoes had been produced in the region. Clearly, manufacturers were reluctant to produce shoes with such low profit margins. The Ministre de Commerce intervened, threatening manufacturers that if they did not devote at least 75 percent of their production to national shoes, they would be sanctioned, and production increased to 450,000 pairs a month.[12] However, by January 24, 1918, *La Baïonnette* was already calling the national shoe "a myth, an allegory." The armistice of November 11, 1918, brought the whole enterprise to an early end.

American Textile Restrictions

The entry of the United States into the war alongside the Allied forces in early April 1917 relieved weary French and British troops and threatened German forces.[13] American troops arrived in Europe in June 1917 and, after training, began participating in trench warfare in October 1917. FIG. 8.10 America mobilized quickly—a standing army of 127,000 soldiers in April 1917 increased to more than 4 million men by the end of the war—but these efforts taxed the limits of government organizational strategies. The United States government implemented measures to ensure that the raw materials and textiles required for the troops were not being used by the general population. These regulations had a direct impact on the French textile industry. As American troops embarked for France, the U.S. government voted to ban the import of wool garments that used more than 4.5 meters of fabric. The resolution, aimed directly at curbing French fashion imports, considered that wasteful lengths of wool detracted from the amount needed for the American Expeditionary Forces.

The resolution passed in August 1917, prompting an immediate response from the French, who were relieved that the fall season's new fashions used less yardage than the regulation required. The French fashion press noted that "all the Couture houses had already decreased the width of their dresses, in such proportions that the quantity of wool used this winter is inferior by 20–25% to that used last winter. The vast majority of these designs do not use more than 4.5 meters of fabric."[14]

Parisian couturiers asked the Ministre de Commerce to relay this message to the American government. *Women's Wear Daily* noted the Chambre Syndicale's cable on August 24, 1917, which promised American buyers that the houses of Beer, Callot Sœurs, Dœuillet, Doucet, Georgette, Jenny, Lanvin, Paquin, Premet, Redfern, Rondeau et Legrand, and Worth had "officially pledged their word that the yardage of woolen fabrics employed will not exceed the average of 4 1/2 meters a gown, instead of the 8 meters that was the average in 1915."[15] Satirical magazines, ever keen to lampoon the latest fashion news, published cartoons featuring gags about the reduced fabric. FIG. 8.11 Unhappy with being told what to do by its own government, the French were even more displeased with being told what to do by the Americans. Regardless, French couturiers promised to maintain the slimmer styles in order to adhere to American regulations. The barrel line, launched in January 1917, used between 3 and 4 meters of fabric —a huge reduction from the 8 meters required for the war crinoline introduced in July and August 1914. However, French couturiers did not adapt their styles to suit the American regulation, as some historians have suggested. The evolution of the fashionable French

FIG. 8.10 The arrival of the first U.S. military contingents in France, Saint-Nazaire, late June 1917. Silver gelatin print. © Excelsior–L'Équipe / Roger-Viollet, RV-72194-49.

N° 169. — 9 Février 1918.

	France et Colonies	Étranger
Trois mois	3.50	4.50
Six mois	6.50	8.50
Un an	12. »	16. »

Les abonnements partent du 1er de chaque mois.

Le Rire ROUGE

ÉDITION DE GUERRE DU JOURNAL "LE RIRE", PARAISSANT LE SAMEDI

25 centimes

F. JUVEN, éditeur
1, rue de Choiseul
PARIS
Téléphone : Central 06.46

Toute demande de changement d'adresse doit être accompagnée de 50 centimes pour frais divers.

Copyright 1918, by LE RIRE, PARIS

LES RESTRICTIONS

— Mais..., quand on est deux, dans leur robe de 4m,50 .., a-t-on droit à un double métrage?

Dessin de A. Guillaume.

FIG. 8.11 Albert Guillaume. In this commentary on wartime fabric restrictions, a soldier and a pregnant woman peer into a shop window where the "national fashion" is on display. Restrictions meant that garments had to be constructed from less than 4.5 meters of fabric, and the caption playfully notes the woman's concern: "But . . . when there are two of us in their 4.5-meter dresses . . . , are we entitled to a double length?" *Le Rire Rouge*, February 9, 1918. Private collection.

silhouette toward a slimmer style was already in place by the time the American textile restriction came to a vote. If anything, the regulation simply confirmed that the shift from the bell to the barrel line was inevitable.

The armistice, signed on November 11, 1918, brought an end to the war and to the restrictions and regulations deemed necessary to the war effort. The national fashion concept was shelved and American textile restrictions were revoked. According to *Women's Wear Daily*, by the time the Treaty of Versailles was signed on June 28, 1919, Paris was "Awake at Last, Eager to Dance and Dress."[16]

1 Jean Jacques Becker, *1917 en Europe: l'année impossible* (Paris: Complexe, 1999).

2 Raymond Poincaré, *Au service de la France: neuf années de souvenirs, IX, L'année trouble, 1917* (Paris: Plon, 1932).

3 André Loez, *14–18, les refus de la guerre. Une histoire des mutins* (Paris: Gallimard, 2010).

4 The Nivelle Offensive was an Allied effort that took place from April 16 to May 9, 1917; it was touted as a way to win the war quickly but ended without significant gain.

5 See Françoise Thébaud, *Les femmes au temps de la guerre de 14* (Paris: Payot, 2013), 211.

6 "Government Control Of Food Supplies In France," *Monthly Review of the U.S. Bureau of Labor Statistics* 4, no. 6 (1917): 915–21.

7 Report on standardized cloth, September 16, 1918, Archives Nationales F/12/7686.

8 Letter from June 26, 1918, Archives Nationales F/12/7686.

9 AN F/12/7686

10 I thank Nicole Pellegrin for bringing Jacques Chauvin's work to my attention. See his article "La Chaussure nationale à prix fixe: un généreux projet on October 20, 1917," *Nouvelle République de la Vienne*, October 20, 2017.

11 Decree published on August 14, 1917 in the *Journal Officiel*. Cited in Chauvin, "La Chaussure nationale à prix fixe."

12 Chauvin, "La Chaussure nationale à prix fixe."

13 President Woodrow Wilson went before a joint session of Congress on April 2, 1917 to request a declaration of war against Germany. Two days later, the U. S. Senate voted in support of the measure. The House voted on April 6, 1917, and war was declared.

14 "Nouvelles syndicales," *Les Élégances Parisiennes*, August 1917.

15 "Question Early Showings of Paris Models," *Women's Wear Daily*, August 24, 1917.

16 "Paris Gay Again, Inspires Couture to New Efforts," *Women's Wear Daily*, May 8, 1919.

9

Midinettes on Strike

MAUDE BASS-KRUEGER

On May 11, 1917, 180 skilled seamstresses from the Jenny couture house congregated at the fashionable Place Vendôme and marched down the rue St. Honoré to the Madeleine chanting for their right to an "English week" (a week with a day and a half of rest on Saturday afternoon and Sunday) and a raise of one franc for the seamstresses and fifty centimes for the apprentices. FIG. 9.1 Protesting a collective decision by the couture houses Beer, Callot Sœurs, Chéruit, Dœuillet, Jenny, Lanvin, Paquin, Poiret, Premet, and Worth to cut a half-day of wages by closing the ateliers on Saturday afternoon, the Jenny workers voiced their concerns in a letter to their director, the designer Jenny Sacerdote, asserting "it is completely impossible to survive during the crisis of the *vie chère* [high cost of living] with this reduction in salary."[1] When Sacerdote did not respond, the seamstresses walked out of the Jenny ateliers, located at 70, Avenue des Champs Elysées, and took to the streets. FIG. 9.2 Incensed by the disparity between the luxurious clothes they sewed, the economic vitality of the couture industry despite the war, and their own desperate finances, one hundred women from the nearby house of Chéruit joined the march that afternoon. During the next eleven days, more than ten thousand women workers from thirty-two couture houses marched through central Paris.[2] FIG. 9.3 The couture seamstresses obtained a raise and the English week after eleven days of strike. In doing so, they set a wheel in motion: by the end of the month, thirty-one thousand female workers from the dress, textile, and leather industries had joined together to demand wage increases. The strike then spread to other sectors. By June, more than seventy-one branches of French industry were in the streets, metalworkers included. Totaling more than 133,000 men and women strikers, the May–June 1917 movement was the biggest labor strike Paris had known, as well as the most feminine. Jean-Louis Robert estimated that women led 80 percent of the Parisian strikes during these two months—a radical increase from the 23 percent of women-led strikes documented in Paris between 1915 and 1916.[3] FIG. 9.4

The strike of the seamstresses, or *midinettes*, remained in the collective memory of the war as a festive assembly of pretty young women who sang their way into the hearts of the ministers—and the public.[4] The moniker "midinettes" for skilled seamstresses employed in the couture industry conveyed a cultural type that merged the ideal female worker with what Patricia Tilburg has called "particularly French notions of the patriotic responsibility of feminine taste."[5] Popular plays, novels, and poems about the midinettes helped create a fiction of the Parisian seamstress who "joined decorousness with diligent labor, bourgeois-style consumption with republican virtue and political deference with erotic submission."[6] Those who have written about the 1917 midinette strike argue that the public embraced the seamstresses' movement not only because of the powerful fantasy created around their earnest labors and innate—and patriotic—fashion-sense, but also because their battle was feminine (and not feminist), non-pacifist, and limited to the world of luxury products.[7] The image of thousands of female seamstresses in tailored suits and trimmed hats demanding their right to a day's rest from sewing fashionable and expensive garments was much more palatable to a war-torn nation than that of the aproned munitions workers or women munitions workers whose strikes at the end of May and during the beginning of June impeded national production and whose cries were at times defiantly anti-war and assuredly political.[8] FIGS. 9.5, 9.6 More than a merry parade of elegant workers whose difficulties within a frivolous, yet exalted, business were embraced by an amused and paternalistic public, the strike revealed an untenable friction between the couturiers and the seamstresses. The financial interests of the couture industry, active and profitable despite the war, became increasingly at odds with the harsh realities of the seamstresses' economic sacrifices and wartime experiences. The midinettes' strike was indeed part of a "multivalent movement," as Laura Lee Downs has written, "erupting as thousands of women were protesting over wages, food prices, and working conditions." But it was also a strike that developed out of, and was intrinsically tied to, the very nature of the wartime couture industry. With war wages, or half wages (*salaires de misère*), membership purges, nationalist rhetoric, international exhibitions, and constant stylistic developments, they tempered the loss of buyers and maintained couture's preeminent reputation throughout the war. The rarefied and moneyed environment of French couture clashed with the seamstresses' more somber wartime experiences.[9]

French couture houses had survived the first shaky months of the war, thanks to the joint efforts made by both workers and employers to scale back wages and drum up foreign sympathy for the industry's precarious situation. By the end of August 1914, the midinettes had agreed to be paid war wages in order to keep their jobs and maintain production levels. The Chambre Syndicale de la Couture Parisienne (Trade Association of

FIG. 9.1 Maurice-Louis Branger. Seamstresses from the Jenny couture house at 70, avenue des Champs Élysées on strike for the right to higher wages and time off on Saturday afternoons and Sundays, Paris, May 18, 1917. Silver gelatin print. © Maurice-Louis Branger / Roger-Viollet, RV-3831-8.

FIG. 9.2 Maurice-Louis Branger. Seamstresses on strike at the Place Vendôme, Paris, May 18, 1917. Silver gelatin print. © Maurice-Louis Branger / Roger-Viollet, RV-1464-12.

FIG. 9.3 Maurice-Louis Branger. Workers' strike in front of the Maison Paquin, Paris, mid-May 1917. The eleven-day strike involved more than 10,000 couture workers from thirty-two different couture houses. Silver gelatin print. © Excelsior–L'Équipe / Roger-Viollet, RV-72197-48.

FIG. 9.4 Restaurant and café staff who joined the demonstrations about the vote for the "English week," Paris, late May 1917. Silver gelatin print. © Excelsior–L'Équipe / Roger-Viollet, RV-72197-28.

FIG. 9.5 Seamstresses in tailored suits and trimmed hats striking for the right to a day's rest from couture work, Paris, late May 1917. Silver gelatin print. © Excelsior–L'Équipe / Roger-Viollet, RV-72195-12.

FIG. 9.6 Apprentice dressmakers drinking beers near the labor council during strikes, Paris, May 30, 1917. Silver gelatin print. © Excelsior–L'Équipe / Roger-Viollet, RV-72191-34.

Parisian Couture) applauded their sacrifice as an act of solidarity, or "*union parfaite*," within the couture industry. Jean Aine-Montaillé, president of the Chambre Syndicale until 1917, later explained that

when the war broke out, because we did not know how long it would last, we took wise and preventative social measures. Rallied by the Minister of Labor and wanting to prevent our workers from suffering prolonged unemployment, we decided . . . to reduce salaries and decrease hours.[10]

The seamstresses were portrayed as selfless and patriotic, and foreign customers were encouraged to support them by buying French couture. American society women sponsored fashion events to raise money for the seamstresses and bought couture dresses—justifying their "implausibly" high prices as a form of charity that "supported the class in Paris that makes the models for the States."[11]

Yet, as the couture industry regained its profits and weathered the new taxes, tariffs, and duties imposed by war, the midinettes continued to make war wages and work overtime to help maintain the luxury industry in the face of war and foreign copying. They had assumed that their salaries would return to normal when business picked up. By January 1915, foreign clients had resumed their purchases of French couture, but the couturiers still considered the situation precarious. As the war ground on, they continued to plead hard times rather than end the war wages, which they had promised to do as soon as conditions allowed. Already by 1915, and certainly by 1916, the export of silk garments increased, the collections resumed their regular schedule, and foreign buyers and clients continued to make the journey to Paris to purchase models. The seamstresses felt that the half wages, which were crucial for the push at the beginning of the war, were no longer mandatory for the economic survival of the couture industry.

The minutes of the Chambre Syndicale, recorded by hand on a weekly basis, show that between May 1915 and May 1917 the association of couturiers was exclusively concerned with the problem of copies and the reputation of the French couture houses abroad. The Chambre twice discussed domestic concerns, but only in relation to charitable works for soldiers. The 1916 and 1917 records indicate that rather than addressing the mounting labor problems at home, the Chambre instead threw itself into eradicating German magazines that paraded as French, establishing an anti-copyright label for clothing, readying garments for international exhibitions, and launching a new silhouette, the barrel silhouette. Indeed, the midinettes' demands for higher wages were not mentioned until their strike was under way. During a session that convened three days before the strike, the couturiers spent the hour debating the "new impulsion that must be given to our propaganda" and congratulating themselves on having received a laudatory telegram from *Women's Wear Daily* in New York.[12]

Jean-Jacques Becker, a French historian of the First World War, has called 1917 "the year of all dangers." Among these dangers were an ideological crisis concerning the morality of war and the Russian revolution, a military crisis that culminated in the mutiny of the French army, a social crisis stemming from increased prices for consumer goods, and a labor crisis among the working class. Unemployment was not a problem. Couture, like other French industries, had full employment in 1917. Records kept by the police during the war show that 378 people were employed at Callot Sœurs, 370 people at Lanvin, 220 at Paquin, 180 at Jenny, 175 at Beer, 170 at Bernard, 150 at Premet, 120 at Chéruit, and 100 at Dœuillet.[13] But despite full employment in a stable industry, the midinettes were increasingly anxious about their immediate future and that of their loved ones on the front lines. The cost of living rose rapidly in 1917, a difficulty made obvious by the fact that the couture workers catered to the whims of a rich and frivolous clientele to whom money was no object. Personal tragedy and low morale fermented in the confines of the female workshops.

The first fissures in the "perfect union" appeared as early as 1916, twelve months before the May strike. In February 1916, the Paris police department noted a growing disconnect between the couturier's practices and the reality of the situation. "Certain couturiers," they noted, "speculate on the war's misery and take advantage by maintaining the war salaries . . . The couture houses, faced with an increase in business, are selling for more than before the war. We have noted that the [male] tailors have returned to earning their prewar salaries."[14] The *New York Times,* in an article entitled "Prices of Paris Clothes Now Higher Than Ever," explained that the buyers could not protest the price, for "it was pay that price or leave the gowns, and no buyer could afford to do the latter after having risked his life to cross the ocean." The *Times* still justified the prices in terms of "aid" for the midinettes, whose plight had been the object of "almost unlimited charity from America." "It is only natural," the article continued, "to suppose that the sewing people reaped quite a little harvest from the wild epidemic of fashion shows that swept our continent since last October."[15]

The profit, however, was not for the workers—an inequality that became apparent as the war ground on. Alice Brisset, a second assistant in a couture house during the war who later became secretary general of the Fédération de l'Habillement (Clothing Union), remembered in a postwar interview that "work hours were endless. The *première*, or head seamstress, would burst into the atelier, saying, 'Ladies, you must work tonight, the client wants her dress.' . . . There was never any talk of paying overtime or of being fed . . . Fatigue made our nerves taut, and on top of that, anxiety had filled our hearts."[16] Brisset emphasized that the all-female environment of the ateliers created a sense of solidarity but also heightened the women's emotions. The women confided their fears to one another while they sewed. But, most importantly, Brisset underlined that the very nature of the couture industry led to their anger. "Paris," she said, "offered the double spectacle of rations and luxury, debauchery. The midinettes were directly confronted with this revolting contrast. I remember making a delivery to a grand hotel on the Champs-Elysées where a certain Mrs. P, a lady of high society, ensconced in silk sheets, received me with such contempt that I was indignant. The wives of profiteers, these nouveaux riches, were demanding and capricious clients." "All this misery," she remembered, "all this anxiety, this fear accumulated, and the strike exploded like a clap of thunder."[17]

The archives of the Paris police department reveal growing discontent in the textile industry after March 1916 over the women's war wages. On March 10, 1916, the police reported that female workers in the Chéruit couture house demanded "the establishment of weekly or hourly salary."[18] On March 12, men and women at the Printemps department store protested their 60 percent pay decrease since the start of the war.[19] On September 25, 1916, 150 men and 50 women from the Section des Couturières et Tailleurs pour Dames united to demand equal work and equal pay.[20] In October workers struck at the Galeries Lafayette department store and the houses of Rossen, Burberys [*sic*], and Maurice Mayer, and then, in January 1917, seamstresses and apprentices at the couture houses Agnès and Bernard et Cie demanded a one franc raise.[21] The union between the workers and the bosses, forged in the first anxious months of the war, lost strength as the initial impetus to "save" an important national industry wound down under the grinding reality of a prolonged conflict. The garment industry, with its militant history and disgruntled workers, was an incubator for the increasing frustrations over living wages on the home front.

Although the demand for the English week and the militancy of the seamstresses who descended into the street on May 11, 1917, had historical antecedents, the unified force of the movement and its positive outcome was unprecedented. Judith Coffin has argued that female militancy in the garment trades "awoke" in the early twentieth century, and in particular during the 1901, 1910, and 1911 strikes over garment pricing and subcontracting conditions.[22] The issue of the English week, Coffin claims, was a tool used by the unions to recruit women during the prewar labor movement. Promoted by activists since the 1890s, the issue gradually took on meaning as a "woman's" demand that pitted time (a woman's need) against money (a male desire).[23] The prewar strikes were, however, diffuse and unsuccessful; the labor unions were increasingly committed to organizing women, but they framed their reforms in terms of gender complementarity and ultimately grew frustrated with their inability to sustain a strong female membership.[24]

The 1917 strike succeeded where the earlier strikes had failed: not only did the seamstresses join together en masse to demand a reduction in hours, as well as an increase in salary, but their demands could no longer be relegated to the category of "women's needs." The prewar dress unions regarded women's work as a "secondary wage" that complemented traditional household functions.[25] But in 1917, with the men off at war, the cost of living had skyrocketed, yet the war wages had remained in place since 1914, so the seamstresses in 1917 were unmistakably striking for their right to a living wage. The nature and form of their demands were informed by their singular experience in the couture industry—a history of female militancy, a decade-old struggle for the English week, the unsustainable disparity between producing luxury goods and living in a war-torn nation, and the intimate relationships fostered in the all-female couture workshops—but their needs were universally understood. As Brisset explained, "It was my first strike, the first big shock of my youth . . . the street belonged to us . . . Our audacity was unheard of . . . Our strike became a popular strike because our fear and anger was in the hearts of everyone."[26]

After eleven days of strike, the Chambre Syndicale ceded to the midinettes' demands and agreed to institute the English week, as well as a seventy-five cent pay increase to the seamstresses and a fifty-cent increase to the apprentices. FIG. 9.7

The raise was voted into law on May 29 and adopted without modification by the Senate on June 7, 1917.[27] The result was interpreted as a joint victory for

FIG. 9.7 Representatives for the Parisian couture houses leaving the Ministry of the Interior after the signing of a "peace" treaty on May 22, 1917. Jeanne Paquin is fourth from the left in the back row and Louise Coudy is third from the right. Silver gelatin print. © Excelsior–L'Équipe / Roger-Viollet, RV-72191-45.

FIG. 9.8 Maurice-Louis Branger. Corset makers and furriers who stopped working to join the seamstresses' demonstrations, Paris, late May 1917. Silver gelatin print. © Excelsior–L'Équipe / Roger-Viollet, RV-72197-36.

the seamstresses and the unions who made up the labor delegations and whose influence forced the government to apply hard pressure to the Chambre Syndicale.[28] Even Brisset was surprised by how quickly the seamstresses' demands were met.[29]

The strike was an important victory for women workers, but it was not presented as a feminist combat by either the women themselves or the press. The midinettes' attitude toward feminism can perhaps best be summed up by one of the articles published in their own newspaper, *La Midinette*. The article, "Why I am not a suffragette," written in 1914 by the fashion journalist Camille Duguet, argued that, although the seamstresses wanted more rights, they were "disgusted by the methods" used by their English peers.[30] Journalists' reports on the strike also focused on the feminine, not feminist, tone set by the vocal women. The image of the midinette was a figure of popular imagination in France that spurred articles and plays devoted to her youthful charms, inexpensive but chic wardrobe, and romantic ambitions.[31] However, these earnest portraits made up only one aspect of the myth surrounding the midinette. The other, a misogynistic and paternalistic fiction, revolved around discussions of the fallen working woman, the "coquette" who sold her body or used her charms to supplement her meager income. The Alsatian soldier André Kahn noted in his diary on May 23 and 26, 1917, that "the couturière's strike is nothing but a little effervescence due to springtime passions. They are agitated because the spring-time excites them and cannot find enough men to satisfy their needs."[32] The midinette Monette Thomas complained in a postwar union meeting that was reported on by the police that "employers represent the midinette as a coquette, [a woman] who is not serious and who relies on the generosity of her lovers despite the fact that we are honest women who have hearts and minds and needs to satisfy just as much as the daughters of the bourgeoisie."[33]

By filtering reports on the strike through the lens of these dual fictions, reporters and observers avoided portraying the seamstresses as unpatriotic, pacifist, or, worse, feminist.[34] Patricia Tilburg has shown how the aestheticization of the working class by way of the Mimi Pinson or midinette archetype had already been used by the press for the garment strikes of 1910 to lighten the symbolic consequences of the strike and transform the political arena "into a site of feminine song and flirtation rather than proletarian anger and political debate."[35] FIG. 9.8 Using similar imagery and rhetoric, the 1917 strike was also portrayed as a peaceful, female-driven act that resulted in important labor legislation and that marked a turning point in the French women's rights movement.[36] By extending the analysis to the changes produced *within* the couture industry itself, it is interesting to note that these changes also reflect the gender-based tensions described above: the strike provoked the resignation of Aine-Montaillé from the Chambre Syndicale and the subsequent election of the Chambre's first female president, Jeanne Paquin, but the seamstresses were openly adverse to Paquin's presidency. Paquin was elected because she represented the industrious seamstress who had risen through the ranks, but her influence was hampered by rumors of bad behavior toward her employees.

Paquin's election underscored the role she played in the negotiations between what she called a "hostile government" and the seamstresses, who, she said, "acted as free women."[37] Paquin was a former seamstress whose success and business acumen were honored by a Légion d'Honneur in 1913. FIG. 9.9 She was entrusted by the Chambre Syndicale to ease negotiations between the couturiers, seamstresses, and government after Aine-Montaillé had refused to negotiate with either the seamstresses or the government, stating that he would "not be the one held responsible for the beginning of a revolution."[38] Opposed to any concessions, Aine-Montaillé resigned on May 26, and Paquin stepped forward to resolve the crisis. In a written appeal to Madame Raymond Poincaré, the wife of the French president, Paquin charged that certain members of the government were hostile toward the seamstresses and asked for her help in arranging a compassionate and swift resolution to the strike.[39] When negotiations succeeded, the Chambre Syndicale voted unanimously to elect Paquin president. Her first act was to create a Caisse de Défense Patronale (Treasury for the Defense of Employers) and a Commission Permanente des Conflits (Standing Committee for the Resolution of Conflicts).[40]

Despite Paquin's success in resolving the May 1917 strike, tensions continued to rise between employers and employees, putting Paquin in the delicate position of trying to keep both sides happy. Whereas the Chambre's minutes before May 1917 bore no trace of internal disputes, the minutes after the midinette's strike tell a far different story. In November 1917, the minutes record a dispute over vacations. In January 1918, the workers demanded a raise adjusted for inflation. In February 1918, Paquin signaled the "exceptional seriousness" of voting for a minimum wage. In March 1918, the couturiers met to discuss paying overtime for work done

FIG. 9.9 Jeanne Paquin. © Roger-Viollet, RV-4496-12.

FIG. 9.10 Jeanne Paquin in the courtyard of the Senate, Paris, July 1918. Silver gelatin print. © Excelsior–L'Équipe / Roger-Viollet, RV-74144-8.

on Saturdays and Sundays.[41] The midinettes, and then the garment workers (55,000 workers in total), went on strike again in 1919 to demand an eight-hour workday, a demand that was accepted by the Chambre, though under duress.[42] If the minutes of the Chambre portray Paquin as a firm proponent of workers' rights, fighting to advance their cause within the limits of the couture industry, lobbying with personal conviction for the minimum wage, and treating the seamstresses' concerns with gravity and diligence, police reports on union meetings tell a different story. FIG. 9.10 Like public perception of the midinettes themselves—hard-working earnest women, on the one hand, immoral coquettes on the other—Paquin's own reputation was scrutinized and attacked.

Police archives show that midinettes who spoke at union meetings did not appreciate their former colleague's accomplishments, considering that she had left the worker's world and now belonged to that of the venal employer. In October 1918, just two weeks before the end of the war, the police department observed that the friction between the midinettes and Paquin was increasing, noting that one union seamstress decried the "former worker who has become a millionaire, who drives an automobile and owns several houses built on the backs of her humble employees," and that another seamstress insinuated that not only had Paquin slept her way up the ladder but she "had killed one of her employees by locking her in a cupboard during a work inspection."[43] Although the male editors of *Les Modes* considered Paquin's election "a big step toward feminism, all the more important in an industry where women are the majority," Paquin became the lightning rod of angry workers and frustrated employers.[44] Incensed that a former worker now negotiated on behalf of the employer, the seamstresses used personal attacks to undermine her influence. The increasingly active role played by the dress unions in the negotiations between seamstresses and couturiers may have also accounted for the deteriorating relationship between Paquin and her employees. The 1917 midinette strike originated from the non-union seamstresses themselves and the labor negotiations were jointly led by the seamstresses and the unions. The 1918 strikes, however, were wholly conceived of and led by the dress unions, a much more militant and aggressive constituency.[45] The Fédération Nationale des Travailleurs de l'Habillement (National Federation of Clothing Workers), the first national federation of garment workers in France, counted only 4,000 members before the war, but the numbers swelled as the war stretched on: from 7,000 in 1917, to 26,000 in 1919 and 56,000 in 1920.[46] Paquin resigned as president of the Chambre Syndicale on July 7, 1920, saying that she felt "specifically targeted by the movement." As the midinettes became unionized, Paquin, accustomed to the prewar style of negotiations that occurred between a couturier and her own workers within the confines of the atelier, lost her ability to mediate between the two worlds. The Chambre Syndicale waited fifty years before electing another woman president—Germaine Emilie Krebs, known as Madame Alix Grès, in 1972.

Within four years, couture's "perfect union" had dissolved into anger, frustration, militancy, and a complete break in the relationship between the couturiers and the seamstresses, as revealed by the attacks on Jeanne Paquin's presidency. The seamstresses' reduced wages and hard work had helped the industry regain its power and prominence during the first months of the war, but the Chambre Syndicale's minutes reveal that the couturiers turned their focus elsewhere: they agonized over German spies within the industry, their reputation abroad, and the problem of copies, to the detriment of their workers' well-being. The successful launch of the war crinolines and the barrel silhouette affirmed the triumph of the French fashion propaganda machine. Although the styles were good for business, their success did little to improve the situation of the workers. The disparity between profits and continued low salaries fostered contempt within the ateliers. Police archives reveal that discontent among the midinettes began brewing as early as 1916, reports that were confirmed by Alice Brisset's experience. The election of Jeanne Paquin as president of the Chambre ultimately provoked the anger of the midinettes rather than appeasing it. Union membership swelled as the seamstresses increasingly turned to organized labor associations to resolve conflicts rather than relying on informal negotiations between couturier and staff. The so-called perfect union between midinettes and couturiers, invincible in their common desire to support French couture at the beginning of the war, was irretrievably broken by the time the last man returned home from the trenches.

1 "Madame . . . il nous est complètement impossible d'arriver à nous suffire dans la crise de vie chère que nous traversons," Procès verbaux of the *Chambre Syndicale de la Couture Parisienne* [CSCP], July 12, 1917.

2 See Jean-Louis Robert, *Les ouvriers, la patrie, et la révolution: Paris 1914–1919* (Paris: Les Annales Littéraires, 1995); Annie Kriegel, *Histoire du mouvement ouvrier*, vol. 1 (Paris: Imprimerie nationale, 1964); Françoise Thébaud, *Les femmes au temps de la guerre de 14* (Paris: Stock, 1986).

3 Robert, *Les ouvriers,* 125.

4 See Margaret H. Darrow, *French Women and the First World War: War Stories of the Home Front* (Oxford: Berg, 2000), 195–97. See Laura Lee Downs, *Manufacturing Inequality: Gender Division in the French and British Metalworking Industries, 1914–1939* (Ithaca, NY: Cornell University Press, 1995), 119–21. Downs argues that the strike's legacy has been downplayed by modern historians because it was female-led, and thus unpolitical.

5 The word midinette came from words *midi*, meaning noon, and *dinette*, or lunch. The seamstresses were freed from the ateliers from noon to one each day for lunch. The term was born in the second half of the nineteenth century and remained in use until the 1950s. Patricia Tilburg explores the construction of the Mimi Pinson type, another cultural shorthand used to refer to the midinettes, in her excellent article "Mimi Pinson Goes to War: Taste, Class and Gender in France, 1900–18," *Gender & History* 23, no. 1 (April 2011), 92–110.

6 Ibid., 94.

7 See Thébaud, *Les femmes*, 258–62; Robert, *Les ouvriers,* 123–34; Downs, *Manufacturing Inequality,* 136–37; Darrow, *French Women,* 197. Downs ascribes the midinettes' success to their "gentle and feminine" tactics. According to Darrow, the seamstresses were no threat because their targets were "the big fashion houses and wealthy women."

8 See Robert, *Les ouvriers,* 134–37; Susan Grayzel, *Women and the First World War* (London: Pearson Education, 2002).

9 Downs, *Manufacturing Inequality,* 137.

10 "Quand éclata la guerre, dont la durée ne pouvait être prévue, nous prîmes des mesures de sage opportunité et de prévoyance sociale. Sollicités par le Ministère du Travail et désirant éviter, dans la mesure possible, à notre personnel et à nos ouvriers un chômage trop prolongé, nous décidâmes, afin de pouvoir conserver plus longtemps nos employées et nos ouvrières et de repartir sur un plus grand nombre de bénéficiaires de nos disponibilités en capital, de réduire les salaires et de diminuer le nombre des heures de présence." CSCP, February 24, 1916.

11 "Paris Holds Fashion Openings Thanks to Patriotic Women," *New York Times*, September 6, 1914; "Prices of Paris Clothes are Higher than Ever," *New York Times*, October 24, 1914.

12 CSCP, May 9, 1917.

13 Archives of the Préfecture de Police, F7 1372, May 13, 1917.

14 "L'attitude de certains patrons qui, spéculant sur la misère présente, en profitent pour imposer des salaires de famine dits 'salaires de guerre' . . . les principales maisons de couture, devant la reprise des affaires, vendent plus cher qu'avant la guerre. [On note le] rétablissement complet des prix d'avant la guerre pour les tailleurs," PPP, BA 1423, February 23, 1916.

15 "Prices of Paris Clothes Now Higher Than Ever," *New York Times*, October 25, 1915.

16 "La durée du travail n'avait pas de limites. La 'première' faisait irruption dans l'atelier, 'Mesdames, vous travaillerez ce soir, la cliente veut sa robe, il faut essayer demain matin.' Et il n'était pas question de payer les heures supplémentaires, ni même d'être nourries . . . La fatigue mettait les nerfs à fleur de peau et, en plus, il y avait l'angoisse dans tous les cœurs." Interview with Alice Brisset transcribed in Madeleine Colin, *Ce n'est pas d'aujourd'hui: femmes, syndicates, luttes de classe* (Paris: Éditions Sociales, 1975), 74.

17 "Et puis Paris offrait le double spectacle de la disette (cartes de pain, cartes de sucre) et du luxe, de la débauche. Les midinettes étaient directement confrontées avec ce contraste révoltant. Je me rappelle être allée faire une livraison dans un grand hôtel des Champs-Elysées où une p . . . [sic] de haut vol, vautrée dans des draps de crêpe de chine, m'avait reçue avec un mépris qui m'avait indignée. Les femmes des profiteurs, des nouveaux riches étaient aussi des clientes exigeantes et capricieuses. Toute cette misère, cette angoisse, cette colère accumulées ont fait éclater la grève comme un coup de tonnerre," ibid, 75.

18 Françoise Thébaud recorded 17 strikes in 1914, 100 in 1915, and more than 300 in 1916 in all sectors of French industry. Thébaud, *Les femmes,* 259. See also PPP, BA 1423, April 10, 1916.

19 PPP, BA 1423, April 12, 1916.

20 PPP, BA 1423, September 25, 1916.

21 Kriegel, *Histoire du mouvement ouvrier*, 159.

22 See Judith Coffin, *The Politics of Women's Work: The Paris Garment Trades, 1750–1915* (Princeton, NJ: Princeton University Press, 1996), 177–92.

23 Because the English week was a reduction in hours without a reduction in pay, the Federation of Clothing Workers thought that the measure would appeal more to women, who wanted more time to "care for the house" than men, who preferred long hours but higher wages. Coffin, *The Politics of Women's Work,* 194.

24 Ibid, 199.

25 Ibid, 197.

26 "C'était ma première grève, mon premier grand choc de jeunesse . . . la rue nous appartenait . . . Notre audace était inouïe . . . Notre mouvement devint très vite populaire car notre colère et notre angoisse étaient dans le cœur de tout le monde." Brisset in Colin, *Ce n'est pas d'aujourd'hui*, 76.

27 CSCP, June 1, 1917.

28 The Syndicat de Défense de la Grande Couture Française (Syndicate for the Defense of French Haute Couture), the Fédération de l'Habillement (Clothing Federation), the Union des Syndicats de la Seine (Union of Labor Unions of the Seine), and the Confédération Générale du Travail (General Confederation of Labor).

29 See John N. Horne, *Labour at War: France and Britain, 1914–1918* (Oxford: Clarendon Press, 1991), 177–79. Horne called the strike a "notable syndicalist victory . . . the very form of the settlement conferred recognition on syndicalism as an institution." See Coffin, *The Politics of Women's Work,* 183–87. For an overview of syndicalism and gender during WWI, see Michelle Zancarini-Fournel, "Femmes, genre et syndicalisme pendant la Grande Guerre," in *1914–1918: combats de femmes, Les femmes, pilier de l'effort de guerre*, ed. Évelyne Morin-Rotureau (Paris: Éditions Autrement, 2004), 98–112.

30 *La midinette* was a cheap circular that featured short articles and miscellaneous items. It was produced by the seamstresses and sold within the community for five centimes. It was published only three times, on February 1, 1914, February 12, 1914, and April 1, 1915. Camille Duguet, "Pourquoi je ne suis pas suffragette," *La Midinette*, February 12, 1914.

31 Tilburg, "Mimi Pinson," 93.

32 "La grève des couturières n'est qu'une petite effervescence due aux ardeurs printanières. Elles s'agitent parce que le printemps les énerve et qu'elles ne trouvent pas assez d'hommes pour les satisfaire," André Kahn, "Journal de guerre d'un juif patriote," cited in Robert, *Les ouvriers*, 125.

33 "[Les patrons] représentent [les midinettes] comme des coquettes, comme étant peu sérieuses et comptant sur la libéralité de leurs amants alors que les ouvrières sont d'honnêtes femmes qui ont un cœur et un cerveau et des besoins à satisfaire au même titre que les filles de bourgeois." APP, BA 1376, September 22, 1918.

34 The image of Mimi Pinson, like that of the midinette, was also used to assuage anxiety about labor militancy and the war. Tilburg, "Mimi Pinson," 93.

35 Ibid., 97.

36 See Thébaud, *Les femmes*; Robert, *Les ouvriers*; Michelle Zancarini-Fournel, "Femmes, genre et syndicalisme pendant la Grande Guerre."

37 Paquin archives, quoted by Dominique Sirop, *Paquin* (Paris: Éditions Adam Biro, 1989), 42.

38 Speech given by Jeanne Paquin, transcribed in CSCP, July 12, 1917.

39 Paquin archives quoted by Sirop, *Paquin*, 42.

40 CSCP, July 5, 1917.

41 CSCP, November 14, 1917, and March 15, 1918.

42 Nancy L. Green, *Ready-to-Wear and Ready-to-Work: A Century of Industry and Immigrants in Paris and New York* (Durham: Duke University Press, 1997), 84, 87–89. Green compares Parisian strike activity, which surged during the war, to New York garment industrial warfare, which peaked before the war and was further diminished during the war. Green argues that the Parisian wartime strike history implies a certain long-term failure to regulate working conditions and abolish seasonality.

43 "[Paquin est une] ancienne ouvrière devenue millionnaire, [qui] roule en automobile et possède de nombreuses maisons de campagne grâce au labeur d'humbles employées." And, "[Elle a] causé la mort d'une de ses apprenties qu'elle avait enfermée dans un placard lors d'une visite d'un inspecteur du travail." PPP, BA 1376, October 23, 1918.

44 "Une grande manifestation de charité du syndicat de la presse parisienne en faveur des éprouvés de la guerre au Petit Palais," *Les Modes* 172 (1917), 9.

45 See Robert, *Les ouvriers*, 274–76.

46 Green, *Ready-to-Wear*, 89. Green notes that although 80% of the garment workers were women, only 20% were union members.

IO

Returning to the Gender Question

MAUDE BASS-KRUEGER & SOPHIE KURKDJIAN

This book begins with two photographs of fashionable women by the Séebergers brothers, one taken before the First World War began and the other in its immediate aftermath. To conclude the book, let us consider two similar images by the Séebergers taken exactly five years apart, the first in June 1914 and the second in June 1919. FIGS. 10.1, 10.2

As in the earlier photographs, the change in the women's appearance is striking: the excess and ostentation of the prewar fashions have given way to the cleaner, more casual lines of the postwar period. The essays in this book have addressed some of the critical changes that occurred during the First World War and led to this simplification of the silhouette. The change in the nature of women's work, including women's increased activity outside the home in order to help the war effort, certainly made simpler styles more practical. The staggering death toll—approximately 1.3 million soldiers died fighting for France, including foreign and colonial soldiers—and the sheer horror of modern trench warfare made frivolity distasteful, not only in mourning but also in daily life. Certain jobs, particularly those formerly held by men, came with new dress codes that required women to don plain dresses, tailored suits, nurse's uniforms, or even overalls. These non-uniform "uniforms" required women to negotiate between the "masculinization" of their labor and their own femininity. Meanwhile, the fashion industry itself changed over the course of the war. Owing to the German invasion of the northeastern regions of France early in the war, manufacturing moved from the northern departments to Lyon, shifting the textiles supplied to the garment industry from predominantly cotton and wool to silk and silk blends. As a consequence, silhouettes became lighter and more fluid. Sensitive to the national mood, designers created fashions for French women that were subdued in color, style, and silhouette. Problems with dyes and colorants made it hard to obtain some of the brighter hues of the prewar palette. Patriotic red, white, and blue became popular, as did silhouettes and styles inspired by men's tailoring and men's military uniforms. The evolution in the silhouette is visible in these photographs, as well as others, and can be explained in part by structural changes brought on by the war, but how did contemporary observers and modern historians interpret them?

Some read the fashionable silhouette of the postwar period as a reflection of the historical moment and a direct outcome of the war: the straight cuts deemphasized the waist, chest, and hips, suggesting that women, having experienced life outside the domestic sphere during the war, were now rejecting the trappings of motherhood; shortened hair and more masculine-looking styles indicated a blurring of sexual difference that had begun during the war as women took over the roles traditionally held by men, both at work and at home; raised hemlines and bare skin emphasized women's supposed sexual, social, and economic emancipation. The women in the photograph from June 1919 could be seen to embody the tropes of the modern woman—emancipated from social mores, financially independent, sexually liberated, and hedonistic. Fashion, this narrative assumes, is a visual marker of the social changes taking place in France.

However, another interpretation construes the changing silhouette of the wartime period as an indication that women deliberately used the new fashions to advance their agenda, proclaim their independence, and signal their new roles. This narrative, developed by the historian Mary Louise Roberts in her discussion of the postwar *garçonne* hairstyle, considers fashion as having a historical dynamic of its own.[1] Here, women gain agency through their fashion choices, and garments become invested with political meaning. Feeling emboldened by new opportunities, women chose styles that reflected and emphasized their emancipated state. What Roberts has written in regards to the postwar bob could also be applicable to the wartime silhouette: "fashion acted as a presentation of self, in part grounded in fantasy and wish fulfillment."[2]

The essays in this book provide examples from both rhetorical sides. On one hand, the (predominantly male) discursive strategies of the wartime press, notably the satirical press, conflated women's social and economic "emancipation" with the "emancipatory" aesthetics of wartime fashions. Wartime styles such as work overalls, the military-inspired suit jacket, and the shortened skirt lengths were seen as visual representations of behaviors that stemmed directly from the war. On the other hand, women also deliberately donned new garb—a nurse's uniform, overalls, a company-issued hat or armband, mourning dress, or a tailored suit—in order to step into their new roles.

Were the new fashions liberating? Much like Poiret's claims to have freed women from corsets while shackling their legs, wartime and postwar fashions helped women move with ease in some respects, while constraining their bodies in others.[3] Despite Poiret's assertions, corsets were not abandoned during this period, although lighter and more flexible versions were introduced. Wartime crinoline-style skirts may have "unhobbled" the legs, but they were heavy and were worn with tight-laced boots that covered the ankles. In the postwar period, the straight silhouettes,

FIG. 10.1 Séeberger Frères. Women at the races wearing hobble skirts and feathered hats, June 1914. Silver gelatin print.
© Bibliothèque nationale de France.

FIG. 10.2 Séeberger Frères. Women at the races wearing the simplified postwar styles, June 1919. Silver gelatin print. © Bibliothèque nationale de France.

which appeared to denote a corsetless waist, were offset by the need to diet and constrain the bust. The new emphasis placed on beauty and youth may have offset the effects of the supposedly "liberated" fashions, yet, even if the fashions themselves were not freeing, women may have felt empowered while wearing them. Today's stilettos are much more constricting than sneakers, for instance, but a woman might feel emboldened by wearing them. How much more "emancipated" women felt while wearing the new wartime silhouettes is hard to determine without first-hand narratives, of which there are too few from the war. Yet each individual experience of possible emancipation through fashion needs to be reframed within the larger French sociopolitical context. Although the evolution of the fashionable silhouette between 1914 and 1919 seems to visually signal tremendous changes in terms of French women's social, economic, and political status, the reality is more nuanced. In many countries the war acted as a catalyst for female enfranchisement. Robust prewar suffrage movements, coupled with supportive public opinion, helped women gain the right to vote in England, Germany, and Armenia in 1918, in Holland and Sweden in 1919, and the United States in 1920. In France, however, women had to wait until the end of the Second World War to vote. The First World War was more of a hindrance to women's suffrage in France than a facilitator. In mid-June and July of 1914, days before war was declared, French suffragettes celebrated what they believed would be an imminent and victorious vote on a suffrage bill. At the start of the conflict, feminists and suffragettes put their demands on hold in order to rally to the support of the nation. The war halted their momentum and reinforced the traditional gender order. A proposition made in 1916 to enfranchise war widows and the mothers of fallen soldiers was deemed insulting by many suffragettes; they wanted the vote in their own name, not that of their departed husbands or sons. After the signing of the armistice, French feminists and suffragists believed that their cause would prevail. The extraordinary service of French women to the nation during the war was certainly a strong argument for female suffrage. But although the French Chamber of Deputies voted overwhelmingly in favor (344 to 97) of a proposition that championed women's rights in 1919, the Senate rejected the bill by a narrow margin (156 to 134) in 1922.

FIG. 10.3 The pronatalist voices had won out over the demands of the feminists. Indeed, during the war, the plummeting birth rate had sharply focused public debate on motherhood and on repopulating the nation. Efforts had been made to couple wartime employment with the needs of working mothers—for instance, photo reportages of war factories often emphasized daycare services at work. FIG. 10.4 But once the war was over, these same women were forced out of their jobs and told to return to the domestic sphere. The *remplaçantes*, the women who replaced men in their jobs during the war, were required to give their jobs back to the returning soldiers. Two days after the armistice was signed, on November 13, 1918, the Ministry of War called on the *munitionnettes* to demobilize within the month. Their service was no longer needed. Men believed that if women wanted to keep working, they should return to more "suitable" (and lower paid) jobs.[4] Calls for equal pay were equally optimistic. Some industries increased their wages for women following the female-led strikes of 1917, but true wage parity remains an issue one hundred years later.

It could be argued that fashions evolved more quickly than women's rights during this period in France, yet the social changes that the new shorter, simpler silhouettes seemed to signal were merely an appearance. The war, in other words, "did not cause a profound change of the hegemonic gender order or long-term improvements of the status of women, even though they might have been of great importance for the contemporaries themselves."[5] Although evidence for or against progress for women in the postwar period varies for each region, class, and ethnicity, historians agree that war-related shifts for women in France were largely temporary. For the French historian Françoise Thébaud, the war was deeply "conservative" in terms of the impact it had on political gender transformations.[6] In the model of the double helix, proposed in 1987 by Margaret R. and Patrice L.-R. Higonnet, the historians argue that "the changes in women's activities during wartime [First and Second World Wars] did not improve their status," because "the female strand on the helix is opposed to the male strand, and position on the female strand is subordinate to position on the male strand."[7] Not only were women's positions inferior to men's during the war, but the war exacerbated the hegemonic gender order, reinforcing classic binary divisions between masculine and feminine gender norms.

These overarching statements can be nuanced: the war also allowed men and women to transgress traditional gender roles as men stepped into more "feminine" jobs, such as nursing, and women took over more "masculine" work, such as factory labor. Additionally, each person experienced the war differently. French

FIG. 10.3 French league for women's rights handing out fliers at the Place de l'Opéra, Paris, 1920. Silver gelatin print. © Bibliothèque Marguerite Durand / Roger-Viollet, 099 B 857.

42 — N° 3854 L'ILLUSTRATION 13 JANVIER 1917

L'ALLAITEMENT DES NOURRISSONS

DANS LES USINES DE GUERRE

Le travail des femmes dans les usines de guerre n'est pas sans soulever des alarmes chez certains docteurs, au nombre desquels se rangent nos puériculteurs les plus éminents, et qui redoutent, tant pour les nourrissons des jeunes mères employées que pour les femmes proches de la maternité, l'influence de conditions de travail défectueuses. Ce problème est d'une importance capitale, car il semble opposer les exigences actuelles de la défense nationale avec celles de l'avenir même de notre pays, menacé dans sa natalité.

Le docteur Pinard, le premier, a démontré dès 1895 que les femmes qui se reposent mettent au monde des enfants plus robustes que celles qui se fatiguent durant la gestation. D'autre part, des statistiques probantes ont démontré la quasi-nécessité de l'allaitement du bébé par la mère, dont l'abstention en tant que nourrice est la cause indirecte de tant de ravages parmi les nouveau-nés. Or, comment des ouvrières pourraient-elles donner le sein pendant les heures de labeur ? Faudrait-il, comme le demande l'illustre professeur, interdire en France le travail dans les usines à toute femme soit en état de gestation, soit allaitant son enfant, soit accouchée depuis moins de six mois, et, par conséquence, grever notre budget des allocations journalières devenues indispensables du fait de cette interdiction? M. Antoine Borrel, député de la Savoie, pour obvier à ces difficultés, a saisi ses collègues d'une proposition de loi tendant à attribuer à toute mère allaitant son enfant une allocation mensuelle de 20 francs.

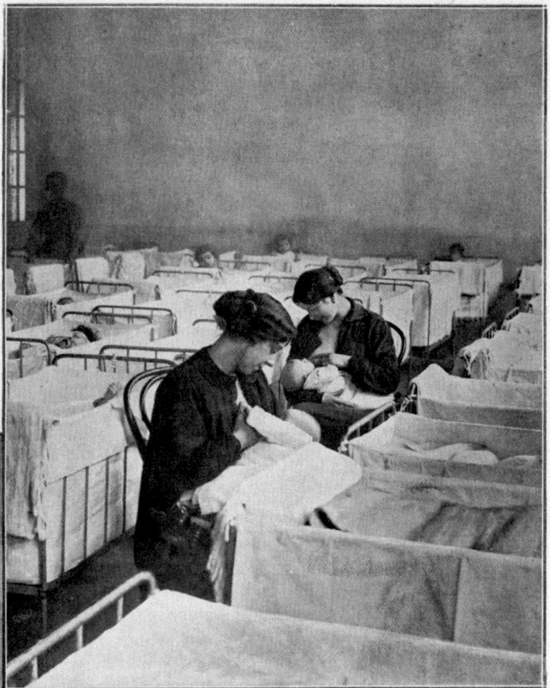

Ouvrières d'une usine de guerre allaitant leurs nourrissons dans une salle spéciale.

Dans une crèche annexée à une usine de guerre : les ouvrières en costume de travail et leurs bébés. — *Phot. Wyndham.*

Ce n'est pas ici le lieu de rechercher dans quelle mesure ce projet est adapté aux conditions actuelles de la vie. Mais, après avoir exposé cette thèse pessimiste, nous tenons à montrer que les alarmes de nos gynécologues sont peut-être excessives, et que dès maintenant le remède est, à la lettre, à côté du mal. Et voici comment.

Mme Pierre Budin, la veuve du grand puériculteur, a mené une campagne inspirée des théories de son mari en faveur des salles d'allaitement annexées aux usines.

Déjà, en temps de paix, une cinquantaine d'industriels français avaient eu l'initiative de réaliser cette ingénieuse combinaison. Quelques établissements de guerre — pas assez nombreux encore — ont suivi cet exemple, et c'est dans l'un d'eux, situé près de Paris, que furent prises les deux touchantes photographies que nous publions.

Une installation de ce genre est très peu coûteuse, quelques centaines de francs, et il est souhaitable de la voir mettre en pratique non seulement dans les usines à munitions, mais partout où travaillent des femmes. Le docteur Henri Bouquet décrivait une de ces salles : « Une grande pièce blanchie à la chaux, quelques berceaux, un casier à vêtements, une table, des chaises, une balance, une petite salle d'isolement, et voilà l'installation terminée. Une gardienne constitue tout le personnel nécessaire. Là, au début de la journée, la mère dépose son enfant. Elle le sait dès lors au calme, surveillé, près d'elle, et son ardeur au travail n'en est que plus grande. A intervalles réguliers, elle vient le voir et lui donner le sein. Le soir elle rentre avec lui à la maison. Est-il rien de plus simple, de plus logique, de moins dispendieux, de plus efficace? » Une garderie d'enfants, pour les bébés sevrés ou mis au biberon, doit compléter l'installation pour qu'elle réponde à tous les besoins. Et il semble bien en effet que ce soit là une solution moyenne, satisfaisant à la fois aux besoins actuels et à l'avenir de notre pays.

FIG. 10.4 "Breastfeeding in War Factories," *L'Illustration*, January 13, 1917, 42. Private collection.

women may have had their "own concept of emancipation" and may have experienced a change in their own self-perception during the war owing to new responsibilities.[8] If the war did not grant new rights to French women in the immediate postwar period, it may have set the foundation for the younger generation to demand change two decades later.

The essays in this book consider fashion as a political force. There was a financial and moral imperative to safeguard the fashion industry itself—the French government relied on the money and soft power wielded by a healthy couture industry—but there was also political symbolism in the very act of wearing clothing during the war. Wartime fashion could signal many things: patriotism, mourning, service to the nation, independence, and practicality. For the defenders of fashion, to wear the new fashions was to support the nation and embrace the new roles and responsibilities offered to women by the war. For the critics, fashion symbolized the turmoil caused by the conflict: the blurring of gender norms, the supposed "emancipation" of women from the domestic sphere, the tension between the front and home, and the feeling that the world had changed forever. The way in which fashion was represented, discussed, marketed, and worn can tell us a great deal about what men and women were thinking about and doing during the war.

The period between 1914 and 1918 was critical for French fashion. Changes in the silhouette that had begun before the war were accelerated by it, the industry became invested with political significance, and society used fashion to debate larger issues. The inclusion of fashion history within the historiography of the First World War broadens our understanding of war culture and offers a new perspective on the history of French women during the war. It also fills a gap in the chronology, as most studies of fashion deal with either the prewar or postwar period—rare are those that cover the first full decades of the twentieth century. Moving forward, we hope that the discussions raised by this book will lead to further studies on the relationship between fashion and war, as well as on transnational comparisons between the French, American, African, and Asian experiences of fashion, war, and gender. More research is needed into the individual voices and the biographical accounts of female consumers and designers of fashion during the war, particularly those that address the intersectionality of female identity. The usefulness of fashion in broadening our understanding of history no longer needs justification; we feel confident that future research will bring to the foreground new sources to expand the narrative set by this book.

1 Mary Louise Roberts, "Samson and Delilah Revisited: The Politics of Women's Fashion in 1920s France," *The American Historical Review* 98, no. 3 (1993): 661.

2 Ibid., 677.

3 "Like all great revolutions, that one had been made in the name of Liberty—to give free play to the abdomen: it was equally in the name of Liberty that I proclaimed the fall of the corset . . . Yes, I freed the bust but I shackled the legs." Paul Poiret, *King of Fashion: The Autobiography of Paul Poiret* (London: V&A, 2009), 36.

4 For a thorough discussion of female employment during the war, see Karen Offen, *Debating the Woman Question in the French Third Republic, 1870–1920* (Cambridge: Cambridge University Press, 2018), 547–612.

5 Christa Hämmerle, Oswald Überegger, Birgitta Bader Zaar, "Introduction: Women's and Gender History of the First World War—Topics, Concepts, Perspectives," in *Gender and the First World War* (New York: Palgrave Macmillan, 2014), 3.

6 Françoise Thébaud, "La Grande Guerre: Le triomphe de la division sexuelle," in *Histoire des Femmes en Occident 5: Le XXe siècle*, ed. Georges Duby and Michelle Perrot (Paris: Plon, 1992), 31–89.

7 Margaret R. Higonnet and Patrice L.-R. Higonnet, "The Double Helix," in *Behind the Lines: Gender and the Two World Wars*, ed. Margaret R. Higonnet, Jane Jenson, Sonia Michel, and Margaret Collins Weitz (New Haven, CT: Yale University Press, 1987), 31–49.

8 Françoise Thébaud, *Les femmes au temps de la guerre de 14* (Paris: Payot, 2013), 426.

PRINCIPAL FRENCH FASHION HOUSES ACTIVE DURING THE WAR

AGNÈS (~1898–1930) AND CH. DRECOLL (1892–1928), THEN MAISON DRECOLL ET SUCCESSEUR DE BEER (1928–1930), THEN AGNÈS-DRECOLL (1930–1963)

Founded around 1898 by Madame Havet, who had worked with Jacques Doucet, the fashion house Agnès moved to the rue Louis-le-Legrand in Paris in 1910, before moving to 7, rue Auber. Agnès was renowned for its turbans and hats. Ch. Drecoll was a Viennese fashion house created by Christoff von Drecoll (1851–1939) in 1892. Von Drecoll sold his label to Berg, Kahn, and Wagner in 1896. In 1903 the company opened a Parisian branch under the name Maison Ch. Drecoll at 4, Avenue de l'Opéra. In 1928, Ch. Drecoll merged with Beer under the name "Maison Drecoll et successeur de Beer" and then merged with Agnès in 1930. Agnès-Drecoll moved to 24, Place Vendôme.

AINE-MONTAILLÉ, 1853–1930

Jean Aine-Montaillé opened his fashion house in 1853 at 1, Place Vendôme, in Paris, before adding a second location at 27, rue Faubourg Saint-Honoré. The house, labeled the "Grande Maison de Noire" (the Great House of Black) by *Le Figaro* (October 30, 1906), gained its reputation primarily through its mourning dress designs. It outfitted wealthy families in Paris, in the provinces, and broad—most notably, for royal mourning periods. Jean Aine-Montaillé was the president of the Chambre Syndicale de la Couture Parisienne from 1913 until 1917.

BEER, 1886–28

Gustav Beer (1855–1908) began his career making artificial flowers before becoming an évantailliste (fan maker), and subsequently a couturier. He opened his first house in Paris, which specialized in lingerie, on the Boulevard Poissonnière in 1886, before moving to 4, Place de l'Opéra in 1893 and then the Place Vendôme in 1900. By 1908, the house employed more than 200 workers. Gustav Beer died that year, leaving the house in the hands of M. Paillon. The house was considered suspicious during the war, owing to its German origins. It would merge with Ch. Drecoll in 1928 under the name "Maison Drecoll et successeur de Beer."

BOUÉ SŒURS, 1899–1957

The house Boué Sœurs, its name based on the maiden names of its founders, Sylvie Montegut (1872–1953) and Baronne Jeanne d'Etreillis (1876–1957), opened in 1899 in Paris. A branch opened in New York in 1915. The label's romantic style is typified by its use of lace with floral motifs, embroidery, and gold and silver textiles, as seen in the collections they showed at the Panama–Pacific International Exposition in San Francisco and the Fête Parisienne in New York in the summer of 1915.

CALLOT SŒURS, 1895–1954

Callot Sœurs was founded by four sisters in 1895, at 24, rue de Taitbout in Paris: Marie Callot-Gerber (1857–1927), Marthe Callot-Bertrand (1859–1920), Regina Callot-Tennyson-Chantrell, and Joséphine Callot-Crimont (1866–1897). The company's success stemmed from its work with ribbons and lace and its blouses, lingerie, and dresses made with gold and silver lamé fabric. Madeleine Vionnet (1876–1975) trained here until 1906. In 1914, Callot Sœurs moved to 9–11, Avenue Matignon.

CHANEL, 1910–

After growing up in an orphanage and learning her craft as a milliner with Lucienne Rabaté (1885–1960), Gabrielle Chanel (1883–1971), known as Coco, opened her first small workshop in Paris in 1909, with the help of her partner, Arthur Capel. There she gained success creating simple hats similar to the ones she would make for herself. She opened her first store in 1910 at 21, rue Cambon under the name Chanel Modes, before adding an additional location, rented by Capel, in Deauville in 1913. This store, named Gabrielle Chanel, at first sold only hats. In 1915, Chanel opened her third store in Biarritz, which sold clothes that were notable for their elegance and simplicity. That same year she began making clothing using a supply of jersey from the textile manufacturer Rodier, a fabric previously reserved for undergarments. These jersey garments—blouses with sailor collars, simple tailored suits—cemented her reputation. In 1918, she opened her first fashion house in Paris on the rue Cambon.

CHÉRUIT, 1898–35

Louise Lemaire-Chéruit (1866–1935) worked with Raudnitz and Cie at 13, rue de la Grange-Batalière in Paris before buying the house with Marie Huet in 1898 and renaming it Chéruit-Huet. It received the Grand Prize at the Exposition Universelle in 1900 and was renowned for its theatrical costumes. In 1902, the house—now named Chéruit—moved to 21, Place Vendôme. In the 1910s, the house employed about one hundred workers and salespersons. Louise Lemaire-Chéruit partnered with the couturiers Louise Boulanger and Julie Wormser in 1909 and retired in 1914. The house continued without her until 1935.

G. DŒUILLET ET CIE., 1898–1937

Georges Dœuillet (1865–1934) began working at the Grande Maison du Blanc in Paris in 1883 before moving to Callot Sœurs. He opened his own fashion house, G. Dœuillet et Cie, in 1898 at 18, Place Vendôme, before moving to number 24 in 1914. He participated in the 1900 Exposition Universelle in the Palais des Fils, Tissue et Vêtements. In 1908 he opened a second store in London, at 25 Albemarle Street. In 1911, he received the Legion d'Honneur, which was presented to him by the couturier Louis Reverdot. He served as president of the Chambre Syndicale de la Couture Parisienne from 1912 until 1913.

DOUCET, 1816–1924

The family of Jacques Doucet (1853–1929) owned a successful store in Paris—founded in 1816 and specializing in lingerie, lacework, and shirts, which he joined in 1875 and reorganized as one of the first made-to-measure fashion houses, at 21, rue de la Paix. His designs paid homage to those of his parents; sophisticated, ethereal, and sensual; his dresses and negligées would often incorporate lace, embroidery, and plissé fabric. Paul Poiret was one of Doucet's assistants between 1898 and 1900, as was Madeleine Vionnet between 1907 and 1912. Doucet gained wealth and reputation dressing actresses and society women. He was an extraordinairy collector of books and works of art and he created a library dedicated to fine arts and archaeology between 1908 and 1914.

JEAN PATOU & CIE., 1914–87

Jean Patou (1887–1936) began working in fashion with his uncle, a furrier. In 1910 he opened a fashion house specializing in furs in Paris. When the first iteration failed, he established Maison Parry, at 4, Rond-point des Champs-Elysées. He expanded in 1914, moving to 7, rue Saint-Florentin and renamed it Jean Patou & Cie. Called to the front in August 1914, Patou was unable to present his first collection. Patou grew his house during the war and became famous in the interwar period for his sportswear outfits, such as those worn by the French female tennis player Suzanne Rachel Flore Lenglen.

JENNY, 1909–40

Jenny Sacerdote, born Jeanne Adèle Bernard (1868–1962), joined the École Normale Supérieure de Sèvres before deciding to reorient herself toward fashion. She was a salesperson at Béchoff-David between 1901–9 at 20, Place Vendôme in Paris before opening her own fashion house, Jenny, at 1, rue de Castiglione in 1909. In 1913, she opened a boutique in Biarritz at 10, rue des Postes, and in 1915, she moved to 70, Avenue des Champs-Élysées in Paris, where Robert Mallet-Stevens decorated her salon. In May 1917, 180 seamstresses from her house went on strike to demand better hours and higher wages. The house moved to 8, rue Royale in 1933 and merged with the house Lucile Paray in 1938, changing its name to Lucile Paray-Jenny. This house closed in 1940.

LANVIN, 1889–

Jeanne Lanvin (1867–1946) started her fashion career in 1880 as a decorator in the hat store of Madame Félix and later as an apprentice with the hatmaker Boni. In 1885, she opened a small boutique on the Faubourg Saint-Honoré in Paris, where she sold her own collection—predominantly hats. She opened a fashion house, Lanvin (Mlle Jeanne) Modes, in 1889, at 16, rue Boissy d'Anglas. She launched a division for young girls and women in 1909 and sold both day and evening dresses. That same year, she joined the Chambre Syndicale de la Couture Parisienne. In 1913, her label created a fur division. She entered wartime at the head of a prosperous business and participated in the Panama–Pacific International Exposition in San Francisco and the Fête Parisienne in New York in 1915. Jeanne Lanvin died in 1946, but her house is still active today.

MARGAINE-LACROIX, 1899–1930

In 1868, Armandine Fresnais-Margaine (1835–1899) founded the house Margaine, which became the house Margaine-Lacroix after being taken over by her daughter, Jeanne-Victorine Margaine-Lacroix (1868–1930) in 1899. The house, situated at 19, Boulevard Haussmann received a gold medal at the Exposition Universelle de Paris in 1889. It also participated in the 1900 Exposition, as part of the Collectivité de la Couture, where it presented three Sylphide dresses. These dresses were remarkable for their lack of corset, which they replaced with an interior construction of jersey and elastic silk. The bodices of these dresses were designed to emphasize this absent corset. The house built on this success with Sylphide girdles in sheepskin and silk Sylphide brassieres. Louis Süe redecorated the interior of the Margaine-Lacroix salons in 1912.

MARTIAL ET ARMAND, 1896–1957

The house Martial et Armand began as the Maison Armand in 1896, situated at 13, rue de la Paix, in Paris, before becoming Maison Martial & Armand in 1902, at 6, rue de la Chaussée d'Antin. It was led by Armand Cahen, Jules Renou, and Martial Finette. In 1902, the house had three locations: 13, rue de la Paix, 10, Place Vendôme, and 125 New Bond Street in London.

PAQUIN, 1891–1956

Founded in 1889 under the name Paquin Lalanne & Cie, and renamed Paquin in 1891, the house was located at 3, rue de la Paix, in Paris. In 1896 the house added a branch in London. In 1907, Jeanne Paquin (1869–1936) took over the directorship of the house after the death of her husband, Isidore Paquin (1862–1907). The house made forays into theatrical costuming and collaborated twice with Léon Bakst in 1912, once for a mini-collection and again for the costumes of the Ballets Russes. That same year, after launching a shop in Buenos Aires, the house opened a store selling furs on Fifth Avenue in New York City. In 1913, Jeanne Paquin collaborated with Georges Barbier, Paul Iribe, and Georges Lepape to create the booklet *L'Eventail et la Fourrure chez Paquin*. She received the Legion d'Honneur in that year for her contributions to art and design. In 1914, Paquin opened a store in Madrid. During the war she contributed to promoting French fashion abroad, showing works in the Panama–Pacific International Exposition in San Francisco and the Fête Parisienne in New York. She was president of the Chambre Syndicale de la Couture Parisienne from 1917 until 1920.

PAUL POIRET, 1903–29

Born to a family of drapery merchants, Paul Poiret (1879–1944) apprenticed with an umbrella merchant and subsequently worked with two of Paris's leading fashion houses—Doucet, between 1898 and 1900, and Worth, between 1901 and 1903. Poiret opened his own house in 1903, and he would eventually branch out into a number of fields—illustration, perfume, textiles, and furniture. In 1908, he worked with Paul Iribe to illustrate his collection in *Les Robes de Paul Poiret racontées par Paul Iribe*, a document that showcases Poiret's innovative aesthetic vision. He repeated this process in 1912, when he asked Georges Lepape to illustrate *Les Choses de Paul Poiret*. In 1911, Poiret launched his perfume division Rosine, named for his youngest daughter, as well as Maison Martine, a furniture and home decorating division named for his second daughter. He was drafted in August 1914 but continued producing collections throughout the war. He created and presided over the Syndicat de Défense de la Grande Couture Française between 1914 and 1918. In 1915, he sent designs to the Panama–Pacific International Exposition in San Francisco and the Fête Parisienne in New York.

REDFERN, 1847–1929

John Redfern (1820–1895) first opened a men's tailor shop in Cowes, England in 1847. He eventually began making women's jackets and skirts for sporting purposes (hunting, equestrianism, tennis, yachting). These tailored dresses and suits would be popularized for daily use after 1885. Redfern & Sons (later Redfern Ltd, in 1892) opened branches in London in 1878, in Paris in 1881, and in the United States, beginning in 1884. John Redfern died in 1895. The Parisian branch, at 242, rue de Rivoli, was headed by Charles Poynter (1853–1929) and was integrated into the Chambre Syndicale de la Couture in 1900. The house, which also made evening wear, managed to establish itself as a major couturier in Paris. In 1916, the label created women's uniforms for the French Red Cross.

VIONNET, 1912–40

Madeleine Vionnet (1876–1975) began her training in fashion in 1888, working initially with a couturier neighbor and then in a workshop the following year. In 1890, she moved to Paris, where she apprenticed with the house Vincent, which was located on the rue de la Paix. After her divorce from Émile Depoutot, whom she had married in 1894, Vionnet moved to London, where she worked with the couturière Kate Reily. In 1900, in Paris once again, Vionnet worked as head of the atelier with the Callot Sœurs and then with Jacques Doucet. In 1912, she opened her own fashion house at 222, rue de Rivoli, where she would take inspiration from ancient Greco-Roman drapery to create distinctly modern designs.

WORTH, 1858–1953

Charles Frederick Worth (1825–1895) was born in England and trained with textile merchants in London before moving to Paris in 1845. He worked with Gagelin, a major textile and clothing store, where he would later open a couture division. He received awards at the Great Exhibition in London in 1851 and the Exposition Universelle in Paris in 1855. In 1858, Worth founded a fashion house with Otto Bobergh, Worth & Bobergh, at 7, rue de la Paix. He is associated with a new perception of the couturier as both a craftsman and an artist. He also introduced the idea of showing his collection on a runway and popularized the ongoing concept of seasonal collections. He quickly gained favor with the Empress Eugénie and the Princess Pauline von Metternich. Upon his death in 1895, Worth's sons took over the business. Gaston Worth (1853–1924) handled business administration and Jean-Philippe Worth (1856–1926) oversaw creative direction.

SELECTED FRENCH FASHION MAGAZINES PUBLISHED DURING THE WAR

L'Art et la Mode, 1880–1956. Publication was suspended between August 1914 and March 1915.

Chiffons, 1907–32.

Les Élégances Parisiennes, 1916–24.

Femina, 1901–74. Publication was suspended between September 1914 and February 1917. Between March 1917 and December 1921, Femina was published under the name *Femina et Vie Heureuse Réunies*.

La Gazette du Bon Ton, 1912–25. Publication suspended between August 1914 and August 1915; one double edition printed in English and French for summer 1915; publication resumed between 1920 and 1925.

La Mode Illustrée, 1860–1937.

La Mode Pratique: revue de la famille, 1891–1951.

Les Modes, 1901–37. Publication was suspended in 1916 and in June 1917.

Les Modes de la Femme de France, 1915–25.

Le Petit Écho de la Mode, 1880–1983.

Le Style Parisien, 1915–16.

TIMELINE CAPTIONS

FIG. T-1 Agence Rol. Suffragette protest at the Tuileries, Paris. Notable writer and feminist Séverine (née Caroline Rémy de Guebhard) at the head of the procession, facing the statue of Condorcet, July 5, 1914. Silver gelatin print. © Agence Rol / Bibliothèque Marguerite Durand / Roger-Viollet RV-75494-25.

FIG. T-2 Louis Rémy Sabattier. Illustration of British soldiers viewing Parisian spring designs including a collared coat over a blouse and tailored skirt (center). *L'Illustration*, February 13, 1915. Private collection.

FIG. T-3 Charles Lansiaux. Newspaper seller, place Denfert-Rochereau, Paris, August 1914. Silver gelatin print. © Charles Lansiaux / BHVP / Roger-Viollet, RV-73737-30.

FIG. T-4 Pierre Brissaud. "Vive Saint-Cyr! Robes d'été de Jeanne Lanvin," *La Gazette du Bon Ton*, July 1914, pl. 72. Pochoir. © Bibliothèque Forney / Roger-Viollet, RV-157622-15.

FIG. T-5 René Viviani. "A Call To French Women," poster urging French farming women to replace men in the fields who have been called to war, August 6, 1914. Archives départementales 71, R guerre 14-18/286.

FIG. T-6 Agence Rol. "Fleeing from the barbarians (civilians fleeing on foot)," 1914. Negative print on glass. © Bibliothèque nationale de France, Département des Estampes et de la photographie, EST EI-13 (408).

FIG. T-7 Anne Rittenhouse. "Couturiers Under Arms" *Vogue*, October 1914, 44. © Condé Nast.

FIG. T-8 Soldier's helmet, 1914-18. Musée de la Grande Guerre du Pays de Meaux, CAPM.2006.1.170.

FIG. T-9 Military kepi, 1914-18. Musée de la Grande Guerre du Pays de Meaux, CAPM2006.1.269.

FIG. T-10 Street in Lille shortly before the city fell to German troops, October 12, 1914. Silver gelatin print. © Ullstein Bild / Roger-Viollet, RV-75258-8.

FIG. T-11 Paul Poiret. "Capote Poiret,"military jacket belonging to the under-lieutenant Jacques Defrasse, 1915. Wool. Musée de la Grande Guerre du Pays de Meaux, CAPM2006.1.12025.

FIG. T-12 A first line trench in the Aisne region, France. *Excelsior*, December 20, 1914. © BHVP / Roger-Viollet, RV-80279-5.

FIG. T-13 Signalwoman at Gare du Nord, Paris. "The new professions for women since the war," *Excelsior*, June 24, 1917. Silver gelatin print. © Excelsior–L'Équipe / Roger-Viollet, RV-72195-53.

FIG. T-14 Fabien Fabiano. Caricature of a woman wearing German fashions. "Élégances Berlinoises," *La Baïonnette*, August 12, 1915. ˝ Bibliothèque Marguerite Durand / Roger-Viollet RV-157096-1.

FIG. T-15 Military chaplain helping a wounded German prisoner during the Second Battle of Ypres (Belgium), April 22, 1915. Silver gelatin print. © PA Archive / Rpger-Viollet, RV-79447-9.

FIG. T-16 "We were separated! We are reunited! / We will be one for eternity." Hand-colored photographic postcard. Private collection.

FIG. T-17 Front cover of the English-language edition of *The 1915 Mode as Shown by Paris, Panama Pacific International Exposition, La Gazette du Bon Ton,* Summer 1915. © BHVP / Roger-Viollet, RV-157095-1.

FIG. T-18 Female mechanic in overalls working on ammunition in a factory, *Excelsior*, February 12, 1917. © Bibliothèque nationale de France.

FIG. T-19 "They will not pass" French soldiers who participated in the battle of Verdun (Meuse), February–December 1916. Silver gelatin print. © TopFoto / Roger-Viollet, RV-88082-24.

FIG. T-20 Dartey, pseudonym of Anette Osterlind. "France" ensemble by Jenny. *Les Élégances Parisiennes,* August 1916, pl. V. © Bibliothéque Forney / Roger-Viollet, RV-157622-23.

FIG. T-21 Battle of the Somme. Civilians and soldiers of the Royal British Army distributing water to wounded soldiers in France, July 1, 1916. Silver gelatin print. © PA Archive / Roger-Viollet, RV-79442-16.

FIG. T-22 "Jersey Suits, Modèles de Gabrielle Chanel," *Les Élégances Parisiennes,* July 1916, pl. XI. © Bibliothéque Forney / Roger-Viollet, RV-157622-20.

FIG. T-23 Weeks. Barrel silhouette evening dress, ca. 1918. Silk georgette, metallic beads, black seed beads. The Museum at FIT, Gift of the Barnard College Theatre Co., 84.69.1.

FIG. T-24 Jules Gervais-Courtellemont. Robert Nivelle, French General, 1916. Autochrome. © Jules Gervais-Courtellemont / Cinémathèque Robert-Lynen / Roger-Viollet, RV-78780-8.

FIG. T-25 Jeanne Paquin. "Matelassé" tailored suit for copyright deposit, August 13, 1917. Silver gelatin print. Archives de Paris, dépôt n° 4540, 13 août 1917, n° de modèle dans la collection: 19, n° de modèle dans le dépôt: 17 D12U10 249. © Archives de Paris / Roger-Viollet, RV-101321-2.

FIG. T-26 A queue of people in front of the grocery stores waiting to buy sugar before the introduction of a food card, Paris, March 5, 1917. Silver gelatin print. © Excelsior–L'Équipe / Roger-Viollet RV-72694-35.

FIG. T-27 Jeanne Lanvin. Dress with elaborate beadwork on the bodice, skirt, and hem, winter 1917. Crêpe, satin. © Patrimoine Lanvin, Paris, JL N° 377.

FIG. T-28 Ch. A. Rethaber. "The Welcome", 1917. Pochoir. © Diktats bookstore.

FIG. T-29 Maurice-Louis Branger. Seamstresses from the Jenny couture house at 70, avenue des Champs Élysées on strike for their right to higher wages and time off on Saturday afternoons and Sundays, May 18, 1917. Silver gelatin print. © Maurice-Louis Branger / Roger-Viollet, RV-3831-8.

FIG. T-30 *Appel aux Femmes*, 1915. Poster. © BHVP / Roger-Viollet RV-101748-31.

FIG. T-31 The arrival of the first U.S. military contingents in France, Saint-Nazaire, late June 1917. Silver gelatin print. © Excelsior–L'Équipe / Roger-Viollet, RV-72194-49.

FIG. T-32 Woman's boots stamped with a "National Shoe" ("Chaussure Nationale") label on the sole, 1914–18. Leather. Paris, Musée des Arts Décoratifs, 53 730B.

FIG. T-33 Lenin delivering a speech on the Red Square, Moscow, 1919. Silver gelatin print. © Iberfoto / Roger-Viollet, RV-100753-17.

FIG. T-34 Smith College Relief Unit suit, 1917. Wool. Smith College Historic Clothing Collection, 1981.13. Jamison, a-e.

FIG. T-35 Neysa McMein. YMCA United War Work Campaign poster for World War I, 1918. Lithograph. Research Library, Western Reserve Historical Society, Cleveland, Ohio, 45.531.

FIG. T-36 Maurice-Louis Branger. Rubble inside the Saint-Gervais church, Paris, after the Good Friday bombing by Big Bertha cannons, March 29, 1918. Silver gelatin print. © Maurice-Louis Branger / Roger-Viollet, RV-1481-16.

FIG. T-37 "Decoration for a cellar [bomb shelter], executed by the Maison Martine," *Les Modes*, no. 177 (1918), 2.

FIG. T-38 Madeleine Vionnet. Postwar evening dress, June 1918. Silk satin, silk embroidery, mousseline de sole. Paris, Musée des Arts Décoratifs – collection UFAC, UF 52 18 9.

FIG. T-39 "What They Signed," *Excelsior*, November 12, 1918. © BHVP / Roger-Viollet, RV-80279-14.

FIG. T-40 Maurice Barbey. Poster for the Society for the Improvement of the Status of Women and the Demand for Women's Rights, ca. 1925–28. © Bibliothèque Marguerite Durand / Roger-Viollet, RV-54759-5.

FIG. T-41 French league for women's rights handing out fliers at the Place de l'Opéra, Paris, 1920. Silver gelatin print. © Bibliothèque Marguerite Durand / Roger-Viollet, 099 B 857.

FIG. T-42 Signing of the Treaty of Versailles between the Allies and Germany in the aftermath of the war. Versailles, June 28, 1919. © PA Archive / Roger-Viollet RV-79445-9.

CHECKLIST OF THE EXHIBITION

1. Prewar

1a. Exhibition Introduction & Timeline

First register for the Chambre Syndicale de la Couture Parisienne. 1910–19. 14⅛ × 9 × 3⅜ in. (35.8 × 23 × 8.5 cm). Fédération de la Haute Couture et de la Mode, Registre 1.
FIG. 6.1

Women wearing fashionable dress. Séeberger Frères (French, 1909–1977). January–February 1919. Bibliothèque nationale de France, 0A 38 boîte 3 (janvier-février 1919, n°1, photo n°39) (Département des Estampes et de la photographie). Reproduction in exhibition.
FIG. I-2

Women wearing fashionable dress. Séeberger Frères (French, 1907–1977). June 1919. Bibliothèque nationale de France, 0A 38 boîte 3 (juin 1919, n°15, photo n°517) (Département des Estampes et de la photographie). Reproduction in exhibition.
FIG. 10.2

Women wearing fashionable dress. Séeberger Frères (French, 1909–1977). January 1914. Bibliothèque nationale de France, 0A 38 boîte 2 (janvier 1914, n°1, photo n°22) (Département des Estampes et de la photographie). Reproduction in exhibition.
FIG. I-1

Women wearing fashionable dress. Séeberger Frères (1909–1977). France. June 1914. Bibliothèque nationale de France, 0A 38 boîte 2 (juin 1914, n°14, et fin, photo n°499) (Département des Estampes et de la photographie). Reproduction in exhibition.
FIG. 10.1

1b. Summer 1914

Dress, "Feuille Morte." Jeanne Lanvin (French, 1867–1946). Summer 1914. Silk. Patrimoine Lanvin, Paris, JL N°220.
FIG. 5c.15

Drawing of "Feuille Morte" dress. Jeanne Lanvin (French, 1867–1946). Summer 1911. Graphite, ink, and gouache. 17¾ × 12⅝ in. (45 × 32 cm). Patrimoine Lanvin, Paris.
FIG. 5c.16

Dress, "Saxe." Jeanne Lanvin (French, 1867–1946). Summer 1917. Crêpe. Patrimoine Lanvin, Paris, JL N°269.
FIG. 5c.23

Dress, "Résurrection." Jeanne Lanvin (French, 1867–1946). Winter 1919–20. Crêpe, velvet, glass beads. Patrimoine Lanvin, Paris, 130 RSC.
FIG. 5a.8

Drawing of "Résurrection" dress and "Charlemagne" coat. Jeanne Lanvin (French, 1867–1946). Winter 1919–20. Graphite, ink, and gouache. 17¾ × 12⅝ in. (45 × 32 cm). Patrimoine Lanvin, Paris.

"The Sun in the Garden: Afternoon dress by Dœuillet." André-Édouard Marty (1882–1974), illustrator. *La Gazette du Bon Ton,* May 1914. Pochoir. 11⅞ × 15¾ in. (30 × 40 cm). Fashion Institute of Technology | SUNY, FIT Library Special Collections and College Archives, New York, NY, USA, TT500.G35, Box 2: Jan. 1914–summer 1915.

"The Romantic Landscape: Tailored suit by Worth." Bernard Boutet de Monvel (French, 1881–1949), illustrator. *La Gazette du Bon Ton,* July 1914. Pochoir. 15¾ × 23⅝ in. (40 × 60 cm). Fashion Institute of Technology | SUNY, FIT Library Special Collections and College Archives, New York, NY, USA, TT500.G35, Box 2: Jan. 1914–summer 1915.

"Long Live Saint-Cyr!: Afternoon dress by Jeanne Lanvin." Pierre Brissaud (French, 1884–1965), illustrator. *La Gazette du Bon Ton,* July 1914. Pochoir. 15¾ × 23⅝ in. (40 × 60 cm). Fashion Institute of Technology | SUNY, FIT Library Special Collections and College Archives, New York, NY, USA, TT500.G35, Box 2: Jan.1914–summer 1915.
FIG. T-4

"We could have been invited too . . . Afternoon dresses and evening dress by Doucet." Pierre Brissaud (French, 1884–1965), illustrator. *La Gazette du Bon Ton*, June 1914. Pochoir. 19⅝ × 23⅝ in. (50 × 60 cm). Fashion Institute of Technology | SUNY, FIT Library Special

Collections and College Archives, New York, NY, USA, TT500.G35, Box 2: Jan. 1914–summer 1915.

1c. Early Days of the War

Illustration of British soldiers viewing spring designs. Louis Rémy Sabattier (French, 1863–1935), illustrator. *L'Illustration,* February 13, 1915. Halftone.15 × 22 in. (39 × 56 cm). Private collection.
FIG. 5.2

"1915:The Hurricane." Georges Lepape (French, 1887–1971), illustrator. *La Gazette du Bon Ton,* July 1915. Pochoir. 11⅞ × 1¾ in. (30 × 40 cm). Fashion Institute of Technology | SUNY, FIT Library Special Collections and College Archives, New York, NY, USA, TT500.G35, Box 2: Jan. 1914–summer 1915.

A sewing room at the Maison Beer. Henri Manuel (French,1874–1947). Paris, France. ca. 1915. Silver gelatin print. 11¾ × 15¾ in. (30 × 40 cm). Private collection.

"Gare de Lyon. Last Kiss Before Departure, August 10–20, 1914," Paris. Charles Lansiaux (French, 1855–1939). August 10–20, 1914. Bibliothèque Historique de la Ville de Paris, 4-EPF-011-0048. Reproduction in exhibition.
FIG. 3.3

French soldiers' cars stock up on equipment and supplies in front of the Belle Jardinière department store, Paris. Charles Lansiaux (French, 1855–1939). September 25, 1914. Bibliothèque Historique de la Ville de Paris, 4-EPF-011-0186. Reproduction in exhibition.
FIG. 5.6

Façade of Galeries Lafayette department store at 38, Boulevard Haussmann, heavily decorated with flags of French allies, Paris. Charles Lansiaux (French, 1855–1939). September 23, 1914. Bibliothèque Historique de la Ville de Paris, 4-EPF-011-0549. Reproduction in exhibition.
FIG. 5.5

Worth delivery garage at 7, rue de la Paix transformed into Ambulance Center no. 152 of the Red Cross of France, Union of French Women, Paris. Charles Lansiaux (French, 1855–1939). Préfecture de Police, Service de l'Identité judiciaire, October 1914. Bibliothèque Historique de la Ville de Paris, 4C EPF 004 0094. Reproduction in exhibition.
FIG. 5.4

Infantry patrol in front of shop of designer Mme. Pouyanne at 4, rue de la Paix, Paris. Charles Lansiaux (French, 1855–1939). Préfecture de Police, Service de l'Identité judiciaire, October 1914. Bibliothèque Historique de la Ville de Paris, 4C EPF 004 0096. Reproduction in exhibition.
FIG. 5.1

Workers at Galeries Lafayette sewing military outfits, Paris. Charles Lansiaux (French, 1855–1839). Préfecture de Police, Service de l'Identité judiciaire, August 1914. Bibliothèque Historique de la Ville de Paris / Photographie de la Préfecture de Police, Service de l'Identité judiciaire, 4C-EPF-004-0995. Reproduction in exhibition.
FIG. 5.7

Dressmakers at Galeries Lafayette working at their counters to help wounded soldiers, Paris. Charles Lansiaux (French, 1855–1839). Préfecture de Police, Service de l'Identité judiciaire. August 1914. Bibliothèque Historique de la Ville de Paris, 4C-EPF-004-0996. Reproduction in exhibition.
FIG. 5.8

2. Wartime

2a. Wartime Fashions

Three women, one wearing a sailor collar blouse. September 1915. Postcard. 5⅜ × 3½ in. (13.7 × 8.9 cm). Private collection.

Eleven women. December 21, 1915. Postcard. 5½ × 3½ in. (14 × 8.9 cm). Private collection.

Woman in a barrel silhouette dress in the town of Vorey (Haute Loire). September 1917. Postcard. 4 × 3 in. (10.2 × 7.6 cm). Private collection.
FIG. 5.14

Woman wearing a tricorn hat and tailored suit in Nantes. July 1918. Postcard. 3⅜ × 5¼ in. (8.6 × 13.3 cm). Private collection.
FIG. 3.14

Three women in blouses and skirts. September 19, 1915. Postcard. 3½ × 5 in. (8.9 × 12.7 cm). Private collection.
FIG. I-4

Six women in tailored suits. Date unknown. Silver gelatin print. 5½ × 3½ in. (14 × 8.9 cm). Private collection.
FIG. I-5

Tailored suit. Probably France. 1915. Wool twill. The Costume Institute, The Metropolitan Museum of Art, Gift of Mme Louis Cerlian, 1940, C.I.40.90.7a,b.
FIG. 16a, b

Suit jacket and skirt. Auguste Champot (French). France. ca. 1915. Silk velvet, fur trim. Museum at the Fashion Institute of Technology, Museum purchase.

Tailored suit. Grands Magasins du Louvre. Paris, France. ca. 1915. Linen, cotton, metal buttons and buckles. Musée des Arts Décoratifs, Paris, Gift of Bujon family, 2012 115 18 1 et 2.
FIG. I-17

Tailored suit. France. 1915–16. Cotton cloth, organdy. Musée des Arts Décoratifs, Paris, Gift of Boulanger family, UF 90 52 28 AB.
FIG. I-18

Women's boots. France. 1914–18. Leather (cow or lamb), linen. Musée de la Grande Guerre du Pays de Meaux, APM.2006.1.10773.

Sailor's uniform shirt. France. 1914–18. Cotton, linen. Musée de la Grande Guerre du Pays de Meaux, APM.2006.1.12057.

Military jacket. France. 1914–18. Wool. Musée de la Grande Guerre du Pays de Meaux, CE2019.4.1.

2b. Hats

"Hats by Suzanne Talbot." *Les Élégances Parisiennes,* April 1916, pl. VII. Watson Library, The Metropolitan Museum of Art, 233.4 El2 Q 1916:1-6. Reproduction in exhibition.

"To Colonel Adrian." *Femina*, March 1917. Bibliothèque Forney, PER D 80 (Res). Reproduction in exhibition.

"A Heroine, Mademoiselle Yolande de Baye." Leopold Reutlinger (French, 1874–1947), photographer. *Femina,* December 1917. Bibliothèque Forney, PER D80 Res. Reproduction in exhibition.
FIG. 3.13

Tricorne hat. Madame l'Hermitte, France. 1914–17. Silk satin, velvet. Musée des Arts Décoratifs, Paris, 70 45 22.
FIG. 3.15

Bicorn hat with bow. Mlle Georgette, France,1914. Silk, silk satin, sparterie, brass, cotton tulle. Palais Galliera – musée de la Mode de la Ville de Paris, Gift of Mme de la Grandville, GAL1958.17.3.

Hat with marquis cocarde. Mlle Georgette. France. ca. 1914–15. Silk velvet, silk ribbon, wool twill, silk taffeta, sparterie, brass, metal thread embroidery. Palais Galliera – musée de la Mode de la Ville de Paris, Gift of Mme de la Grandville, GAL1958.17.2.

Soldier's helmet. France. 1914–18. Metal, leather (cow or lamb). Musée de la Grande Guerre du Pays de Meaux, CAPM.2006.1.170.
FIG. T-8

Military kepi (cap). France. 1914–18. Wool, silk, leather (cow or lamb), metal. Musée de la Grande Guerre du Pays de Meaux, CAPM.2006.1.269.
FIG. T-9

2c. The Evolution of the Wartime Silhouette

"Sport and traveling coats by Martial & Armand." *Les Élégances Parisiennes,* June 1916, pl. XVIII. Watson Library, The Metropolitan Museum of Art, 233.4 El2 Q 1916:1-6. Reproduction in exhibition.
FIG. 5.10

"Longchamp (I), or She Won!" Georges Lepape (French, 1887–1971), illustrator. *La Gazette du Bon Ton,* Summer 1915. Pochoir. 19⅝ × 15¾ in. (50 × 40 cm). Fashion Institute of Technology | SUNY, FIT Library Special Collections and College Archives, New York, NY, USA, TT500.G35, Box 2: Jan. 1914–summer 1915.
FIG. 6.14

"Longchamp (II), or She lost!" Georges Lepape (French, 1887–1971). *La Gazette du Bon Ton*, Summer 1915. Pochoir. 19⅝ × 15¾ in. (50 × 40 cm). Fashion Institute of Technology | SUNY,

FIT Library Special Collections and College Archives, New York, NY, USA, TT500.G35, Box 2: Jan. 1914–summer 1915.
FIG. 1.6

"France" ensemble by Jenny. Dartey, pseudonym of Anette Osterlind (1882–1954), illustrator. *Les Élégances Parisiennes,* August 1916, pl. V. Watson Library, The Metropolitan Museum of Art, 233.4 El2 Q 1916:1–6. Reproduction in exhibition.
FIG. 5c.37

"The New Line: designs by Jenny and Premet." *Les Élégances Parisiennes,* October 1917, pl. XI. Watson Library, The Metropolitan Museum of Art, 233.4 El2 Q 1916–1917:7-12. Reproduction in exhibition.

Evening dress. Weeks. Paris, France. ca. 1918. Silk georgette, metallic beads, black seed beads. Museum at the Fashion Institute of Technology, Gift of the Barnard College Theatre Co.
FIG. 5a.3

Day dress. Callot Sœurs. Paris, France. Summer 1917. Silk charmeuse, filet lace, metallic flower. Museum at the Fashion Institute of Technology, Gift of Rosalie Davidson.
FIG. 5A.2a,b

"Some New Tailored Suits by Lanvin." *Les Élégances Parisiennes,* December 1917, pls. VIII–IX. Watson Library, The Metropolitan Museum of Art, 233.4 El2 Q 1916–1917:7-12. Reproduction in exhibition.
FIG. 5.12

2d. Wartime Fashions, Evolution, Department Stores

Au Printemps department store catalogue. Winter 1918–19. Paper, ink. Bibliothèque Forney, CC 274"1918"déc.

Grands Magasins du Louvre department store catalogue. February 1916. Paper, ink. Bibliothèque Forney, CC 268 "1916"févr.
FIG. I-11

Belle Jardinière department store catalogue. June 1914. Paper, ink. Bibliothèque Forney, CC 110"1914"juin.

2e. Textiles & Colors

Dress. Chéruit. Paris, France. August 26, 1918. Silver gelatin print. 7 × 4½ in. (18 × 11.5 cm). Archives de Paris, dépôt n°4777, 26 août 1918, n° de modèle dans la collection: 56, n° de modèle dans le dépôt: 52, D12U10 672.

Textile sample for dress design. Chéruit. Paris, France. August 26, 1918. Silk. 5⅞ × 6¼ in. (15 × 16 cm). Archives de Paris, dépôt n°4777, 26 août 1918, n° de modèle dans la collection: 36, n° de modèle dans le dépôt: 34, D12U10 672 (3).

Textile sample for dress design. Chéruit. Paris, France. August 26, 1918. Silk. 3⅞ × 6⅞ in. (10 × 17.5 cm). Archives de Paris, dépôt n°4777, 26 août 1918, n° de modèle dans la collection: 47, n° de modèle dans le dépôt: 45, D12U10 672 (4).

Textile sample for dress design. Chéruit. Paris, France. August 26, 1918. Silk. 11¼ × 5½ in. (28.5 × 14 cm). Archives de Paris, dépôt n°4777, 26 août 1918, n° de modèle dans la collection: 56, n° de modèle dans le dépôt: 52, D12U10 672 (4).

Drawing and textile sample for "Garibaldi" design. Worth. Paris, France. March 26, 1917. Paper, fabric. Drawing: 10¼ × 8½ in. (26 × 21.5 cm).; swatch: 3⅛ × 1½. (8 × 4 cm). Archives de Paris, Modèle Garibaldi (dépôt n°4439, 26 mars 1917, n° de modèle dans la collection: 8927, n° de modèle dans le dépôt: 36) D12U10 397.

Drawing and textile sample for "Général" design. Worth. Paris, France. February 1918. Paper, fabric. Drawing: 10¼ × 8½ in. (26 × 21.5 cm).; swatches: 3¾ × 1¾ in. (17 × 4.5 cm)., 3⅞ × 1⅛ in. (9.8 × 3 cm). Archives de Paris, Modèle Général (dépôt n°4694, 21 février 1918, n° de modèle dans la collection: 9360, n° de modèle dans le dépôt: 1) D12U10 398.

Drawing and textile sample for "Rosinette" design. Worth. Paris, France.

February 14, 1918. Paper, fabric. Drawing: 10¼ × 8½ in. (26 × 21.4 cm).; swatches: 3⅞ × 1⅝ in. (9.8 × 4 cm)., 2½ × ¾ in. (6.5 × 1.8 cm)., 2⅜ × 1½ in. (6 × 3.7 cm). Archives de Paris, Modèle Rosinette (dépôt n°4684, 14 février 1918, n° de modèle dans la collection: A0256, n° de modèle dans le dépôt: 44) D12U10 398.

FIG. 5b.7

Drawing and textile sample for "Vauban" design. Worth. Paris, France. February 14, 1918. Paper, fabric. Drawing: 10¼ × 8½ in. (26 × 21.4 cm).; swatches: 4⅛ × 1⅜ in. (10.5 × 3.5 cm)., 3 × 1⅜ in. (7.8 × 3.5 cm). Archives de Paris, Modèle Vauban (dépôt n°4684, 14 février 1918, n° de modèle dans la collection: 8961, n° de modèle dans le dépôt: 40) D12U10 398.

FIG. 5b.8

Drawing and textile sample for "Kiri" design. Worth. Paris, France. February 14, 1918. Paper, fabric. Drawing: 10¼ × 8½ in. (26 × 21.5 cm).; swatches: 5½ × 2 in. (14 × 5 cm)., 5½ × 1⅜ in. (14 × 3.5 cm). Archives de Paris, Modèle Kiri (dépôt n°4684, 14 février 1918, n° de modèle dans la collection: 6367, n° de modèle dans le dépôt: 24) D12U10 398.

FIG. 5b.9

Drawing and textile sample for "Madelon" design. Worth. Paris, France. February 14, 1918. Paper, fabric. Drawing: 10¼× 8½ in. (26 × 21.5 cm).; swatches: 6¼ × 1⅝ in. (16 × 4), 4¾ × 1½ in. (12.2 × 3.8 cm). Archives de Paris, Modèle Madelon (dépôt n°4684, 14 février 1918, n° de modèle dans la collection: 6369, n° de modèle dans le dépôt: 25) D12U10 398.

FIG. 5b.10

Dress. Chéruit. Paris, France. August 26, 1918. Silver gelatin print. 7 × 4½ in. (17.8 × 11.6 cm). Archives de Paris, dépôt n°4777, 26 août 1918, n° de modèle dans la collection: 36, n° de modèle dans le dépôt: 34, D12U10.

Dress. Chéruit. Paris, France. August 26, 1918. Silver gelatin print. 7 × 4½ in. (18 × 11.5 cm). Archives de Paris, dépôt n°4777, 26 août 1918, n° de modèle dans la collection: 47, n° de modèle dans le dépôt: 46, D12U10 672.

"Some traveling and car coats by Premet, Beer, and Martial & Armand." *Les Élégances Parisiennes,* August 1916, pls. VIII–IX. Watson Library, The Metropolitan Museum of Art, 233.4 El2 Q 1916: 1-6. Reproduction in exhibition.

FIG. 5.9

Textile sample for dress design. Chéruit. Paris, France. August 26, 1918. Wool. 3 × 3 in. (7.5 × 7.5 cm). Archives de Paris, dépôt n°4777, 26 août 1918, n° de modèle dans la collection: 56, n° de modèle dans le dépôt: 52, D12U10 672 (4).

Design notes for "Marmouset" design. Paquin. Paris, France. August 13, 1917. Paper. 4⅛ × 5⅜ in. (10.5 × 13.8 cm). Archives de Paris, Modèle Marmouset, dépôt n°4540, 13 août 1917, n° de modèle dans la collection: 1, n° de modèle dans le dépôt: 1 D12U10 249.

Design notes for "Matelassé" design. Paquin. Paris, France. August 13, 1917. Paper. 4⅛ × 5⅜ in. (10.5 × 13.8 cm). Archives de Paris, Modèle Matelassé, dépôt n°4540, 13 août 1917, n° de modèle dans la collection: 19, n° de modèle dans le dépôt: 17, D12U10 249.

Design notes for "Pochette" design. Paquin. Paris, France. August 13,1917. Paper. 4⅛ × 5⅜ in. (10.5 x 13.7 cm). Archives de Paris, Modèle Pochette, dépôt n°4540, 13 août 1917, n° de modèle dans la collection: 47, n° de modèle dans le dépôt: 38, D12U10 249.

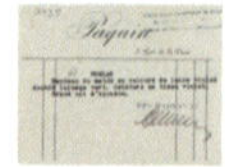

Design notes for "Prélat" design. Paquin. Paris, France. August 13, 1917. Paper. 4⅛ × 5⅜ in. (10.5 x 13.7 cm). Archives de Paris, Modèle Prélat, dépôt n°4540, 13 août 1917, n° de modèle dans la collection: 49, n° de modèle dans le dépôt: 61, D12U10 249.

Design notes for "Kiki" design. Paquin. Paris, France. February 21, 1918. Paper. 4⅛ × 5⅜ in. (10.5 × 13.8 cm). Archives de Paris, Modèle Kiki, dépôt n°4693, 21 février 1918, n° de modèle dans la collection: 202, n° de modèle dans le dépôt: 33, D12U10 250.

3. Designers & Press

3a. Poiret, Summer 1914

Two women and a soldier wearing a Poiret military coat. ca. 1915. Postcard. 3⅜ × 5⅜ in. (8.6 × 13.7 cm). Private collection.

FIG. 1.1

"The New Necklace: Evening dress by Paul Poiret." Georges Lepape (French, 1887–1971), illustrator. *La Gazette du Bon Ton,* January 1914, pl. X. Pochoir. 11⅞ × 15¾ in. (30 × 40 cm). Fashion Institute of Technology | SUNY, FIT Library Special Collections and College Archives, New York, NY, USA, TT500.G35, Box 2: Jan. 1914–summer 1915.

Evening coat. Paul Poiret (French, 1879–1944), designer. Paris, France. Spring 1917. Silk satin, silk fringe. Museum at the Fashion Institute of Technology, Museum purchase.

Military jacket. Paul Poiret (French, 1879–1944), designer. Paris, France. 1915. Wool. Musée de la Grande Guerre du Pays de Meaux, APM.2006.1.12025.
FIG. T-11

3b. Chanel

Jersey costumes by Gabrielle Chanel. (French, 1883–1971) *Les Élégances Parisiennes,* July 1916, pl. XI. Lithograph. 16⅜ × 12 in. (41.5 × 30.5 cm). Watson Library, The Metropolitan Museum of Art, 233.4 El2 Q 1916:1-6.
FIG. 5c.43

Hat design by Gabrielle Chanel. Louis Strimpl (Czech, 1880–1937), illustrator. *Modes d'Hiver 1914–1915,* December 1, 1914. CHANEL Patrimoine Collection, Paris.
FIG. 5c.40

Woman's hat. Gabrielle Chanel (French, 1883–1971). Paris, France. Spring–Summer 1917. Satin, silk embroidery, satin ribbon. 13⅜ × 12⅝ × 5⅛ in. (34 × 32 × 13 cm).; size: 22 in. (56 cm).; circumference: 40½ in. (103 cm). CHANEL Patrimoine Collection, Paris.
FIG. 5c.41

Blouse. Gabrielle Chanel (French, 1883–1971) Paris, France. 1916. Silk. CHANEL Patrimoine Collection, Paris.
FIG. 5c.44

3c. Lanvin

Embroidery sample. Jeanne Lanvin (French, 1867–1946) Paris, France. 1918–19. Beaded and rhinestone sequins on silk. 9½ × 12 in. (24 × 30.5 cm). Patrimoine Lanvin, Paris, Album perlé servis 1918–19.
FIG. 5c.21

Embroidery sample. Jeanne Lanvin (French, 1867–1946) Paris, France. 1918–19. Acetate sequins. 10⅝ × 8¼ in. (27 × 21 cm). Patrimoine Lanvin, Paris.
FIG. 5c.22

"Madame" dress. Jeanne Lanvin (French, 1867–1946). Paris, France.1917. Crêpe, crêpe georgette, Cornely machine embroidery. Patrimoine Lanvin, Paris, 079-RJ-1917-madame.
FIG. 5c.19, 5c.20

Dress. Jeanne Lanvin (French, 1867–1946). Paris, France. Winter 1917. Crêpe, satin. Patrimoine Lanvin, Paris, JL N°377.
FIG. 5c.24

3d. Fashion & Patriotism

"Tricolor Bouquet." Étienne Adrien Drian (French, 1885–1961), illustrator. *La Gazette du Bon Ton*, Summer 1915. Pochoir. 11¾ × 15¾ in. (30 × 40 cm). Fashion Institute of Technology | SUNY, FIT Library Special Collections and College Archives, New York, NY, USA, TT500.G35, Box 2: Jan. 1914–summer 1915.
FIG. 6.5

"The Bulletin." Étienne Adrien Drian (French, 1885–1961), illustrator. *La Gazette du Bon Ton*, Summer 1915. Pochoir. 11¾ × 15¾ in. (30 × 40 cm). Fashion Institute of Technology | SUNY, FIT Library Special Collections and College Archives, New York, NY, USA, TT500.G35, Box 2: Jan. 1914–summer 1915.
FIG. 6.8

"Following the Operations." Étienne Adrien Drian (French, 1885–1961), illustrator. *La Gazette du Bon Ton*, Summer 1915. Pochoir. 11¾ × 15¾ in. (30 × 40 cm). Fashion Institute of Technology | SUNY, FIT Library Special Collections and College Archives, New York, NY, USA, TT500.G35, Box 2: Jan. 1914–summer 1915.
FIG. 6.6

"Without her car." Étienne Adrien Drian (French, 1885–1961), illustrator. *La Gazette du Bon Ton*, Summer 1916. Pochoir. 11¾ × 15¾ in. (30 × 40 cm). Fashion Institute of Technology | SUNY, FIT Library Special Collections and College Archives, New York, NY, USA, TT500.G35, Box 2: Jan. 1914–summer 1915.
FIG. 6.9

"The Marseillaise." Étienne Adrien Drian (French, 1885–1961), illustrator. *La Gazette du Bon Ton*, Summer 1917. Pochoir. 11¾ × 15¾ in. (30 × 40 cm). Fashion Institute of Technology | SUNY, FIT Library Special Collections and College Archives, New York, NY, USA, TT500.G35, Box 2: Jan. 1914–summer 1915.
FIG. 6.7

"Avenue du Bois." Étienne Adrien Drian (French, 1885–1961), illustrator. *La Gazette du Bon Ton*, Summer 1918. Pochoir. 11¾ × 15¾ in. (30 × 40 cm). Fashion Institute of Technology | SUNY, FIT Library Special Collections and College Archives, New York, NY, USA, TT500.G35, Box 2: Jan. 1914–summer 1915.
FIG. 6.10

4. France-America & France-Germany

"The Allies" scarf. Raoul Dufy (French, 1977–1953), designer. Paris, France. ca. 1914–15. Woodcut on silk scarf, pochoir coloration. 19⅝ × 19⅝ in. (50 × 50 cm). Bibliothèque Forney, TI 235042 PF.

4a. Wartime Vogue

"This Number a Forecast of Autumn Fashions" cover. Helen Dryden (American, 1882–1972), illustrator. British *Vogue*, September 15, 1916. Lithograph. 12¾ × 9¾ in. (32.5 × 25 cm). Diktats bookstore.
FIG. 6.19

"Long live France!" cover. Georges Lepape (French, 1887–1971), illustrator. British *Vogue*, Early November, 1917. Lithograph. 12¾ × 9¾ in. (32.5 × 25 cm). Diktats bookstore.
FIG. 6.24

"Long live France!" Georges Lepape (French, 1887–1971), illustrator. Pochoir. 25½ × 19¾ in. (64.5 × 50 cm). Diktats bookstore.

Cover illustration, Georges Lepape (French, 1887–1971), illustrator. Continental *Vogue*, early August 1918. Lithograph. 12¾ × 9¾ in. (32.5 × 25 cm). Diktats bookstore.
FIG. 6.22

"The Heart of France" cover. Georges Lepape (French, 1887–1971), illustrator. Continental *Vogue*, early December 1918. Lithograph. 12¾ × 9¾ in. (32.5 × 25 cm). Diktats bookstore.
FIG. 6.21

Cover illustration of woman waving a white flag. Alice de Warenne Little, illustrator. Continental *Vogue*, early July 1918. Lithograph. 12¾ × 9¾ in. (32.5 × 25 cm). Diktats bookstore.
FIG. 6.23

"We'll get them" cover. Helen Dryden (American, 1882–1972), illustrator. Continental *Vogue*, late July 1918. Lithograph. 12¾ × 9¾ in. (32.5 × 25 cm). Diktats bookstore.
FIG. 6.20

"After the Storm" cover. Georges Lepape (French, 1887–1971), illustrator. Continental *Vogue*, late April 1919. Lithograph. 12¾ × 9¾ in. (32.5 × 25 cm). Diktats bookstore.

4b. French Fashion in America

San Francisco Panama–Pacific International Exposition catalogue belonging to Jeanne Lanvin. 1915. Paper. 8⅝ × 6⅝ × 1½ in. (22 × 17 × 4 cm). Patrimoine Lanvin, Paris.
FIG. 6.2

"Letters from a Parisian Woman." Francine, author. *Le Style Parisien*, November 1915. Halftone. 18 × 12⅞ in. (45.5 × 32.5 cm). Diktats bookstore.
FIG. 5c.29

"Evening coats by Premet, Chéruit, and Jenny." Dartey, pseudonym of Anette Osterlind (1882–1954), illustrator. *Le Style Parisien*, November 1915, pl. XIX. Lithograph. 18 × 12⅞ in. (45.5 × 32.5 cm). Diktats bookstore.
FIG. 5c.38

"Letters from a Parisian Woman." Francine, author. *Le Style Parisien*, July 1915. Halftone. 18¼ × 12¼ in. (46.4 × 31.1 cm). Research Library, Western Reserve Historical Society, Cleveland, Ohio, GT 500 S938.

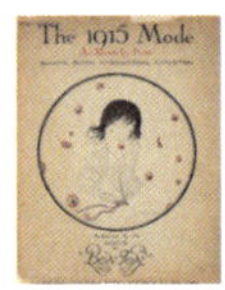

The 1915 Mode as Shown by Paris: Panama–Pacific International Exposition, La Gazette du Bon Ton (American edition), Summer 1915. Bibliothèque Historique de la Ville de Paris, 717446. Reproduction in exhibition.
FIG. 6.3

Evening dress. Callot Sœurs. Paris, France. 1915–16. Silk, metallic thread. The Costume Institute, The Metropolitan Museum of Art, C.I.51.97.1a,b.
FIG. 6.17

Model in Callot Sœurs "Déesse" dress shown at the Fête Parisienne in New York. Philippe Ortiz (French), photographer. 1915. Silver gelatin print. 6⅝ × 4½ in. (17 × 11.5 cm). Diktats bookstore.
FIG. 6.18

"The Fête Parisienne in New York." Dartey, pseudonym of Anette Osterlind (French, 1882–1954), illustrator. *Le Style Parisien*, November 1, 1915, pl. XV. Lithograph. 18 x 12⅞ in. (45.5 x 32.5 cm). Diktats bookstore.
FIG. 6.15

"The Fête Parisienne in New York." Dartey, pseudonym of Anette Osterlind (French, 1882–1954), illustrator. *Le Style Parisien,* November 2, 1915, pl. V. Lithograph. 18 x 12⅞ in. (45.5 x 32.5 cm). Diktats bookstore.
FIG. 5c.31

Model wearing Lanvin dress in black silk faille. Philippe Ortiz (French), photographer. 1915. Silver gelatin print. 7¼ × 5¼ in. (13 × 18 cm). Diktats bookstore.
FIG. 5c.32

"The Fête Parisienne in New York." *Le Style Parisien*, December 1915, pl. XXI. Lithograph. 18 × 12⅞ in. (45.5 × 32.5 cm). Diktats bookstore.
FIG. 6.16

4c. America Entering the War

"The Welcome." Ch. A. Rethaber, illustrator. 1917. Pochoir. 19 × 24½ in. (47.5 × 62.5 cm). Diktats bookstore.
FIG. T-28

Poster for YMCA United War Work Campaign, Neysa McMein (American, 1888–1949), designer. United States. 1918. Lithograph. 48.5 × 34.5 in. (123.2 × 87.6 cm). Research Library, Western Reserve Historical Society, Cleveland, Ohio, 45.531.
FIG. T-35

Practical Hints on Paris: Offered by the American People through the American Red Cross. Compiled by W. Thallon Daus, Capt. A.R.C. 1919. Hachette & Co. Paper, ink. 5¼ x 4⅜ in. (13.25 x 11cm). Private collection.

4d. Wartime Restrictions, 1917 USA

Caricature of French "national fashion," Albert Guillaume (French, 1873–1942), illustrator. *Le Rire Rouge*, February 9, 1918.Halftone. 9¼ × 12¼ in. (23.5 × 31.1 cm). Private collection.
FIG. 8.11

"4.5 meters? 3.5 meters? 2.5 meters?" *Femina,* September 1917. Halftone. 13½ × 10½ in. (34.5 × 26 cm). Bard Graduate Center.

4e. France-Germany: Copies & Counterfeits

"Berlin Elegance," cover caricature, *La Baïonnette,* August 12, 1915. Halftone. 12¼ × 9 in. (31 × 23 cm). Bard Graduate Center.
FIG. 7.2

"May Hats," *Feminina, L'Ideal Parisien, Magazine Illustré Universel,* May 1, 1911. Bibliothèque nationale de France, JO-50683. (Département Droit, économie, politique). Reproduction in exhibition.
FIG. 7.1

5. Identity

5a. Women at Work

"The new professions for women since the war," cover. *Excelsior,* June 24, 1917. Halftone. 14¾ × 21 in. (37.5 × 53.5 cm). Private collection.
FIG. 4.3

"Not all of them are in Biarritz or Deauville." Paul Iribe (French, 1883–1935), illustrator. *La Baïonnette,* October 4, 1917. Halftone. 9¼ × 12¼ in. (23.5 × 31.1 cm). Private collection.
FIG. 4a.3

Commercial catalogue for the Companie d'Applications Mécanique, Ouvrières au travail, May 13, 1916. Bibliothèque Forney, CC 1647 "1916" déc.

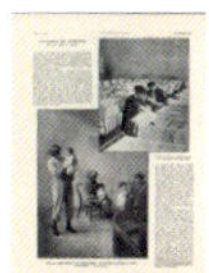

"Breastfeeding infants in war factories." *L'Illustration,* January 13, 1917. Halftone. 15¾ × 15⅜ in. (40 × 39 cm). Private collection.
FIG. 10.4

"Factory workers on the rue de Tolbiac, Paris." March 1915. Bibliothèque Historique de la Ville de Paris,4C-EPF-004-1053. Reproduction in exhibition.
FIG. 4a.6

Illustration of *remplaçante*. Étienne Adrien Drian (French, 1885–1961), illustrator. *La Femme et la Guerre* (Paris: Devambez), 1920. Lithograph. 18⅞ × 15 in. (48 × 38 cm). Bibliothèque Marguerite Durand, F°M° 32 Res.
FIG. 1.8a

Illustration of *remplaçante*. Étienne Adrien Drian (French, 1885–1961), illustrator. *La Femme et la Guerre* (Paris: Devambez), 1920. Lithograph. 18⅞ × 15 in. (48 × 38 cm). Bibliothèque Marguerite Durand, F°M° 32 Res.
FIG. 1.8b

Illustration of *remplaçante*. Étienne Adrien Drian (French, 1885–1961), illustrator. *La Femme et la Guerre* (Paris: Devambez), 1920. Lithograph. 18⅞ × 15 in. (48 × 38 cm). Bibliothèque Marguerite Durand, F°M° 32 Res.
FIG. 1.8c

Illustration of *remplaçante*. Étienne Adrien Drian (French, 1885–1961), illustrator. *La Femme et la Guerre* (Paris: Devambez), 1920. Lithograph. 18⅞ × 15 in. (48 × 38 cm). Bibliothèque Marguerite Durand, F°M° 32 Res.
FIG. 1.8d

"Munitionettes in our war factories." *Les Modes*, 1917. Watson Library, The Metropolitan Museum of Art, 233.4 M722 1917–1918. Reproduction in exhibition.
FIG. 4a.5

Women working in a munitions factory. Maurice-Louis Branger (French, 1874–1950), photographer. 1914–18. Roger-Viollet, BRA-108615. Reproduction in exhibition.

Women working in a munitions factory. Maurice-Louis Branger (French, 1874–1950), photographer. 1914–18. Roger-Viollet, BRA-108622. Reproduction in exhibition.

Delivery woman for the Printemps department store. Paris. *Excelsior*, June 24, 1917. Roger-Viollet, EXL-12672. Reproduction in exhibition.
FIG. 4.1c

Motorist. Paris. *Excelsior*, June 24, 1917. Roger-Viollet, EXL-12678. Reproduction in exhibition.
FIG. 4.1h

Signalwoman at the Gare du Nord. Paris. *Excelsior*, June 24, 1917. Roger-Viollet, EXL-12683. Reproduction in exhibition.
FIG. 4.1d

Postwoman. Paris. *Excelsior*, June 24, 1917. Roger-Viollet, EXL-12686. Reproduction in exhibition.
FIG. 4.1b

Station manager of the Compagnie du Métropolitain. Paris. *Excelsior*, June 24, 1917. Roger-Viollet, EXL-12688. Reproduction in exhibition.
FIG. 4.1f

Conductor for the trolley company. Paris. *Excelsior*, June 24, 1917. Roger-Viollet, EXL-12708. Reproduction in exhibition.
FIG. 4.1e

Cyclist newspaper carrier. Paris. *Excelsior*, June 24, 1917. Roger-Viollet, EXL-12713. Reproduction in exhibition.
FIG. 4.1g

Gas company collection clerk. Paris. *Excelsior*, June 24, 1917. Roger-Viollet, EXL-12714. Reproduction in exhibition.
FIG. 4.1a

Woman in overalls. Paris. *Excelsior*, June 24, 1917. Roger-Viollet, EXL-12724. Reproduction in exhibition.
FIG. 4a.1

Chimney sweeps. Paris. *Excelsior*, late November 1917. Roger-Viollet, EXL-14684. Reproduction in exhibition.
FIG. 4.1j

5b. Nurses

"The most beautiful fashion." Léo Fontan (French, 1884–1965), illustrator. Louis Icart (French, 1888–1950), illustrator. *La Baïonnette*, October 21,1915. Halftone. 18½ × 12⅜ in. (47 × 31.5 cm). Private collection.
FIG. 1a.6

Caricature of a woman in fashionable dress and a woman in a nurse's uniform. Fabien Fabiano (French, 1883–1962), illustrator. *La Baïonnette*,

December 21, 1916. Halftone. 9¼ × 12¼ in. (23.5 × 31.1 cm). Private collection.

Poster for Société Française de Secours aux Blessés Militaires. Lucien Jonas (French, 1880–1947), designer. 1917. © Bibliothèque Forney/Roger-Viollet, RV-86432-31, AF 93175 - GF. Reproduction in exhibition.
FIG. 1.17

Aux Trois Quartiers department store catalogue. October 1917. Paper, ink. Bibliothèque Forney, CC276 "1917"oct.

"The Day Off." Harry B. Lachman (American, 1886–1975), photographer. *Femina*, June 1917. Halftone. 13½ × 10½ in. (34.5 × 26 cm). Diktats bookstore.
FIG. 1.18

Women in nurses' uniforms. *Le Petit Écho de la Mode*, January 24, 1915. Halftone. 15¾ × 19⅝ in. (40 × 50 cm). Bibliothèque Forney, PER D59 Rés Fol.

"Dresses to wear beneath the nurses' uniform." *La Mode Pratique*, May 15, 1915. Halftone. 14½ × 8.85 in. (37 × 22.5 cm). Bibliothèque Forney, PER D66 Rés Fol.

"The White Angels." Georges Lepape (French, 1887–1971), illustrator. *Femina*, June 1, 1917. Halftone. 13½ × 10½ in. (34.5 × 26 cm). Bard Graduate Center.
FIG. 1a.5

"The Coquetry of an Angel: Regulations did not foresee this." G. Léonnec (French), illustrator. *La Vie Parisienne*, May 13, 1916. Halftone. 12 × 15⅞ in. (30.5 × 40.3 cm). Bibliothèque Forney, PER U 13 Res Fol.
FIG. 1.19

"Galeries Lafeyette. The sale of elegant outfits for women has been replaced by nurse's uniforms." Préfecture de Police, Service de l'Identité judiciaire. August 1914. Bibliothèque Historique de la Ville de Paris © Préfecture de Police, Service de l'Identité judiciaire / BHVP / Roger-Viollet, RV-76464-5, 4C-EPF-004-0997. Reproduction in exhibition.
FIG. 1a.2

U.S. military nurse's uniform. Belle Jardinière. Paris, France. ca. 1916. Wool twill. Museum at the Fashion Institute of Technology, Gift of Margaret Larson.

Nurse's bag. France. 1914–18. Cotton canvas, felt emblem on wool patch. Musée des Arts Décoratifs, Paris, Gift of Branly family, 53 290.
FIG. 1.14

The Duchesse of Vendôme as a nurse. Maurice-Louis Branger (French, 1874–1950), photographer. 1915. Roger-Viollet Collection, BHVP, BRA-101 566. Reproduction in exhibition.
FIG. 1.13

"The Two Fashions." *La Baïonnette*, October 21, 1915. Halftone. 18¼ × 12¼ in. (46.4 × 31.1 cm). Private collection.

Nurse's uniform belonging to Sidonie Pocquet. France. 1914–18. Wool, cotton, linen. Musée de la Grande Guerre du Pays de Meaux, CAPM.2006.1.7925, CAPM.2006.7937, APM.2006.1.12089, APM.2006.1.12094 à 96, APM.2006.1.12101.
FIG. 1a.10

Nurses preparing bandages. 1914–18. Silver gelatin print. 5½ × 3½ in. (14 × 9 cm). Musée de la Grande Guerre du Pays de Meaux, don Lalanne, CE2019.2.1.
FIG. 1a.12

"Hymn to France." 1914–18. Postcard. 5 × 3½ in. (13 × 9 cm). Musée de la Grande Guerre du Pays de Meaux, 2006.1.14235.0.
FIG. 1a.1

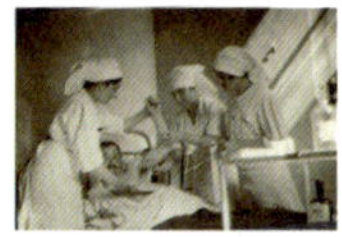

Nurses cleaning the wound on a soldier's arm. 1914–18. Silver gelatin print. 2⅝ × 1¾ in. (6.8 × 4.3 cm). Musée de la Grande Guerre du Pays de Meaux, don Lalanne, CE2019.2.2.
FIG. 1a.3

Treatment room at a French military hospital.1914–18. Stereoscopic plate. 4⅛ × 1¾ in. (10.5 × 4.5 cm). Musée de la Grande Guerre du Pays de Meaux, 2006.1.4972.
FIG. 1a.4

"The Double Wound." Louis Icart (French, 1888–1950), illustrator. *La Baïonnette*, October 21, 1915. Halftone. 9¼ × 12¼ in. (23.5 × 31.1 cm). Musée de la Grande Guerre du Pays de Meaux, CAPM.2006.8.3.0.
FIG. 1.20

Group of French soldiers in convalescence posing with

nurses. July 7, 1915. Postcard. 5⅜ × 3⅜ in. (13.7 × 8.5 cm). Musée de la Grande Guerre du Pays de Meaux, PM.2006.1.14129.18.
FIG. 1a.7

French nurse smoking a cigarette. 1914–18. Silver gelatin print. 1⅞ × 2⅝ in. (4.7 × 6.7 cm). Musée de la Grande Guerre du Pays de Meaux,A PM.2006.1.14128.17.
FIG. 1a.8

Anor Marvel Bertuleit, U.S. Army Nurse Corps. ca. 1918. Silver gelatin print. 6¾ × 10¾ in. (17.1 × 27.3 cm). Private collection.

Nurse's blouse and apron belonging to Louise Daniel. 1914–18. Cotton, linen. Musée de la Grande Guerre du Pays de Meaux, CE2019.1.1 et CE2019.1.2.
FIG. 1a.9

Extract from Sidonie Pocquet's nurse's booklet. 1914–18. Paper. 4⅜ × 6¾ in. (11 × 17.2 cm). (closed.) Musée de la Grande Guerre du Pays de Meaux, Yannick Marques, APM.2006.1.5811.0.
FIG. 1a.11

French uniform for YMCA Pennsylvania Division of the U.S. Army. H. J. Nicoll & Co Ltd. England. 1910s. Wool, cotton, viscose. The Costume Institute, The Metropolitan Museum of Art, C.I.40.45a-h.

Woman's ambulance driver uniform. John Shannon & Son Ltd. England. 1915. Wool, silk lining. Palais Galliera – musée de la Mode de la Ville de Paris, Gift of Mme Munaut d'Auras, GAL 1986.118.1.

Smith College Relief Unit suit, Abercrombie and Fitch. United States. 1917. Wool. Smith College Historic Clothing Collection, 1981.13.Jamison.a-e.
FIG. T-34

5c. Charity

Poster for Semaine de la Haute Garonne. Henri Rachou (French, 1856–1944), illustrator. March 5–12, 1916. Bibliothèque Historique de la Ville de Paris, 1 AFF 001338. Reproduction in exhibition.
FIG. 1.11

5d. Couture Copyright Deposits

"Intimate Dinner Dresses." *Les Élégances Parisiennes*, January 1917. Watson Library, The Metropolitan Museum of Art, 233.4 El2 Q 1916-1917:7-12. Reproduction in exhibition.

"Two Alpaca Dresses." *Les Élégances Parisiennes*, May 1916. Watson Library, The Metropolitan Museum of Art, 233.4 El2 Q 1916-1917:7-12. Reproduction in exhibition.

"Suit and Coats by Redfern and Dœuillet." *Le Style Parisien*, January 6, 1916, pl. XI. Lithograph. Diktats bookstore.

"Kiki" design for copyright deposit. Paquin. February 21, 1918. Silver gelatin print. 7 × 9½ in. (18 × 24 cm). Archives de Paris, Modèle Kiki, dépôt n°4693, 21 février 1918, n° de modèle dans la collection: 202, n° de modèle dans le dépôt: 33 D12U10 250.
FIG. 5c.10

"Marmouset" design for copyright deposit. Paquin. August 13, 1917. Silver gelatin print. 7 × 9½ in. (18 × 24 cm). Archives de Paris, Modèle Marmouset, dépôt n°4540, 13 août 1917, n° de modèle dans la collection: 1, n° de modèle dans le dépôt : 1 D12U10 249.
FIG. I-10

"Matelassé" design for copyright deposit. Paquin. August 13, 1917. Silver gelatin print. 7 × 9½ in. (18 × 24 cm). Archives de Paris, Modèle Matelassé, dépôt n°4540, 13 août 1917, n° de modèle dans la collection: 19, n° de modèle dans le dépôt: 17 D12U10 249.
FIG. 5c.11

"Pochette" design for copyright deposit. Paquin. August 13, 1917. Silver gelatin print. 7 × 8⅞ in. (17.8 × 22.8 cm). Archives de Paris, Modèle Pochette, dépôt n°4540, 13 août 1917, n° de modèle dans la collection: 47, n° de modèle dans le dépôt: 38 D12U10 249.
FIG. 5c.12

"Prélat" design for copyright deposit. Paquin. August 13, 1917. Silver gelatin print. 7 × 9½ in. (17.8 × 24 cm). Archives de Paris, Modèle Prélat, dépôt n°4540, 13 août 1917, n° de modèle dans la collection: 49, n° de modèle dans le dépôt: 61 D12U10 249.
FIG. 5c.13

6. Social Upheaval

6a. Mourning

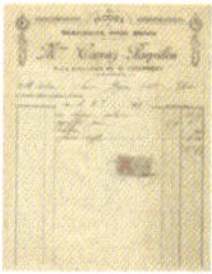

Bill for mourning wear from "Mode, spécialités pour deuil, Mme Carraz-Parpillon, Chambéry." November 17, 1915. 10⅞ × 8½ in. (27.5 × 21.5 cm). Private collection.

Mourning dress. France. 1915. Artificial silk. Private collection.
FIG. 3a.6

Souvenir brooch. France. 1914–18. Silver plated metal, copper. 1⅛ × 1 in. (3 × 2.5 cm). Private collection.

Souvenir brooch, France. 1914–18. Silver plated metal, copper. 1⅜ × ¾ in. (3.5 × 2 cm). Private collection.

Cornflower brooch. France. 1914–18. Painted metal, glass. 1⅝ × ¾ in. (4 × 2 cm). Private collection.

"Proper Mourning." *Femina*, March 1917. Halftone. 13½ × 10½ in. (34.5 × 26 cm). Bibliothèque Forney, PER D80 Rés.
FIG. 3a.9

Advertising poster for Maison Debray for mourning garments, "À la religieuse." Pol de Czernichowski (1876–1916). ca. 1896. © Bibliothèque Forney/Roger-Viollet, RV-86435-8, BF E150220. Reproduction in exhibition.
FIG. 3a.10

Au Printemps department store catalogue. March 1918. Paper, ink. Bibliothèque Forney, CC 274"1918"mars.
FIG. 5.13

"Mourning and Half Mourning." *Les Élégances Parisiennes,* February 1917, pl. XX. Watson Library, The Metropolitan Museum of Art, 233.4 El2 Q 1916-1917:7-12. Reproduction in exhibition.
FIG. 3a.3

Cover illustration of three women in mourning dress. *Le Petit Écho de la Mode,* October 25, 1914. Halftone. 15 × 11 in. (38 × 28 cm). Bibliothèque Forney / Roger-Viollet, RV-157622-3, PER D59 Rés Fol.
FIG. 3a.4

Women in mourning dress meet at the restaurant Marguery, Paris, to discuss their wartime experiences. Charles Lansiaux (French, 1855–1939). September 26, 1915. Bibliothèque Historique de la Ville de Paris © Charles Lansiaux/BHVP/ Roger-Viollet, RV-73734-29, 4-EPF-011-0560. Reproduction in exhibition.
FIG. 3a.8

Widow standing in front of posters on the base of the Lion of Belfort statue, place Denfert-Rocherau, Paris. 1914–18. Bibliothèque Historique de la Ville de Paris © BHVP/ Roger-Viollet, RV-77106-24, 4C EPF-003-0024. Reproduction in exhibition.
FIG. 3a.1

Mourning ensemble. France. 1916–17. Jacket: silk, wood beads; dress: cashmere, silk, wood beads. Musée des Arts Décoratifs, Paris, Gift of Daujat family, 70 45 A B.
FIG. I-15

Mourning hat. Jane Blanchot. France. ca. 1915. Silk velvet. Musée des Arts Décoratifs, Paris, Gift of Musée de Romans, UF 81 26 29.

Mourning hat. Henriette Epel. France. ca. 1915. Silk velvet. Musée des Arts Décoratifs, Paris, UF 81 26 32.

Mourning dress. France. ca. 1920. Cotton, linen, silk, satin, lace. Musée de la Grande Guerre du Pays de Meaux, APM.2006.1.12099.
FIG. 3a.7

Mourning muff. France. 1914-1918. Taffeta embossed with artificial fibers. Palais Galliera – musée de la Mode de la Ville de Paris, GAL 2001.253.17a.

7. Social Upheaval, II

7a. Caricatures

Caricature showing fashionable women whispering about war secrets. Raymond de la Nézière (French, 1865–1953), illustrator. *La Baïonnette,* September 16, 1915. Halftone. 9¼ × 12⅜ in. (23.5 × 31.4 cm). Private collection.
FIG. 3.17

Caricature of a woman shopping while her soldier husband waits in the background. Louis Icart (French, 1888–1950), illustrator. Édouard Touraine, pseudonym of André Bonnafond (French, 1882–1916), illustrator. *La Baïonnette,* April 20, 1916. Halftone. 18¼ × 12¼ in. (46.4 × 31.1 cm). Private collection.
FIG. 3.1a

"The Heroes are Thirsty." Abel Faivre (French, 1867–1945), illustrator. *Le Rire Rouge,* June 2, 1917. Halftone. 8½ × 11½ in. (21.6 × 29.2 cm). Private collection.

"The Helmet." SAT, illustrator. *Fantasio,* March 1, 1916. Halftone. 16⅞ × 11½ in. (42.9 × 29.2 cm). Private collection.
FIG. 3.12

"Unexpected Wish." Henri Armengol (French, 1884–1944), illustrator. *La Baïonnette,* November 25, 1915. Halftone. 18½ × 12⅜ in. (47 × 31.4 cm). Private collection.
FIG. I-14

Woman working in a factory. Jean Villemot (French, 1880–1958), illustrator. *La Baïonnette,* October 4, 1917. Halftone. 9¼ × 12⅜ in. (23.5 × 31.4 cm). Private collection.
FIG. 4a.4

"Soldiers on Leave." Louis Icart (French, 1888–1950), illustrator. *Le Rire Rouge,* March 11, 1916. Halftone. 8¾ × 11⅛ in. (22.2 × 28.3 cm). Private collection.
FIG. 3.9

"The Feminine Emancipation." Chas Laborde (French, 1886–1941), illustrator. *Le Rire Rouge,* May 18, 1918. Halftone. 9⅛ × 12 in. (23.2 × 30.5 cm). Private collection.
FIG. 2.2

"Conductrice." Albert Guillaume (French, 1873–1942), illustrator. *Le Rire Rouge,* November 27, 1915. Halftone. 8⅜ × 11⅝ in. (21.3 × 29.5 cm). Private collection.
FIG. I-8

"The Arrival of the Soldier on Leave." George-Alfred Pavis (French, 1886–1951), illustrator. *Le Rire Rouge,* March 24, 1917. Halftone. 8¾ 11½ in. (22.2 × 29.2 cm). Private collection.
FIG. 3.2

Caricature of a woman in a tailored suit and two uniformed officers. Fabien Fabiano (French, 1883–1962), illustrator. *Le Rire Rouge,* April 8, 1916. Halftone. 9¼ × 12⅛ in. (23.5 × 30.8 cm). Private collection.
FIG. 3.10

Caricature of a man and woman in a bar both wearing work overalls. Bernard Villemot (French, 1911–1989), illustrator. *La Baïonnette,* October 4, 1917. Halftone. 9 × 12¼ in. (22.9 × 31.1 cm). Private collection.
FIG. 4a.2

7b. Shell Casings

Shell casing. France. 1914–18. Brass. 11½ in. (29.4 cm). Musée de la Grande Guerre du Pays de Meaux, don Danzé, CE2011.1.9.1 et CE2011.1.9.2.

Shell casing. France. 1914–18. Brass. 9 in. (23 cm). Musée de la Grande Guerre du Pays de Meaux, don Verney, CE2019.5.1.

Shell casing. France. 1914–18. Brass. 13¾ in. (35 cm). Musée de la Grande Guerre du Pays de Meaux, don Danzé, CE2011.1.17.

Shell casing. France. 1914–18. Brass. 12¼ in. (31 cm). Musée de la Grande Guerre du Pays de Meaux, don Danzé, CE2011.1.24.2.

7c. Wartime restrictions, France

"Restrictions, Shortages." Fabien Fabiano (French, 1883–1962), illustrator. *Le Rire Rouge,* May 26, 1917. Halftone. 9⅛ × 12⅛ in. (23.2 × 30. 8 cm). Private collection.

"The Art of Being a Seamstress." *Le Petit Écho de la Mode,* April 7, 1918. Halftone. 15 × 11⅚ in. (38 × 30 cm). Bibliothèque Forney, PER D59 Rés Fol.

"Transformation of a Sheath Dress into a Bell Dress." *La Mode Pratique,* March 11, 1916. Halftone. 14⅛ × 21¼ in. (36 × 54 cm). Bibliothèque Forney, Per. Fol D 66 (1916).

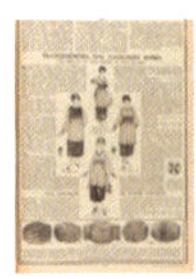

"Let's Transform our Old Dresses." *La Mode Pratique,* November 17, 1917. Halftone. 14⅛ × 21¼ in. (36 × 54 cm). Bibliothèque Forney, Per Fol D 66 (1917).

7d. Families

"At the Tuileries. The convalescent father walks with his wife and baby, April 1915." Paris. Charles Lansiaux (French, 1855–1939), photographer. April 1915. Silver gelatin print. 11¾ × 15¾ in. (30 × 40 cm). Bibliothèque Historique de la Ville de Paris, 4-EPF-011-0499.
FIG. 3.4

"A soldier on leave visiting his family. June 1915." Charles Lansiaux (French, 1855–1839). Bibliothèque Historique de la Ville de Paris, 4-EPF-011-497. Reproduction in exhibition.
FIG. 3.5

"Nothing beats a holiday to exalt love / On which the soul feeds both night and day." Hand-colored postcard. 5½ × 3½ in. (14 × 8.9 cm). Private collection.
FIG. 3.18

"For you our beautiful flowers / We give them to you with our heart." Hand-colored postcard. 5½ × 3½ in. (14 × 8.9 cm). Private collection.
FIG. 3.19

"The barometer is a beautiful device / Only one kiss brings the sun!" Hand-colored postcard. 5½ × 3½ in. (14 × 8.9 cm). Private collection.
FIG. 3.20

"Your lips have such sweet flavors for me / That I can only love them and our three [French] colors." Hand-colored postcard. 5½ × 3½ in. (14 × 8.9 cm). Private collection.
FIG. 3.21

"I picked these flowers for you." Hand-colored postcard. 5½ × 3½ in. (14 × 8.9 cm). Private collection.

"Two hearts united." Hand-colored postcard. 5½ × 3½ in. (14 × 8.9 cm). Private collection.
FIG. 3.22

"Vision of love: It's not too expensive to pay with a heart / The gift that love makes you with a flower." Hand-colored postcard. 5½ × 3½ in. (14 × 8.9 cm). Private collection.
FIG. 3.23

"We were separated! We are reunited! / We will be one for eternity." Hand-colored postcard. 5½ × 3½ in. (14 × 8.9 cm). Private collection.
FIG. 3.24

"Festival of Love: Champagne and flowers, warm and floating shade, experience the thrill of our singing soul!" Hand-colored postcard. 5½ × 3½ in. (14 × 8.9 cm). Private collection.
FIG. 3.25

"Happy Easter: A cry of love rises from the bronze bell / Whose flight passes in a dream, among the serene sky!" Hand-colored postcard. 5½ × 3½ in. (14 × 8.9 cm). Private collection.
FIG. 3.26

"Promise to love me always!" Hand-colored postcard. 5½ × 3½ in. (14 × 8.9 cm). Private collection.
FIG. 3.27

"The dawn of love by lighting our eyes / A thousand radiant hopes arise." Hand-colored postcard. 5½ × 3½ in. (14 × 8.9 cm). Private collection.
FIG. 3.28

"My heart is always with you." Hand-colored postcard. 5½ × 3½ in. (14 × 8.9 cm). Private collection.
FIG. 3.29

"From the dear home, the sweet image / Is engraved on the heart when the gun rages." Hand-colored postcard. 5½ × 3½ in. (14 × 8.9 cm). Private collection.
FIG. 3.30

"This kiss will give me the strength to win." Hand-colored postcard. 5½ × 3½ in. (14 × 8.9 cm). Private collection.
FIG. 3.31

"Do you love me? Everything makes me believe in this hope, your confusion, your eyes, even your silence!" Hand-colored postcard. 5½ × 3½ in. (14 × 8.9 cm). Private collection.
FIG. 3.32

"The gift of a flower is a precious pledge, but know what it entails." Hand-colored postcard. 5½ × 3½ in. (14 × 8.9 cm). Private collection.
FIG. 3.33

"Stay hopeful: France first! It is our duty; to be cherished brings hope!" Hand-colored postcard. 5½ × 3½ in. (14 × 8.9 cm). Private collection.
FIG. 3.34

"Who cares about the sad hour / Only our love exists!" Hand-colored post-card. 5½ × 3½ in. (14 × 8.9 cm). Private collection.
FIG. 3.35

7e. Mode nationale

Caricature showing woman in "national fashion" contrasted with Parisian fashions. Gerda Wegener (Danish, 1886–1940), illustrator. *La Baïonnette*, December 27, 1917. Halftone. 9¼ × 12¼ in. (23.5 × 31.1 cm). Private collection.
FIG. 8.7

"A shop on the Avenue des Gobelins in Paris selling the "National Shoes." Préfecture de Police, Service de l'Identité judiciaire, photographer. July 1918. Bibliothèque Historique de la Ville de Paris,4C-EPF-004-1159. Reproduction in exhibition.
FIG. 8.5

Woman's boot stamped with "chaussure nationale" on the sole. France. 1914–18. Leather. Musée des Arts Décoratifs, Paris, Gift of Hillemand family, 53 730 B.
FIG. 8.6a,b

"The National Fashion? Show Us Your Legs!" Henry Fournier (French, 1871–1919), illustrator. *La Baïonnette*, December 27, 1917. Halftone. 9¼ × 12¼ in. (23.5 × 31.1 cm). Private collection.
FIG. 8.8

"The Soldier's Opinion." *La Baïonnette*, December 27, 1917. Halftone. 9¼ × 12¼ in. (23.5 × 31.1 cm). Private collection.
FIG. 8.9

7f. 1917 Strike

"After the Seamstresses, The Hat-Makers Have Gone On Strike." *Excelsior*, May 22, 1917. Halftone. 14¾ × 21 in. (37.5 × 53.5 cm). Private collection.
FIG. I-19

"Call to Women" poster. Comité intersyndical contre l'exploitation de la femme. 1915. Bibliothèque Historique de la Ville de Paris, 1-AFF130. Reproduction in exhibition.
FIG. T-30

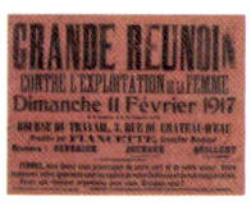

"Great Meeting Against the Exploitation of Women" poster. Comité intersyndical contre l'exploitation de la femme.1917. Bibliothèque Historique de la Ville de Paris, 1AFF 003130. Reproduction in exhibition.

Parisian fashion workers on strike. Maurice-Louis Branger (French, 1874–1950), photographer. May 18, 1917. Roger-Viollet, BRA-104917. Reproduction in exhibition.
FIG. 9.1

Parisian fashion workers on strike at the Place Vendôme. Maurice-Louis Branger (French, 1874–1950), photographer. May 18, 1917. Roger-Viollet, BRA-104920. Reproduction in exhibition.
FIG. 9.2

Parisian fashion workers on strike in front of the Maison Paquin. Maurice-Louis Branger (French, 1874–1950), photographer. Mid-May 1917. Roger-Viollet, EXL-11999. Reproduction in exhibition.
FIG. 9.3

Parisian fashion workers on strike. Maurice-Louis Branger (French, 1874–1950), photographer. Late May 1917. Roger-Viollet, EXL-12070. Reproduction in exhibition.
FIG. 9.8

8. Post-war

8a. Emancipation?

"Fine Example." Albert Guillaume (French, 1873–1942), illustrator. *Le Rire Rouge*, November 17, 1917. Halftone. 8¼ × 11⅝ in. (21 × 29.5 cm). Private collection.

"For the French Rebirth." Abel Faivre (French, 1867–1945), illustrator. *Le Rire Rouge*, July 22, 1916. Halftone. 9¼ × 12¼ in. (23.5 × 31.1 cm). Private collection.

"We want "Labor" machines / Typists' strike!" poster. 1919. Bibliothèque Forney © Bibliothèque Forney / Roger-Viollet, RV-157623-1, AF 215124 GF. Reproduction in exhibition.

"National Day for Mothers of Large Families" poster. 1920. Bibliothèque Historique de la Ville

de Paris, 1 AFF 001252. Reproduction in exhibition.
FIG. 1.21

"Women Must Vote: New Era, New Suffrage" poster. Maurice Barbey (French, ca. 1880–after 1939). 1924. Bibliothèque Historique de la Ville de Paris, 4-AFF-000267. Reproduction in exhibition.
FIG. 1.22

La Garçonne. Victor Margueritte (French, 1866–1942), author. Paris: E. Flammarion, 1922. 7¼ x 5 in. (18.5 x 12.5 cm). Bard Graduate Center.

"Suffragette protest at the Tuileries, Paris. Notable writer and feminist Séverine at the head of the procession, facing the statue of Condorcet." Agence Rol. July 5, 1914. Silver gelatin print. 11¾ × 15¾ in. (30 × 40 cm). Bibliothèque Marguerite Durand, 099 B 686.
FIG. T-1

French league for women's rights handing out flyers at the Place de l'Opéra, Paris. 1920. Silver gelatin print. 11¾ × 15¾ in. (30 × 40 cm). Bibliothèque Marguerite Durand, 099 B 857.
FIG. 10.3

Poster for public conference by Maria Vérone on women's suffrage. Ligue française de l'enseignement. February 8, 1920. Bibliothèque Marguerite Durand, AFF 33a. Reproduction in exhibition.

Evening dress. Callot Sœurs (1885–1952). Paris, France. ca. 1919, Silk. Museum at the Fashion Institute of Technology, Museum purchase.
FIG. 5a.7

Fashionable woman at the races at Auteuil. Maurice-Louis Branger (French, 1874–1950), photographer. ca. 1910. Silver gelatin print. 11¾ × 15¾ in. (30 × 40 cm). Diktats bookstore.

Fashionable woman at the Grand Prix de Longchamps. Séeberger Frères (French, 1909–1977), photographer. ca. 1910. Silver gelatin print. 11¾ × 15¾ in. (30 × 40 cm). Diktats bookstore.

Three fashionable women at the races. Séeberger Frères (French, 1909–1977), photographer. ca. 1920. Silver gelatin print. 11¾ × 15¾ in. (30 × 40 cm). Diktats bookstore.

Dress. Madeleine Vionnet (French, 1876–1975). Paris, France. 1918. Crêpe de Chine, velvet. Musée des Arts Décoratifs, Paris, Gift of Vionnet family, UF 52 18 19.
FIG. 5a.5

Evening dress. Madeleine Vionnet (French, 1876–1975) Paris, France. June 1918. Silk satin, silk embroidery, silk chiffon. Musée des Arts Décoratifs, Paris, Gift of Vionnet family, UF 52 18 9.
FIG. 5a.6

"Suits by Agnès and Mme. Havet." G. Dupon-Emera (French), photographer. *Les Modes*, 1918. Halftone. 22 × 13¾ in. (56 × 35 cm). Watson Library, The Metropolitan Museum of Art, 233.4 M722 1917–1918.
FIG. 5d.8

Evening dress. House of Worth. Paris, France. 1918. Silk, metal, glass. Western Reserve Historical Society. Chisholm Halle Costume Wing, Western Reserve Historical Society, Cleveland, Ohio, 83.19.7.
FIG. 5a.4

BIBLIOGRAPHY

Adlington, Lucy. *Great War Fashion, Tales from the History Wardrobe.* London: The History Press, 2014.

Aftalion, Albert. *L'industrie textile en France pendant la guerre, Publication de la Dotation Carnegie pour la paix international.* Paris: P.U.F., 1924.

L'Art et le Droit. Paris: Marchal & Godde, 1914.

Atwood, Kathryn J. *Women Heroes of World War I: 16 Remarkable Resisters, Soldiers, Spies and Medics.* Chicago: Chicago Review Press, 2014.

Audoin-Rouzeau, Stéphane. *À travers leurs journaux: 14–18 les combattants des tranchées.* Paris: Armand Colin, 1986.

Audoin-Rouzeau, Stéphane, and Annette Becker. "Violence et consentement: la 'culture de guerre' du premier conflit mondial." In *Pour une histoire culturelle,* ed. Jean-Paul Rioux and Jean-François Sirinelli. Paris: Seuil, 1997.

Barbusse, Henri. *Le Feu.* Paris: Flammarion, 1916.

Barbusse, Henri. *Under Fire,* trans. W. Fitzwater Wray. London: Dent, 1926.

Bard, Christine. *Les Filles de Marianne: Histoire des féminismes, 1914–1940.* Paris: Fayard, 1995.

Bard, Christine. *Les Garçonnes: Modes et Fantasmes des Années Folles.* Paris: Flammarion, 1998.

Bard, Christine*, Une histoire politique du pantalon. Paris: Le Seuil, 2010.*

Bass-Krueger, Maude. "The Culture of Dress History in France: The Past in Fashion, 1814–1900." Doctoral dissertation, Bard Graduate Center, 2016.

Bass-Krueger, Maude. "From the 'union parfaite' to the 'union brisée': The French Couture Industry and the Midinettes during the Great War." *Costume* 47, no. 1 (2013), 28–44.

Bass-Krueger, Maude. "La mode en France durant la Première Guerre Mondiale: Approches d'histoire culturelle," MA thesis, Institut d'Études Politiques de Paris, 2008.

Bass-Krueger, Maude, Hayley Dujardin, Amy de la Haye, and Sophie Kurkdjian, eds. *Fashion, Society, and the First World War.* London: Bloomsbury, forthcoming.

Becker, Annette. *Les Cicatrices rouges 14–18: France et Belgique occupées.* Paris: Fayard, 2010.

Becker, Annette. *Oubliés de la Grande Guerre: Humanitaire et culture de guerre.* Paris: Noesis, 1998.

Becker, Jean Jacques. *1917 en Europe: l'année impossible.* Paris: Complexe, 1999.

Becker, Paula. "Knitting for Victory—World War I"; posted https://www.historylink.org/File/5721, 2004.

Bertheau, M. E. "L'Engagement des Infirmières Laïques pendant la Première Guerre Mondiale: Amorce de Professionnalisation des Soins en Milieu Militaire." *Médecine et Armées* (2016).

Beurier, Joëlle. *Images et violence, 1914–1918. Quand le Miroir racontait la Grande Guerre.* Paris: Editions Nouveau Monde, 2007.

Blanchard, Raoul. "L'effort industriel de Lyon pendant la guerre." *Revue de Géographie Alpine* (1919), 593–600.

Bonton, Jeanne. "La Mode Française et la Contrefaçon Allemande," *La France Universelle* (July 22, 1916), 15.

Brachet-Champsaur, Florence. "De l'odalisque de Poiret à la femme nouvelle de Chanel: une victoire de la femme." In Evelyne Morin-Rotureau, *1914–1918: Combats de Femmes.* Paris: Autrement, 2004.

Brucker, Jérémie. "Le front de l'arrière en 1914–1918: des femmes mobilisées par—et pour—l'habit?" In Maude Bass-Krueger et al., *Fashion, Society, and the First World War.* London: Bloomsbury, forthcoming.

Brucker, Jérémie. "Le vêtement professionnel en France des années 1880 à nos jours." Forthcoming PhD thesis, Université d'Angers.

Brucker, Jérémie. "Le vêtement professionnel et l'inspection du travail, entre normes et pratiques." *Modes pratiques. Revue d'histoire du vêtement et de la mode.* Volume 1 (Paris: IRHIS-École Duperré, 2015), 308–27.

Bulletin Bimensuel / Association Générale du Commerce et de l'Industrie des Tissus et des Matières Textiles, Paris, May 1917.

Bulletin de la Ligue anti-allemande. Organe de défense des intérêts économiques français et coloniaux (August 1, 1916).

Cabanes, Bruno. *August 1914; France, the Great War, and a Month that Changed the World Forever,* trans. Stephanie O'Hara. New Haven: Yale University Press, 2016.

Capdevila, Luc, François Rouquet, and Fabrice Virgili, eds. *Hommes et femmes dans la France en guerre, 1914–1945.* Paris: Payot, 2003.

Capy, Marcelle. *Une voix de femme dans la mêlée.* Paris: Librairie Paul Ollendorff, 1917.

Carles, Emilie. *A Life of Her Own: A Country Woman in Twentieth-Century France,* trans. Avriel H. Goldberger. New Brunswick, NJ: Rutgers University Press, 1991.

Cère, Émile. *Madame Sans-Gêne et les femmes soldats: 1792–1815.* Paris: E. Plon, Nourrit, 1894.

Charles-Roux, Edmonde. *L'Irrégulière. L'itinéraire de Coco Chanel.* Paris: Grasset, 2016.

Charton, Charles. *Pour Nos Soldats: Guide du Poilu. Avant, pendant, après.* Paris: H. Charles-Lavauzelle, 1916.

Chase, Edna Woolman. *Always in Vogue.* New York: Doubleday, 1954.

Chauvin, Jacques. "La Chaussure nationale à prix fixe: un généreux projet." *Nouvelle République de la Vienne* (October 20, 2017).

Clermont, Camille. *Souvenirs de parisiennes en temps de guerre.* Paris: Berger-Levrault, 1918.

Coffin, Judith. *The Politics of Women's Work: The Paris Garment Trades, 1750–1915.* Princeton, NJ: Princeton University Press, 1996.

Colin, Madeleine. *Ce n'est pas d'aujourd'hui: femmes, syndicates, lutes de classe.* Paris: Editions Sociales, 1975.

Colines, J."Elegances Parisiennes." *La Femme de France* (December 24, 1917).

Colombel, Marguerite (Mme Emmanuel). *Journal d'une infirmière d'Arras: août-septembre-octobre 1914.* Paris: Publications Bloud et Gay, 1916.

Courson, Comtesse Roger de. *La femme française pendant la guerre.* Paris: P. Lethielleux, n.d.

Courtine, Jean-Jacques, ed. *Histoire du Corps.* Volume 20: *Les Mutations du Regard.* Paris: Points, 2011.

d'Arguibert, Maïten. *Journal d'une famille française pendant la guerre.* Paris: Perrin, 1916.

Darmon, Pierre. *Vivre à Paris pendant la Grande Guerre.* Paris: Fayard, 2002.

Darrow, Margaret H. "French Volunteer Nursing and the Myth of War Experience in World War I." *The American Historical Review* 101 no. 1 (February 1996).

Darrow, Margaret H. *French Women and the First World War: War Stories of the Home Front.* Oxford: Berg, 2000.

Darrow, Margaret H. "Mademoiselles in Uniform." In *Cutting a New Pattern: Uniformed Women in the Great War,* ed. Bart Hacker and Margaret Vining. Washington DC: Smithsonian Institution Scholarly Press, forthcoming.

Dawbarn, Charles. *Makers of New France* (London: Mill & Boon, 1915).

Delétang, Louise. *Journal d'une ouvrière parisienne pendant la guerre.* Paris: Eugène Figuière, 1935.

Deruyk, Réné. *Louise de Bettignies (1880–1918).* Hazebrouk: La Voix du Nord, 1998.

Devarennes, Alexandre. *La femme française pendant la guerre.* Documentary film, 1917–18. Établissement de Communication et de Production Audiovisuelle de la Défense (ECPAD).

Donnay, Maurice. *Lettre à une Dame Blanche.* Paris: Société Littéraire de France, 1917.

Dorgelès, Roland. *Les Croix de bois.* Paris: Albin Michel, 1919.

Downs, Laura Lee. *Manufacturing Inequality: Gender Division in the French and British Metalworking Industries, 1914–1939.* Ithaca, NY: Cornell University Press, 1995.

Duboys-Fresney, Catherine, and Georgette Perrin. *Le Métier d'Infirmière en France.* Paris: Presses Universaires, 2009.

Duguet, Camille. "Pourquoi je ne suis pas suffragette." *La midinette* (February 12, 1914).

Dunbar-Nelson, Alice Ruth. "I Sit and Sew." In *The Dunbar Speaker and Entertainer,* ed. Alice Dunbar-Nelson. Napierville, IL: Nichols, 1920.

Edwardians in Colour: The Wonderful World of Albert Kahn. Five-part documentary film based on photographs from the Albert Kahn Museum. BBC, 2007–.

Edwards, Nina. *Dressed for War: Uniform, Civilian Clothing and Trappings, 1914 to 1918.* London: I.B. Tauris, 2014.

Exposition Internationale de San Francisco, 1915, general report. Paris: E. Larose, 1915.

Fee, Elizabeth, and Mary Garofalo, "Florence Nightingale and the Crimean War." *American Journal of Public Health* (September 2010).

Fell, Alison S. *Women as Veterans in Britain and France After the First World War.* Cambridge: Cambridge University Press, 2018.

Feyel, Gilles. "Naissance, Constitution Progressive et Épanouissement d'un Genre de Presse aux Limites Floues: Le Magazine." *Réseaux* 105 (January 2001).

Formont, Maxime. *La dame blanche.* Paris: A. Lemerre, 1917.

Fraboulet, Danièle, and Pierre Vernus. *Genèse des organisations patronales en Europe (XIXe-XXe siècle).* Paris: PUR, 2012.

Frader, Laura Levine. *Breadwinners and Citizens: Gender in the Making of the French Social Model.* Durham, NC: Duke University Press, 2008.

Fréjaville, Gustave. "Les petites amazones." *L'Opinion: Journal de la Semaine* (September 8, 1917).

Frois, Marcel. *La santé et le travail des femmes pendant la guerre.* Carnegie Endowment for International Peace, Histoire économique et sociale de la guerre mondiale, no. 23. Paris: Presses universitaires de France, 1926.

Ganeva, Mila. *Women in Weimar Fashion: Discourses and Displays in German Culture.* London, Camden House, 2011.

Gaudriault, Raymond. *La Gravure de Mode Féminine en France.* Paris: Editions de l'Armateur, 1983.

Géraldy, Paul. *Les femmes et la guerre.* Paris: Devambez, 1920.

Ghelerter, Donna. "Knitting in America During the First World War." MA thesis, Fashion Institute of Technology, 1989.

Gibson, Craig, *Behind the Front: British Soldiers and French Civilians, 1914–1918.* Cambridge: Cambridge University Press, 2014.

Godfroy, Léonie. *Souvenirs d'ambulance et de captivité.* Paris: Librairie de "L'Eclair," [1917?].

Gordon, Hampden. *Our Girls in Wartime.* London: John Lane, 1916.

Gosling, Lucinda. *Knitting for Tommy: Keeping the Great War Soldier Warm.* Stroud: History Press, 2014.

"Government Control Of Food Supplies In France," *Monthly Review of the U.S. Bureau of Labor Statistics,* 4, no. 6 (1917): 915–21.

Gramont, Elisabeth de, Duchesse de Clermont-Tonnerre. *Mémoires: Clair de lune et taxi-auto.* Paris: Brasset, 1932.

Grayzel, Susan R. "Defence Against the Indefensible: The Gas Mask, The State and British Culture during and after the First World War." *Twentieth Century British History* 25, no. 3 (2014), 418–34.

Grayzel, Susan R. "Mothers, Marraines and Prostitutes: Morale and Morality in First World War France." *International History Review* 19, no. 1 (February 1997), 66–82.

Grayzel, Susan R. *The First World War: A Brief History with Documents.* Boston: Bedford/St Martins, 2012.

Grayzel, Susan R. *Women and the First World War.* London: Pearson Education, c2002.

Grayzel, Susan R. *Women's Identities at War: Gender, Motherhood, and Politics in Britain and France during the First World War.* Chapel Hill: University of North Carolina Press, 1999.

Grayzel, Susan R., and Tammy M. Proctor, eds. *Gender and the Great War.* Oxford: Oxford University Press, 2017.

Green, Nancy L. *Ready-to-Wear and Ready-to-Work: A Century of Industry and Immigrants in Paris and New York.* Durham, NC: Duke University Press, 1997.

Grossiord, Sophie. *Roman d'une Garde-Robe: Le Chic d'une Parisienne de la Belle Époque aux Années 30.* Paris: Paris Musées, 2013.

Groult, Holly. *The Force of Beauty: Transforming French Ideas of Femininity in the Third Republic.* Baton Rouge, LA: Louisiana State University Press, 2015.

Gueno, Jean-Pierre. *Paroles de poilus: Lettres et carnets du front (1914–1918).* Paris: J'ai Lu, 2013.

Guiche, Gustave. *Les deux soldats.* Paris: Faquelle, 1917.

Gunthert, André, and Emmanuelle Toulet. *Paris 14–18: La guerre au quotidien.* Paris : Bibliothèques, 2014.

Hämmerle, Christa, Oswald Überegger, and Birgitta Bader Zaar. "Introduction: Women's and Gender History of the First World War—Topics, Concepts, Perspectives." In *Gender and the First World War* (New York: Palgrave Macmillan, 2014).

Hanna, Martha. *Your Death Would Be Mine: Paul and Marie Pireaud in the Great War.* Cambridge, MA: Harvard University Press, 2006.

Hauser, Henri, and Henri Hitier. *Enquête sur la Production Française et la Concurrence Etrangère,* 6 volumes. Paris: Association national d'expansion économique, 1917.

Hélys, Marc, pseudonym of Maria Léra, *Cantinière de la Croix-Rouge 1914–1916.* Paris: Perrin, 1917.

Héry, Evelyne. "Quand le baccalauréat devient mixte." *Clio: Histoire, Femmes, Société* 18 (December 2003), 77–90.

Higonnet, Margaret R., and Patrice L.-R. Higonnet. "The Double Helix." In *Behind the Lines: Gender and the Two World Wars,* ed. Margaret R. Higonnet, Jane Jenson, Sonia Michel, and Margaret Collins Weitz, 31–49. New Haven, CT / London: Yale University Press, 1987.

Higonnet, Margaret R., ed. *Lines of Fire: Women Writers of the World War I.* New York: Plume, 1999.

Hill, Daniel Delis. *As Seen in Vogue: A Century of American Fashion Advertising.* Lubbock, TX: Texas Tech University Press, 2004.

Horne, John N. *Labour at War: France and Britain, 1914–1918.* Oxford: Clarendon Press, 1991.

Horne, John, and Alan Kramer. *German Atrocities, 1914: A History of Denial.* New Haven, CT: Yale University Press, 2001.

Horne, John, and Alan Kramer. *German Atrocities, 1914–1997.* London: Cambridge University Press, 1998.

Huss, Marie-Monique. *Histoires de famille 1914/1918: cartes postales et culture de guerre.* Paris: Noesis, 2000.

"Jeanne Lanvin," *La Renaissance de l'Art Français et des Industries de Luxe* (January 1924), 7.

Jeanneney, Jean-Noël. *Jours de guerre, 1914–1918. Les trésors des archives photographiques du journal Excelsior.* Paris: Editions Les Arènes, 2013.

Jensen, Kimberly. *Mobilizing Minerva: American Women in the First World War.* Champaign, IL: University of Illinois Press, 2008.

Jones, Geoffrey. "Globalization and Beauty: A Historical and Firm Perspective," *EurAmerica* 41, no. 4 (December 2011), 886

Keene, Jennifer. *Doughboys, the Great War and the Remaking of America.* Baltimore, MD: Johns Hopkins University Press, 2006.

Keene, Jennifer. *World War I: The American Soldier*

Experience. Lincoln, NE: University of Nebraska Press, 2011.

Kleinert, Annemarie. *Le Journal des dames et des modes, ou la conquête de l'Europe féminine* (1797–1839). Stuttgart: Thorbecke, 2001.

Knežević, Jovana. "Gender and Occupation." In *Gender and the Great War*, ed. Susan R. Grayzel and Tammy M. Proctor. Oxford: Oxford University Press, 2017, 133–48.

Knibiehler. Yvonne et al. *Cornettes et blouses blanches: Les infirmières dans la société française (1880–1980)*. Paris: Hachette, 1984.

Kriegel, Annie. *Histoire du mouvement ouvrier*. Volume 1. Paris: Imprimerie nationale, 1964.

Kurkdjian, Sophie. "The Cultural Value of Parisian Fashion." In *Paris, Capital of Fashion*, ed. Valerie Steele. London: Bloomsbury, 2019.

Kurkdjian, Sophie. *Lucien Vogel et Michel de Brunhoff: parcours croisés de deux editeurs de presse illustrée au XXe siècle*. Paris: Fondation Varenne, 2013.

La Boulaye, M. de. *Croix et cocarde*. Paris: Plon-Nourrit, 1919.

La Ville Lumière: Anecdotes et Documents Historiques, Éthnographiques, Littéraires, Artistiques. Paris: Direction et Administration, 1909.

Lafon, Alexandre, and Céline Piot. *Aimer et Travailler: Léonie Bonnet, Une Infirmière dans la Grande Guerre*. Paris: Editions d'Albret, 2008.

Lapauze, Henri. "Dans le Royaume de la Mode." *La Renaissance de l'Art Français et des Industries de Luxe* (November 1923), 1.

Le Naour, Jean-Yves. *Misères et tourments de la chair durant la Grande Guerre: les mœurs sexuelles des Français, 1914–1918*. Paris: Aubier, 2002.

Lentz-Smith, Adrienne. *Freedom Struggles: African Americans and World War I* . Cambridge, MA: Harvard University Press, 2011.

Leroux-Hugon, Véronique, Jacques Poirier, and Philippe Ricou. "L'Histoire de l'École d'Infirmières de la Salpêtrière." In *Histoire des Sciences Médicales* 31 (1997), 189.

"Les journaux de mode," *L'Ami: Journal Paroissial de Ménilmontant* (February 1916), 12.

"Les Journaux de Mode Allemands," *Bulletin de la Ligue Anti-Allemande: Organe de Défense des Intérêts Économiques Français et Coloniaux* (December 1, 1915), 5–6.

Lesage, Marguerite. *Journal de guerre d'une française*. Paris: Editions de la diffusion du livre, 1938.

"Les Lycées et Collèges de jeunes filles et Les Victimes de la Guerre." *L'Enseignement secondaire des jeunes filles: revue mensuelle,"* January 15, 1915.

Loez, André. *14–18, les refus de la guerre. Une histoire des mutins*. Paris: Gallimard, 2010.

Macdonald, Lynn. *1915: The Death of Innocence*. Reprint ed., Baltimore, MD: Johns Hopkins Press, 2000.

Machen, Emily. "Soldiers of Faith behind the Lines: religious women and community patriotism during the First World War," *Women's History Review* 22, no. 1 (2013), 31–50.

Martineau, Juliette. *Journal d'une infirmière*. Angers: Imprimerie G. Grassin, 1916.

McPhail, Helen. *The Long Silence: Civilian Life Under the German Occupation of Northern France, 1914–1918*. London: I. B.Tauris, 1999.

Meader, Joyce. *Knitskrieg: A Call to Yarns*. London: Unicorn, 2016.

Mignon, Alfred. *Le Service de Santé pendant la guerre 1914–1918*. Volume 4. Paris: Masson, 1926-27.

[Ministère des affaires étrangères]. *The Deportation of Women and Girls from Lille*. New York: George H. Doran Company, 1916.

Morand, Paul. *L'Allure Chanel*. Paris: Gallimard, 2014.

Morin-Rotureau, Evelyne. *1914–1918: combats de femmes. Les femmes, pilier de l'effort de guerre*. Paris: Autrement, 2004.

Nicot, Lucien. *L'Allemagne à Paris*. Paris, E. Dentu, 1887.

Offen, Karen. *Debating the Woman Question in the French Third Republic, 1870–1920*. Cambridge: Cambridge University Press, 2018.

Office central des oeuvres de bienfaisance, *Paris charitable pendant la guerre*. Paris: Plon, 1915.

"Original oder Kopie? *Das Journal des Dames et des Modes* und seine zahlreichen Varianten," *Francia* (1993), 99–120

Orr, Andrew. *Women and the French Army during the World Wars, 1914–1940*. Bloomington, IN: Indiana University Press, 2017.

Palais Galliera, *Jeanne Lanvin,* exh. cat. Paris: Paris Musées, 2015.

Perreux, Gabriel. *La Vie Quotidienne des Civils en France pendant la Grande Guerre*. Paris: Hachette, 1964.

Perrot, Michelle. "Sur le Front des Sexes: Un Combat Douteux." *Vingtième siècle* 3 (July 1984), 69–76.

Philippe, Nathalie. *Vie quotidienne en France occupée: journaux de Maurice Delmotte, 1914–1918*. Paris: L'Harmattan, 2007.

Picon, Jérôme. *Jeanne Lanvin*. Paris: Flammarion, 2002.

Poincaré, Raymond. *Au service de la France: neuf années de souvenirs, IX, L'année trouble, 1917*. Paris: Plon, 1932.

Poiret, Paul. *En Habilant l'Époque.* Paris: Grasset, 1986.

Poiret, Paul. *King of Fashion: The Autobiography of Paul Poiret.* London: V&A, 2009.

Poitelon, Jean-Claude. "À Propos du Catalogue Collectif des Périodiques." *Bulletin des Bibliothèques de France* (BBF), no. 1 (1967), 5–8.

Pompon, "La Croix Rose," *La Vie Parisienne* 53, no. 2 (January 9, 1915).

Pope, Jessie. "Socks." In *War Poems.* London: Grant Richards, 1915.

Pouillard, Véronique. "Design Piracy in the Fashion Industries of Paris and New York in the Interwar Years." *Business History Review* 85 (2011), 319–44.

Pouillard, Véronique. "In the Shadow of Paris? French Haute Couture and Belgian Fashion Between the Wars." In Regina Lee Blaszczyk, *Producing Fashion: Commerce, Culture, and Consumers (Hagley Perspectives on Business and Culture*). Philadelphia: University of Pennsylvania Press, 2007.

Pourcher, Yves. *Les jours de guerre: La vie des français au jour le jour entre 1914 et 1918.* Paris: Plon, 1994.

Proctor, Tammy. *Civilians in a World at War, 1914–1918.* New York: New York University Press, 2010.

Prost, Antoine, and Jay Winter. *Penser la Grande Guerre: un essai d'historiographie.* Paris: Seuil, 2004.

Proust, Marcel. *Le Temps Retrouvé.* Paris: Gallimard, 1927.

Rapport Général sur l'Industrie Française, sa situation, son avenir, Ministre du Commerce, de l'Industrie, des Postes et Télégraphes, des Transports maritimes et de la Marine marchande. 3 volumes. Paris: Imprimerie Nationale, 1919.

"Rapports et délibérations - Conseil général des Hautes-Alpes." Gap: Eds. Vollaire, 1916.

"Rapports…Délibérations du Conseil Général de L'Allier." Moulins: Fudez Frères, 1915.

Rasche, Adelheid. "Two Drecoll Houses of Fashion in Paris—A New Discovery," symposium "Les Échanges Franco-Allemands dans la Mode," October 6–7, 2016, in Paris, October 10–11, 2016, in Berlin.

Rearick, Charles. "Madelon and the Men—in War and Memory." *French Historical Studies* 17 no. 4 (Fall 1992), 1001–1034.

Reed, John. "German France." *Metropolitan Magazine,* New York, March 1915.

Reynolds, Siân. *France Between the Wars: Gender and Politics.* London: Routledge, 1996.

Rittenhouse, Anne. "The Women Who Create the Mode in Paris." *Vogue* 10 (November 15, 1914), 52.

Robert, Jean-Louis. "La CGT et la famille ouvrière 1914–1918: première approche," *Le Mouvement social* 116 (July–September 1981).

Robert, Jean-Louis. *Les ouvriers, la patrie, et la révolution: Paris 1914–1919.* Paris: Les Annales Littéraires, 1995.

Roberts, Mary Louise. *Civilization Without Sexes: Reconstructing Gender in Postwar France, 1917–1927.* Chicago: University of Chicago Press, 1994.

Roberts, Mary Louise. "Prêt-à-Déchiffrer: La Mode de l'Après-Guerre et la Nouvelle Histoire Culturelle." *Mouvement Social* 1 (1996), 57–74.

Roberts, Mary Louise. "Samson and Delilah Revisited: The Politics of Women's Fashion in 1920s France." *The American Historical Review* 98, no. 3 (1993), 657–684.

Ruault, L. *Cents ans de Croix rouge française au service de l'humanité.* Paris: Hachette, 1963.

Sammons, Jeffrey T., and John H. Morrow Jr. *Harlem's Rattlers and the Great War: The Undaunted 369th Regiment and the African American Quest for Equality.* Lawrence, KS: University of Kansas Press, 2014.

Schaepdrijver, Sophie de. *Gabrielle Petit: The Death and Life of a Female Spy in the First World War.* London: Bloomsbury Press, 2015.

Seebohm, Caroline. *The Man who was Vogue, the Life and the Times of Condé Nast.* London: Weidenfeld and Nicolson, 1982.

Sem. *Le Vrai et le Faux Chic: La Mode Vue par Sem.* Paris: Succès, 1914.

Shearer, Joanna. "Dressing Up For War: Women and Militarism in the Writings of French Women Journalists in the First World War." *Minerva: Journal of Women and War* 1, no. 2 (July 2008), 66–76.

Sirop, Dominique. *Paquin, 1891–1956.* Tokyo: Fondation de la Mode, 1990.

Sirop, Dominique. *Paquin.* Paris: Éditions Adam Biro, 1989.

Smith, Leonard V., Stéphane Audoin-Rouzeau, and Annette Becker. *France and the Great War.* Cambridge: Cambridge University Press, 2003.

Steele, Valerie. *The Corset: A Cultural History.* New Haven, CT: Yale University Press, 2001.

Stewart, Mary Lynn. *Dressing Modern Frenchwomen: Marketing Haute Couture, 1919–1939.* Baltimore, MD: Johns Hopkins University Press, 2008.

Stewart, Mary-Lynn. "Copying and Copyrighting Haute Couture: Democratizing Fashion, 1900–1930s." *French Historical Studies* 28, no. 1 (2005), 103–30.

Strauss, Paul. "Le travail féminin dans les usines de guerre." *Revue philanthropique* 19 (1917).

Tardif, Fernand. *La Vendée deux ans de guerre 1914–1916.* La Roche-sur-Yon: Hamonnet, 1916.

Taylor, Lou. *Mourning Dress: A Costume and Social History.* London: George Allen and Unwin, 1983.

Thébaud, Françoise. "La Grande Guerre: Le triomphe de la division sexuelle." In *Histoire des Femmes en Occident 5: Le XXe siècle*, ed. Georges Duby and Michelle Perrot. Paris: Plon, 1997.

Thébaud, Françoise. "Le Mouvement Nataliste dans la France de l'Entre-Deux-Guerres: l'Alliance Nationale pour l'Accroissement de la Population Française." *Revue d'Histoire Moderne & Contemporaine* (1985), 276–301.

Thébaud, Françoise. *Les femmes au temps de la guerre de 14.* Paris: Payot, 2013. First published in 1986 by Éditions Stock.

Tilburg, Patricia. "Mimi Pinson Goes to War: Taste, Class and Gender in France, 1900–18." *Gender & History* 23, no. 1 (April 2011), 92–110.

Toulouse, Dr. Edouard. *La réforme sociale: Question sexuelle de la femme.* Paris: Bibliothèque Charpentier, 1918.

Troy, Nancy. *Couture Culture: A Study in Modern Art and Fashion.* Cambridge, MA: MIT Press, 2002.

Turquan, Joseph. *1870–1871: Les Femmes de France pendant l'invasion.* Paris: Berger-Levrault, 1893.

Union des Syndicats patronaux des industries textiles de France. Rapport présenté à MM. les Ministres du Commerce et du Travail sur les industries textiles en France leur importance avant la guerre, leur situation pendant la guerre, ce qu'elles désirent pour après la guerre. 10 décembre 1915. Paris: rue du Louvre, 1918.

"Variétés: Femmes de France," *Journal des Débats Politiques et Littéraires* (August 25, 1918).

Vars, M. *Association générale du commerce et de l'industrie des tissus et des matières textiles. Conférence faite par M. Vars sur la Société suisse de surveillance* économique *(S.S.S.), 4 mars 1916.* Paris : impr. de Levé, n.d.

Veillon, Dominique. *La mode sous l'Occupation. Débrouillardise et coquetterie dans la France en guerre (1939–1945).* Paris: Payot, 1990.

Vigarello, Georges. *Histoire de la Beauté: Le Corps et l'Art d'Embellir de la Renaissance à Nos Jours.* Paris: Editions du Seuil, 2004.

Weiss, Louise. *Mémoires d'une européenne.* Volume I: *1893–1919.* Paris: Payot, 1968.

Wheelwright, Julie. *The Fatal Love: Mata Hari and the Myth of Women in Espionage.* London: Collins & Brown, 1992.

Williams, Chad L. *Torchbearers of Democracy: African American Soldiers in the World War I Era.* Chapel Hill, NC: University of North Carolina Press, 2010.

Witt-Guizot, François de. *La femme et la guerre: Comment une femme peut-elle servir la France en temps de guerre? Deux conferences données à l'Action sociale de la Femme, Paris, 25 avril-6 mai, 1912.* Autun: Imprimerie Pernot, 1913.

Zancarini-Fournel, Michelle. "Femmes, genre et syndicalism pendant la Grande Guerre." In *1914–1918: combats de femmes, Les femmes, pilier de l'effort de guerre*, ed. Évelyne Morin-Rotureau, 98–112. Paris: Éditions Autrement, 2004.

Zanon, Johanna. "De la Baïonnette aux Ciseaux: Les Premières Années de Jean Patou." In Maude Bass-Krueger et al., *Fashion, Society, and the First World War.* London: Bloomsbury, forthcoming.

INDEX

CREDIT PAGE

Photographs were taken or supplied by the lending institutions, organizations, or individuals credited in the picture captions and are protected by copyright; many names are not repeated here. Individual photographers are credited below. Permission has been sought for use of all copyrighted illustrations in this volume. In several instances, despite extensive research, it has not been possible to locate the original copyright holder. Copyright owners of these works should contact the Bard Graduate Center, 18 West 86th Street, New York, NY 10024.

© 2019 Artists Rights Society (ARS), New York / ADAGP, Paris:
Figs. 1.6, 1.8a–d, 1a.5, 3.1a, 3.9, 6.5–10, 6.14, 6.21, 6.22, 6.24

© Françoise Cochennec / Galliera / Roger-Viollet RV-101359-1:
Fig. 5a.1

© MAD, Paris / Christophe Dellière:
Figs. T-32, I-15, I-17, I-18, 1.14, 1.15, 3.15, 8.6a

© MAD, Paris / Patrick Gries:
Figs. T-38, 5a.5, 5a.6

© MAD, Paris / Jean Tholance:
Fig. 5c.18

Yannick Marques:
Fig. 1a.11

Image copyright © The Metropolitan Museum of Art.
Image source: Art Resource, NY:
Figs. T-34, I-16, 5c.27, 6.17

© M Toussaint:
Fig. 5c.41

Bruce M. White:
Figs. T-27, I-19, 3a.6, 4.3, 5.2, 5a.8, 5c.15–17, 5c.19–24, 10.4